Essential ActionScript 2.0
by Colin Moock

Copyright © 2004 O'Reilly Media, Inc. All rights reserved.
Printed in the United States of America.

Published by O'Reilly Media, Inc., 1005 Gravenstein Highway North, Sebastopol, CA 95472.

O'Reilly Media, Inc. books may be purchased for educational, business, or sales promotional use. Online editions are also available for most titles (*safari.oreilly.com*). For more information, contact our corporate/institutional sales department: (800) 998-9938 or *corporate@oreilly.com*.

Editor:	Bruce Epstein
Production Editor:	Sarah Sherman
Cover Designer:	Ellie Volckhausen
Interior Designer:	David Futato

Printing History:

June 2004:	First Edition.

 This book uses RepKover™, a durable and flexible lay-flat binding.

ISBN: 0-596-00652-7
[M]

Essential ActionScript 2.0

Colin Moock

Beijing · Cambridge · Farnham · Köln · Paris · Sebastopol · Taipei · Tokyo

to gray, the wonderkid

Table of Contents

Part I.   The ActionScript 2.0 Language

Part II. Application Development

Part III.   Design Pattern Examples in ActionScript 2.0

Foreword

I came to Macromedia in the summer of 2000, shortly after graduating from college, to start working as a software engineer on the Flash team. In my first days at the company, the team was working tirelessly to ship Flash 5, and everyone was too busy to give me much work to do, let alone guide me in the ways of Macromedia corporate life. Little did I realize that as I was learning my way around the complex C++ architecture of the Flash authoring tool, ActionScript was also beginning its own career in the web development industry. Flash 5 was a landmark release for the Flash authoring tool: it brought ActionScript from an interface that required point-and-click interaction to a full-fledged scripting language based on the ECMAScript standard, with a real text editor. I arrived just as the Flash team was putting real scripting power in the hands of Flash developers. Over the next two releases of Flash, I participated in the continuation of that effort, first by producing the ActionScript debugger in Flash MX and, most recently, by developing the ActionScript 2.0 compiler. My past few years are inextricably linked to this language, and it has contributed to my growth, just as I have contributed to its growth.

In the beginning, my feelings about ActionScript were similar to the feelings a lot of traditional developers have when coming to the language. I found myself comfortable with its flexibility, yet frustrated with its limitations. I was happy to bring features such as the debugger to life, because it helped Flash meet my own expectations of a programming environment. I enjoyed working to close the gaps in Flash's capabilities, feature by feature. With Flash MX, we made strides by greatly improving the code editor and by enabling users to debug their ActionScript. However, ActionScript 1.0 still had one frustrating limitation that we did not address in Flash MX: it was possible to write code that employed object-oriented programming (OOP) techniques, but doing so was complex and unintuitive and not well integrated with Flash concepts like library symbols.

With Flash MX 2004 and ActionScript 2.0, we have arrived at yet another major landmark in ActionScript's evolution. ActionScript 2.0 offers a more sophisticated syntax for the OOP constructs that ActionScript has always supported. ActionScript 2.0 is easier to learn than its predecessor, and it is closer to other industry-standard programming languages, such as Java and C#. It gives developers the framework needed to build and maintain large, complex applications. In addition, our implementation required minimal changes to the Flash Player, meaning that ActionScript 2.0 can be exported to Flash Player 6, which was already nearly ubiquitous at the time of Flash MX 2004's release.

In the short time that ActionScript has been around, developers have found it to be extraordinarily powerful. Flash places few constraints on the developer's access to the *MovieClip* hierarchy and object model, permitting them to do anything, anywhere. This flexibility has stirred the creativity of our users, enabling them to grow into ActionScript and experiment with it. However, the lack of structure in ActionScript 1.0 made applications difficult to scale up, leading to unwieldy projects that teams found challenging to maintain and organize. It was too easy to write poor code, not to mention place code in locations almost impossible to find by others unfamiliar with the project. ActionScript 2.0 aspires to address these pitfalls by encouraging a structure that all developers can adhere to and understand. Moreover, the ActionScript 2.0 compiler provides developers with feedback on errors that otherwise wouldn't be found until they manifested as bugs at runtime. Still, ActionScript continues to provide extensive and unique control over graphical elements. We strove to ensure that ActionScript is a powerful language moving forward, without treading on the toes of already-seasoned scripters.

ActionScript 2.0 was also the basis for several other notable elements of Flash MX 2004.

The following are all written in ActionScript 2.0:

- The second generation of components (i.e., the v2 components)
- The new Screens metaphor, which includes Slides and Forms (available only in Flash MX Professional 2004)
- The sophisticated data integration capabilities
- The multilingual resource support offered by the Strings panel

Building significant, large-scale features using ActionScript 2.0 provided valuable testing and validation to those of us working on the compiler and informed many of our design decisions. More importantly, these features give Flash developers comprehensive, working examples of ActionScript 2.0 in action (see the *Macromedia/Flash MX 2004/en/First Run/Classes* folder under your application's installation folder). Likewise, the benefits of ActionScript 2.0 are readily apparent in these features, which all consist of classes that are well organized in the *mx.** class hierarchy. In addition, it is easier than ever to determine which code corresponds to the different components, as ActionScript 2.0 has made it possible to eliminate troublesome relics of ActionScript's past, such as the `#initclip` pragma (compiler directive).

ActionScript started life as a few scripting commands inserted by mouse clicks. Five years later, it is a full-featured object-oriented language with which large, complex applications can be developed. Furthermore, it presents a clean, simple syntax that is easy to read and straightforward for a beginner to pick up. In my two releases of the Flash authoring tool, I have learned more and more about ActionScript each step of the way, and now I am proud to have helped redefine it. Colin Moock's previous book, *ActionScript for Flash MX: The Definitive Guide*, was indispensable to me, even as I've worked on the new face of ActionScript. It is the single book you'll find within easy reach at the desk of every engineer on the Flash team. Many of our engineers here were already looking forward to this new book, *Essential ActionScript 2.0*, before it shipped. And with good reason. In this volume, Moock has once again applied his insightful, conversational style to complex topics, teaching not only the syntax of ActionScript 2.0 but also the theory and principles of OOP. He has thoroughly researched the relationships between ActionScript 2.0, its predecessor, and other languages, and he illustrates their differences in precise detail. Moock's intimate familiarity with Flash and ActionScript is evident in this instructive and approachable text, which certainly is an essential companion for anyone wishing to learn and master the ActionScript 2.0 language.

—Rebecca Sun
Senior Software Engineer
Macromedia Flash Team
March 2004

Preface

In September 2003, Macromedia released Flash MX 2004, and, with it, ActionScript 2.0—a drastically enhanced version of Flash's programming language.

ActionScript 2.0 introduces a formal *object-oriented programming* (OOP) syntax and methodology for creating Flash applications. Compared to traditional timeline-based development techniques, ActionScript 2.0's OOP-based development techniques typically make applications:

- More natural to plan and conceptualize
- More stable and bug-free
- More reusable across projects
- Easier to maintain, change, and expand on
- Easier to test
- Easier to codevelop with two or more programmers

Those are some extraordinary qualities. So extraordinary, in fact, that they've turned this book into something of a zealot. This book wants you to embrace ActionScript 2.0 with a passion.

This Book Wants You

This book wants you to use object-oriented programming in your daily Flash work. It wants you to reap the benefits of OOP—one of the most important revolutions in programming history. It wants you to understand ActionScript 2.0 completely. And it will stop at nothing to get what it wants.

Here's its plan...

First, in Part I, *The ActionScript 2.0 Language*, this book teaches you the fundamentals of object-oriented concepts, syntax, and usage. Even if you have never tried object-oriented programming before, Part I will have you understanding and applying it. Chapter 1 gives an overview of ActionScript 2.0. Chapter 2 teaches you the basics of OOP and helps you decide how much is right for your projects. Chapters 3 through 10 offer details on classes, objects, methods, properties, inheritance, composition, interfaces, packages, and myriad other core OOP concepts. If you already know a lot about OOP because you program in Java or another object-oriented language, this book helps you leverage that prior experience. It draws abundant comparisons between Flash-based OOP and what you already know. Along the way, it introduces OOP into your regular routine through exercises that demonstrate real-world Flash OOP in action.

In Part II, *Application Development*, this book teaches you how to structure entire applications with ActionScript 2.0. In Chapter 11, you'll learn best practices for setting up and architecting an object-oriented project. In Chapters 12 and 13, you'll learn how user interface components and movie clips fit into a well-structured Flash application. In Chapter 14, you'll see how to parcel up and share code with other developers. All this will help you build more scalable, extensible, stable apps. It's all part of this book's plan.

Finally, in Part III, *Design Pattern Examples in ActionScript 2.0*, you'll explore a variety of approaches to various programming situations. You'll see how to apply proven and widely accepted object-oriented programming strategies—known as *design patterns*—to Flash. The design patterns in Part III cover two key topics in Flash development: event broadcasting and user interface management. After an introduction to design patterns in Chapter 15, we'll explore four common patterns in Chapters 16 through 19. Once you've tried working with the patterns presented in Part III, you'll have confidence consulting the larger body of patterns available online and in other literature. And you'll have the skills to draw on other widely recognized object-oriented practices. You see, this book knows it won't be with you forever. It knows it must teach you to find your own solutions.

This book doesn't care whether you already know the meaning of the words "class," "inheritance," "method," "prototype," or "property." If you have no idea what OOP is or why it's worthwhile, this book is delighted to meet you. If, on the other hand, you're already a skilled object-oriented developer, this book wants to make you better. It wants you to have the exhaustive reference material and examples you need to maximize your productivity in ActionScript 2.0.

This book is determined to make you an adept object-oriented programmer. And it's confident it will succeed.

What This Book Is Not

While this book is zealous about core ActionScript 2.0 and object-oriented programming, it does not cover every possible ActionScript-related topic. Specifically, you won't find much discussion of companion technologies, such as Flash Remoting or

Flash Communication Server, nor will you find a dictionary-style Language Reference, as you do in *ActionScript for Flash MX: The Definitive Guide* (O'Reilly). Whereas that book describes the Flash Player's native functions, properties, classes, and objects, this book teaches you how to use those classes and objects, and how to fit them into your own custom-built structures. The built-in library of classes available in the Flash Player changed only incrementally in Flash Player 7, so *ActionScript for Flash MX: The Definitive Guide,* continues to be a worthwhile reference—even to ActionScript 2.0 developers. It makes the perfect companion to *Essential ActionScript 2.0*.

This book does not cover the Screens feature (including Slides and Forms), which is supported only in Flash MX Professional 2004. Screens are used to develop user interfaces visually (in the tradition of Microsoft Visual Basic) and to create slideshow presentations (in the tradition of Microsoft PowerPoint). Although the feature is not a direct topic of study, you'll certainly be prepared to explore Screens on your own once you understand the fundamentals taught by this text.

This book is also not a primer on programming basics, such as conditionals (*if* statements), loops, variables, arrays, and functions. For a gentle introduction to programming basics in Flash, again see *ActionScript for Flash MX: The Definitive Guide*.

Finally, this book does not teach the use of the Flash authoring tool, except as it applies to application development with ActionScript 2.0. For help with the authoring tool, such as creating graphics or timeline animations, you should consult the in-product documentation or any of the fine third-party books available on the topic, including O'Reilly's own *Flash Out of the Box*, by Robert Hoekman, scheduled for release in the second half of 2004.

Who Should (and Shouldn't) Read This Book

You should read this book if you are:

- An intermediate ActionScript 1.0 or JavaScript programmer who understands the basics of variables, loops, conditionals, functions, arrays, and other programming fundamentals.

- An advanced ActionScript 1.0 or ActionScript 2.0 programmer who wants hard facts about best practices for OOP in ActionScript 2.0, including detailed syntax and usage information, language idiosyncrasies, and sample application structures.

- A Flash designer who does some programming and is curious to learn more about application development.

- A programmer migrating to Flash development from another language, such as Java, C++, Perl, JavaScript, or ASP. (Be prepared to learn the fundamentals of the Flash authoring tool from the sources mentioned earlier. You should also read Chapter 13, *Movie Clips*, in *ActionScript for Flash MX: The Definitive Guide*, available online at: *http://moock.org/asdg/samples*.)

You should not read this book if you are a Flash designer/animator with little or no programming experience. (Start your study of ActionScript with *ActionScript for Flash MX: The Definitive Guide* instead.)

ActionScript 2.0 Versus ActionScript 1.0

Chapter 1 introduces ActionScript 2.0 in more detail, but this discussion provides a brief orientation for ActionScript 1.0 developers.

ActionScript 1.0 and ActionScript 2.0 have the same core syntax. Basics like conditionals, loops, operators, and other non-object-oriented aspects of ActionScript 1.0 can be used verbatim in ActionScript 2.0 and are still an official part of the language. In addition, object creation, property access, and method invocation have the same syntax in ActionScript 1.0 and ActionScript 2.0. So, generally speaking, ActionScript 2.0 is familiar to ActionScript 1.0 developers. The main difference between the two versions of the language is object-oriented syntax and authoring tool support for object-oriented development.

In ActionScript 1.0, object-oriented programming had an unintuitive syntax and nearly no authoring tool support (e.g., no compiler messages, no class file structure, no type checking, poor connections between code and movie assets, etc.). With ActionScript 1.0, object-oriented programming was an awkward, esoteric undertaking. With ActionScript 2.0, it is a natural endeavor. ActionScript 2.0's more traditional OOP implementation makes ActionScript 2.0 skills more transferable to and from other languages.

If you're an ActionScript 1.0 programmer and have already been applying OOP techniques, ActionScript 2.0 will be a delight (and a relief) to work with. If you're an ActionScript 1.0 programmer who doesn't use OOP, you don't need to learn OOP in ActionScript 1.0 before you learn it in ActionScript 2.0. Now is the perfect time to explore and adopt this important methodology. OOP offers to increase your productivity, make your projects easier to manage, and improve your code's quality and reusability.

Although this book doesn't spend a lot of time focusing on how to upgrade your code from ActionScript 1.0 to ActionScript 2.0, after reading it, you should have no trouble doing so. The book focuses on giving you a strong fundamental understanding of ActionScript 2.0 and I didn't want to unnecessarily distract from that focus by talking too much about obsolete ActionScript 1.0 code. That said, keep an eye out for the numerous ActionScript 1.0 notes that look like this:

 Such notes directly compare an ActionScript 1.0 technique with the analogous ActionScript 2.0 technique, so you can see the difference between the old way of doing things and the new, improved way.

Finally let's be clear about what I mean by "programming in ActionScript 2.0 versus ActionScript 1.0." If you are just creating timeline code and not using ActionScript 2.0 classes, static datatypes, or other OOP features, then it is really moot whether you refer to your code as "ActionScript 1.0" or "ActionScript 2.0." Without using OOP features, ActionScript 2.0 code looks indistinguishable from ActionScript 1.0 code. So when I say, "we're going to learn to program in ActionScript 2.0," of necessity, I'm assuming you're creating a meaningful OOP application in which you're developing one or more classes. For an example, consider an online form that merely sends an email. You might implement that form entirely on the Flash timeline using only variables and functions. If that's generally all you want to do with your applications, then frankly, this book might be overkill for your current needs. However, given the chance, this book will expand your horizons and teach you how to be a skilled object-oriented programmer and to tackle larger projects. So when I say "programming in ActionScript 2.0," I mean "developing object-oriented applications in ActionScript 2.0." The emphasis is on "object-oriented development" rather than ActionScript 2.0, per se, as ActionScript 2.0 is just a means to that end. You may ask, "Is this book about ActionScript 2.0 syntax, object-oriented design, or object-oriented programming?" The answer is, "All of the above."

For more information about ActionScript 2.0 and ActionScript 1.0 in relation to Flash Player 6 and Flash Player 7, see Chapter 1.

Deciphering Flash Versions

With the introduction of the Studio MX family of products, including Flash MX, Macromedia abandoned a standard numeric versioning system for its Flash authoring tool. Subsequent to Flash MX, Macromedia incorporated the year of release in the product name (products released after September use the following year in the product name). With the 2004 release, Macromedia also split the Flash authoring tool into two versions: Flash MX 2004 and Flash MX Professional 2004, as discussed in Table P-1. The principal features specific to the Professional edition are:

- Screens (form- and slide-based content development)
- Additional video tools
- Project and asset management tools
- An external script editor
- Databinding (linking components to data sources obtained via web services, XML, or record sets)
- Advanced components (however, Flash MX Professional 2004 components work happily in Flash MX 2004)
- Mobile device development tools

The techniques taught in this book can be used in both Flash MX 2004 and Flash MX Professional 2004, although I note the rare circumstances in which the two versions differ as pertaining to development in ActionScript 2.0. Unlike the Flash authoring tool, the Flash Player is still versioned numerically; at press time, the latest version is Flash Player 7. Table P-1 describes the naming conventions used in this book for Flash versions.

Table P-1. Flash naming conventions used in this book

Name	Meaning
Flash MX	The version of the Flash authoring tool that was released at the same time as Flash Player 6.
Flash MX 2004	The standard edition of the Flash authoring tool that was released at the same time as Flash Player 7. In the general sense, the term "Flash MX 2004" is used to refer to both the standard edition (Flash MX 2004) and the Professional edition (Flash MX Professional 2004) of the software. When discussing a feature that is limited to the Professional edition, this text states the limitation explicitly.
Flash MX Professional 2004	The Professional edition of the Flash authoring tool that was released at the same time as Flash Player 7. The Professional edition includes some features not found in the standard edition (see preceding list). The Professional edition is not required for this book or to use ActionScript 2.0.
Flash Player 7	The Flash Player, version 7. The Flash Player is a browser plugin for major web browsers on Windows and Macintosh. At press time, Flash Player 6, but not Flash Player 7, was available for Linux. There are both ActiveX control and Netscape-style versions of the plugin, but I refer to them collectively as "Flash Player 7."
Flash Player $x.0.y.0$	The Flash Player, specifically, the release specified by major version number x and major build number y, as in Flash Player 7.0.19.0. The minor version number and minor build number of publicly released versions is always 0.
Standalone Player	A version of the Flash Player that runs directly as an executable off the local system, rather than as a web browser plugin or ActiveX control.
Projector	A self-sufficient executable that includes both a *.swf* file and a Standalone Player. Projectors can be built for either the Macintosh or Windows operating system using Flash's File → Publish feature.

Example Files and Resources

The official companion website for this book is:

http://moock.org/eas2

You can download the example files for this book at:

http://moock.org/eas2/examples

More example Flash code can be found at the Code Depot for *ActionScript for Flash MX: The Definitive Guide*:

http://moock.org/asdg/codedepot

For a long list of Flash-related online resources, see:

http://moock.org/moockmarks

For an extensive collection of links to hundreds of ActionScript 2.0 resources, see:

http://www.actionscripthero.com/adventures

Typographical Conventions

In order to indicate the various syntactic components of ActionScript, this book uses the following conventions:

Menu options
> Menu options are shown using the → character, such as File → Open.

`Constant width`
> Indicates code examples, code snippets, clip instance names, frame labels, property names, variable names, and symbol linkage identifiers.

Italic
> Indicates function names, method names, class names, package names, layer names, URLs, filenames, and file suffixes such as *.swf*. In addition to being italicized in the body text, method and function names are also followed by parentheses, such as *duplicateMovieClip()*.

`Constant width bold`
> Indicates text that you must enter verbatim when following a step-by-step procedure. **`Constant width bold`** is also used within code examples for emphasis, such as to highlight an important line of code in a larger example.

`Constant width italic`
> Indicates code that you must replace with an appropriate value (e.g., *`your name here`*). *`Constant width italic`* is also used to emphasize variable, property, method, and function names referenced in comments within code examples.

> This is a warning. It helps you solve and avoid annoying problems or warns of impending doom. Ignore at your own peril.

> This is a tip. It contains useful information about the topic at hand, often highlighting important concepts or best practices.

> This is a note about ActionScript 1.0. It compares and contrasts ActionScript 1.0 with ActionScript 2.0, helping you to migrate to ActionScript 2.0 and to understand important differences between the two versions of the language.

Using Code Examples

This book is here to help you get your job done. In general, you may use the code in this book in your programs and documentation. You do not need to contact us for permission unless you're reproducing a significant portion of the code. For example, writing a program that uses several chunks of code from this book does not require permission. Selling or distributing a CD-ROM of examples from O'Reilly books does require permission. Answering a question by citing this book and quoting example code does not require permission. Incorporating a significant amount of example code from this book into your product's documentation does require permission.

We appreciate, but do not require, attribution. An attribution usually includes the title, author, publisher, and ISBN. For example: "*Essential ActionScript 2.0* by Colin Moock. Copyright 2004 O'Reilly Media, Inc., 0-596-00652-7"

If you feel your use of code examples falls outside fair use or the permission given above, feel free to contact us at permissions@oreilly.com.

We'd Like to Hear from You

We have tested and verified the information in this book to the best of our ability, but you may find that features have changed (or even that we have made mistakes!). Please let us know about any errors you find, as well as your suggestions for future editions, by writing to:

O'Reilly Media, Inc.
1005 Gravenstein Highway North
Sebastopol, CA 95472
(800) 998-9938 (in the United States or Canada)
(707) 829-0515 (international/local)
(707) 829-0104 (fax)

We have a web page for the book, where we list errata, examples, or any additional information. You can access this page at:

http://www.oreilly.com/catalog/0596006527

To comment or ask technical questions about this book, send email to:

bookquestions@oreilly.com

For more information about our books, conferences, software, Resource Centers, and the O'Reilly Network, see our web site at:

http://www.oreilly.com

Acknowledgments

Sometimes you're given the opportunity to thank someone but you know you won't be able to fully express the magnitude of your appreciation. You can say what you want, but ultimately you just have to trust that the person knows how deeply grateful you are. I trust that Rebecca Sun, Macromedia's lead ActionScript 2.0 developer, knows.

I'm in a similar boat with Derek Clayton. I've been working with Derek for years on Unity, our commercial framework for creating multiuser applications (see *http:// moock.org/unity*). Derek's been a programming mentor to me since I met my first *if* statement, and he's been a friend for even longer. I learn something from him almost every day. This book is filled with the wisdom he has imparted to me over the years.

Bruce Epstein, my editor. What can you say? He is, quite simply, the best. No hyperbole can exaggerate his merit, nor do it justice, so I shall attempt none.

I'd also like to thank all of the members of O'Reilly's editorial, production, interior design, art, marketing, and sales teams including Glenn Bisignani, Claire Cloutier, Colleen Gorman, Tim O'Reilly, Rob Romano, Sarah Sherman, Ellen Troutman, and Ellie Volckhausen. Also my thanks to the copy editor, Norma Emory, for helping to ensure the text's consistency, readability, and accuracy.

Then there are the members of Macromedia's Flash team, who have been a constant source of inspiration, knowledge, and friendship to me since there was a "Flash." I believe that anyone interested in computers is indebted to the whole Flash team for constantly pioneering new forms of computer-based communication. Above all, for his unending support and kindness, I owe Gary Grossman a lifetime of deep bows, obsequious "thank yous," and long handshakes. Specific members of the Flash team, past and present, that I'm honored to know and work with are: Nigel Pegg, Michael Williams, Erica Norton, Waleed Anbar, Deneb Meketa, Matt Wobensmith, Mike Chambers, Chris Thilgen, Gilles Drieu, Nivesh Rajbhandari, Tei Ota, Troy Evans, Lucian Beebe, John Dowdell, Bentley Wolfe, Jeff Mott, Tinic Uro, Robert Tatsumi, Michael Richards, Sharon Seldon, Jody Zhang, Jim Corbett, Karen Cook, Jonathan Gay, Pete Santangeli, Sean Kranzberg, Michael Morris, Kevin Lynch, Ben Chun, Eric Wittman, Jeremy Clark, and Janice Pearce.

I was extraordinarily fortunate to have some truly wonderful technical reviewers and beta readers for this book. Rebecca Sun lent her sage eye to the entire text. Gary Grossman reviewed key sections, including Chapter 10. The following keen beta readers guided me throughout the writing process: Alistair McLoed, Chafic Kazoun, Jon Williams, Marcus Dickinson, Owen Van Dijk, Peter Hall, Ralf Bokelberg, Robert Penner, and Sam Neff. Special thanks to Mark Jonkman and Nick Reader for their consistently thorough examinations of the manuscript.

Love to my wife, Wendy, who completes me. To my family and friends. And to the trees, for providing the answer to any question, the splendor of any dream, and the paper upon which this book is printed.

—Colin Moock
Toronto, Canada
March 2004

The ActionScript 2.0 Language

Part I teaches you the fundamentals of object-oriented concepts, syntax, and usage in ActionScript 2.0. Even if you have never tried object-oriented programming before, Part I will have you understanding and applying it. Part I covers classes, objects, methods, properties, inheritance, composition, interfaces, packages, and myriad other core OOP concepts. Beyond teaching you the basics of OOP, it helps you decide how much OOP is right for your projects, and how to structure your classes and their methods.

ActionScript 2.0 Overview

Over the course of this book, we'll study ActionScript 2.0 and object-oriented programming in Flash exhaustively. There's lots to learn ahead but, before we get into too much detail, let's start with a quick summary of ActionScript 2.0's core features and Flash Player 7's new capabilities. If you have an ActionScript 1.0 background, the summary will give you a general sense of what's changed in the language. If, on the other hand, you're completely new to Flash or to ActionScript, you may want to skip directly to Chapter 2.

ActionScript 2.0 Features

Introduced in Flash MX 2004 and Flash MX Professional 2004, ActionScript 2.0 is a major grammatical overhaul of ActionScript as it existed in Flash 5 and Flash MX (retroactively dubbed *ActionScript 1.0*). ActionScript 2.0 adds relatively little new runtime functionality to the language but radically improves object-oriented development in Flash by formalizing objected-oriented programming (OOP) syntax and methodology.

While ActionScript 1.0 could be used in an object-oriented way, it lacked a traditional, official vocabulary for creating classes and objects. ActionScript 2.0 adds syntactic support for traditional object-oriented features. For example, ActionScript 2.0 provides a *class* keyword for creating classes and an *extends* keyword for establishing inheritance. Those keywords were absent from ActionScript 1.0 (though it was still possible to create prototypical objects that could be used as classes). The traditional OOP syntax of ActionScript 2.0 makes the language quite familiar for programmers coming from other OOP languages such as Java and C++.

Most of the new OOP syntax in ActionScript 2.0 is based on the proposed ECMAScript 4 standard. Its specification is posted at *http://www.mozilla.org/js/language/es4*.

Here are some of the key features introduced in ActionScript 2.0. Don't worry if these features are new to you; the remainder of the book covers them in detail:

- The *class* statement, used to create formal classes. The *class* statement is covered in Chapter 4.

- The *extends* keyword, used to establish inheritance. In ActionScript 1.0 inheritance was typically established using the prototype property but could also be established via the __proto__ property. Inheritance is covered in Chapter 6.

- The *interface* statement, used to create Java-style interfaces (i.e., abstract datatypes). Classes provide implementations for interfaces using the *implements* keyword. ActionScript 1.0 did not support interfaces. Interfaces are covered in Chapter 8.

- The official file extension for class files is *.as*. Formerly, classes could be defined in timeline code or in external *.as* files. ActionScript 2.0 now requires classes to be defined in external class files. Class files can be edited in Flash MX Professional 2004's script editor or in an external text editor.

- Formal method-definition syntax, used to create instance methods and class methods in a class body. In ActionScript 1.0, methods were added to a class via the class constructor's prototype property. See Chapter 4.

- Formal getter and setter method syntax, which replaces ActionScript 1.0's *Object.addProperty( )* method. See Chapter 4.

- Formal property-definition syntax, used to create instance properties and class properties in a class body. In ActionScript 1.0, instance properties could be added in several ways—via the class constructor's prototype property, in the constructor function, or on each object directly. Furthermore, in ActionScript 1.0, class properties were defined directly on the class constructor function. See Chapter 4.

- The *private* and *public* keywords, used to prevent certain methods and properties from being accessed outside of a class.

- Static typing for variables, properties, parameters, and return values, used to declare the datatype for each item. This eliminates careless errors caused by using the wrong kind of data in the wrong situation. See Chapter 3 for details on type mismatch errors.

- Type casting, used to tell the compiler to treat an object as though it were an instance of another datatype, as is sometimes required when using static typing. See Chapter 3 for details on casting.

- Classpaths, used to define the location of one or more central class repositories. This allows classes to be reused across projects and helps make source files easy to manage. See Chapter 9.

- Exception handling—including the *throw* and *try/catch/finally* statements—used to generate and respond to program errors. See Chapter 10.

- Easy linking between movie clip symbols and ActionScript 2.0 classes via the symbol Linkage properties. This makes *MovieClip* inheritance easier to implement than in ActionScript 1.0, which required the use of #initclip and *Object. registerClass( )*. See Chapter 13.

Features Introduced by Flash Player 7

In addition to the ActionScript 2.0 language enhancements, Flash Player 7 introduces some important new classes and capabilities. These are available only to Flash Player 7–format movies playing in Flash Player 7 or later. (For information on export formats, see "Setting a Movie's ActionScript Version and Player Version," later in this chapter.) Although these features are not the direct topic of study in this book, we'll cover a few of them during our exploration of ActionScript 2.0.

The key new features of Flash Player 7 include:

- New array-sorting capabilities
- The *ContextMenu* and *ContextMenuItem* classes for customizing the Flash Player context menu that appears when the user right-clicks (Windows) or Ctrl-clicks (Macintosh) on a Flash movie
- Cross-domain policy files for permitting data and content to be loaded from an external domain
- ID3 v2 tag support for loaded MP3 files
- Mouse wheel support in text fields (Windows only)
- Improved *MovieClip* depth management methods
- The *MovieClipLoader* class for loading movie clips and images
- The *PrintJob* class for printing with greater control than was previously possible
- Support for images in text fields, including flowing text around images
- Improved text metrics (the ability to obtain more accurate measurements of the text in a text field than was possible in Flash Player 6)
- Cascading stylesheet (CSS) support for text fields, allowing the text in a movie to be formatted with a standard CSS stylesheet
- Improved ActionScript runtime performance
- Strict case sensitivity

The topic of this book is the core ActionScript 2.0 language. As such, the preceding Flash Player features are not all covered in a detailed manner. For more information on the new features in Flash Player 7, see Flash's online help under Help → Action-Script Reference Guide → What's New in Flash MX 2004 ActionScript.

Flash MX 2004 Version 2 Components

Flash MX introduced *components*—ready-to-use interface widgets and code modules that implement commonly needed functionality. Flash's built-in components make it relatively easy to create desktop-style Flash applications. Flash MX 2004 introduces the new *v2 components*, rewritten from scratch in ActionScript 2.0 and built atop version 2 of the Macromedia Component Architecture, which provides a much richer feature set than its predecessor. The new architecture necessitates new ways of developing and using components (see Chapter 12 for component usage). Officially, the v2 components require Flash Player 6.0.79.0 or higher; however, tests show that many v2 components work in earlier releases of Flash Player 6 (especially Flash Player 6.0.40.0 and higher). If you want to use a v2 component in a version prior to Flash Player 6.0.79.0, you should test your application extensively.

A single application produced in either Flash MX 2004 or Flash MX Professional 2004 can include both v2 components and Flash MX's v1 components, provided the v1 components have been updated to support ActionScript 2.0 and the movie is exported in ActionScript 2.0 format.

Don't confuse v1 and v2 components with the version of ActionScript in which they are written. Granted, v2 components are written in ActionScript 2.0 and there are no ActionScript 1.0 versions of the v2 components. However, although v1 components were written originally in ActionScript 1.0, versions updated to compile under ActionScript 2.0 are available.

The v1 component update for ActionScript 2.0 is available at the Flash Exchange (*http://www.macromedia.com/exchange/flash*), in the User Interface category, under the title "Flash MX Components for Flash MX 2004."

If nonupdated v1 components (i.e., those written in ActionScript 1.0) are used with v2 components in the same movie, some compile-time and runtime errors may occur, depending on the components used.

Do not mix ActionScript 1.0 OOP techniques with ActionScript 2.0 code. If you are using classes, inheritance, and other OOP features, make sure all your code is upgraded to ActionScript 2.0.

Key new v2 component features include:

- A new listener event model for handling component events, which lets many external objects receive a single component's events
- CSS-based stylesheet support, making it easier to change text attributes across components

- Focus management to support tabbing between user interface elements
- Depth management to manage the visual stacking of components on screen
- Richer accessibility support (i.e., better support for screen readers)
- Richer skinning (i.e., graphic replacement) support
- Encapsulation of component assets in a single file, allowing easier component management and sharing

The v2 components tend to be larger than their v1 counterparts. This is especially true if using only one or two components, as the v2 architecture is optimized for applications that use at least three or four different component types. Therefore, if you need only one or two components, and you don't need focus management or accessibility support, you'll get faster (smaller) downloads using the v1 components.

Beware that the default theme ("halo") for the v2 components does not support custom colors for scrollbars and buttons. That is, the scrollTrackColor and buttonColor style properties do not work with the default v2 component theme in Flash MX 2004 and Flash MX Professional 2004. To set the color of buttons and scrollbars on v2 components, you must apply a new theme to the document. See Help → Using Components → About Themes → Applying a Theme to a Document.

Table 1-1 shows the complete set of components in Flash MX 2004 and Flash MX Professional 2004. Professional components that are not available in Flash MX 2004 will still work in that version of the software. That is, a *.fla* document that contains a component specific to the Professional edition will open normally and work properly in Flash MX 2004. Macromedia's End User License Agreement for Flash MX 2004 does not explicitly prohibit the use of Professional-only components in the standard edition of the software.

Table 1-1. The v1 and v2 components

Component	Flash MX	Flash MX 2004	Flash Pro	Notes
Accordion	a		v2	
Alert	b, c		v2	
Button	v1	v2	v2	
CheckBox	v1	v2	v2	
ComboBox	v1	v2	v2	
Data Components			v2	Includes DataHolder, DataSet, RDBMSResolver, WebServiceConnector, XMLConnector, and XUpdateResolver
DataGrid	b		v2	
DateChooser	c, d		v2	
DateField			v2	
Label	a	v2	v2	

Table 1-1. The v1 and v2 components (continued)

Component	Flash MX	Flash MX 2004	Flash Pro	Notes
List	v1	v2	v2	
Loader	b	v2	v2	
Media Components	b		v2	MediaController, MediaDisplay, MediaPlayback
Menu	d		v2	
MenuBar			v2	
NumericStepper		v2	v2	
ProgressBar	b, c	v2	v2	
RadioButton	v1	v2	v2	
ScrollPane	v1	v2	v2	
TextArea	v1	v2	v2	
TextInput	v1	v2	v2	
Tree	c		v2	
Window	c	v2	v2	

ᵃ Similar component available in DRK3 (http://www.macromedia.com/software/drk/productinfo/product_overview/volume3).
ᵇ Similar component available in DRK1 (http://www.macromedia.com/software/drk/productinfo/product_overview/volume1).
ᶜ Similar component available in Flash UI Component Set 2 at the Flash Exchange (http://www.macromedia.com/exchange/flash).
ᵈ Similar component available in DRK2 (http://www.macromedia.com/software/drk/productinfo/product_overview/volume2).

In Chapter 12, we'll learn how to program graphical, OOP applications that use the v2 components.

ActionScript 1.0 and 2.0 in Flash Player 6 and 7

ActionScript 1.0 is based on the ECMAScript 3 standard (as is JavaScript 1.5), whereas ActionScript 2.0 is based on the emerging ECMAScript 4 standard (as is the theoretical JavaScript 2.0). As we learned in the Preface, under "ActionScript 2.0 Versus ActionScript 1.0," this common heritage gives the two versions a strong family resemblance; they share the same syntax for most non-OOP features, such as loops, conditionals, and operators.

Although ActionScript 2.0 is now the preferred version of ActionScript, ActionScript 1.0 syntax continues to be fully supported by Flash Player 7 and is not deprecated. As we'll see shortly, you can author either ActionScript 1.0 or ActionScript 2.0 in Flash MX 2004 and Flash MX Professional 2004 (but you cannot author ActionScript 2.0 in Flash MX). With a few minor exceptions, noted throughout the text, ActionScript 2.0 code is also backward compatible with Flash Player 6. However, ActionScript 2.0 is not compatible with older versions such as Flash Player 5 or Flash Player 4.

If you're an ActionScript 1.0 programmer, you can think of ActionScript 2.0 as a syntactic façade over ActionScript 1.0. That is, both ActionScript 2.0 and ActionScript 1.0

compile to the same *.swf* bytecode (with a few minor additions for ActionScript 2.0). To the Flash Player, at runtime, there's effectively no difference between ActionScript 1.0 and ActionScript 2.0 (barring the aforementioned minor additions). For example, once an ActionScript 2.0 class, such as *Rectangle*, is compiled to a *.swf* file, it exists as a *Function* object at runtime, just as an older ActionScript 1.0 function declaration used as a class constructor would. Similarly, at runtime, an ActionScript 2.0 *Rectangle* instance (r) is given a `__proto__` property that refers to `Rectangle.prototype`, again making it look to the Flash Player just like its ActionScript 1.0 counterpart.

But for the most part, you don't need to worry about these behind-the-scenes compiler and runtime issues. If you're moving to ActionScript 2.0 (and I think you should!), you can permanently forget ActionScript 1.0's prototype-based programming. In fact, most ActionScript 1.0 techniques for dynamically manipulating objects and classes at runtime are considered bad practice in ActionScript 2.0, and will actually lead to compiler errors when mixed with ActionScript 2.0 code. But never fear, this book highlights problematic ActionScript 1.0 practices and show you how to replace them with their modern ActionScript 2.0 counterparts.

Setting a Movie's ActionScript Version and Player Version

Flash MX 2004 lets you export *.swf* files (a.k.a. movies) in a format compatible with specific versions of the Flash Player. Don't confuse this with the version of the Flash Player the end user has installed (which is beyond your control except for checking their Player version and suggesting they upgrade when appropriate).

To set the version of a *.swf* file, use the drop-down list under File → Publish Settings → Flash → Version. For maximum compatibility, always set your *.swf* file's Flash Player version explicitly to the lowest version required, and no higher. If the *.swf* file version is higher than the end user's version of the Flash Player, it might not display correctly, and most code execution will fail.

Setting the version of a Flash movie has the following effects:

- The movie will be compatible with (i.e., playable in) the specified version of the Flash Player (or later versions). In earlier versions, most ActionScript code will either not execute properly or not execute at all.

- The movie will play properly in the most recent version of the Flash Player, even if it uses features that have changed since the specified version was released. In other words, the newest Flash Player will always play older format *.swf* files properly. For example, ActionScript identifiers in a Flash Player 6–format *.swf* file playing in Flash Player 7 are *not* case sensitive, even though identifiers in Flash Player 7–format *.swf* files *are* case sensitive. However, there's one exception: the security changes to the rules of cross-domain data loading in Flash Player 7 affect Flash Player 6–format *.swf* files in some cases. For details see *http://moock.org/asdg/technotes/crossDomainPolicyFiles*.

When exporting Flash Player 6– and Flash Player 7–format movies from either Flash MX 2004 or Flash MX Professional 2004, you can tell Flash whether to compile your code as if it is ActionScript 1.0 or ActionScript 2.0. Naturally, you should make this choice at the beginning of development, as you don't want to rewrite your code at the end. To specify which version of the ActionScript compiler to use when creating a *.swf* file, use the drop-down list under File → Publish Settings → Flash → Action-Script Version.

 Throughout the remainder of the text, this book assumes you are using ActionScript 2.0's compiler.

When the ActionScript version is set to ActionScript 1.0, the following changes take effect:

- ActionScript 2.0 syntax is not recognized and ActionScript 2.0 features, such as type checking (including post-colon syntax) and error handling, can either cause compiler errors (for Flash Player 6–format movies) or simply fail silently (for Flash Player 7–format movies).
- Flash 4–style "slash syntax" for variables is allowed (but this coding style is deprecated and not recommended).
- Reserved words added in ActionScript 2.0 such as *class*, *interface*, and *public* can be used as identifiers (but this practice makes code difficult to update and is highly discouraged).

The following runtime features of ActionScript 2.0 will not work in *.swf* files exported to a Flash Player 6–format *.swf* file, no matter which version of the Flash Player is used:

- Exception handling (see Chapter 10).
- Case sensitivity. (Scripts exported in Flash Player 6–format *.swf* files are not case sensitive, even in Flash Player 7. But beware! ActionScript 1.0 code in a Flash Player 7–format *.swf* file is case sensitive when played in Flash Player 7. See Table 1-2.)
- Type casting (see "Runtime Casting Support" in Chapter 3).

Table 1-2 outlines case sensitivity for various possible permutations of the *.swf* file version and the user's Flash Player version. Note that runtime case sensitivity is unrelated to the ActionScript compiler version chosen and is dependent only on the format of the exported *.swf* file and the Flash Player version. In other words, both ActionScript 1.0 and 2.0 are case sensitive when exported in Flash Player 7–format . *swf* files and played in Flash Player 7. In other cases, code is case insensitive subject to the exceptions cited in the footnotes to Table 1-2. Consult my book *ActionScript for Flash MX: The Definitive Guide* (O'Reilly) for a full discussion of case sensitivity and its implications in Flash Player 6.

Table 1-2. Runtime case sensitivity support by language, file format, and Flash Player version

Movie compiled as either ActionScript 1.0 or 2.0 and	Played in Flash Player 6	Played in Flash Player 7
Flash Player 6–format *.swf* file	Case insensitive[a]	Case-insensitive[a]
Flash Player 7–format *.swf* file	Not supported[b]	Case-sensitive

[a] Identifiers (i.e., variable and property names), function names, frame labels, and symbol export IDs are case insensitive in Flash Player 6–format *.swf* files. However, reserved words such as "if" are case sensitive, even in Flash Player 6.

[b] Flash Player 6 cannot play Flash Player 7–format *.swf* files.

Changes to ActionScript 1.0 in Flash Player 7

In a Flash Player 7–format *.swf* file running in Flash Player 7, some ActionScript 1.0 code behaves differently than it does in Flash Player 6. These changes bring Flash Player 7 closer to full ECMAScript 3 compliance. Specifically:

- The value undefined converts to the number NaN when used in a numeric context and to the string "undefined" when used in a string context (in Flash Player 6, undefined converts to the number 0 and to the empty string, "").

- Any nonempty string converts to the Boolean value true when used in a Boolean context (in Flash Player 6, a string converts to true only if it can be converted to a valid nonzero number; otherwise, it converts to false).

- Identifiers (function names, variable names, property names, etc.) are case sensitive. For example, the identifiers firstName and firstname refer to two different variables in Flash Player 7. In Flash Player 6, the identifiers would refer to a single variable. (However, as usual, frame labels and symbol linkage IDs are not case sensitive.)

The preceding changes affect you only when you are updating a Flash Player 6–format movie to a Flash Player 7–format movie in order to use a feature unique to Flash Player 7. That is, if you upgrade your movie, you must test and possibly modify your code to make sure that it operates the same in Flash Player 7 format as it did in Flash Player 6 format. If you do not need Flash Player 7 features in your movie, you can continue to export it to Flash Player 6 format and it will usually run in Flash Player 7 exactly as it did in Flash Player 6. This last point cannot be emphasized enough.

Macromedia goes to great lengths to ensure that movies exported in older versions of the *.swf* format, such as Flash Player 6 format, continue to operate unchanged even if played in a later Player, such as Flash Player 7. However, when you publish a movie in Flash Player 7 format, you must be mindful of the changes implemented since the previous version of the *.swf* format. That is, the changes needed in your ActionScript depend on the *.swf* file version, not the Flash Player version.

Of course, any newly created *.swf* files exported in Flash Player 7 format (and not just those upgraded from Flash Player 6–format *.swf* files) must obey the new conventions, so keep them in mind moving forward. Remember that these new conventions bring ActionScript in line with other languages such as JavaScript and Java, making it easier to port code to or from other languages.

Flash 4 Slash Syntax Is Not Supported in ActionScript 2.0

In Flash 4 and subsequent versions, variables could be referenced with so-called "slash syntax." For example, in Flash 4, the following code is a reference to the variable x on the movie clip ball:

```
/ball:x
```

That syntax generates the following error if you attempt to use it with the Action-Script 2.0 compiler, whether exporting in Flash Player 6 or Flash Player 7 format:

```
Unexpected '/' encountered
```

Let's Go OOP

Now that we've had a taste of what ActionScript 2.0 has to offer, we can start our study of object-oriented programming with Flash in earnest. When you're ready to get your hands dirty, move on to Chapter 2!

Object-Oriented ActionScript

Ironically, Flash users who are new to object-oriented programming (OOP) are often familiar with many object-oriented concepts without knowing their formal names. This chapter demystifies some of the terminology and brings newer programmers up to speed on key OOP concepts. It also serves as a high-level overview of OOP in ActionScript for experienced programmers who are making their first foray into Flash development.

Procedural Programming and Object-Oriented Programming

Traditional programming consists of various instructions grouped into *procedures*. Procedures perform a specific task without any knowledge of or concern for the larger program. For example, a procedure might perform a calculation and return the result. In a procedural-style Flash program, repeated tasks are stored in *functions* and data is stored in *variables*. The program runs by executing functions and changing variable values, typically for the purpose of handling input and generating output. Procedural programming is sensible for certain applications; however, as applications become larger or more complex and the interactions between procedures (and the programmers who use them) become more numerous, procedural programs can become unwieldy. They can be hard to maintain, hard to debug, and hard to upgrade.

Object-oriented programming (OOP) is a different approach to programming, intended to solve some of the development and maintenance problems commonly associated with large procedural programs. OOP is designed to make complex applications more manageable by breaking them down into self-contained, interacting modules. OOP lets us translate abstract concepts and tangible real-world things into corresponding parts of a program (the "objects" of OOP). It's also designed to let an application create and manage more than one of something, as is often required by user interfaces. For example, we might need 20 cars in a simulation, 2 players in a game, or 4 checkboxes in a fill-in form.

Properly applied, OOP adds a level of conceptual organization to a program. It groups related functions and variables together into separate *classes*, each of which is a self-contained part of the program with its own responsibilities. Classes are used to create individual objects that execute functions and set variables on one another, producing the program's behavior. Organizing the code into classes makes it easier to create a program that maps well to real-world problems with real-world components. Parts II and III of this book cover some of the common situations you'll encounter in ActionScript, and show how to apply OOP solutions to them. But before we explore applied situations, let's briefly consider the basic concepts of OOP.

Key Object-Oriented Programming Concepts

An *object* is a self-contained software module that contains related functions (called its *methods*) and variables (called its *properties*). Individual objects are created from *classes*, which provide the blueprint for an object's methods and properties. That is, a class is the template from which an object is made. Classes can represent theoretical concepts, such as a timer, or physical entities in a program, such as a pull-down menu or a spaceship. A single class can be used to generate any number of objects, each with the same general structure, somewhat as a single recipe can be used to bake any number of muffins. For example, an OOP space fighting game might have 20 individual *SpaceShip* objects on screen at one time, all created from a single *SpaceShip* class. Similarly, the game might have one *2dVector* class that represents a mathematical vector but thousands of *2dVector* objects in the game.

 The term *instance* is often used as a synonym for *object*. For example, the phrases "Make a new *SpaceShip* instance" and "Make a new *SpaceShip* object" mean the same thing. Creating a new object from a class is sometimes called *instantiation*.

To build an object-oriented program, we:

1. Create one or more classes.
2. Make (i.e., *instantiate*) objects from those classes.
3. Tell the objects what to do.

What the objects *do* determines the behavior of the program.

In addition to using the classes we create, a program can use any of the classes built into the Flash Player. For example, a program can use the built-in *Sound* class to create *Sound* objects. An individual *Sound* object represents and controls a single sound or a group of sounds. Its *setVolume( )* method can raise or lower the volume of a sound. Its *loadSound( )* method can retrieve and play an MP3 sound file. And its duration property can tell us the length of the loaded sound, in milliseconds. Together, the built-in classes and our custom classes form the basic building blocks of all OOP applications in Flash.

Class Syntax

Let's jump right into a tangible example. Earlier, I suggested that a space fighting game would have a *SpaceShip* class. The ActionScript that defines the class might look like the source code shown in Example 2-1 (don't worry if much of this code is new to you; we'll study it in detail in the coming chapters).

Example 2-1. The SpaceShip class

```
class SpaceShip {
  // This is a public property named speed.
  public var speed:Number;

  // This is a private property named damage.
  private var damage:Number;

  // This is a constructor function, which initializes
  // each SpaceShip instance.
  public function SpaceShip () {
    speed - 100;
    damage = 0;
  }

  // This is a public method named fireMissile().
  public function fireMissile ():Void {
    // Code that fires a missile goes here.
  }

  // This is a public method named thrust().
  public function thrust ():Void {
    // Code that propels the ship goes here.
  }
}
```

Notice how the *SpaceShip* class groups related aspects of the program neatly together (as do all classes). Variables (properties), such as speed and damage, related to spaceships are grouped with functions (methods) used to move a spaceship and fire its weapons. Other aspects of the program, such as keeping score and drawing the background graphics can be kept separate, in their own classes (not shown in this example).

Object Creation

Objects are created (*instantiated*) with the *new* operator, as in:

```
new ClassName()
```

where *ClassName* is the name of the class from which the object will be created.

For example, when we want to create a new *SpaceShip* object in our hypothetical game, we use this code:

```
new SpaceShip()
```

The syntax for creating objects (e.g., *new SpaceShip( )*) is the same in ActionScript 2.0 as it was in ActionScript 1.0. However, the syntax for defining classes in ActionScript 2.0 differs from ActionScript 1.0.

Most objects are stored somewhere after they're created so that they can be used later in the program. For example, we might store a *SpaceShip* instance in a variable named ship, like this:

```
var ship:SpaceShip = new SpaceShip();
```

Each object is a discrete data value that can be stored in a variable, an array element, or even a property of another object. For example, if you create 20 alien spaceships, you would ordinarily store references to the 20 *SpaceShip* objects in a single array. This allows you to easily manipulate multiple objects by cycling through the array and, say, invoking a method of the *SpaceShip* class on each object.

Object Usage

An object's methods provide its capabilities (i.e., behaviors)—things like "fire missile," "move," and "scroll down." An object's properties store its data, which describes its state at any given point in time. For example, at a particular point in a game, our ship's current state might be speed is 300, damage is 14.

Methods and properties that are defined as *public* by an object's class can be accessed from anywhere in a program. By contrast, methods and properties defined as *private* can be used only within the source code of the class or its subclasses. As we'll learn in Chapter 4, methods and properties should be defined as *public* only if they must be accessed externally.

To invoke a method, we use the dot operator (i.e., a period) and the function call operator (i.e., parentheses). For example:

```
// Invoke the ship object's fireMissile() method.
ship.fireMissile();
```

To set a property, we use the dot operator and an equals sign. For example:

```
// Set the ship's speed property to 120.
ship.speed = 120;
```

To retrieve a property's value, we use the dot operator on its own. For example:

```
// Display the value of the speed property in the Output panel.
trace(ship.speed);
```

Encapsulation

Objects are said to *encapsulate* their property values and method source code from the rest of the program. If properly designed, an object's private properties and the internal code used in its methods (including public methods) are its own business;

they can change without necessitating changes in the rest of the program. As long as the method names (and their parameters and return values) stay the same, the rest of the program can continue to use the object without being rewritten.

Encapsulation is an important aspect of object-oriented design because it allows different programmers to work on different classes independently. As long as they agree on the names of the public methods through which they'll communicate, the classes can be developed independently. Furthermore, by developing a specification that shows the publicly available methods, the parameters they require, and the values they return, a class can be tested thoroughly before being deployed. The same test code can be used to reverify the class's operation even if the code within the class is *refactored* (i.e., rewritten to enhance performance or to simplify the source code without changing the previously existing functionality).

In Chapter 4, we'll learn how to use the *private* modifier to prevent a method or property from being accessed by other parts of a program.

Datatypes

Each class in an object-oriented program can be thought of as defining a unique kind of data, which is formally represented as a *datatype* in the program.

 A class effectively defines a custom datatype.

You are probably already familiar with custom datatypes defined by built-in Action-Script classes, such as the *Date* class. That is, when you create a *Date* object using *new Date( )*, the returned value contains not a string or a number but a complex datatype that defines a particular day of a particular year. As such, the *Date* datatype supports various properties and methods uniquely associated with dates.

Datatypes are used to impose limits on what can be stored in a variable, used as a parameter, or passed as a return value. For example, when we defined the speed property earlier, we also specified its datatype as *Number* (as shown in bold):

```
// The expression ":Number" defines speed's datatype.
public var speed:Number;
```

Attempts to store a nonnumeric value in the speed property generate a compile-time error.

If you test a movie and Flash's Output panel displays an error containing the phrase "Type mismatch," you know that you used the wrong kind of data somewhere in your program (the compiler will tell you precisely where). Datatypes help us guarantee that a program isn't used in unintended ways. For example, by specifying that the datatype of speed is a number, we prevent someone from unintentionally setting speed to, say, the string "very fast." The following code generates a compile-time error due to the datatype mismatch:

```
public var speed:Number = "very fast";  // Error!
                                         // You can't assign a String to a
                                         // variable whose type is Number.
```

We'll talk more about datatypes and type mismatches in Chapter 3.

Inheritance

When developing an object-oriented application, we can use *inheritance* to allow one class to adopt the method and property definitions of another. Using inheritance, we can structure an application hierarchically so that many classes can reuse the features of a single class. For example, specific *Car*, *Boat*, and *Plane* classes could reuse the features of a generic *Vehicle* class, thus reducing redundancy in the application. Less redundancy means less code to write and test. Furthermore, it makes code easier to change—for example, updating a movement algorithm in a single class is easier and less error prone than updating it across several classes.

A class that inherits properties and methods from another class is called a *subclass*. The class from which a subclass inherits properties and methods is called the subclass's *superclass*. Naturally, a subclass can define its own properties and methods in addition to those it inherits from its superclass. A single superclass can have more than one subclass, but a single subclass can have only one superclass (although it can also inherit from its superclass's superclass, if any). We'll cover inheritance in detail in Chapter 6.

Packages

In a large application, we can create *packages* to contain groups of classes. A package lets us organize classes into logical groups and prevents naming conflicts between classes. This is particularly useful when components and third-party class libraries are involved. For example, Flash MX 2004's GUI components, including one named *Button*, reside in a package named *mx.controls*. The GUI component class named *Button* would be confused with Flash's built-in *Button* class if it weren't identified as part of the *mx.controls* package. Physically, packages are directories that are collections of class files (i.e., collections of *.as* files).

We'll learn about preventing naming conflicts by referring to classes within a package, and much more, in Chapter 9.

Compilation

When an OOP application is exported as a Flash movie (i.e., a *.swf* file), each class is *compiled*; that is, the compiler attempts to convert each class from source code to *bytecode*—instructions that the Flash Player can understand and execute. If a class contains errors, compilation fails and the Flash compiler displays the errors in the Output panel in the Flash authoring tool. The error messages, such as the datatype mismatch error described earlier, should help you diagnose and solve the problem. Even if the movie compiles successfully, errors may still occur while a program is running; these are called *runtime errors*. We'll learn about Player-generated runtime errors and program-generated runtime errors in Chapter 10.

Starting an Objected-Oriented Application

In our brief overview of OOP in Flash, we've seen that an object-oriented application is made up of classes and objects. But we haven't learned how to actually start the application running. Every Flash application, no matter how many classes or external assets it contains, starts life as a single *.swf* file loaded into the Flash Player. When the Flash Player loads a new *.swf* file, it executes the actions on frame 1 and then displays the contents of frame 1.

Hence, in the simplest case, we can create an object-oriented Flash application and start it as follows:

1. Create one or more classes in *.as* files.
2. Create a *.fla* file.
3. On frame 1 of the *.fla* file, add code that creates an object of a class.
4. Optionally invoke a method on the object to start the application.
5. Export a *.swf* file from the *.fla* file.
6. Load the *.swf* file into the Flash Player.

We'll study more complex ways to structure and run object-oriented Flash applications in Chapters 5, 11, and 12.

But How Do I Apply OOP?

Many people learn the basics of OOP only to say, "I understand the terminology and concepts, but I have no idea how or when to use them." If you have that feeling, don't worry, it's perfectly normal; in fact, it means you're ready to move on to the next phase of your learning—*object-oriented design* (OOD).

The core concepts of OOP (classes, objects, methods, properties, etc.) are only tools. The real challenge is designing what you want to build with those tools. Once you understand a hammer, nails, and wood, you still have to draw a blueprint before you can actually build a fence, a room, or a chair. Object-oriented design is the "draw a blueprint" phase of object-oriented programming, during which you organize your entire application as a series of classes. Breaking up a program into classes is a fundamental design problem that you'll face daily in your OOP work. We'll return to this important aspect of OOP regularly throughout this book.

But not all Flash applications need to be purely object-oriented. Flash supports both procedural and object-oriented programming and allows you to combine both approaches in a single Flash movie. In some cases, it's sensible to apply OOP only to a single part of your project. Perhaps you're building a web site with a section that displays photographs. You don't have to make the whole site object-oriented; you can just use OOP to create the photograph-display module. (In fact, we'll do just that in Chapters 5 and 7!)

So if Flash supports both procedural and object-oriented programming, how much of each is right for your project? To best answer that question, we first need to understand the basic structure of every Flash movie. The fundamental organizing structure of a Flash document (a *.fla* file) is the *timeline*, which contains one or more *frames*. Each frame defines the content that is displayed on the graphical canvas called the *Stage*. In the Flash Player, frames are displayed one at a time in a linear sequence, producing an animated effect—exactly like the frames in a filmstrip.

At one end of the development spectrum, Flash's timeline is often used for interactive animation and motion graphics. In this development style, code is mixed directly with timeline frames and graphical content. For example, a movie might display a 25-frame animation, then stop, calculate some random feature used to display another animation, and then stop again and ask the user to fill in a form while yet another animation plays in the background. That is, for simple applications, different frames in the timeline can be used to represent different program *states* (each state is simply one of the possible places, either physical or conceptual, that a user can be in the program). For example, one frame might represent the welcome screen, another frame might represent the data entry screen, a third frame might represent an error screen or exit screen, and so on. Of course, if the application includes animation, each program state might be represented by a range of frames instead of a single frame. For example, the welcome screen might include a looping animation.

When developing content that is heavily dependent on motion graphics, using the timeline makes sense because it allows for precise, visual control over graphic elements. In this style of development, code is commonly attached to the frames of the timeline using the Actions panel (F9). The code on a frame is executed immediately before the frame's content is displayed. Code can also be attached directly to the graphical components on stage. For example, a button can contain code that governs what happens when it is clicked.

Timeline-based development usually goes hand-in-hand with procedural programming because you want to take certain actions at the time a particular frame is reached. In Flash, "procedural programming" means executing code, defining functions, and setting variables on frames in a document's timeline or on graphical components on stage.

However, not all Flash content necessarily involves timeline-based motion. If you are creating a video game, it becomes impossible to position the monsters and the player's character using the timeline. Likewise, you don't know exactly when the user is going to shoot the monster or take some other action. Therefore, you must use ActionScript instead of the timeline to position the characters in response to user actions (or in response to an algorithm that controls the monsters in some semi-intelligent way). Instead of a timeline-based project containing predetermined animated sequences, we have a nonlinear project in which characters and their behavior are represented entirely in code.

This type of development lends itself naturally to objects that represent, say, the player's character or the monsters. At this end of the development spectrum lies traditional object-oriented programming, in which an application exists as a group of classes. In a pure object-oriented Flash application, a *.fla* file might contain only a single frame, which simply loads the application's main class and starts the application by invoking a method on that main class. Of course, OOP is good for more than just video games. For example, a Flash-based rental car reservation system might have no timeline code whatsoever and create all user interface elements from within classes.

Most real-world Flash applications lie somewhere between the extreme poles of timeline-only development and pure OOP development. For example, consider a Flash-based web site in which two buttons slide into the center of the screen and offer the user a choice of languages: "English" or "French." The user clicks the preferred language button, and both buttons slide off screen. An animated sequence then displays company information and a video showing a product demo. The video is controlled by a *MediaPlayback* component.

Our hypothetical web site includes both procedural programming and OOP, as follows:

- Frames 2 and 3 contain preloader code.
- Frame 10 contains code to start the button-slide animation.
- Frames 11–25 contain the button-slide animation.
- Frame 25 contains code to define button event handlers, which load a language-specific movie.
- In the loaded language-specific movie, frame 1 contains code to control the *MediaPlayback* component.

In the preceding example, code placed directly on frames (e.g., the preloader code) is procedural. But the buttons and *MediaPlayback* component are objects derived from classes stored in external *.as* files. Controlling them requires object-oriented programming. And, interestingly enough, Flash components are, themselves, movie clips. Movie clips, so intrinsic to Flash, can be thought of as self-contained objects with their own timelines and frames. Components (indeed, any movie clip) can contain procedural code internally on their own frames even though they are objects. Such is the nature of Flash development—assets containing procedural code can be mixed on multiple levels with object-oriented code.

As mentioned in the Preface, this book assumes you understand movie clips and have used them in your work. If you are a programmer coming to Flash from another language, and you need a crash course on movie clips from a programmer's perspective, consult Chapter 13 of *ActionScript for Flash MX: The Definitive Guide* (O'Reilly), available online at *http://moock.org/asdg/samples*.

Flash's ability to combine procedural and object-oriented code in a graphical, time-based development environment makes it uniquely flexible. That flexibility is both powerful and dangerous. On one hand, animations and interface transitions that are trivial in Flash might require hours of custom coding in languages such as C++ or Java. But on the other hand, code that is attached to frames on timelines or components on the Stage is time-consuming to find and modify. So overuse of timeline code in Flash can quickly (and quietly!) turn a project into an unmaintainable mess. Object-oriented techniques stress separation of code from assets such as graphics and sound, allowing an object-oriented application to be changed, reused, and expanded on more easily than a comparable timeline-based program. If you find yourself in the middle of a timeline-based project faced with a change and dreading the work involved, chances are the project should have been developed with object-oriented principles from the outset. Although OOP may appear to require additional up-front development time, for most nontrivial projects, you'll recoup that time investment many times over later in the project.

Ultimately, the amount of OOP you end up using in your work is a personal decision that will vary according to your experience and project requirements. You can use the following list to help decide when to use OOP and when to use procedural timeline code. Bear in mind, however, that these are just guidelines—there's always more than one way to create an application. Ultimately, if the software works and can be maintained, you're doing something right.

Consider using OOP when creating:

- Traditional desktop-style applications with few transitions and standardized user interfaces
- Applications that include server-side logic
- Functionality that is reused across multiple projects
- Components
- Games
- Highly customized user interfaces that include complex visual transitions

Consider using procedural programming when creating:

- Animations with small scripts that control flow or basic interactivity

- Simple applications such as a one-page product order form or a newsletter subscription form
- Highly customized user interfaces that include complex visual transitions

You'll notice that the bulleted item "Highly customized user interfaces that include complex visual transitions" is included as a case in which you might use both OOP and procedural programming. Both disciplines can effectively create that kind of content. However, remember that OOP in Flash is typically more maintainable than timeline code and is easier to integrate into version control systems and other external production tools. If you suspect that your highly customized UI will be used for more than a single project, you should strongly consider developing it as a reusable class library or set of components with OOP.

Note that in addition to Flash's traditional timeline metaphor, Flash MX Professional 2004 introduced a *Screens* feature (which includes both *Slides* and *Forms*). Screens provide a facade over the traditional timeline metaphor. Slides and Forms are akin to the card-based metaphors of programs like HyperCard. Slides are intended for PowerPoint style slide presentations, while Forms are intended for VB developers used to working on multipage forms. Like timeline-based applications, Screens-based applications include both object-oriented code (i.e., code in classes) and procedural-style code (i.e., code placed visually on components and on the Screens of the application). As mentioned in the Preface, this book does not cover Screens in detail, but the foundational OOP skills you'll learn in this text will more than equip you for your own exploration of Screens.

On with the Show!

In this chapter, we summarized the core concepts of OOP in Flash. We're now ready to move on with the rest of Part I, where we'll study all of those concepts again in detail, applying them to practical situations along the way. If you're already quite comfortable with OOP and want to dive into some examples, see Chapters 5, 7, 11, and 12, and all of Part III, which contain in-depth studies of real-world object-oriented code.

Let's get started!

CHAPTER 3

Datatypes and Type Checking

ActionScript 2.0 defines a wide variety of datatypes. Some datatypes are native to the language itself (e.g., *String*, *Number*, and *Boolean*). Others are included in the Flash Player and are available throughout all Flash movies (e.g., *Color*, *Date*, and *TextField*). Still other datatypes are defined by components that can be added individually to Flash movies (e.g., *List*, *RadioButton*, and *ScrollPane*).

For a primer on ActionScript's datatypes, see Chapter 3 of *ActionScript for Flash MX: The Definitive Guide* (O'Reilly), available online at *http://moock.org/asdg/samples*.

In addition to using ActionScript 2.0's datatypes, developers can add new datatypes to a program by creating classes (covered in Chapter 4) and interfaces (covered in Chapter 8). Every value in ActionScript 2.0 belongs to a datatype, whether built-in or programmer-defined. When we work with a value, we must use it only in ways supported by its datatype. For example, we can call *getTime( )* on a *Date* object, but we must not call *gotoAndPlay( )* on a *Date* object, because the *Date* class does not support the *gotoAndPlay( )* method. On the other hand, we can call *gotoAndPlay( )* on a movie clip because that method is defined by the *MovieClip* class.

In order for an object-oriented program to work properly, every operation performed on every object should succeed. That is, if a method is invoked on an object, the object's class must actually define that method. And if a property is accessed on an object, the object's class must define that property. If the object's class does not support the method or property, that aspect of the program will fail. Depending on how we write our code, either the failure will be silent (i.e., cause no error message), or it will cause an error message that appears in the Output panel. The error message helps us diagnose the problem.

We certainly strive to use objects appropriately. We don't intentionally call *gotoAndPlay( )* on a *Date* object, because we know that the *gotoAndPlay( )* method isn't supported by the *Date* class. But what happens if we make a typographical error? What if we accidentally invoke *geTime( )* (missing a "t") instead of *getTime( )* on a *Date* object?

```
someDate.geTime( )  // WRONG! No such method!
```

Our call to *geTime( )* will fail because the *Date* class defines no such method.

And what happens if we invoke *indexOf( )* on a value we think is a *String*, but the value turns out to be a *Number*? The call to *indexOf( )* will fail, because the *Number* class doesn't support the *indexOf( )* method. Example 3-1 demonstrates this situation.

Example 3-1. A mistaken datatype assumption

```
// WRONG! This code mistakenly assumes that getDay( ) returns
// a string indicating the day (e.g., "Monday", "Tuesday"),
// but getDay( ) actually returns a number from 0 to 6.
var today;
today = new Date().getDay( );
if (today.indexOf("Friday") == 1) {
  trace("Looking forward to the weekend!");
}

// The correct code should be:
var today;
today = new Date().getDay( );
// Sunday is 0, Monday is 1, ... Friday is 5.
if (today == 5) {
  trace("Looking forward to the weekend!");
}
```

In a large program, these kinds of problems can be exceedingly difficult and time-consuming to track down. In both the *geTime( )* example and the *indexOf( )* example, unless ActionScript reports an error in the Output panel, we'll have a hard time identifying the issue and locating its cause in our program.

To help us recognize and isolate datatype-related problems in our code, we use ActionScript 2.0's *type checking* capabilities. That is, we can ask ActionScript to check the values in our program and warn us with an error message if it detects a value being used in some inappropriate way. But there's a catch: in order to provide this service, ActionScript 2.0 requires that you formally declare the datatype of every variable, property, parameter, and return value that you want checked. To declare the datatype of a variable or property, we use this general form, referred to as *post-colon syntax*:

    var *variableOrPropertyName*:*datatype*

Specifying an item's datatype is often called *datatype declaration*. For example, this line of code *declares* that the datatype of the variable count is *Number*:

    var count:Number;

We'll learn more about datatype syntax later in this chapter.

As a best practice, in an ActionScript 2.0 program, you should declare the datatype of every variable, property, function parameter, method parameter, function return value, and method return value.

ActionScript 2.0 performs type checking on every variable, property, parameter, and return value that has a declared datatype. If your code attempts to store incompatible types of data in an item that has a declared datatype, a *type error* appears in the Output panel at compile time. Later we'll learn precisely what constitutes an "incompatible type," but for now, you can just assume intuitively that two types are incompatible when they don't match (i.e., *String* and *Number*, *Array* and *Sound*, etc.).

 Variables, properties, parameters, and return values *without* a declared datatype are *not* type checked. If you omit the datatype, omit the colon used in post-colon syntax as well.

Type checking helps us guarantee that a program will run the way we intend it to. To see how, let's return to Example 3-1 in which a programmer mistakenly attempted to invoke *indexOf( )* on a numeric value. The source of the programmer's problem was the incorrect assumption that *Date.getDay( )* returns a string, when in fact, it returns a number. The programmer originally assigned the return value of *getDay( )* to the variable today without specifying today's datatype:

```
var today;
today = new Date().getDay( );
```

Because the code doesn't specify the datatype of the variable today, the ActionScript 2.0 compiler has no way of knowing that the programmer expects today to contain a string. The compiler, hence, allows any type of data to be stored in today. The preceding code simply stores the return value of *getDay( )* into today. Because the return value of *getDay( )* is a number, today stores a number, not a string. This eventually leads to a problem with the program.

In ActionScript 2.0, the programmer can prevent the problem from going unnoticed by declaring the intended datatype of the variable today, as follows (changes shown in bold):

```
// ":String" is the datatype declaration
var today:String;
today = new Date().getDay( );
```

In this case, the programmer is still "wrong." His assumption that *getDay( )* returns a string is still a problem, but it is no longer a *hidden* problem. Because the programmer has stated his assumption and intent, the ActionScript 2.0 compiler dutifully generates this error:

```
Type mismatch in assignment statement: found Number where String is
required.
```

This error message should elicit great joy. Why? Because *known* errors are usually trivial to fix once you understand the error message. The error message states that the code requires a string but encountered a number instead. We need to work backward to understand the message's meaning. Why did the code "require" a string? It

---

was just obeying the programmer's request! The compiler thinks the code requires a string because (and for no other reason than) the programmer declared today's datatype as *String*. The error message tells the programmer that he is breaking his own constraints; the programmer declared a string-only data container (the variable today) and tried to place a numeric value (the return value of *getDay( )*) into it.

An inexperienced developer might immediately say, "Aha! The problem is that awful number where a string belongs! I must change the number into a string!" Don't fall into that trap, and don't be misled by the error message.

The programmer originally assumed that *Date.getDay( )* returns a *String* when it in fact returns a *Number*. But the programmer has no control over the value returned by *getDay( )*, which is defined by the *Date* class and not the programmer. So the solution is to accommodate the return value's correct datatype by storing it in a variable of type *Number* instead of type *String*. Example 3-2 demonstrates.

Example 3-2. Fixing a datatype mismatch error

```
// This line declares today's type as a Number.
var today:Number
// Assign the return value of getDay() to today. In this version,
// the variable's datatype matches the datatype of the value returned
// by getDay(), so no type mismatch error occurs.
today = new Date().getDay();

// Sunday is 0, Monday is 1, ... Friday is 5.
if (today == 5) {
  trace("Looking forward to the weekend!");
}
```

Example 3-3 demonstrates an alternative case in which the programmer really does need a string for display purposes. As usual, *getDay( )* returns a number, so in this case, the programmer must manually convert the number to a human-readable string. The trick is to use the number returned by *getDay( )* to extract a string from an array of day names.

Example 3-3. One way to derive a string from a number

```
// This line declares today's type as a Number
// and assigns the return value of getDay() to today.
var today:Number = new Date().getDay();

// Populate an array with the names of the days.
var dayNames:Array = ["Sunday", "Monday", "Tuesday", "Wednesday",
                      "Thursday", "Friday", "Saturday"];
// Make a new variable that stores the human-readable day.
var todayName:String = dayNames[today];

// Display the human-readable day in a text field.
currentDay_txt.text = todayName;
// Display the human-readable day in the Output panel.
trace(todayName);
```

So there are two ways to solve a type mismatch error. One way is to declare your variable to be of the correct type and write (or rewrite if necessary) your code to deal with the datatype accordingly. The alternative is to write extra code to convert the returned data to the datatype you desire.

Regardless, without ActionScript 2.0's type checking, the original datatype mismatch might have gone unnoticed.

 ActionScript 1.0 had no form of type checking whatsoever and generated no type-based errors. This left developers with the arduous chore of hunting down unintentional typos and misuses of objects.

ActionScript 2.0's approach to datatyping is called *static typing*. In static typing, the datatype of variables and other data containers is fixed at compile time so that the compiler can guarantee the validity of every method called and property accessed in the program. Because datatypes are fixed in a statically typed language, the compiler can say, "I know this variable contains a *Date* object, and I know that the *Date* class doesn't define a method by the name *geTime( )* (remember our earlier typo?), so I'll warn the programmer with an error message." Handy indeed.

 In ActionScript 1.0, methods were often added to a class via the prototype object. This technique is not recognized by the ActionScript 2.0 compiler in most cases. Therefore, if you are compiling code for ActionScript 2.0, invoking a prototype-based method on a variable with a declared datatype may cause a compile-time error. In ActionScript 2.0, there is no way to add a method to most classes at runtime; the practice is considered officially illegitimate. You should define all methods in class files, prior to compiling. See "Built-in Dynamic Classes" for exceptions to this rule. See "Class Attributes" in Chapter 4 for related information.

The converse of static typing is *dynamic typing*, in which each value is associated with a datatype at runtime, not at compile time. With dynamic typing, data containers such as variables can change datatypes at runtime because type information is associated with each value, not with each data container. In a dynamically typed language, such as Python or Smalltalk, type mismatch errors can occur at runtime but they can't be detected a priori at compile type. ActionScript 2.0 does not provide any dynamic type facilities and generates no runtime type errors. ActionScript 1.0, by contrast, provided no type checking at all and therefore could not be considered statically typed nor dynamically typed—rather, it was considered *untyped*. ActionScript 1.0 effectively let you do whatever you wanted with any kind of data. For example, in ActionScript 1.0, you could change the type of a variable from one type to another without errors:

```
// ActionScript 1.0 code...
var x = 10;          // Look ma, I'm a number!
x = "hello world";   // Now I'm a string!
```

And you could access a nonexistent method or property without errors:

```
// ActionScript 1.0 code...
var s = new Sound( );
s.thisMethodDoesntExist( );   // No error in ActionScript 1.0!
```

As we learned earlier, the preceding code—without any modifications—would not cause errors even in ActionScript 2.0! That's because ActionScript 2.0's type checking is an opt-in system. In order to activate type checking, you must specify the datatype of the variable, property, parameter, or return value being used. Hence, to cause the preceding ActionScript 1.0 code to generate helpful errors in ActionScript 2.0, we declare the variables' datatypes, as follows:

```
// ActionScript 2.0 code...
var x:Number = 10;   // Here, x's datatype starts as Number.
x = "hello world";   // This attempt to store a string in x causes an error!

var s:Sound = new Sound( );
s.thisMethodDoesntExist( );   // ERROR! No such method...

// Here's the output:
**Error** Scene=Scene 1, layer=Layer 1, frame=1:line 3: Type mismatch in
assignment statement: found String where Number is required.
x = "hello world";   // This attempt to store a string in x causes an error!

**Error** Scene=Scene 1, layer=Layer 1, frame=1:Line 6: There is no method
 with the name 'thisMethodDoesntExist'.
s.thisMethodDoesntExist( );   // ERROR! No such method...
```

Because ActionScript 2.0 lets you circumvent type checking by omitting type declarations, its specific variety of static typing is called *weak static typing*, where "weak" means that the language will check for type errors at compile time if told to do so but also offers programmers ways to disable the type checking system. Languages such as Java that do not let the programmer circumvent type checking are called *strongly typed*. Generally speaking, it pays to develop all ActionScript 2.0 projects with datatyping enabled for all variables, properties, parameters, and return values (i.e., by declaring their types using post-colon syntax). Even when upgrading Action-Script 1.0 code, try to add as much type information as you can; the more information you provide, the more feedback you'll get from the compiler when you do something wrong.

 Macromedia's documentation uses the term "strict data typing" to refer to ActionScript's type checking capabilities. Although Macromedia uses "strict" as a synonym for "static," they are not technically the same. So be aware that the terms "strict," "static," and "strong" are often interchanged recklessly in common discussion, as are "weak" and "dynamic."

Why Static Typing?

There's plenty of debate about whether static typing (compile-time type checking) is better than dynamic typing (runtime type checking). But there's no question that a programmer benefits from being alerted to potential or actual type mismatch errors. Next to syntax errors (grammatical and typographical errors), datatype errors are the most common kind of error in an object-oriented program. If a syntax error occurs, a program won't compile. If a type mismatch error occurs, a program may be able to run, but it wouldn't likely be able to perform one or more requested operations. Such errors often lead to program failures. Some compilers merely warn of type mismatch errors but still allow compilation to continue. However, ActionScript 2.0's static typing facilities prevent the movie from compiling if type mismatch errors exist. Compared to ActionScript 1.0's complete lack of type checking, this is a great step forward for the language.

You must address all type mismatch errors to get your movie to compile. If type checking is new to you, you may feel that this requirement adds unnecessary work. You might be tempted to simply eliminate the datatype declarations that are causing the type mismatch errors in order to get your movie to compile. That's a little like going upstairs when your basement is flooded. Avoiding the problem doesn't solve anything in the long run. Here's a laundry list of reasons that explains why you should stay the course and learn to love type checking:

- Type checking guarantees the validity of most operations at compile time, catching potential errors before they ever occur. Once a program type checks (i.e., compiles without producing type errors), most careless errors are eliminated, so you can focus on correcting any errors in logic.

- Specifying type information throughout your code helps to ensure you follow your own OOP architectural plan. Similarly, it guarantees you'll use another developer's class as intended. If you misuse a class, you'll hear about it from the compiler.

- Type checking reduces the amount of manual data-verification code you need in your methods (though you'll still have to do some data verification, such as when parsing user input or server results).

- Some programmers find static typing easier to read because statically typed code expresses important information about values and dependencies in a program's source code.

 In Flash MX 2004, when you specify datatypes in your code, the Flash authoring tool provides *code hints* for built-in classes and components. A code hint is a pop-up menu that lists the properties and methods of objects as you type them. This isn't a traditional OOP benefit, but it's a nice side effect. It also eliminates the need to use suffixes such as "_mc" to activate code hinting, as was necessary in Flash MX.

As noted earlier, static typing is not universally accepted as the best way to implement type checking. The jury is split, but many well-known programmers argue in favor of dynamic typing over static typing. Dynamic type checking is often less restrictive and can make code easier to change than statically typed code. Those arguments aside, ActionScript 2.0 will be statically typed for the foreseeable future because static typing is part of the ECMAScript 4 specification on which ActionScript 2.0 is based. However, if type theory debates titillate you, you should enjoy these articles:

- *Static Type Checking*, by Dave Harris, at *http://ootips.org/static-typing.html*
- *Strong Typing vs. Strong Testing*, by Bruce Eckel, at *http://mindview.net/WebLog/log-0025*

The main advantage of static type checking is that it can check all your code at compile time, whereas dynamic type checking requires that you execute the code in order to verify it. To be sure that all your code is executed, you need to perform *unit testing* on each module (writing classes specifically to test the output of other classes). Mr. Eckel argues that combining religious unit testing with dynamic type checking offers all the error-catching benefits of strong typing and more. For a quick-and-dirty example showing how to write a unit test in Java, see *http://c2.com/cgi/wiki?CodeUnitTestFirstExampleTwo*. For an ActionScript 2.0 unit testing tool, see *http://www.as2unit.org*.

In some languages, static typing improves runtime performance. ActionScript 2.0's static typing does not improve runtime performance.

Type Syntax

Now that we've had a general introduction to type checking in ActionScript 2.0, let's study the syntax more formally. ActionScript 2.0's compile-time type checking can be applied to:

- A variable
- A property
- A function or method parameter
- A function or method return value

To enable type checking for any of the preceding items, we declare the item's type using post-colon syntax, as discussed earlier and in the next section. Declaring an item's type tells the compiler what kind of data it should contain. Armed with that knowledge, the compiler can warn us of two possible error conditions:

- If a value of an incompatible type is stored in a variable, passed as a function parameter, or returned by a function, the compiler generates a *type mismatch* error.

- If a nonexistent property or method is accessed through a typed variable, function parameter, or function return value, the compiler generates an error explaining that the property or method cannot be found.

The compiler selectively type checks only items that have their types declared. Unfortunately, Flash MX 2004 does not provide a way to force the ActionScript compiler to report which items have no datatype declared. Hence, type errors can slip through if you're not vigilant about declaring datatypes. (For comparison, in Java, a program will not compile if any datatype declarations are missing.)

Declaring Variable and Property Datatypes

To declare the datatype of a variable or property, use the following syntax:

```
var variableOrPropertyName:datatype;
```

where *variableOrPropertyName* is the name of the variable or property, and *datatype* is the type of data that the variable or property can legally contain. For example, the following code creates a variable called currentTime and declares its datatype as *Date*. It then assigns a new *Date* instance to the variable, which is legal, because the class of the instance is compatible with the datatype of the variable:

```
// Create a variable that can contain only data
// compatible with the Date datatype.
var currentTime:Date;

// Store a Date instance in the currentTime variable.
currentTime = new Date( );
```

We could also reduce the preceding two lines to a single step:

```
var currentTime:Date = new Date( );
```

If you mistakenly refer to a nonexistent datatype in a datatype declaration or elsewhere, the compiler will return the following message:

```
The class '<NONEXISTENT_TYPE>' could not be loaded.
```

Once a variable's datatype is declared, it is fixed until the variable is destroyed. Attempts to assign any value not compatible with the original type cause a type mismatch error at compile time. For example, this code attempts to assign a *Number* to currentTime, whose datatype was declared as *Date*:

```
var currentTime:Date;
currentTime = 10;
```

That code yields the following compile-time error:

```
Type mismatch in assignment statement: found Number where Date is required.
```

Attempts to access any property or method on currentTime that is not defined by the *Date* class likewise yields an error. For example, this code:

```
// Create a typed variable.
var currentTime:Date = new Date( );

// Attempt to access the nonexistent _width property.
currentTime._width = 20;
// Attempt to access the nonexistent sort( ) method.
currentTime.sort( );
```

yields the following errors:

```
There is no property with the name '_width'.
There is no method with the name 'sort'.
```

Note that in order to report nonexistent methods and properties, ActionScript 2.0 prevents new properties or methods from being added to individual objects after they have been created (unlike ActionScript 1.0, which allows such additions). For example, in ActionScript 2.0, the following code is illegal, but in ActionScript 1.0, it is allowed:

```
var currentTime:Date = new Date( );
currentTime.name = "Day One";  // Illegal in ActionScript 2.0, but
                               // legal in ActionScript 1.0.
```

As we'll learn in Chapter 4, ActionScript 2.0 provides a special means of creating classes whose instances allow new properties and methods to be added at runtime. However, instances of these classes cannot, by definition, be checked for nonexistent methods and properties. Later in this chapter, under "Bypassing Type Checking on a Per-Use Basis," we'll see that ActionScript 2.0's type checking can also be disabled on a per-object basis.

But remember that type checking is intended to help you write better code more quickly. Don't try to avoid it by, say, changing the datatype of a variable as follows:

```
var currentTime:Date;
var currentTime:Number;
```

In ActionScript 2.0, the preceding code does not change the datatype of currentTime to *Number*. The second line is simply ignored and later attempts to assign a numeric value to currentTime will generate errors.

However, due to a bug in the ActionScript 2.0 compiler in Flash MX 2004, the following code *does* change the datatype of currentTime from *Date* to *Number*:

```
var currentTime:Date;
var currentTime:Number = 10;  // Redeclare with assignment.
currentTime = 11;             // currentTime's datatype is now Number.
```

The preceding code redeclares the datatype of the variable currentTime and also reassigns its value. The reassignment causes the (buggy) change in the variable's datatype. Such code is ill advised, as the official behavior will very likely change in the future.

Instead of redeclaring a variable's datatype, you should use two separate variables when you need to store values of two different datatypes. That said, you can safely reuse a loop counter when its datatype is the same across multiple loops in the same script, function, or method. Just remember to omit the keyword *var*, the colon, and the datatype on the second and subsequent loops. For example:

```
// First loop: declare i as a Number.
for (var i:Number = 0; i < 10; i++) {
  trace(i);
}
// Second loop: reuse i, but don't include var or :Number.
for (i = 15; i > 0; i--) {
  trace(i);
}
```

In a loop in which a different datatype is required, use a new variable:

```
// Use p instead of i.
for (var p:String in someObj) {
  // List properties of an object.
  trace("Found property: " + p);
}
```

Naturally, local variables within one function have no relation to local variables within a separate function. So you could have a local variable declared as a number in one function and a different local variable of the same name declared as a string in another function.

Declaring Method Parameter and Return Value Datatypes

The following code shows how to declare the datatype of method or function parameters and return values:

```
function methodName (param1Name:param1Type,
                     param2Name:param2Type):returnType {
  // ...
}
```

where *methodName* is the name of the method or function, *param1Name* and *param2Name* are the names of the parameters, *param1Type* and *param2Type* are the parameters' datatypes, and *returnType* is the datatype of the function's return value. This example shows a function with two parameters but, naturally, a function declaration may have zero or more parameter:datatype pairs, separated by commas. Functions that return no value should specify a *returnType* of *Void*. But note that the *Void* type is reserved for use only as a function *returnType*. To declare a variable or parameter with a datatype that can accommodate any value, use the *Object* type, as described in the later section, "Compatible Types."

The following code creates a function, *largerThanTen( )*, that checks whether a numeric value is greater than ten. It requires a single numeric argument and returns a Boolean result (either true or false):

```
function largerThanTen (n:Number):Boolean {
  return n > 10;
}
```

If we pass a nonnumeric value to the function, the compiler issues a type mismatch error, indicating the location of the error in your code by line number. For example, the following code:

```
largerThanTen("colin");
```

yields this error (line number omitted):

```
Type mismatch.
```

If, within the function, we access a nonnumeric property or method on n, the compiler generates an error. For example, the following code:

```
function largerThanTen (n:Number):Boolean {
  n.charAt(0);
  return n > 10;
}
```

yields this error:

```
There is no method with the name 'charAt'.
```

Returning anything but a *Boolean* value from the function also causes a type mismatch error. We'll revisit return-value type mismatch errors with examples when we study methods in the next chapter.

Finally, storing the return value of a function or method in a variable or property of an incompatible type causes a type mismatch error. For example, the following code attempts to store a numeric return value in a *String* variable:

```
function sum (x:Number, y:Number):Number {
  return x+y;
}
var result:String = sum(10, 20);
```

In response, the compiler generates the following error:

```
Type mismatch in assignment statement: found Number where String is required.
```

Refer to the discussion accompanying Examples 3-2 and 3-3 for ways of addressing this sort of type mismatch error.

Accessing nonexistent methods and properties on a typed return value also causes an error. This attempt to call *getYear( )* on a numeric return value:

```
sum(10, 20).getYear( );
```

yields this error:

```
There is no method with the name 'getYear'.
```

Remember, these errors are your best friends. Don't think of them as scolding you or complaining about something that's not your problem. You should thank the compiler for telling you when you've made a mistake, just as you'd thank your neighbor for pointing out that you left your keys in your front door. Every time the compiler generates a datatype-related error, think to yourself, "Wow, I just saved a few minutes or maybe a few hours tracking down that problem myself!"

In an object-oriented Flash application, be sure to provide a datatype for each property, variable, method parameter, and method return value. If you omit the datatype of an item, ActionScript 2.0 performs no type checking on it and cannot warn you about datatype-related errors in your code.

In Chapter 4, we'll study method definition again, in much greater detail.

Why Post-Colon Syntax?

As we've learned in this section, ActionScript 2.0 uses the following, slightly unusual syntax for type declarations:

```
variableOrPropertyName:datatype = value;
```

By contrast, Java and C++ use:

```
datatype variableName = value;
```

In *JavaScript 2.0: Evolving a Language for Evolving Systems*, Waldemar Horwat (one of the creators of the ECMAScript 4 specification) explains the reason for this difference at *http://www.mozilla.org/js/language/evolvingJS.pdf*.

 Embarrassingly, this is a decision based purely on a historical standards committee vote—this seemed like a good idea at one time. There is no technical reason for using [post-colon] syntax, but it's too late to reverse it now (implementations using this syntax have already shipped), even though most of the people involved with it admit the syntax is a mistake.

Compatible Types

The following discussion assumes an understanding of inheritance in OOP. If you're not familiar with that concept, you may want to skip this section for now and return to it once you've read Chapter 6.

Earlier we learned that a variable of one type can store only a value of a *compatible type*. Intuitively, we understand that the *String* type is incompatible with the *Number* type (that is, putting aside for a moment that it is possible to convert between strings and numbers, we know that a string is not a number). But the phrase "compatible type" has a very precise technical meaning. A type, X, is compatible with another type, Y, if X is of type Y, or if X is any subtype of Y.

For example, suppose we have a class, *Ball*, and a subclass, *Basketball*. A variable of type *Ball* can store a *Basketball* instance because the *Basketball* type is a subtype (i.e., subclass) of *Ball*:

```
var ball1:Ball = new Basketball( );  // Legal!
```

The preceding code works because the compiler knows that every *Basketball* instance has (through inheritance) all the properties and methods of the *Ball* class. The converse, however, is not true; every *Ball* instance does not necessarily have the properties and methods of the *Basketball* class. Therefore, the following code yields a compile-time type mismatch error:

```
var ball2:Basketball = new Ball( );  // Illegal!
```

On first glance, you might think that the preceding examples seem backward, but they are not. In the first example, we store a *Basketball* instance in the variable ball1, whose declared datatype is *Ball*. The compiler allows this even though the *Basketball* subclass might define methods and properties not supported by the *Ball* superclass. However, the compiler displays an error if we try to access a method or property on ball1 that isn't supported by the *Ball* class (i.e., the datatype of ball1) even if such method or property is defined for the *Basketball* class. For example, suppose that the *Basketball* subclass defines an *inflate( )* method but the *Ball* superclass does not. The second line of the following code example causes the compiler to display an error:

```
var ball1:Ball = new Basketball( );  // Legal, so far...
ball1.inflate( );                    // But this causes a compiler error!
```

Thus, the compiler gives us a little rope and we have to avoid the temptation to hang ourselves. As programmers, we need to be smart enough not to access methods and parameters of the *Basketball* class on ball1, unless they are also supported by the *Ball* class.

 The compiler checks the datatype of the variable (ball1)—not the class of the object actually stored in the variable—to determine what methods and properties are available.

That explanation might be clear, but it is admittedly counterintuitive. You may be wondering whether there is some way to make use of the *Basketball*-ness of the *Basketball* instance stored in ball1, even though the variable's datatype is *Ball*. We'll answer that question under "Casting," later in this chapter. And we'll revisit our *Basketball* and *Ball* classes under "Polymorphism and Dynamic Binding" in Chapter 6.

Now let's return to the converse example in which we attempted to store a *Ball* instance in the variable ball2, whose datatype is *Basketball*:

```
var ball2:Basketball = new Ball( );  // Illegal!
```

What would happen if the compiler allowed the preceding assignment? At some point later in the program, we might try to access methods and properties of the *Basketball* subclass on the ball2 instance, but those methods and properties would not be supported (the object we stored in ball2 is a *Ball*, not a *Basketball*!). Therefore, the compiler prevents us from storing a *Ball* instance in a *Basketball*-typed variable to prevent potential runtime errors resulting from accessing methods or properties of the *Basketball* class on an instance of the *Ball* class.

In the following example, if the first line were allowed by the compiler, we'd get into trouble later. The second line seems reasonable at compile time (it invokes the *inflate( )* method on what it thinks is a *Basketball* instance). But at runtime, the interpreter would attempt to invoke *inflate( )* on what is in fact a *Ball* instance (stored in ball2). The invocation would fail because the *Ball* class doesn't define the *inflate( )* method:

```
var ball2:Basketball = new Ball(); // If this were allowed at compile time...
ball2.inflate();                   // this would cause a runtime error!
```

Make sense? If not, remember that all basketballs are balls, but not all balls are basketballs. We can treat any basketball as a ball (even if we don't take advantage of all its features), but we can't treat any ball like a basketball. For example, inflating a bowling ball wouldn't work very well!

 The rule of thumb is to declare the variable to be of a more general type than the content placed in it (i.e., you can place data of the subtype's class within a variable declared to be of the supertype's class).

The ability to use subtypes wherever a given type is expected enables an important OOP feature: *polymorphism*. We'll return to subtypes and polymorphism in Chapter 6.

Handling Any Datatype

In ActionScript 2.0, we can make a variable, property, parameter, or return value accept data of any type by specifying *Object* as the datatype. For example, here we declare the datatype of container as *Object*. We can subsequently store an instance of any class in it without error:

```
var container:Object = new Date(); // No error.
container = new Color();            // No error.
```

This technique works because the *Object* class is the superclass of all ActionScript classes, so all types are compatible with the *Object* type (primitive values such as the Boolean true or the string "hello world" are not, strictly speaking, instances of any class but are still considered compatible with the *Object* type).

But be careful not to overuse this technique, as it effectively disables the compiler's ability to generate type errors for the variable, property, parameter, or return value in question. The compiler won't complain when you refer to a nonexistent property or method on an item whose datatype is *Object*. For example, the following code generates no errors:

```
var container:Object = new Date(); // No error.
trace(container.toString());        // Execute toString() normally.
container.blahblahblah();           // Invoke nonexistent method. No error.
trace(container.foobarbaz);         // Access nonexistent property. No error.
```

The *toString( )* method executes normally because it is supported by all objects, but no error occurs for the invocation of *blahblahblah( )* and the access of foobarbaz, despite the fact that they are not defined by any class.

Using the *Object* datatype is not the only way to elude ActionScript 2.0's type checking; we'll discuss several others shortly, under "Circumventing Type Checking."

Compatibility with null and undefined

In an object-oriented ActionScript 2.0 program, it's typical to store null or undefined in a variable as an indication of an absence of data or an uninitialized variable. Knowing this, you might wonder how a variable can store null if its datatype is, say, *MovieClip*. Rest easy—unlike other values, the null and undefined types can be used anywhere, regardless of the type of container they are stored in:

```
var target:MovieClip = null;  // Legal.

function square (x:Number):Number {
  return x*x;
}
square(null);  // Legal.

function square (x:Number):Number {
  if (x == 0) {
    return null;  // Legal.
  }
  return x*x;
}
```

Declaring something's type to be *Object* makes it a universal recipient, like a person with type AB positive blood who can accept any type of blood you give her. On the other hand, null and undefined are universal donors, like people with type O negative blood whose blood can be transfused into any other person without harm.

This flexibility allows us to use the null type to indicate an empty value for any data container. For example, here we construct a new *TextFormat* object, using null for arguments we wish to leave empty:

```
// Specify emphasis format, but not other font information.
var tf:TextFormat = new TextFormat(null, null, null, true);
```

Compatibility with undefined also allows ActionScript to assign undefined to parameters, variables, and properties that have never been assigned a value. For example, here we define a method that displays a message on screen, complete with the message sender's name. If the name of the message sender is not provided, ActionScript sets the sentBy parameter to undefined, in which case the method uses the name "Anonymous":

```
public function displayMsg (msg:String, sentBy:String):Void {
  // Use "Anonymous" if a name was not supplied.
  if (sentBy == undefined) {
    sentBy = "Anonymous";
  }
  // Display the message in a text field.
  output.text = sentBy + ": " + msg;
}
```

Built-in Dynamic Classes

We saw earlier that trying to dynamically add a property to the *Date* class generates a compile-time error in ActionScript 2.0. To allow new properties and methods to be added to a class's instances without generating a compile-time error, we can use a *dynamic class*. You can define your own dynamic classes, but some built-in classes are dynamic by default. Due partially to the architecture of the Flash Player and partially to the heritage of ActionScript 1.0, the following native ActionScript 2.0 classes are dynamic:

- *Array*
- *ContextMenu*
- *ContextMenuItem*
- *Function*
- *FunctionArguments* (a.k.a. the *Arguments* object)
- *LoadVars*
- *MovieClip*
- *Object*
- *TextField*

When you attempt to access a nonexistent property or method on an object of one of the preceding dynamic classes, the ActionScript 2.0 compiler does not generate an error. For example, the following code yields no error:

```
var dataSender:LoadVars = new LoadVars();
dataSender.firstName = "Rebecca";  // No error, even though
                                   // the LoadVars class doesn't
                                   // define the firstName property.
```

However, type mismatch errors may still occur when using the preceding dynamic classes. For example, the following code creates a variable of type *Array* and attempts to place a *Date* instance into it:

```
var list:Array = new Date( );
```

It yields the following error:

```
Type mismatch in assignment statement: found Date where Array is required.
```

 As we emphasized earlier, in ActionScript 1.0, unlike in ActionScript 2.0, it was possible to add a new property or method to any object at runtime. Furthermore, ActionScript 1.0 allowed you to add new methods and properties to an entire class at runtime (via the class's prototype object). ActionScript 2.0 considers adding new properties and methods to classes or objects at runtime bad form. We'll cover this limitation, its motivation, and its workarounds in Chapter 6, under "Augmenting Built-in Classes and Objects."

Circumventing Type Checking

We learned earlier that ActionScript 2.0's type checking is an "opt-in" system. That is, type checking occurs only when the programmer supplies type information (i.e., declares an item's datatype) in a program's source code. If you are sadistic and prefer to check your code manually for type errors, simply do not declare type information for variables, properties, parameters, and return values. When no type information is supplied for a data container, the compiler skips type checking for it. For example, the following code creates a variable, x, but does not declare x's datatype:

```
var x = 10;
```

Because the variable x is not typed, type checking is not (indeed cannot be) performed, and x's datatype can be changed without generating an error:

```
x = "hello";  // Change from Number to String.
```

Furthermore, accessing nonexistent properties and methods on x causes no error:

```
trace(x._width);   // No error. Returns undefined if _width doesn't exist.
x.flyToTheMoon( );  // No error.
                    // Fails silently if flyToTheMoon( ) doesn't exist.
```

Likewise, when a function or method parameter's type is not supplied, the parameter can accept values of any type without generating a compile-time error. And when a function's or method's return type is not supplied, the function or method can return values of any type without generating a compile-time error. The following code shows a method that declares no parameter types or return type. No matter what the types of the parameters, the method adds them together and returns the result. The result can legally belong to any datatype:

```
function combine (x, y) {
  return x + y;
```

```
}
// Pass values with different datatypes to x and y.
// No errors occur because the parameters x and y are not typed.
trace(combine(4,5));                    // Displays: 9
trace(combine("hello ", "world"));      // Displays: hello world
trace(combine(_root, "hello world"));   // Displays: _level0hello world
```

While the preceding code may seem more convenient because of its flexibility, it actually causes more work and problems than a typed version would. When the method is not typed, the program code—not the compiler—must decide whether the method's return value is useful or nonsensical. The program becomes responsible for guarding against basic data errors rather than relying on the compiler to do so automatically. For example, if we wanted to be sure that the result of *combine(4, 5)* were a number, we'd have to use:

```
if (typeof combine(4, 5) == "number") {
  // Okay to proceed...
} else {
  trace("Unusable value returned by combine().");
}
```

The preceding code successfully safeguards against nonnumeric uses of *combine( )*, but it takes five lines to do so! What's more, it is required every time the program uses the *combine( )* method, and similar code would be needed for any other calls to methods without return types. That is, absent compile-time datatype checking, the programmer has to implement a lot of runtime datatype checking.

With datatypes declared, the *combine( )* method would look like this:

```
function combine (x:Number, y:Number):Number {
  return x + y;
}
```

In which case, the following code:

```
combine("ten", 5);
```

would *automatically* generate a type mismatch error at compile time. With the typed version of the method, we can omit the earlier five lines of type checking code because the compiler checks the datatypes for us and displays an error when a type is misused.

Creating Parameters That Accept Multiple Types

Occasionally it's convenient to create a function or method whose parameters accept more than one type of data. For example, you might want our recent *combine( )* method to work with both strings and numbers. Or you might want to be able to send both XML objects and strings to a server, as does the built-in *XMLSocket* class via its *send( )* method. The *XMLSocket.send( )* method's only parameter, data, can accept a *String* object, an *XML* object, or an item of any other datatype, allowing the developer to choose what's appropriate for a given situation. The following calls to *XMLSocket.send( )* are both legal:

```
theSocket.send("Hello World");        // Send a string.

var doc:XML = new XML("<P>Hello World</P>");
theSocket.send(doc);                  // Send an XML instance.
```

As we learned earlier under "Handling Any Datatype," we can use any type of data wherever the *Object* datatype is declared. Hence, we can make a parameter that accepts any type of data by specifying *Object* as the parameter's datatype. Again, this technique works because the *Object* class is the superclass of all ActionScript classes, so all types are compatible with the *Object* type.

The following function defines a parameter, msg, that can accept any type of data. Within the body of the function, we invoke *toString( )* on whatever value was passed for msg:

```
function output (msg:Object):Void {
   trace(msg.toString( ));
}
```

The *toString( )* method is defined by the *Object* class, so it is guaranteed to work on any value passed for msg.

But our earlier warning applies here: be careful not to overuse this technique, as it effectively disables the compiler's ability to generate type errors for the parameter in question.

To restore the compiler's ability to type check msg, we must *cast* the generic msg value to the desired datatype (we'll cover casting soon). For example, the following rewrite of the *output( )* function checks the datatype of msg. If msg is a string, the function traces the text to the Output panel as-is. If msg is an instance of the *XML* class, the function assigns it to a new variable, doc, whose declared type is *XML*. Casting msg to the *XML* type using XML(msg), tells the compiler to treat msg as an *XML* object. The function then uses doc instead of msg to access the data, thereby enjoying the benefits of type checking. Specifically, if we access non-*XML* methods and properties on doc, the compiler generates errors:

```
function output (msg:Object):Void {
   // Use typeof to detect the datatype of primitive values.
   if (typeof msg == "string") {
     trace(msg);
   }

   // Use instanceof to check the class of an object.
   if (msg instanceof XML) {
     var doc:XML = XML(msg);
     trace(doc.firstChild.firstChild.nodeValue);
   }
}
```

Some languages (e.g., Java) address the need for multiple parameter types with so-called *method overloading*. Method overloading lets multiple methods have the same name but define unique parameter types. When an overloaded method is called, the compiler determines which version of the method to execute based on the datatype(s) of the passed argument(s). ActionScript 2.0 does not support method overloading. However, we'll see how to simulate overloaded methods and constructor functions in Chapter 4.

Allowing Property and Method Creation on a Class's Instances

As of the introduction of ActionScript 2.0, the compiler normally generates an error when you attempt to access a nonexistent property or method on an object. (A nonexistent property or method is one that is not defined by the object's class.) If, however, you feel you must create a class that allows new properties or methods to be added to its instances at runtime, you can disable nonexistent property and method checking by declaring the class *dynamic*. For much more information, see "Class Attributes" in Chapter 4.

Do not take this technique lightly. Dynamic classes let you create instances that have unknown properties and methods, which can cause unexpected results in the rest of your program (or when incorporated into a different program).

Bypassing Type Checking on a Per-Use Basis

As we just learned, omitting the datatype for a data container disables type checking for all uses of that container. However, type checking may also be sidestepped for a single use of a data value in one of two ways.

First, we can use the [ ] operator to access methods and properties without concern for compile-time type checking. For example, the following code generates an error because the *Sound* class does not define the property url:

```
var song:Sound = new Sound( );
song.url = "track3.mp3";  // Error!
```

But if we use the [ ] operator when referring to url, no error occurs, and a new url property is added to the *song* object:

```
var song:Sound = new Sound( );
song["url"] = "track3.mp3";
trace(song["url"]);          // Displays: track3.mp3
```

This technique adds a new property (in this case, url) to the object instance (in this case, song), not to the class itself (in this case, *Sound*). We still haven't fully addressed the question of how to add methods or properties to a class dynamically. We'll cover that in Chapter 6, under "Augmenting Built-in Classes and Objects." All we've done here is bypass some of the type checking otherwise performed by the ActionScript compiler.

Alternatively, we can cast the value to the desired type (casting is covered next, so if it's new to you, you may want to skip ahead for now). For example, the following code casts someValue to the *TextField* class so that it can be stored in the variable tf, whose type is *TextField*:

```
var tf:TextField = TextField(someValue);
```

In ActionScript 2.0, casting data to a datatype always succeeds at compile time. That is, the preceding code convinces the compiler that whatever the actual type of someValue, it should be treated as a legitimate *TextField* object. In reality, the cast operation may fail at runtime, but we're talking only about compile-time type checking here.

Once again, do not take either of these techniques for bypassing compile-time type checking lightly!

 It's considered extremely bad form to add a new property (i.e., one not defined by the object's class) to a single object instance. It can also be dangerous to cast an object to a class if the object is not actually an instance of that class.

You may fool the compiler but, as we'll learn next, at runtime you can easily end up with a null reference instead of the object you thought you cast. In the vast majority of cases, you should not circumvent the type checking system. (However, as discussed in the next section, casting certainly has other valid uses.)

Casting

In drama, when we say that an actor is "cast" in a role, we mean that the person will portray a particular character in a play or a movie. In programming, the term *cast* has very much the same meaning, but it applies to objects instead of people. When we cast an object in ActionScript 2.0, we make the object pretend to be an instance of another datatype. Casting is used to tell the compiler the type of an object when the compiler can't determine the object's type on its own.

To fully understand casting in ActionScript 2.0, you first need to understand *inheritance*, which we haven't covered yet. If you're new to the concept of inheritance, you may want to skip this section and return to it after reading Chapter 6.

The syntax of casting in ActionScript 2.0 is:

```
Type(object);
```

where *object* is the object to cast and *Type* is the datatype to which the object will appear to belong.

Java and C++ developers accustomed to the cast syntax (*Type*)*object* should note that in ActionScript 2.0's cast syntax, the parentheses surround the object, not the type name. That is, ActionScript's type casting resembles the form of a function call.

Here's a very simple example of casting, in which we store a generic *Object* in the variable obj, then assign obj to the variable tf, whose type is *TextField*. Before assigning obj to tf, we cast obj to the *TextField* datatype:

```
var obj:Object    = new Object();
var tf:TextField = TextField(obj);
```

For the sake of type checking, the expression TextField(obj) tricks the compiler into believing that obj is a *TextField*. Without the cast, the compiler would generate a type mismatch error. With the cast, the compiler generates no error because it considers the variable obj to be a *TextField* instance, which is compatible with the datatype of tf. Refer to the earlier discussion under "Compatible Types" for an explanation of why storing an *Object* instance in a *TextField* variable would generate a type mismatch error if not for the manual casting to the *TextField* type. Refer to the same discussion to understand why casting isn't required in this example:

```
var tf:TextField = someClip.createTextField("output", 1, 0, 0, 100, 20);
var obj:Object    = tf;
```

Casting does not convert an object from one class to another. It merely tells the compiler to treat the object or datum as though it were an instance of the specified datatype.

 Casting does not change the class of the object or datum being cast.

In the earlier type casting example, the compiler allows obj to be stored in tf because the cast operation tells it to treat obj as a *TextField* instance. But if we actually use a *TextField* method or property on tf at runtime, nothing will happen because, in reality, obj isn't a *TextField* instance! Refer again to the discussion under "Compatible Types" for more details on this subject.

Why, then, would you ever want to perform a cast operation? You should use a cast to tell the compiler the type of an object when it can't figure that out for itself. For example, suppose we have a game with a class, *EnemyManager*, that handles enemy spaceships. The *EnemyManager* class keeps track of three kinds of spaceships, represented by the classes *Cruiser*, *Bomber*, and *Fighter*, which are all subclasses of *EnemyShip*. The *EnemyManager* class defines a method for retrieving the closest ship to the player—*EnemyManager.getClosestShip( )*. Of course, the closest ship might be a *Cruiser*, a *Bomber*, or a *Fighter*, all of which are compatible with the *EnemyShip* datatype. Hence, the *getClosestShip( )* method has a return type of *EnemyShip*, allowing it to return a *Cruiser*, a *Bomber*, or a *Fighter*. Here's the skeletal method definition:

```
public function getClosestShip ():EnemyShip {
  // Closest ship calculation not shown...
  return closestShip;
}
```

Now suppose that once per second, the closest ship to the player should perform an action appropriate to its type. If the closest ship is a *Bomber*, it should invoke *bomb( )*. If the closest ship is a *Cruiser*, it should invoke *evade( )*. If the closest ship is a *Fighter*, it should invoke *callReinforcements( )* and *fire( )*. You might try to write code that makes the closest ship act appropriately as follows (see "Runtime Casting Support" later in this chapter for details on the use of the *instanceof* operator in this context):

```
var ship:EnemyShip = theEnemyManager.getClosestShip();
if (ship instanceof Bomber) {
  ship.bomb();
} else if (ship instanceof Cruiser) {
  ship.evade();
} else if (ship instanceof Fighter) {
  ship.callReinforcements();
  ship.fire();
}
```

That code is nearly correct, but it also generates compile-time type errors. The ship variable is of type *EnemyShip*, but the *EnemyShip* class doesn't define the methods *bomb( )*, *evade( )*, *callReinforcements( )*, or *fire( )*. Those methods are defined by the *Bomber*, *Cruiser*, and *Fighter* classes, so the compiler complains that there are no such methods when they are invoked on ship. Of course, the code first checks the class of the ship object before calling methods on it, so the programmer knows that, at runtime, ship will contain an instance of the class with the necessary methods. But the compiler isn't smart enough to consider the preceding *if* statements; the compiler blindly checks ship's datatype without regard to when or if a particular section of code is reached.

Solution? Tell the compiler the datatype of the ship variable by casting it to the appropriate class before invoking methods on it. Here's the code:

```
var ship:EnemyShip = theEnemyManager.getClosestShip();
if (ship instanceof Bomber) {
  Bomber(ship).bomb();                 // Cast to Bomber
} else if (ship instanceof Cruiser) {
  Cruiser(ship).evade();               // Cast to Cruiser
} else if (ship instanceof Fighter) {
  Fighter(ship).callReinforcements();  // Cast to Fighter
  Fighter(ship).fire();                // Cast to Fighter
}
```

Note that you can't just cast ship to a new class, such as *Fighter*, and then use it as if it belongs to the new class, because casting won't permanently change ship's datatype. This won't work:

```
} else if (ship instanceof Fighter) {
    ship = Fighter(ship);         // Doesn't change ship's datatype
    ship.callReinforcements();    // Still generates compile-time error
    ship.fire();                  // Still generates compile-time error
}
```

However, if you need to call many methods on an object, you can create a new variable, such as fightShip, and use it to store the value of ship cast to the *Fighter* class. For example:

```
} else if (ship instanceof Fighter) {
    fightShip:Fighter = Fighter(ship);  // Cast to Fighter
    fightShip.callReinforcements();     // Now this works
    fightShip.fire();                   // And so does this
}
```

Casting Terminology

Before we continue, let's pause to consider some common casting terminology. Casting an object to one of its supertypes is known as an *upcast*. Normally a *supertype* is a superclass, but it could also be a *superinterface* (see Chapter 8). For example, if *Basketball* is a subclass of *Ball*, then the following operation is considered an upcast:

```
var bball:Basketball = new Basketball();
var genericBall:Ball = Ball(bball);     // Upcast of bball
```

Conversely, casting an object to one of its *subtypes* (i.e., subclass or *subinterface*) is known as a *downcast* because it casts the object's type to a type further down the type hierarchy. Reusing our *Basketball* example, the following operation is considered a downcast:

```
var b:Ball = new Ball();
var bball:Basketball = Basketball(b)  // Downcast of b
```

We also used downcasting in the earlier *EnemyShip* example when we cast the ship variable to the *Bomber*, *Cruiser*, or *Fighter* subclass.

An upcast is said to "widen" the object's type because a supertype is more generalized than its subtype. A downcast is said to "narrow" the object's type because a subtype is more specialized than its supertype.

An upcast is also described as a *safe cast* because it always succeeds. An instance of a subtype can always be safely treated as an instance of any of its supertypes because it is guaranteed (through inheritance) to have all of its supertypes' methods and properties.

Conversely, a downcast is described as an *unsafe cast* because it is not guaranteed to succeed. An instance of a supertype is not necessarily also an instance of one of its subtypes and, therefore, may not have its subclasses' methods and properties. We'll consider the result of a failed downcast shortly.

Don't confuse explicit casting with merely assigning objects of one datatype to variables of another datatype, as described earlier under "Compatible Types." To reiterate, if *Basketball* is a subclass of the *Ball* class, this assignment operation is legal:

```
var ball1:Ball = new Basketball();  // Assignment without casting
```

And this is a safe cast (an upcast):

```
var ball1:Ball = Ball(new Basketball());  // Safe upcast
```

In this context, an explicit upcast is unnecessary, because storing the *Basketball* instance in the ball1 object automatically casts the instance to the *Ball* class. The automatic cast is called an *implicit upcast*.

Let's look at the converse situation, which we also discussed earlier in this chapter. This assignment operation is illegal because you can't assign an instance of supertype *Ball* to a variable of subtype *Basketball*:

```
var ball2:Basketball = new Ball();  // Illegal!
```

However, the following is legal but considered an unsafe cast (a downcast):

```
var ball3:Basketball = Basketball(new Ball());  // Legal, but unsafe
```

In this case, an explicit downcast is necessary to prevent a type mismatch error when storing the *Ball* instance in the ball3 variable, whose type is *Basketball*. Furthermore, the programmer must take care not to access methods and properties of the *Basketball* class on ball3, except for those inherited from the *Ball* class. Again, see the detailed discussion earlier in this chapter under "Compatible Types." Therefore, when downcasting, it's wise to add error-checking code that guarantees the validity of the cast attempt (as we did in the earlier *EnemyShip* example).

Earlier in this chapter we asked whether there is some way to make use of the *Basketball*-ness of a *Basketball* instance stored in a variable whose datatype is *Ball*. As you may have guessed by now, we can use manual type checking before downcasting to achieve our goal safely. The following is legal at compile time (because of the downcast) and works as intended at runtime (because we perform manual type checking to ensure the *inflate( )* invocation will succeed):

```
var ball1:Ball = new Basketball();  // Legal, so far...
if (ball1 instanceof Basketball) {  // Include manual type checking
  Basketball(ball1).inflate();      // Downcast prevents compiler error!
}
```

The next section describes in greater detail how to check the validity of a downcast (which can be done only at runtime).

Runtime Casting Support

In Flash Player 7–format *.swf* files, a successful cast operation returns the object specified between parentheses. For example:

```
SomeType(someObj); // If cast succeeds, returns someObj
```

A cast operation succeeds at runtime if the datatype of *someObj* is compatible with the datatype specified by *SomeType*. (It is considered compatible if *someObj* belongs to the class specified by *SomeType* or a subclass of *SomeType*.) For example, in the following code, the cast operation, Color(obj), succeeds and, therefore, returns obj. The cast succeeds because the object's original class, *Color*, matches the datatype specified in the cast operation (also *Color*):

```
var obj:Object = new Color( );
trace(Color(obj));          // In Flash Player 7, displays:
                            // [object Object]
```

Notice that the cast operation succeeds or fails based on the actual runtime datatype of the value stored in obj, not the datatype of the obj variable itself (which is *Object*, not *Color*!).

 Compile-time type checking relies on the datatype of the variable (container). Conversely, runtime type casting relies on the datatype of the instance stored in the variable (it ignores the variable's datatype).

A failed cast operation returns the value null. A cast operation fails at runtime if the datatype of *someObj* is not compatible with the datatype specified by *SomeType*. For example, in the following code, the cast operation returns null because obj does not belong to the *TextField* type:

```
var obj:Object = new Object( );
trace(TextField(obj));          // Displays: null
```

A cast succeeds only if the object specified can be proven to belong to the type specified. The proof is made with the *instanceof* operator. Hence, a cast, *SomeType*(*someObj*), succeeds only if *someObj* instanceof *SomeType* returns true. The *instanceof* operator returns true if *someObj* belongs to the class specified by *SomeType* or a subclass of *SomeType*. Therefore, casting to the *Object* class always succeeds because *someObj* instanceof Object always returns true. That is, Object(*someObj*) always returns *someObj*. However, if *someObj* is null, the cast will fail; in other words, the cast *SomeType*(null) always returns null.

When using the ActionScript 2.0 compiler and exporting a movie in either Flash Player 6– or Flash Player 7–format, casting to the null or undefined datatypes returns undefined (whether the movie is running in Flash Player 6 or Flash Player 7). For example:

```
var obj:Object = new Object( );
/// Displays underfined in Flash Player 6 and 7, when the
/// .swf formate is Player 6 or Player 7 and the
/// ActionScript version is 2.0
trace(null(obj));
```

But in Flash Player 6–format .swf files, there is no other runtime support for casting, no matter what the version of the Flash Player. A cast operation in a Flash Player 6–format .swf file is always ignored; instead, it returns the uncast value. For example, the following code attempts to cast an *Object* instance to the *TextField* type. In theory, the cast should fail and return null because the instance does not belong to the *TextField* type. However, in Flash Player 6, the cast returns the *Object* instance:

```
var obj:Object = new Object();
// When exported to Flash Player 6 format, displays: [object Object]
// (Would display null if exported to Flash Player 7 format)
trace(TextField(obj));
```

Never lie when you cast! It's never sensible to use a cast to lie to the compiler about the type of an object.

If you cast an object to an incompatible datatype, the compiler may be fooled, but you still won't be able to use the object as an instance of that datatype at runtime. As we just learned, in Flash Player 7–format *.swf* files, a cast that fails returns the value null at runtime, which will almost certainly break some aspect of your program:

```
var obj:Object = new Object();
trace(TextField(obj));  // If exported to Flash Player 7 format,
                        // displays: null
```

You should perform only those casts you know to be valid.

If you cannot guarantee that a cast will succeed, you should first use *instanceof* to check whether the cast will succeed at runtime before attempting the cast operation.

For example, the following code checks the actual type of obj at runtime before attempting to cast it to *TextField*:

```
var obj:Object = new Object();
var tf:TextField;

if (obj instanceof TextField) {
  tf = TextField(obj);
} else {
  trace("Warning! Cannot cast obj to a TextField.");
}
```

Casting Does Not Affect Method or Property Selection

If a superclass defines a method or property that is overridden by a subclass, casting does not affect which version of a method or property is used. When an overridden method is invoked on an instance of the subclass, the subclass's version of the method is always used, even if the subclass instance is cast to the superclass.

For exhaustive coverage of method and property access in superclasses and subclasses, see Chapter 6.

Casting Versus Conversion

We learned earlier that casting does not convert an object from one datatype to another. The point is worth reiterating. Casting merely tells the compiler to treat the object as though it were an instance of the specified datatype. Conversion, on the other hand, *does* change an object from one datatype to another. ActionScript 2.0 includes built-in tools for converting a value to a *Boolean*, a *Number*, or a *String*. For complete details, see "Datatype Conversion" in Chapter 3 of *ActionScript for Flash MX: The Definitive Guide,* available online at: *http://moock.org/asdg/samples.*

There is no built-in mechanism for converting an object from one class to another (besides those mentioned in the preceding paragraph). If you need to convert between classes, you'll have to manually create a method that takes a source object of class *X* as a parameter and returns a new object of class *Y* as a result. This requires custom code that reads the state of the class *X* instance and meaningfully translates it to a corresponding instance of class *Y*. Such translation is not always logical or possible. For example, it might make perfect sense to convert a *2dPoint* instance to a *3dPoint* instance, but it wouldn't make sense to convert a *Button* instance to a *Date* instance.

ActionScript 2.0's Lenient Compile-Time Casting

As we've seen, in ActionScript 2.0, all casts—even unsafe casts—are trusted by the compiler. If you tell the compiler that an object is a *MovieClip*, a *Ball*, or even the *Mouse*, it believes you (how's that for unconditional love?). An ActionScript 2.0 cast never generates a compile-time error, even if it might fail at runtime and even if the compiler could theoretically determine the failure in advance.

Invalid casts (i.e., casts that lie about the real datatype of an object) are caught only at runtime and, even then, only if you exported the movie to Flash Player 7 format.

Note that in Java unsafe casts that can be proven invalid at compile time generate a compile-time error. It's neither typical nor appropriate to cast across a type hierarchy. In ActionScript 2.0, you should perform upcasts or downcasts only between subclasses and superclasses, despite the fact that the compiler lets you cast to any datatype. Again, remember that *converting* between two datatypes (e.g., a *Number* and a *Boolean*) is legitimate, but *casting* between such types is not. Reread the previous section.

Problems Casting to String, Number, Boolean, Date, and Array

The class constructors for the built-in datatypes *String, Number, Boolean, Date,* and *Array* all have global functions by the same name. The *String( ), Number( ), Boolean( ),* and *Array( )* functions perform data conversion. The *Date( )* function returns the current time as a string. These global functions have the same syntax as a cast. For example, to convert a value to a number, we use:

```
Number(value)
```

Because of this overlap, it is effectively impossible to cast to the datatypes *String*, *Number*, *Boolean*, *Date*, and *Array*. For example, suppose we have an object we know is an array:

```
var obj:Object = [1, 2, 3];
```

To cast obj to the *Array* type, we'd theoretically use:

```
Array(obj);
```

But attempting to cast to the *Array* type unfortunately performs a data conversion and returns a new array whose first element is the array [1, 2, 3]. For example:

```
var arr:Array = Array(obj);
trace(arr[0]);  // Displays: 1,2,3
trace(arr[1]);  // Displays: undefined
trace(arr[2]);  // Displays: undefined
```

The only workaround for this regrettable situation is to forego datatyping for the target container, as in:

```
// Don't bother casting obj to an array.
// Just ignore datatyping for the arr variable.
var arr = obj;
```

You might encounter this problem when, say, processing a method parameter whose type is unknown. As an example, let's return to our earlier function, *output( )*:

```
function output (msg:Object):Void {
  if (typeof msg == "string") {
    trace(msg);
  }

  if (msg instanceof XML) {
    var doc:XML = XML(msg);
    trace(doc.firstChild.firstChild.nodeValue);
  }
}
```

As we learned earlier, *output( )* treats its msg parameter differently depending on whether that parameter is an *XML* object or a string. When msg is an *XML* object, the function casts it to the *XML* type and then displays specific data from the *XML* document:

```
var doc:XML = XML(msg);
trace(doc.firstChild.firstChild.nodeValue);
```

Now let's assume we want to perform an analogous operation on an *Array* object. When an *Array* object is passed to *output( )*, we want to print each of its elements on its own line. We'd sensibly expect to use the following code, which casts msg to the *Array* type (see the line in bold):

```
function output (msg:Object):Void {
  if (typeof msg == "string") {
    trace(msg);
  }
```

```
    if (msg instanceof Array) {
      var arr:Array = Array(msg);  // Cast to Array here
      trace(arr.join("\n"));
    }
  }
```

Unfortunately, due to the existence of the global *Array( )* function, the would-be cast in the preceding code actually *converts* the existing array in msg to a new, single-element array, which is stored in arr. If we test the function as follows:

```
output([1, 2, 3]);
```

the Output panel displays:

```
1,2,3
```

Notice that there's no newline character between elements because the entire array passed to *output( )* is now the first and only element in arr!

To fix the problem, we're forced to operate on msg directly, without first casting it to *Array*, as indicated in bold:

```
function output (msg:Object):Void {
  // Use typeof to detect the datatype of primitive values.
  if (typeof msg == "string") {
    trace(msg);
  }

  // Use instanceof to check the class of an object.
  if (msg instanceof Array) {
    trace(msg.join("\n"));   // No cast here.
  }
}
```

With our revised version of *output( )*, the following test:

```
output([1, 2, 3]);
```

causes the Output panel to display the desired result (each element on its own line):

```
1
2
3
```

Datatype Information for Built-in Classes

When working with static typing and ActionScript 2.0's built-in classes, you must observe the declared datatypes for each class. For example, if you store a *TextFormat* object in a typed variable, you must use the correct datatypes when assigning values to its properties. The following code generates an error because the TextFormat.align property requires a *String*, but a *Boolean* is used:

```
var tf:TextFormat = new TextFormat();
tf.align = true;  // Error! Boolean values not allowed.
```

Unfortunately, Macromedia's documentation does not provide type information for the methods and properties of the built-in classes nor for the Flash MX 2004 components. For your benefit, the type information is listed in Appendix A.

Type information can also be retrieved from the source code of the classes in the installation folder for Flash MX 2004, as follows:

/Macromedia/Flash MX 2004/en/First Run/Classes

Component class definitions are found in the */mx/* directory, one directory below the */Classes/* directory listed previously.

Note that although source code for components is included in full, the built-in class definitions are *intrinsic*, meaning that they do not include method bodies or other implementation information. They do, however, contain datatype information as specified in Appendix A. For more details on intrinsic definitions, see Chapter 6.

ActionScript 2.0 Type Checking Gotchas

ActionScript 2.0's type checking system has its quirks and limitations. The remainder of this chapter covers some anomalies to keep in mind when working with ActionScript 2.0.

Global Variables Can't Be Typed

To create a global variable in ActionScript, we add a property to the _global object, as follows:

```
_global.varname = value;
```

The preceding property-definition syntax is a carryover from ActionScript 1.0 and does not support datatype declarations. It is, therefore, impossible to use type checking with a global variable. For example, this causes a compile-time syntax error:

```
_global.author:String = "moock";  // Output panel displays: Syntax error.
```

As an alternative, you should consider using a class property in lieu of globals, as discussed under "Property Attributes" in Chapter 4.

Type Checking and Timeline Code

When code is placed on a frame in a timeline, the properties and methods of movie clips are not type checked. For example, the following attempt to assign a *String* value to the numeric property _y does not generate a compile-time type mismatch error when the code is placed on a frame in a timeline:

```
_root._y = "test";  // No error. (Should be a type mismatch error.)
```

Similarly, the following attempt to store a number returned by *getBytesLoaded( )* in a *String* variable does not generate an error when the code is placed on a frame:

```
// No error. (Should be a type mismatch error.)
var msg:String = _root.getBytesLoaded( );
```

Furthermore, assigning the current *MovieClip* instance (this) to a non-*MovieClip* variable or passing the current *MovieClip* instance (this) to a non-*MovieClip* function parameter causes no error. For example, when placed on a frame in a timeline, the following examples yield no error:

```
var x:String = this;  // No error. (Should be a type mismatch error.)

function square(x:Number):Number {
  return x * x;
}
square(this);  // No error. (Should be a type mismatch error.)
```

These problems occur only within code on a frame in a timeline, because on a timeline, nested movie clips are treated as dynamic properties of the containing movie clip. ActionScript 2.0 does not type check dynamic properties. However, within an ActionScript 2.0 class, type checking works properly with *MovieClip* instances.

To ensure proper type checking for movie clips within timeline code, first assign the *MovieClip* instance in question to a variable of type *MovieClip*, and use that variable in place of the *MovieClip* instance reference. For example, this code generates type mismatch errors at compile time (remember, compile-time errors are your friend, so although this code generates errors, it demonstrates the proper way to achieve type checking in timeline code):

```
var theRoot:MovieClip = _root;
theRoot._y = "test";                     // Type mismatch error!
var msg:String = theRoot.getBytesLoaded( );  // Type mismatch error!

var thisMC:MovieClip = this;
var x:String = thisMC;                    // Type mismatch error!
function square(x:Number):Number {
  return x * x;
}
square(thisMC);                           // Type mismatch error!
```

Type Checking XML Instances

Unbeknownst to many developers, the built-in *XML* class is actually a subclass of the *XMLNode* class, which was undocumented by Macromedia until Flash MX 2004. Furthermore, all child nodes of an *XML* instance are instances of the *XMLNode* class, not of the *XML* class! The relationship between the *XML* and *XMLNode* classes can be a source of confusion when working with ActionScript 2.0's type checking. The following code demonstrates the issue. It creates a new *XML* instance, stores the instance in a variable, xmlDoc, then attempts to assign one of its child nodes to a new variable, xmlFragment:

```
var xmlDoc:XML = new XML("<P>Hello world</P>");
var xmlFragment:XML = xmlDoc.firstChild;  // Error.
```

The preceding code causes a type mismatch error because xmlDoc.firstChild is an *XMLNode* instance, not an *XML* instance. To fix the error, we simply declare the datatype of xmlFragment as *XMLNode* instead of *XML* (change shown in bold):

```
var xmlDoc:XML = new XML("<P>Hello world</P>");
var xmlFragment:XMLNode = xmlDoc.firstChild;  // No error
```

The preceding code does not cause a type mismatch error because—as we learned earlier under "Compatible Types"—the compiler knows that every *XML* instance has, through inheritance, all the properties and methods of the *XMLNode* class (remember that the *XML* class is a subclass of the *XMLNode* class despite their names, which might imply the opposite).

In general, when you want a variable to store an *XML* instance or any of its children, you should set the variable's datatype to *XMLNode*.

No Type Checking with the [] Operator

When a property or method is accessed via the [ ] operator, the compiler does not perform type checking. For example, the following code attempts to execute a non-existent method. No error occurs when the method is accessed via the [ ] operator:

```
var d:Date = new Date( );
d["noSuchMethod"]( );  // No compile-time error, but fails
                       // silently at runtime.
d.noSuchMethod( );     // Compile-time error.
```

Similarly, the following code mistakenly attempts to store a *String* property (name_txt.text) in a *Number* variable (userID). No error occurs when the property is accessed via the [ ] operator:

```
target_mc.createTextField("tf", 0, 0, 0, 400, 400);
var name_txt:TextField = target_mc.tf;
name_txt.border = true;
name_txt.text = "Type your name...";
var userID:Number = name_txt["text"];  // No error. At runtime, userID
                                       // stores a string value.
var userID:Number = name_txt.text;     // Compile-time error.
```

Therefore, to take advantage of type checking, you should rewrite any old code that uses the [ ] operator to access methods or properties. Use the dot operator (a period) instead of [ ], as is a best practice in ActionScript 2.0 regardless, unless you're dynamically generating the name of a property or method. Although the lack of type checking when using the [ ] operator might seem an oversight, it is necessary because it allows access to properties and methods whose names are determined dynamically at runtime.

Array Elements and Type Checking

In other object-oriented languages, the canonical example of casting portrays a programmer retrieving an object from an array of objects whose types are unknown and casting that object to a known type.

For example, here we have an *XML* instance:

```
var doc:XML = new XML("<P>hello world</P>");
```

Suppose we store that *XML* instance in an array, like this:

```
var items:Array = new Array();
items.push(doc);
```

Because the array, items, does not keep track of the datatypes of its elements, the following code should generate a type mismatch error:

```
var otherDoc:XML = items[0];
```

The programmer knows that the element items[0] is an *XML* instance, but the compiler doesn't recognize this fact. Rather, the compiler treats each array element as a generic *Object*. The sensible solution here is to cast the value items[0] to the *XML* datatype:

```
var otherDoc:XML = XML(items[0]);
```

However, even without that cast, the code generates no errors at compile time. Why not? Because, as we learned in the previous section, the compiler skips type checking for values accessed with the [] operator.

The compiler also generates no errors when accessing nonexistent properties and methods on an array's elements. For example, this code generates no error even though neither the *XML* class nor the *Object* class defines the method *fixAllBugs( )*.

```
items[0].fixAllBugs();  // No error.
```

This unfortunate lack of error messages means that you must effectively type check all objects used through array elements yourself. Remember to be extra careful when working with arrays.

Up Next: Creating Classes— Your Own Datatypes!

As we've seen in this chapter, datatypes and type checking are an essential part of programming in ActionScript 2.0. Now that you're familiar with how datatypes work and how they help you write better code, it's time to move on. In Chapter 4 you'll learn how to define your own datatypes by creating classes. Learning to create a class is the first hands-on step down the path of the object-oriented programmer.

Classes

This chapter covers the syntax and theory behind classes in ActionScript 2.0 and assumes a prior basic understanding of the concepts discussed in Chapter 2. Classes are the foundational structure of all object-oriented programs, making them arguably the most important aspect of OOP. As such, classes are predictably intricate. This chapter is correspondingly lengthy and detailed but, even so, newer programmers can use it to learn the basics of creating and using classes.

If this is your first real exposure to programming with classes, you may want to concentrate on the first few pages of each of the following sections:

- "Defining Classes"
- "Constructor Functions (Take 1)"
- "Properties"
- "Methods"
- "Completing the Box Class"

Then you can dive right into Chapter 5, which shows, step-by-step, how to create a real-world class in the Flash authoring environment. We'll address the big-picture questions in Chapter 5. (I decided to cover the syntax and mechanics first so you'd have a strong foundation moving forward.)

Just remember to return to the present chapter whenever you need detailed reference material on implementing and using classes in ActionScript 2.0.

Defining Classes

A *class* is a template for the creation of *objects* (or, synonymously, *instances*). Classes are the building blocks of an object-oriented program. Every object-oriented application includes at least one class, and typical applications include several or dozens of classes. From classes, a program generates the objects that determine the things the program can do.

We saw earlier that classes are used to group properties and methods into a coherent bundle. A typical class might define a spaceship or a scrollbar in terms of how it looks, what it does when the user clicks on it, or how it interacts with other objects.

To create, or *define*, an ActionScript 2.0 class, we use a *class* declaration, which starts with the class keyword, as follows:

```
class ClassIdentifier {
}
```

where *ClassIdentifier* is the name of the class (which, by convention, should start with a capital letter). For example, the following code defines a class named *Box*, albeit one that doesn't do anything interesting yet:

```
class Box {
}
```

We'll use the *Box* class as an example throughout this chapter. Eventually, our *Box* will represent and control an on-screen rectangular shape. You might use a similar class in a drawing-tool application. The *Box* class is intentionally generic, allowing you to map its concepts onto your own classes. In subsequent chapters, we'll explore more applied scenarios.

 A class definition *must* reside in an external plain text file that has the extension *.as*. Use of the class keyword anywhere else—such as on a keyframe or a button—generates a compile-time error. Furthermore, each *.as* file can contain only one class definition and must have a filename exactly matching the name of the class it contains (case sensitivity matters!).

For example, the *Box* class must be stored in a file named *Box.as*. If *Box.as* erroneously contains a class named, say, *Circle*, the compiler generates the following error when the *Box* class is instantiated:

```
The class 'Circle' needs to be defined in a file whose relative
path is 'Circle.as'.
```

We'll learn more about the file structure of an object-oriented Flash application in Chapters 5 and 11. For now, our focus is mainly on the code that goes into a class.

 ActionScript 1.0 had no formal *class* statement. Classes were defined using the *function* statement, as in:

```
function Box () {
}
```

ActionScript 1.0 class definitions were allowed anywhere that code was legal (e.g., a frame, a button, or a movie clip) but were conventionally stored in external *.as* files and brought into a *.fla* file using the #include directive, which is not required in ActionScript 2.0.

Everything between the curly braces in a *class* declaration constitutes the *class definition block*, or more informally, the *class body*. The class body can contain:

- A constructor function (used to initialize instances of the class)
- Variable definitions (the class's properties)
- Function definitions (the class's methods)
- #include directives, which can include files containing properties, methods, and constructor functions
- Metadata tags used in Flash MX 2004 components
- Comments

Nothing else is permitted—class definitions cannot be nested, and no other code can appear in a class definition. For example, the following code is illegal because the *if* statement is not one of the six legal items listed:

```
class Box {
  if (100 == 10*10) {
    trace("One hundred is ten times ten");
  }
}
```

In other words, you cannot place raw code directly into a *class* statement. All code must either define a property or be part of a method or constructor function.

However, you can work around this limitation by adding a so-called *class method* that runs the first time an instance is constructed, but never again. The following code demonstrates the approach, using techniques we haven't yet covered. If the code seems foreign to you, try returning to it when you've finished reading this chapter:

```
class Box {
  private static var inited:Boolean = false;

  public function Box () {
    if (!inited) {
      init();
    }
  }

  private static function init():Void {
    if (100 == (10*10)) {
      trace("One hundred is ten times ten");
    }
    inited = true;
  }
}
```

 In ActionScript, a class's methods and properties are referred to collectively as its *members*. For example, we might say "radius is not a member of *Box*," meaning that the *Box* class does not define any methods or properties named radius.

Further, the term *instance member* refers to either an *instance property* or an *instance method* (covered later), while the term *class member* refers to either a *class property* or a *class method* (also covered later). The terms *static member*, *static property*, and *static method* are sometimes used as synonyms for the terms *class member*, *class property*, and *class method*. We'll learn much more about instance and class members throughout this chapter.

Class Attributes

Class definitions can be modified with one or both of two *attributes*: *dynamic* and *intrinsic*. Attributes dictate how a class and its instances can be used in a program. Attributes must be listed before the keyword class in a class definition. For example, to add the *dynamic* attribute to the *Box* class, we'd use:

```
dynamic class Box {
}
```

ActionScript 2.0 does not support ECMAScript 4's *final* attribute (which prevents a class from being subclassed), nor does it support a Java-style *abstract* modifier (which prevents instances of a class from being created). For one way to simulate an abstract class, see "Constructor Functions (Take 2)," later in this chapter.

The dynamic attribute

By default, a class's members must be defined exclusively within the *class* statement. Any attempt to add a property or method to an individual instance of a class or the class itself from outside the class definition causes a compile-time error. However, when a class is defined with the *dynamic* attribute, new properties and methods can legally be added both to the class's instances and to the class itself. For example, suppose we define the *Box* class without the *dynamic* attribute, as follows:

```
class Box {
}
```

Further, suppose we create a *Box* instance and attempt to give it a new property named size:

```
var b:Box = new Box();
b.size = "Really big";
```

When that code is compiled, the following error appears in the Output panel:

```
There is no property with the name 'size'.
```

because the size property isn't declared within the *Box* class definition, and properties cannot be added dynamically, so the compiler thinks you are trying to access a nonexistent property.

But if we add the *dynamic* attribute to the class definition:

```
dynamic class Box {
}
```

then the preceding size property addition is allowed and does not cause an error at compile time. Similarly, when the *Box* class is not dynamic, the following attempt to define a new class property is illegal:

```
// Illegal when Box class is not dynamic.
Box.classPurpose = "Represent a four-sided figure";
```

But again, when the *Box* class is dynamic, the preceding property definition is legal.

The size and classPurpose properties are examples of *dynamic properties*, which can be added at runtime only to classes declared with the *dynamic* attribute (and to instances of such classes).

Generally speaking, you should not rely on dynamic classes in your application development. It's considered bad form to augment a single object with a new dynamic property or method. If the property or method rightly applies to all instances of the class, add it to the class definition. If the property or method does not apply to all instances of the class, the following approach is preferred over using a dynamic class:

1. Create a subclass of the original class.

2. Add the new property or method to the subclass definition (i.e., don't add it dynamically at runtime).

3. Create the object as an instance of the subclass instead of the superclass.

The *dynamic* attribute is provided primarily to give the built-in ActionScript classes special behavior. For example, the *MovieClip* and *Object* classes are both defined as *dynamic*, which allows all *MovieClip* and *Object* instances to take on new properties and methods. If the *MovieClip* class were not dynamic, any attempt to create a variable on a Flash timeline frame would fail. Similarly, the *Array* class is declared *dynamic* so that any array can define named elements (in addition to numbered elements). Note, however, that even though the built-in *Object* class is dynamic, a compiler bug in Flash MX 2004 makes attempts to add class properties to the *Object* class fail when they occur in a class body. For example, if the following line of code appears in any class body, the compiler generates an error:

```
Object.someProp = "Hello world";
```

In general, subclasses of a dynamic class are also dynamic. This guarantees that features in the superclass that rely on the *dynamic* class definition work properly in any subclass. However, *subclasses* of the *MovieClip* and *Object* classes are, by default, not dynamic, because every class is a subclass of *Object*, but not all classes should be dynamic by default. With the exception of *MovieClip* and *Object*, there is no way to make a subclass of a dynamic class nondynamic.

In ActionScript 1.0, all classes were effectively dynamic. Properties and methods could be added to any instance or class at runtime without error.

The intrinsic attribute

The *intrinsic* attribute is used only when distributing a compiled class without also distributing the class's source code, such as in the case of the built-in Flash Player classes. A class defined with the *intrinsic* attribute includes no method bodies or property values; it simply specifies property and method names and datatypes for the sake of compile-time type checking.

For example, the following code shows the *intrinsic* class definition for the Flash Player's built-in *LoadVars* class:

```
dynamic intrinsic class LoadVars {
    var contentType:String;
    var loaded:Boolean;
    var _customHeaders:Array;

    function load(url:String):Boolean;
    function send(url:String,target:String,method:String):Boolean;
    function sendAndLoad(url:String,target,method:String):Boolean;
    function getBytesLoaded():Number;
    function getBytesTotal():Number;
    function decode(queryString:String):Void;
    function toString():String;
    function onLoad(success:Boolean):Void;
    function onData(src:String):Void;
    function addRequestHeader(header:Object, headerValue:String):Void;
}
```

The *LoadVars* class is compiled into the Flash Player itself, so its source code is not available to the ActionScript compiler at authoring time. The compiler uses the preceding *intrinsic* class definition to perform type checking on *LoadVars* instances at compile time. The Flash MX 2004 and Flash MX Professional 2004 authoring tools include *intrinsic* class definitions for all built-in classes and objects. For details, see "Datatype Information for Built-in Classes" in Chapter 3.

We'll learn more about *intrinsic* class definitions in Chapter 14.

Constructor Functions (Take 1)

Generally speaking, when we create an object, we also want to initialize it. For example, when we create an instance of our *Box* class, we might want to:

- Initialize the new instance's size (i.e., set its width and height properties)
- Represent the new instance on screen (i.e., call the *draw()* method)

To initialize and perform setup tasks for new objects of a class, we create a *constructor function*. The constructor function executes automatically each time an instance is created. Typically, when we create a class, we immediately add an empty constructor function to it. Then, as we develop the class, we add any necessary initialization code to the constructor function.

Let's now add an empty constructor function to our *Box* class. In the following code, lines 2 and 3 are the *Box* class's constructor function (or, more succinctly, "the *Box* constructor"):

```
class Box {
  public function Box () {
  }
}
```

Now that our *Box* class has an empty constructor function, we'll give the class some properties and methods. Once we add properties and methods, we can use them in the *Box* constructor to initialize *Box* instances.

However, we have a lot to learn about properties and methods in the upcoming sections before we can finish our *Box* constructor. Hence, we'll leave it empty for now and return to it later, under "Constructor Functions (Take 2)." For the sake of brevity, until we return to the *Box* constructor, we'll omit it from all intervening code samples. This omission is legal, if uncommon. When no constructor is provided for a class, ActionScript adds an empty one automatically at compile time.

Properties

As we learned in Chapter 2, classes use *properties* to store information. But some information relates to a class as a whole (e.g., the default size for all *SpaceShip* objects) and some information relates to individual objects (e.g., the current speed or position of each *SpaceShip* instance). Consequently, properties come in different varieties:

Class properties
　　Named data containers associated with a class

Instance properties
　　Named data containers associated with objects (i.e., *instances* of the class)

> Together, class properties and instance properties are sometimes referred to as *fixed properties*, in opposition to the *dynamic properties* discussed earlier. Again, dynamic properties are generally considered bad OOP form and should be avoided, although they are necessary for things like named array elements.

In our coverage of properties, we'll concentrate first on instance properties because they are by far the most common type of property. We'll also largely ignore dynamic properties because they are considered bad form in ActionScript 2.0 despite being somewhat common in ActionScript 1.0.

In ActionScript and ECMAScript 4, instance properties are sometimes called *instance variables,* and class properties are sometimes called *class variables* (following Java's terminology). Instance variables and class variables should not be confused with the normal ActionScript variables that can be created without reference to an object or a class. To keep things clear, we'll avoid the terms *instance variable* and *class variable,* but you should expect to see them in other technical documentation and even in ActionScript compiler error messages. Furthermore, to avoid awkward wordiness, we'll often use the shorter term, *property*, to mean *instance property*. Unless otherwise noted, you should assume that all properties discussed in this book are instance properties, not class properties. On the other hand, we'll nearly always refer to class properties by the full name, "class property," unless the context makes the type of property abundantly clear.

Finally, don't confuse instance properties—which are declared once for the class, but for which each instance maintains it own value—with the dynamic properties discussed under "The dynamic attribute." Dynamic properties are properties defined solely for a single instance (not for all instances).

Instance properties typically store information that describes an object's state. Instance properties:

- Are stored individually on each instance of a class
- Are accessed through instances only
- Can be set uniquely for one instance without affecting any other instances

The key thing to remember is that an instance property is declared once for the entire class, but each instance of the class maintains its own value. For example, every movie clip has its own _rotation instance property that indicates the amount, in degrees, that the clip is rotated. The _rotation instance property is declared once in the *MovieClip* class, but each movie clip (each an instance of the *MovieClip* class) defines its own value for _rotation. If we have two *MovieClip* instances, circle_mc and square_mc, we can set the instance property _rotation to 45 on circle_mc and to 120 on square_mc, causing each instance to be rotated individually on screen.

To define an instance property, we use the *var* statement within the body of a class definition. The general syntax is:

```
var propertyName:datatype = value;
```

where *propertyName* is the property's identifier (case sensitive in ActionScript 2.0), *datatype* is the built-in or custom datatype of the property, and *value* is the optional default value for the property (*value* must be a *compile-time constant expression*, as discussed later).

 Properties must be declared *outside* of class methods and instance methods (discussed later). Any variables declared within a method are considered local variables.

If *datatype* is omitted, no type checking is performed on the property (allowing it to store any value). For example:

```
var propertyName = value;  // No type checking for this property.
```

If the default value is omitted, then the default is undefined:

```
var propertyName:datatype;   // Property set to undefined.
```

 In ActionScript 1.0, instance properties were typically defined in the class constructor function and could contain values of any datatype (it was not possible to restrict a property to a specific datatype). For example:

```
function Box (w, h) {
  // Define properties width and height.
  this.width = w;
  this.height = h;
}
```

Default instance property values were set on the prototype of the class:

```
// Set default value of width to 20.
Box.prototype.width = 20;
```

Let's see what an ActionScript 2.0 instance property definition looks like in real life by adding height and width properties to our *Box* class:

```
class Box {
  var width:Number;
  var height:Number;
}
```

Notice that lines 2 and 3 of the preceding code sample end with ":Number", which, as we learned in Chapter 3, is the *type declaration* of each property definition. It indicates that our width and height properties must store numeric data (i.e., data of the *Number* datatype). As a result, any attempt to assign a nonnumeric value to the width or height properties will cause a compile-time error. For example, the following code attempts to assign the *String* value "tall" to the numeric property height:

```
var b:Box = new Box( );
b.height = "tall";
```

which results in the following error:

```
Type mismatch in assignment statement: Found String where Number is required.
```

In ActionScript 2.0, all properties must be declared explicitly using *var*, whether or not you also specify their datatype or initial value. That is, you must use at least the following minimal declaration before making reference to the height property in later code:

```
var height;
```

Making reference to a property that doesn't exist causes an error (unless the class that defines the property is declared *dynamic*). For example, the following code attempts to assign a value to the nonexistent description property:

```
var b:Box = new Box( );
b.description = "A square object";
```

which results in the following error:

```
There is no property with the name 'description'.
```

To fix the problem, you could add the line shown in bold to the *Box* class definition:

```
class Box {
  var width:Number;
  var height:Number;
  var description:String;
}
```

 In ActionScript 1.0, a reference to a nonexistent property did not generate an error. The interpreter simply created a new property of the specified name the first time it was encountered at runtime.

Even if our *Box* class defines a property by the name `description`, it's often considered bad form to access properties directly from outside a class, as does the code:

```
var b:Box = new Box();
b.description = "A square object";
```

When a property is accessible to code outside a class, code that uses the property becomes dependent on the class definition, limiting its flexibility. If, for example, we were to rename the `description` property to `desc`, we'd also have to change all code outside the class that referred to `description`. If enough external code relies on a class's property name, changing the name can become unfeasible. Furthermore, when a property is accessible outside a class, class-external code might unwittingly assign illogical or illegal values to the property. For example, code external to the *Box* class might assign a negative or fractional value to the `height` property, which may not be considered legal by the *Box* class. In order to prevent external access to a class's properties, we use the *private* attribute.

What luck, we're discussing the *private* property attribute next!

Property Attributes

We saw earlier that class definitions could be modified by the *dynamic* and *instrinsic* attributes. Property definitions can also be modified with three possible attributes—*public*, *private*, and *static*—which control how and where the property can be accessed. These attributes must be listed before the keyword var in a property definition. For example, to add the *public* attribute to the `height` property of our *Box* class, we'd use:

```
class Box {
  public var height:Number;
}
```

When a property has more than one attribute, the attributes can appear in any order. However, the *public* or *private* attribute is conventionally placed before the *static* attribute, as in:

```
public static var someProperty:someDataType = someValue;
```

Furthermore, the *public* and *private* attributes cannot both be used to modify the same property definition; they are mutually exclusive.

Restricting property access with the private and public attributes

The *private* and *public* attributes are known as *access control modifiers* because they determine whether a property is accessible outside of the class that defines it. To make a property inaccessible to code outside of a class, we use the *private* attribute. For example, to make our *Box* class's height and width properties inaccessible to code outside of the *Box* class, we use:

```
class Box {
  private var width:Number;
  private var height:Number;
}
```

Now suppose we place the following code somewhere outside of the *Box* class:

```
var b:Box = new Box( );
b.height = 10;
```

When that code is compiled, the following error appears in the Output panel:

```
The member is private and cannot be accessed.
```

The somewhat unusual exception to this rule is that code in a subclass can access private properties defined by its superclass. In most other OOP languages (e.g., Java and C++), private members are accessible within a single class only, *not* its subclasses. There is no way to impose a similar restriction in ActionScript 2.0.

> In ActionScript 2.0, a property defined as *private* is accessible only to code in the property's class or subclasses.

By defining a class's properties as *private*, we keep the class's information safely encapsulated, preventing other code from relying too heavily on the internal structure of the class or accidentally assigning invalid values to properties.

When a *private* property represents some aspect of an object that should be externally modifiable (e.g., the height of a box), we must provide an *accessor method* as an external means of making the modification. We'll learn more about accessor methods when we cover methods, later in this chapter.

If a property definition does not include the *private* attribute, the property is considered public, meaning that it is accessible to code anywhere (not just to code within the class that defines the property). That is, all properties are public unless otherwise specified. If, however, we wish to show that a property is public by intention, not just by default, we can use the optional *public* attribute, as follows:

```
class Box {
  public var width:Number;
  public var height:Number;
}
```

AS 1.0

ActionScript 1.0 had no access control modifiers. All properties were effectively public.

In general, it's good form to specify either the *public* or *private* attribute explicitly for every property. When a property is defined as *public*, we can rest assured that the programmer made a conscious decision to *expose* the property (i.e., make it publicly accessible). A designation of *public* says "use this property freely without worrying that it may become private in the future." By the same token, no property should be made public unless it is specifically required to be so by the class's architecture. If you are unsure whether to make a property public or private, make it private. Down the road, you can easily make the property public if required. By contrast, if you start with a public property, you'll have a tough time changing it to private later if external code already relies on it.

In other languages, access control modifiers are sometimes referred to as *visibility modifiers*. In the ECMAScript 4 standard, however, the term *visibility* is used to describe whether a property or method is enumerable via a *for-in* loop.

Note that ActionScript does not support the *protected* access control modifier found in Java and C++. The rules governing ActionScript's access control modifiers are relatively simple (albeit nonstandard): *private* properties are accessible to code in a class and its subclasses; *public* properties are accessible from anywhere. The rules for Java and C++ access control modifiers are somewhat more complex. For comparison, Table 4-1 lists the meanings of *public*, *protected*, and *private* in ActionScript, Java, and C++. In all cases, the *public* and *private* attributes are mutually exclusive. (Note that Table 4-1 focuses strictly on access modifiers in various languages and, therefore, does not include other property attributes such as *static*.)

Table 4-1. Access control modifiers in ActionScript, Java, and C++

Access control modifier	ActionScript	Java	C++
public	No access restrictions	No access restrictions	No access restrictions
private	Class and subclass access only	Class access only	Class access only
no modifier	Same as public	Access allowed from class's own package only	Same as private
protected	Not supported	Access allowed from class's own package and class's subclasses in any other package	Access allowed from class and subclass only

Defining class properties with the static attribute

The *static* attribute determines whether a property is associated with instances of the class or with the class itself. By default, property definitions create instance properties. To indicate that a property should be treated as a class property instead of an instance property, we precede it with the keyword `static`, which is traditionally placed after the keyword `public` or `private` and before the keyword `var`. Because the *static* attribute is used to define a class property, class properties are sometimes called *static properties*.

Our *Box* class could define a class property, `numSides`, that indicates the number of sides all *Box* instances have, as follows:

```
class Box {
   public static var numSides:Number = 4;
}
```

Class properties are accessed through a class directly, independent of any object instance. They are used to store information that relates logically to an entire class, as opposed to information that varies from instance to instance.

Unlike instance properties, class properties can be initialized to any value, not just compile-time constant expressions. However, the values available in a class depend on the compiler's progress through the class. For example, in the case:

```
public static var x = y;
public static var y = 10;
```

x is set to undefined because y hasn't been defined at the time x is assigned a value. But in the case:

```
public static var y = 10;
public static var x = y;
```

x is set to 10 because y is defined before x. A class property can also retrieve values from methods that return values that are resolvable at compile time.

Within the class that defines a class property (and any of its subclasses), a class property can be accessed either by name directly, as in `numSides`, or through the class, as in `Box.numSides`. For example, this code, if written within the class definition:

```
trace("A box has " + numSides + " sides.");
```

is synonymous with this code:

```
trace("A box has " + Box.numSides + " sides.");
```

Outside of its defining class, a class property can be accessed only through the class name, as in `Box.numSides` (and only if the property is not declared *private*). For example, because numSides is defined as *public*, we can use the following code outside the *Box* class definition:

```
// Displays: A box has 4 sides.
trace("A box has " + Box.numSides + " sides.");
```

By contrast, the following code, which does not qualify the property name numSides with the class name *Box*, is valid only inside the *Box* class (or any of its subclasses):

```
trace("A box has " + numSides + " sides.");
```

You cannot access a class property through a reference to an instance of a class. For example, if we attempt to access numSides through b (a *Box* instance), as follows:

```
var b:Box = new Box( )
b.numSides;
```

the following error appears in the Output panel:

```
Static members can only be accessed directly through classes.
```

A class property stores only a single value. If that value changes due to, say, a method call on a particular instance, the change is universal. In Example 4-1, we add two methods to our *Box* class, one to set the value of Box.numSides and one to retrieve it. No matter which instance invokes the methods, they operate on a single numSides property value. (We haven't studied methods yet, so you may want to return to this code later once you're familiar with method definitions.)

Example 4-1. Accessing a static property through a method

```
// The Box class, with methods to set and retrieve the
// value of the class property, numSides.
class Box {
  // The class property.
  private static var numSides:Number = 4;

  // The method that sets numSides.
  public function setNumSides (newNumSides:Number):Void {
    numSides = newNumSides;
  }

  // The method that retrieves numSides.
  public function getNumSides ():Number {
    return numSides;
  }
}

// *** Code placed somewhere outside the Box class.***
// Make two unique Box instances.
var box1:Box = new Box();
var box2:Box = new Box();

// Check the value of numSides for each instance.
trace(box1.getNumSides());  // Displays: 4
trace(box2.getNumSides());  // Displays: 4

// Set numSides through instance box1.
box1.setNumSides(5);
// Retrieve numSides through instance box2.
trace(box2.getNumSides());  // Displays: 5
```

Example 4-1. Accessing a static property through a method (continued)

```
                        // Both box1 and box2 accessed the single
                        // value for numSides.
```

You may be saying, "Wait a minute! I thought class properties cannot be accessed via instances but only directly through the class. Why does the code access numSides through the box1 and box2 instances?" You are correct that class properties cannot be accessed directly via an instance. The following is invalid:

```
box2.numSides
```

However, Example 4-1 does not access the class property numSides directly through an instance. Instead, it accesses the class property through a method, *getNumSides( )*, which is accessible to instances of the class. And if you're wondering, "Is there such a thing as a static method?" Yes, there is. We'll discuss static methods later.

Within a single class, the same identifier cannot be used for a class property and an instance property. Attempting to create two properties with the same name, whether class or instance properties, always causes a compile-time error.

Class properties are useful for sharing data across objects of a class or even between classes. For example, in Chapter 5 we'll study an *ImageViewer* class that creates a rectangular region for displaying an image on screen. The *ImageViewer* class needs to know which depths it should use when creating the movie clips that make up the rectangular region. The depths are the same for every *ImageViewer* instance, so they are best implemented as class properties. Here's an excerpt of the *ImageViewer* class that defines the depth-related properties:

```
class ImageViewer {
  // Depths for visual assets
  private static var imageDepth:Number - 0;
  private static var maskDepth:Number = 1;
  private static var borderDepth:Number = 2;

  // Remainder of class definition not shown...
}
```

A class property might also provide default values to use when constructing instances of a class. Here we add defaultHeight and defaultWidth as class properties to the *Box* class. If values for h and w aren't supplied to the *Box* constructor, it uses the defaults (we'll cover constructor functions in detail later):

```
class Box {
  private var width:Number;
  private var height:Number;

  private static var defaultWidth:Number = 30;
  private static var defaultHeight:Number = 20;
```

```
public function Box (w:Number, h:Number) {
  if (w == undefined) {
    w = defaultWidth;
  }
  if (h == undefined) {
    h = defaultHeight;
  }
  width  = w;
  height = h;
}
}
```

We might similarly add maxHeight and maxWidth class properties to use to check for a valid *Box* size when constructing *Box* instances.

Class properties can also be handy for storing global counters for a class, such as a property to track the number of instances that have been created. Or, a class property might have nothing to do whatsoever with its instances—some classes are simply collections of related class properties and are never actually instantiated. The built-in *Math* class is a good example of this; it consolidates numerical constants such as PI and numerical functions such as *max( )* and *min( )*.

As another example, consider a typical application in which we might have an *AppStartupSettings* class that maintains a set of application-wide startup parameters as class properties:

```
class AppStartupSettings {
  public static var CONFIG_LOCATION:String = "config.xml";
  public static var SOUND_ENABLED:Boolean = true;
  public static var SHOW_TIP:Boolean = true;
}
```

In some cases, we might want to guarantee that the preceding settings never change (i.e., make the property values *constant*). The ECMAScript 4 standard provides a means of making that guarantee, via the *final* attribute, but ActionScript 2.0 does not support *final*. Following a common convention in other languages, we use ALL CAPS when naming static properties that should not be modified by a program (i.e., should be treated as constants by other programmers).

 ActionScript 1.0 did not have a formal means of defining class properties. By convention, class properties were defined on a class's constructor function, as follows:

```
// Class constructor
function Box () {
}
// Class property
Box.numSides = 4;
```

Furthermore, ActionScript 1.0 class properties could be accessed via the class constructor only, as in Box.numSides (never as numSides).

Global variables versus class properties

In addition to class properties, ActionScript supports *global variables*, which are created like this:

```
_global.someVariable = someValue;
```

Notice that no datatype is specified when a global variable is created. ActionScript 2.0 does not support static typing for global variables.

Global variables are accessible from anywhere in a program and were commonly used in ActionScript 1.0. While global variables are legal in ActionScript 2.0, using them is considered unsafe OOP practice. In an OOP application, information needed across classes should be stored in class properties, both for the sake of organization and to prevent variable name collisions (i.e., cases in which separate classes or *.swf* files create global variables of the same name). Java, for comparison, does not support global variables at all and expects all cross-class data to be stored in static variables (the equivalent of ActionScript's class properties).

In general, you should try to place your class properties in the classes that use them. If more than one class needs access to the same information, consider creating a separate class, such as the earlier *AppStartupSettings* class, that provides a central point of access to the information.

Subclasses and class properties

If you're new to the concept of overriding properties and defining subclasses with the *extends* keyword, you should skip this section for now and return to it once you've read Chapter 6.

When a class property in a superclass is not overridden by a subclass, the property maintains a single value that is accessible via both the subclass and the superclass. For example, suppose an *Employee* class defines a class property, defaultSalary. Further suppose a *Manager* class extends the *Employee* class but does not override the defaultSalary property. Here's the code, greatly simplified to show only the defaultSalary property definition:

```
// Employee class
class Employee {
  public static var defaultSalary:Number = 34000;
}

// Manager class
class Manager extends Employee {
}
```

In this situation, the references to the properties Employee.defaultSalary and Manager.defaultSalary are synonymous:

```
trace(Employee.defaultSalary);  // Displays: 34000
trace(Manager.defaultSalary);   // Displays: 34000
```

Furthermore, changes made to defaultSalary via Employee.defaultSalary are reflected in Manager.defaultSalary and vice versa:

```
trace(Employee.defaultSalary);   // Displays: 34000
Manager.defaultSalary = 40000;
trace(Employee.defaultSalary);   // Displays: 40000
Employee.defaultSalary = 50000;
trace(Manager.defaultSalary);    // Displays: 50000
```

By contrast, when a property in a superclass is overridden by a subclass, the property in the subclass maintains a unique value, distinct from the property's value in the superclass. Let's rewrite our *Manager* class so that it overrides the *Employee* class property defaultSalary (changes shown in bold):

```
// Employee class
class Employee {
  public static var defaultSalary:Number = 34000;
}

// Manager class
class Manager extends Employee {
  // Override defaultSalary
  public static var defaultSalary:Number = 60000;
}
```

Now the properties Employee.defaultSalary and Manager.defaultSalary are different:

```
// Check defaultSalary's value for each class
trace(Employee.defaultSalary);   // Displays: 34000
trace(Manager.defaultSalary);    // Displays: 60000
```

And changes made to Employee.defaultSalary are separate from Manager.defaultSalary and vice versa:

```
// Change Manager's defaultSalary value
Manager.defaultSalary = 70000;
// Check defaultSalary's value for each class
trace(Employee.defaultSalary);   // Displays: 34000
trace(Manager.defaultSalary);    // Displays: 70000

// Change Employee's defaultSalary value
Employee.defaultSalary = 20000;
// Check defaultSalary's value for each class
trace(Employee.defaultSalary);   // Displays: 20000
trace(Manager.defaultSalary);    // Displays: 70000
```

For more information on overriding properties, see Chapter 6.

 A bug in ActionScript 2.0 prevents access to inherited class properties before the superclass that defines the property is used in a script.

For example, in the following code, the class property Employee.defaultSalary is inherited by *Manager*:

```
// Code in Employee.as
class Employee {
  public static var defaultSalary:Number = 34000;
}
```

```
// Code in Manager.as
class Manager extends Employee {
}
```

If, outside of the *Employee* and *Manager* classes, we attempt to access Manager.defaultSalary before referencing the *Employee* class, then the property will be undefined:

```
// Fails when this code appears outside of Employee.as and Manager.as
trace(Manager.defaultSalary);  // Displays: undefined
```

To fix the problem, we simply refer to the *Employee* class before accessing the property:

```
// Refer to Employee
Employee;
// Now it works
trace(Manager.defaultSalary);  // Displays: 34000
```

Note, however, that the inherited class property bug does not cause problems for code inside the subclass. For example, the following code in *Manager* works without any special reference to *Employee*:

```
class Manager extends Employee {
  function paySalary ():Void {
    // This reference is valid because Employee is referenced
    // in the Manager class definition.
    var salary:Number = Manager.defaultSalary;

    // Remainder of method not shown...
  }
}
```

Compile-Time Constant Expressions

Earlier, we learned that an instance property definition can assign a default value to a property, provided that the value is a so-called *compile-time constant expression*. A compile-time constant expression is an expression whose value can be fully determined at compile time (i.e., it does not rely on any values set at runtime). Specifically, a compile-time constant expression may include only:

- null, numeric, boolean, and string constants
- The following operators (used only on numbers, booleans, strings, null, or undefined): + (unary and binary), - (unary and binary), ~, !, *, /, %, <<, >>, >>>, <, >, <=, >=, instanceof, ==, !=, ===, !==, &, ^, |, &&, ^^, ||, and ?: (ternary operator)

- *Array* literals, *Object* literals, and instances of the following classes: *Array*, *Boolean*, *Number*, *Object*, and *String*
- References to other compile-time constant expressions

Examples of valid compile-time constant expressions are:

```
4 + 5
"Hello" + " world"
null
[4, 5]
new Array(4, 5)
{a: 5, b: 10}
new Object()
```

The following code assigns the value of DEFAULT_HEIGHT to height, which is legal because DEFAULT_HEIGHT contains a compile-time constant expression:

```
class Box {
  private var DEFAULT_HEIGHT:Number = 10;
  private var height:Number = DEFAULT_HEIGHT;
}
```

Compile-time constant expressions cannot contain function calls, method calls, object construction, or any other value that cannot be entirely determined at compile time. For example, the following code attempts to use *parseInt( )* in the calculation of an instance property value:

```
private var area = parseInt("100.5");
```

which results in the following error:

```
A class's instance variables may only be initialized to compile-time
constant expressions.
```

This code attempts illegally to assign an object as the initial value of the property target:

```
private var target:MovieClip = _root;  // ERROR!
                                        // References to objects are
                                        // not compile-time constants.
```

Fortunately, it's easy to work around the compile-time constant requirement placed on instance properties. Simply move the initialization code to the class's constructor function. For example, to initialize an area property for our *Box* class, we would use the following code:

```
class Box {
  // Property definition
  private var width:Number;
  private var height:Number;
  private var area:Number;

  // Constructor
  public function Box (w:Number, h:Number) {
    width = w;
    height = h;
```

```
    // Initialize area. This is perfectly legal within a constructor.
    area = width * height;
  }
}
```

Enumerating Properties with for-in loops

Even if you are familiar with core ActionScript 1.0 syntax such as *for-in* loops (and this book assumes you are), you may not be aware of their subtle interaction with object-oriented aspects of the language. Specifically, although the *for-in* statement lets us list (a.k.a. *enumerate*) properties of an object, not all properties are enumerable. The following example displays the enumerable properties of obj in the Output panel:

```
for (var prop:String in obj) {
  trace("property name: " + prop);
  trace("property value: " + obj[prop]);
}
```

By default, instance properties (i.e., properties not declared as *static*) are not enumerable with a *for-in* loop. For example, suppose our *Box* class defines two public properties, width and height, and initializes them both to the value 15:

```
class Box {
  public var width:Number  = 15;
  public var height:Number = 15;
}
```

When we create a new *Box* object, its width and height properties are set to 15:

```
var b:Box = new Box( );
trace(b.width);   // Displays: 15
trace(b.height);  // Displays: 15
```

But when we enumerate the properties of the *Box* object, width and height are not listed:

```
// This loop generates no output
for (var prop:String in b) {
  trace("property name: " + prop);
  trace("property value: " + b[prop]);
}
```

 According to the ECMAScript 4 specification, instance properties should remain non-numerable even after value assignment. However, in ActionScript 2.0, due to the legacy architecture of ActionScript 1.0, an instance property becomes enumerable after it is assigned a value (unless that value assignment is part of the property declaration). That is, in ActionScript 2.0, a property whose value is initialized at declaration time is not enumerable unless and until it is subsequently assigned another value. You should not rely on this deviation because ActionScript may become more ECMAScript-compliant in the future.

By contrast, class properties (i.e., properties declared as *static*) are enumerable with a *for-in* loop. For example, suppose our *Box* class defines two class properties, maxWidth and maxHeight, and initializes them both to 250:

```
class Box {
  public static var maxWidth:Number  = 250;
  public static var maxHeight:Number = 250;
}
```

We can use a *for-in* loop to list the *Box* class's class properties:

```
for (var prop:String in Box) {
  trace("property name: " + prop);
  trace("property value: " + Box[prop]);
}

// Displays:
property name: maxHeight
property value: 250
property name: maxWidth
property value: 250
```

Perhaps surprisingly, class properties are enumerable even when they are declared *private*.

Dynamic properties (new properties added to an individual instance of a class declared as *dynamic*) are also enumerable, as shown in this example:

```
// The dynamic class definition
dynamic class Box {
  public var width:Number  = 15;
  public var height:Number = 15;
}

// Create an instance
var b:Box = new Box( );

// Add a new dynamic property to the instance
b.newProp = "hello world";

// Enumerate b's properties
for (var prop in b) {
  trace("property name: " + prop);
  trace("property value: " + b[prop]);
}

// Displays:
property name: newProp
property value: hello world
```

Notice in the preceding example that the dynamic property, newProp, is enumerated, but the instance properties width and height are not.

ActionScript 2.0 does not support ECMAScript 4's *enumerable* attribute, which makes an instance property visible to the *for-in* statement. To make an instance property enumerable, you can use the undocumented *ASSetPropFlags( )* function. For details, see *http://chattyfig.figleaf.com/flashcoders-wiki/index.php?ASSetPropFlags*

Methods

Methods are functions that determine the behavior of a class. They implement the tasks that instances of the class or the class itself can perform. For example, Action-Script's built-in *Sound* class has a method named *loadSound( )* that can retrieve an external MP3 file for playback in the Flash Player.

To define methods for our own classes, we use the *function* statement within the body of a class definition, as follows:

```
class ClassName {
  function methodName (param1:type, param2:type,...paramn:type):returnType {
    statements
  }
}
```

where *methodName* is the identifier for the method; *param1:type*, *param2:type*, ...*paramn:type*, is a list of the method's parameters; *returnType* is the datatype of the method's return value; and *statements* is zero or more statements executed when the method is invoked. Each parameter definition (e.g., *param1:type*) consists of a parameter name (*param1*), a colon (:), and a type identifier (*type*), indicating the datatype of the parameter.

 In ActionScript 1.0, methods could be defined in several ways. Most commonly, methods were defined by assigning a function to a property of a class constructor's prototype, as follows:

```
ClassName.prototype.methodName = function (param1, param2,...
paramn) {
  statements
};
```

Although the ActionScript 2.0 compiler does not generate an error when a prototype-based method is declared, it does generate an error when a prototype-based method is invoked on or referenced through an object whose class is not dynamic. Generally speaking, prototype-based methods should not be used when exporting to ActionScript 2.0.

Within the body of a method, parameters are referred to directly by name. For example, the following method, *square( )*, defines a parameter, x, and refers to it directly in the method body:

```
function square (x:Number):Number {
  return x * x;
}
```

If a parameter's *type* is omitted in the method definition, no type checking is performed for that parameter (allowing the parameter to accept value of any datatype). Similarly, if *returnType* is omitted, no type checking is performed for the return value. (Whenever you omit the datatype, omit the colon as well.) However, if a method returns no value, its *returnType* should be set to Void (with a capital "V"), indicating that the method does not return a value.

 Don't confuse the *Void* datatype with the rarely used *void* operator. The former starts with a capital "V," while the latter starts with a lowercase "v." Use *Void* (with a capital "V") when specifying a method return type for a method that doesn't return a value. If you use lowercase *void* instead, you'll get the following error, which can be very confusing if you don't know the subtle cause:

```
A type identifier is expected after the ':'.
```

If your method's *returnType* is *Void*, make sure it doesn't return any value. When a method specifies *Void* as its *returnType* but returns a value, the following error appears in the Output panel at compile time:

```
A function with return type Void may not return a value.
```

In most cases, the preceding error is a helpful debugging tool. It means that you probably designed the method to return no value but have strayed from the original design and implemented the method with a return value. If that happens, you should either:

- Alter your design so that it reflects the method's return type (i.e., specify the return value's correct datatype in the function declaration)
- Stick to your original design by altering your method so it does not return a value (in which case *Void* is the correct return datatype for the function declaration)

Conversely, when a method specifies a *returnType* other than *Void* but returns a value that does not match the specified type, the compiler generates the error:

```
The expression returned must match the function's return type.
```

And when a method specifies a *returnType* other than *Void* but contains no *return* statement whatsoever, the compiler generates the error:

```
A return statement is required in this function.
```

The general rule, then, is to be sure your method's implementation actually complies with the parameter and return types it specifies.

Right, enough theory. Let's see what a method definition looks like in real life by adding a *getArea( )* method to our *Box* class:

```
class Box {
  private var width:Number = 0;
  private var height:Number = 0;

  // Here's the method definition
```

```
    function getArea ():Number {
      return width * height;
    }
  }
```

The *getArea( )* method definition starts with the `function` keyword, followed by the method name, getArea. The *getArea( )* method takes no parameters, so its parameter list is simply an empty set of parentheses, ( ). The post-colon datatype, `:Number`, specifies that *getArea( )* returns a value of the *Number* type. When called, *getArea( )* returns the value of `width` multiplied by `height`, which will be a numeric value (as advertised).

By specifying our method's return type explicitly, we make debugging easier down the road. If we initially design our method to return a number, but then in the method body we accidentally return, say, a string, the compiler will warn us accordingly.

The final section of our method definition is the statement block, delineated by opening and closing curly braces:

```
  {
    return width * height;
  }
```

Notice that we refer to the properties `width` and `height` directly by name. Within the body of a method, properties are referred to directly, without any qualifying reference to an object (in the case of instance properties) or a class (in the case of class properties). In the next section, "Referring to the Current Object with the Keyword this," we'll learn one exception to this rule.

In a method definition, the method *signature*—consisting of the method name and parameter list—uniquely identifies the method among all other methods in the class. In some languages (most notably Java), a method is considered completely different from all other methods if any aspect of its signature differs from that of other methods. Hence, in Java, two methods might have the exact same name and the exact same number of parameters but be considered unique because, say, the first parameter of one method has a different datatype than the first parameter of the other! In Java, methods that have the same name but different signatures are known as *overloaded* methods. ActionScript doesn't support method overloading; every method in an ActionScript class must have a unique name (unique within that class). When two methods within a class have the same name, the compiler generates the following error:

```
The same member name may not be repeated more than once.
```

In our *getArea( )* method definition, getArea( ) is the method's *signature*. The `:Number` datatype is not considered part of the signature.

You may wonder why the return datatype is not part of the signature. In a language that supports overloading, the compiler decides which method to execute based on the name of the method called and, if necessary, the datatypes of the arguments in the method call. Although in theory a compiler could also check the return datatype to differentiate between two methods with the same names and same parameter types, in practice nothing in the method invocation expression can sufficiently indicate which return type (and hence, which method) is required. Thus, the return datatype is not used to identify a method's signature, but simply to perform type checking on the return types.

Returning to our *getArea( )* method, note that the whitespace adjacent to the curly braces in our *getArea( )* definition is not dictated by ActionScript's grammatical rules; it's a matter of personal style. Some developers place the opening curly brace on the first line of the method definition, as shown earlier and throughout this book. Others place it on a line of its own, as in:

```
function getArea ( ):Number
{
  return width * height;
}
```

Both styles are technically valid; only you can decide which god you pray to.

Referring to the Current Object with the Keyword this

From within a method body, you'll often want to refer to the object on which the method was invoked—the so-called *current object*. Consider the expression b. getArea( ). When that code runs, it invokes *getArea( )* on the object b, but within the *getArea( )* method body there is no such variable as b. So how do we refer to the current object—the object on which *getArea( )* was invoked—from within *getArea( )*? To refer to the current object within a method, we use the this keyword. You might ask whether we couldn't alternatively pass in the object reference as a parameter. In theory, we could, but using this helps our class to remain encapsulated, eliminating the need for the outside world to worry about the object's internal requirements. The this reference to the current object allows an object to refer to itself without the need for an additional parameter, and is therefore much cleaner.

Let's take a look at several practical situations that require this. Note that neither of the following situations is exceedingly common. The this keyword is certainly important when you need it, but if you're a newer programmer, you may want to wait until that need arises before studying the next sections in detail.

Passing the current object to a method

The this keyword is most often used when passing the current object to another object's method, as in:

```
function someMethod ( ):Void {
  // Pass this as a parameter to a completely separate object
  someOtherObject.someOtherMethod(this);
}
```

Let's build an example that follows this pattern, in which we need to pass the current object (this) to a method of another class.

First, we'll add a *resetDimensions( )* method to the *Box* class:

```
function resetDimensions ( ):Void {
  height = 1;
  width  = 1;
  trace("Dimensions reset!");
}
```

Now suppose we want to call *resetDimensions( )* whenever the user clicks the mouse. To handle mouse clicks, we give the *Box* class an *onMouseDown( )* method that simply invokes *resetDimensions( )*:

```
function onMouseDown ( ):Void {
  resetDimensions();
}
```

However, an instance of the *Box* class won't receive mouse events unless we register it to do so. Here we define another method, *enableReset( )*, that can register a *Box* instance to receive *Mouse* event notifications:

```
function enableReset ( ):Void {
  Mouse.addListener(this);
}
```

The *enableReset( )* method will be called elsewhere in our hypothetical program, but only on *Box* instances that should respond to mouse clicks. If we wanted all *Box* instances to respond to mouse clicks, then we would add an *enableReset( )* call to the *Box* constructor function.

Now take a closer look at the body of the *enableReset( )* method. The command:

```
Mouse.addListener(this);
```

passes the current *Box* object, this, to the *Mouse* class's *addListener( )* method. The code says literally "*Mouse* class, please start sending mouse event notifications to the current object (i.e., to this, the *Box* instance that called *enableReset( )*)." Henceforward, whenever the mouse is clicked, *Box.onMouseDown( )* executes, resetting the *Box* instance's dimensions. Without the this keyword, we couldn't have told the *Mouse* class that the current object wants to receive mouse events.

To complete the example, we should also define *disableReset( )*, a method to stop the *Mouse* class from sending events to a particular *Box* instance. We again use this to tell the *Mouse* class which *Box* wants to cancel event notifications:

```
function disableReset ( ):Void {
  Mouse.removeListener(this);
}
```

Here's how we'd use *enableReset( )*:

```
var b:Box = new Box();
// When enableReset() is called, the value of this in the enableReset()
// method definition stores a reference to our Box instance, b.
b.enableReset();
// From now on, b.onMouseDown() fires whenever the mouse is clicked.
```

When an object registers as a listener of another object, it should always unregister itself before it is deleted.

For example, in the preceding usage example, we registered b to receive mouse events. Suppose we were to delete our *Box* instance, b, as follows:

```
delete b;
```

Even though the reference to the *Box* instance stored in b is gone, another reference to that instance still exists in the *Mouse* class's list of registered listeners! We did not delete the *Box* instance, we only deleted the variable, b. The instance itself lives on due to the *Mouse* class's reference to it. This sloppiness can cause erratic behavior in a program and could become a serious waste of memory. A class should always provide a means of cleaning up stray object references before an object is deleted. That is, ActionScript doesn't *garbage-collect* an object (i.e., free up the memory used by an object) until no more references to it remain. Typically, cleanup is done in a custom *die( )* or *destroy( )* method that must be invoked before an object is deleted. (The name of the method is up to you, but it should indicate that it wipes the object's slate clean.) For example, here's a *die( )* method for our *Box* class:

```
function die ():Void {
  disableReset();  // Unregister the object so the Mouse class
                   // deletes the reference to it.
}
```

By providing a *die( )* method, a class guarantees a safe means of deleting its instances. A developer using the class simply calls *die( )* before deleting each instance. For example:

```
var b:Box = new Box();
b.enableReset();
b.die();
delete b;
```

Note that the *die( )* method should not attempt to delete the *Box* instance itself. It is illegal for an object to delete itself. We'll return to this topic in Chapter 5.

Managing parameter/property name conflicts

When an instance property or a class property has the same name as a method parameter, the parameter takes precedence. That is, uses of the duplicate name in the method will refer to the parameter, not the property. However, we can still access the property by preceding the name with the this keyword (known as *disambiguating* the method parameter from the property.) For example, the following method, *setHeight( )*, has a parameter, height, whose name is identical to the instance property height:

```
class Box {
  // Instance property height
```

```
    private var height:Number;

    // Method with parameter height
    function setHeight (height:Number):Void {
      // Method body not shown
    }
  }
```

Within the body of *setHeight( )*, if we don't include a qualifier, the compiler assumes that the identifier height refers to the method parameter, not the instance property of the same name. The height parameter is said to *shadow* the height property. But we can still access the height property explicitly using the this keyword. The this keyword contains a reference to the current object; hence, just as with any other object, we can use the dot operator to access its properties or invoke its methods, as follows:

```
function setHeight (height:Number):Void {
  // Sets height property (this.height) to the
  // value of height parameter (height).
  this.height = height;
}
```

In the preceding *setHeight( )* method, the value of the height parameter is assigned to the height property. The this keyword tells the compiler that this.height is the property, while height, on its own, is the parameter.

You will encounter many code examples in which the programmer purposely uses the same name for a parameter and an instance property. To keep things more clearly separated, however, you may wish to avoid using parameter names that have the same name as properties. For example, you could rewrite the preceding *setHeight( )* method so it uses h instead of height as a parameter name:

```
function setHeight (h:Number):Void {
  // Sets height instance property (height) to value of h parameter
  height = h;
}
```

In this case, because the parameter is named h, not height, the unqualified reference (height) refers to the instance property. We'll see later under "Local Variables" that local variables can also shadow properties of the same name.

Redundant use of the keyword this

Even when the this keyword is not required, using it is perfectly legal. Therefore, in the example at the end of the preceding section, it is legal to explicitly qualify height by preceding it with this, as follows:

```
this.height = h;
```

Likewise, the following rewrite of our earlier *Box.getArea( )* method is legal:

```
function getArea ():Number {
  return this.width * this.height;
}
```

However, using this when not required is redundant. For the sake of easier reading, many developers (and this book) avoid redundant uses of this. Even the single-line *getArea( )* method is much less verbose without this:

```
function getArea ():Number {
  return width * height;
}
```

Methods that make redundant use of this require more work to produce and take longer to read. However, some programmers prefer to always use this when referring to instance properties and methods, simply to distinguish them from local variables. Other programmers prefer to use variable name prefixes instead, where local variable names start with l_, and all property and method names start with m_ (meaning member).

 In ActionScript 1.0, within method and constructor function bodies, the this keyword was not redundant—it was a required part of all instance property and method references.

Inside an ActionScript 2.0 class definition, use of the this keyword is legal only within instance methods and constructor functions. Within a class method (discussed in the next section), use of the this keyword generates the following compile-time error:

```
'this' is not accessible from this scope.
```

And anywhere else in a class definition, use of the this keyword generates this error:

```
This statement is not permitted in a class definition.
```

Method Attributes

Earlier, we saw how the *public*, *private*, and *static* attributes could control access to properties and make some properties pertain to an entire class rather than to individual instances of the class. Likewise, method definitions can be modified using the same three attributes, with an analogous effect. Method attributes must be listed before the function keyword in a method definition. For example, to add the *private* attribute to the *getArea( )* method of our *Box* class, we'd use:

```
class Box {
  private function getArea ():Number {
    return width * height;
  }
}
```

When a method has more than one attribute, the attributes can appear in any order. However, the *public* or *private* attribute is conventionally placed before the *static* attribute, as in:

```
private static function getArea ():Number {
  return width * height;
}
```

Furthermore, the *public* and *private* attributes cannot both be used to modify the same method definition; they are mutually exclusive.

Controlling method access with the public and private attributes

The *public* and *private* method attributes are analogous to the *public* and *private* property attributes; they determine from where a method can be accessed. A *public* method is accessible to all code, anywhere. A *private* method can be accessed from within the class that defines the method (and its subclasses). If a method definition does not include the *private* attribute, the method is considered public. That is, all methods are public unless otherwise specified. If, however, we wish to show that a method is public by intention, not just by default, we can use the optional *public* attribute, as shown next. In general, it's good form to specify the *public* or *private* attribute explicitly for every method.

```
class Box {
  // Define properties...
  private var width:Number = 10;
  private var height:Number = 10;

  // Define getArea() with an explicit use of the public attribute
  public function getArea ( ):Number {
    return width * height;
  }
}
```

When a *private* method is accessed outside of the class that defined it (or any of its subclasses), the following error occurs at compile time:

```
The member is private and cannot be accessed.
```

The *public* and *private* attributes are used to put the OOP "black box" principle into strict practice. In OOP, each object can be thought of as a black box that is controlled by an external assortment of metaphoric knobs. The object's internal operations are unknown (and unimportant) to the person using those knobs—all that matters is that the object performs the desired action. A class's public methods are the knobs by which a programmer can specify inputs (i.e., tell the class to perform some operation). A class's private methods can perform other internal operations. Each class should publicly expose only methods that the outside world needs to instruct it to do something. Methods needed to carry out those instructions should be kept internal (i.e., defined as *private*). For example, a driver doesn't need to know how a car's engine works; to drive the car, he simply uses the gas pedal to accelerate and the steering wheel to turn. Making the car accelerate when he steps on the gas pedal is the manufacturer's concern, not his. The somewhat arbitrary nature of the external "knobs" is apparent if you compare a car to, say, a motorcycle. On a motorcycle, the rider typically accelerates by turning the handle grip rather than depressing a gas pedal. In both vehicles, however, the driver's action (the input) supplies gasoline to the engine, which is ultimately used to power the wheels (the output).

As you manufacture your own classes, you should focus as much energy designing the way the class is used as you do implementing how it works internally. Remember to put yourself in the "driver's seat" regularly. Ideally, the signatures for your class's public methods should change very little or not at all each time you make an internal change to the class. If you put a new engine in the car, the driver should still be able to use the gas pedal. Stay mindful that each change to a public method's signature will force a change everywhere that the method is used. As much as possible, keep the volatility of your classes behind the scenes, in private methods. Likewise, strive to create stable, generic public methods that aren't likely to be visibly affected if, say, the gravity of the physics environment changes or a new field is added to the database.

 In OOP terms, an object's public methods and properties are sometimes called the object's *interface* to the outside world. In Action-Script, the term *interface* has a more specific technical meaning, covered in Chapter 8. To avoid confusion, we'll use the term *"interface"* in the ActionScript-specific sense only.

The *ImageViewer* class in Chapter 5 uses private methods to render an image on screen, crop it to a particular height and width, and surround it with a border. In the following excerpt from the *ImageViewer* class, the *buildViewer( )*, *createMainContainer( )*, *createImageClip( )*, *createImageClipMask( )*, and *createBorder( )* methods are all private. In theory, this means we could entirely change how the image is rendered without affecting any code that uses *ImageViewer* objects:

```
private function buildViewer (x:Number,
                              y:Number,
                              w:Number,
                              h:Number):Void {
  // Create the clips to hold the image, mask, and border.
  // Each of the following methods is declared private (not shown).
  createMainContainer(x, y);
  createImageClip( );
  createImageClipMask(w, h);
  createBorder(w, h);
}
```

Consider what would happen if our *createBorder( )* method were public and a developer used it to resize the border around the image. That seems sensible enough, but the developer probably doesn't know that in order to resize the border, she must also resize the image mask! The latter is an internal detail that's specific to our implementation and shouldn't be the developer's concern. What the developer really needs is a public method, *setSize( )*, that handles resizing the image viewer but hides the implementation details required to do so. The *setSize( )* method describes the object's behavior in generic terms rather than in relation to our specific implementation. Hence, *setSize( )*'s external use is unlikely to change even if we fundamentally change the rendering approach in the *ImageViewer* class. It's wise to define the *createBorder( )* method as *private* in the first place, averting problems caused by its unintended use.

Then, when dynamic resizing becomes a requirement of our class, we can add public methods to expose that functionality to the world at large (which is filled with dangerous, nosy, meddling developers).

Defining class methods with the static attribute

Earlier, we saw that the *static* attribute determines whether a property is associated with instances of a class or with the class itself. Likewise, when used with methods, the *static* attribute determines whether the method is associated with instances of the class or with the class itself. Normally, method definitions create so-called *instance methods*—methods that are accessed only through instances. By contrast, methods defined with the *static* attribute create so-called *class methods*, which are accessed through a class rather than through a particular instance (just like the class properties we learned about earlier).

Class methods (sometimes referred to as *static methods*) provide functionality that relates to an entire class, not just an instance of that class. For example, Action-Script's built-in *TextField* class defines a class method named *getFontList( )*, which returns a list of fonts on the user's system. The result of the *getFontList( )* method is the same for all text fields, not specific to each text field. Therefore, it should logically be declared *static*. Because *getFontList( )* is *static*, we access it through the *TextField* class directly, not through a *TextField* instance. For example, here we store the return value of *getFontList( )* in a variable, fonts:

```
var fonts:Array = TextField.getFontList();
```

There are two reasons you should care if a method is a class method:

- You need to know whether it is a class method in order to access it properly (if it's a class method, access it through the class; otherwise, access it through an instance of the class).

- Knowing whether it is a class method tells you whether it affects a particular instance or whether it applies to the entire class.

Knowing that *TextField.getFontList( )* is a class method (as identified by Appendix A) a developer should infer that it returns a font list that is independent of a single text field. If *getFontList( )* were not a class method (that is, if it were accessed through an instance of the *TextField* class), a developer might instead assume that it returned a list of fonts used in a particular text field rather than all the fonts on the user's system.

Class methods can also be used to provide access to private class properties or to compare some aspect of two instances of a class. For example, the following code adds a class method, *findLarger( )*, to our *Box* class. The *findLarger( )* method returns the larger of two *Box* instances, or if the instances are the same size, it returns the first instance:

```
class Box {
  public static function findLarger (box1:Box, box2:Box):Box {
    if (box2.getArea() > box1.getArea()) {
```

```
        return box2;
    } else {
        return box1;
    }
}

// Remainder of class not shown...
}

// Usage example:
var biggestBox:Box = Box.findLarger(boxInstance1, boxInstance2);
```

Let's add another class method, *getNumBoxes( )*, to the *Box* class. The *getNumBoxes( )* method returns the value of a private class property, numBoxes, which tracks how many box instances currently exist:

```
class Box {
    private static var numBoxes:Number = 0;

    public static function getNumBoxes ():Number {
        return numBoxes;
    }

    // Remainder of class not shown...
}

// Usage example:
var boxCount:Number = Box.getNumBoxes();
```

Some classes define class methods only (that is, they define no instance methods). In such a case, the class exists solely to contain a group of related functions, but objects of the class are never instantiated. For example, you might define a *SystemSettings* class that contains the following class methods: *setSoundEnabled( )*, *setIntroEnabled( )*, and *setScaleOnResize( )*. Those class methods are accessed via *SystemSettings* directly, so a *SystemSettings* instance need never be created. The built-in *Mouse* class similarly defines the following class methods: *show( )*, *hide( )*, *addListener( )*, and *removeListener( )*. Those class methods are accessed through *Mouse* directly (as in, Mouse.hide( )), not through an instance of the *Mouse* class.

Class methods have two limitations that instance methods do not. First, a class method cannot use the this keyword, as discussed earlier. Second, class methods can access class properties only (unlike instance methods, which can access both instance properties and class properties). A moment's consideration reveals why this is so: an instance should be able to access its own properties (instance properties) plus the properties common to all objects of the class (the class properties, of which there is only one set). Likewise, a class method should be able to access class properties. But it makes no sense for a class method to access an instance property, because each instance has its own set of instance properties. There would be no simple way for a class method to know which instance's properties are of interest.

Therefore, any attempt to access an instance property from a class method results in the following compile-time error:

```
Instance variables cannot be accessed in static functions.
```

However, a class method can legally create an instance of a class and then access its instance properties, as shown here:

```
class SomeClass {
  private static var obj:SomeClass;
  private var prop:Number = 10;

  public static function doSomething ():Void {
    // Create an instance of SomeClass and store it
    // in the class property obj.
    obj = new SomeClass();

    // Access an instance property, prop, of instance stored in obj.
    trace(obj.prop);  // Displays: 10
  }
}
```

In the preceding code, *SomeClass* defines a class property, obj, and an instance property, prop. When the class method *doSomething( )* is invoked, it creates an instance of *SomeClass*, stores it in obj, and accesses the instance property, prop. We'll revisit this theoretical structure when we study the Singleton pattern in Chapter 17.

Let's be clear that class properties (declared using static var) and instance properties (declared using var) are both declared *outside* of class methods and instance methods. Any variables declared within a method using the var keyword are considered local variables. For example, you can't declare a class property by simply using var or static var within a class method. Use of the static keyword within a method causes the following error:

```
Attribute used outside class.
```

AS 1.0

ActionScript 1.0 did not have a formal means of defining class methods. By convention, class methods were defined on a class's constructor function, as follows:

```
// Class constructor
function Box () {
}
// Class method
Box.findLarger = function (box1, box2) {
  if (box2.getArea() > box1.getArea()) {
    return box2;
  } else {
    return box1;
  }
};
```

ActionScript 1.0 class methods could be accessed via the class constructor only, as in Box.findLarger() (not findLarger()). Furthermore, in an ActionScript 1.0 class method, the this keyword was legal; it referred to the class constructor function.

```
// Class constructor
function Box () {
}
// Class method
Box.showThis = function () {
  trace(this == Box);  // Displays: true
};
```

Accessor Methods

Earlier we learned that it's good OOP practice to declare a class's instance properties as *private*, meaning that they cannot be read or modified by code outside of the class. However, most objects must expose some means of examining and changing their state (i.e., provide a publicly accessible means of retrieving and assigning the object's properties). To allow external code to read and modify private properties, we create so-called *accessor methods,* which come in two varieties:

- Those that retrieve a property's value
- Those that set a property's value

Traditionally, an accessor method that retrieves a property's value is known as a *getter method*, and an accessor method that sets a property's value is known as a *setter method*. In ActionScript 2.0, however, those terms have a more specific technical meaning. They refer to special methods that are invoked automatically when a property is accessed, as described under "Getter and Setter Methods," later in this chapter. To avoid confusion, we'll use the terms "getter method" and "setter method" when referring only to ActionScript's special automatic methods.

In general, an accessor method that retrieves a property's value looks like this:

```
public function getPropertyName ():returnType {
  return propertyName;
}
```

By convention, the retrieval method is named get*PropertyName*, where get is used literally and *PropertyName* is the name of the property being retrieved, except that the first letter is capitalized.

An accessor method that assigns a property's value looks like this:

```
public function setPropertyName (param:type):Void {
  propertyName = param;
}
```

By convention, the assignment method is named set*PropertyName*, where set is used literally and *PropertyName* is the name of the property whose value is being assigned (again, with the first letter capitalized). When the method is called, the parameter *param* receives the value being assigned to the property.

Recall that our *Box* class defines two properties, width and height, both of which are declared *private*. Let's add accessor methods for those properties so that code outside of the *Box* class can retrieve and assign their values. In accordance with accessor-method naming conventions, we'll call our methods *getWidth( )*, *setWidth( )*, *getHeight( )*, and *setHeight( )*. Here's the code:

```
class Box {
  private var width:Number;
  private var height:Number;

  // Accessor to retrieve width
  public function getWidth ():Number {
    return width;
  }
  // Accessor to assign width
  public function setWidth (w:Number):Void {
    width = w;
  }

  // Accessor to retrieve height
  public function getHeight ():Number {
    return height;
  }
  // Accessor to assign height
  public function setHeight (h:Number):Void {
    height = h;
  }
}
```

The *getWidth( )* method simply returns the value of the width property. The *setWidth( )* method defines a parameter, w, which can accept values of the *Number* datatype only. When invoked, *setWidth( )* stores value of w in the *private* property width:

```
width = w;
```

Accessor methods that assign a property value traditionally have one of the following return values (we chose the first option):

- No return value (i.e., return type *Void*), if the assignment operation has no result, as is the case for *setHeight( )*
- A Boolean, indicating whether the operation was successful (according to the method's own logic)
- The old property value
- The new property value (perhaps adjusted to make it fall within legal range)

The *getHeight( )* and *setHeight( )* methods are structured exactly like the *getWidth( )* and *setWidth( )* methods but apply to the height property rather than to width.

Here's a sample use of our new accessor methods:

```
var b:Box = new Box( );
b.setWidth(300);
b.setHeight(200);
trace(b.getWidth( ));    // Displays: 300
trace(b.getHeight( ));   // Displays: 200
```

Here, we can start to see the real benefits of a typed language. By specifying the w parameter's datatype as *Number*, we guarantee that the *setWidth( )* method assigns only numeric values to the width property, as required by its property definition (private var width:Number). If some code erroneously attempts to pass *setWidth( )* nonnumeric data, the compiler will warn us of the specific location of the problem! For example, suppose we place the following code on frame 1 of a movie:

```
var b:Box = new Box( );
b.setWidth("really short");
```

When we attempt to export the movie, the compiler displays the following error in the Output panel:

```
**Error** Scene=Scene 1, layer=Layer 1, frame=1:Line 2: Type mismatch.
    b.setWidth("really short");
```

Specifying w's datatype guarantees that our class cannot be used in ways that will cause runtime problems that would be difficult to track down. We can further insulate our program from the effects of erroneous data by implementing custom limitations on the argument values supplied to the *setWidth( )* method. For example, the following code restricts the legal values of w to numbers greater than 0 and less than infinity. It also ensures that w's value is neither the special *NaN* numeric value nor null. While both *NaN* and null are legitimate values of the *Number* type, they would cause problems for our program. (Remember from Chapter 3 that null is a legal value of any datatype.)

```
public function setWidth (w:Number):Boolean {
  if (isNaN(w) || w == null
     || w <= 0 || w > Number.MAX_VALUE) {
    // Invalid data, so return false to indicate a lack of success
    return false;
  }
  // Otherwise, it was successful, so return true to indicate success
  width = w;
  return true;
}
```

Our revised *setWidth( )* method returns a Boolean value indicating whether width was set successfully. External code can rely on the Boolean result to handle cases in which invalid data is passed to the method. For example, the following code attempts to set the width property based on a user input text field. If the input is not valid, the code can recover, presumably by displaying an error message:

```
var b:Box = new Box( );
// Check the Boolean return value of the call to setWidth( )
if (b.setWidth(parseInt(input_txt.text))) {
  // No problems...proceed as planned
} else {
  // ERROR! Invalid data...display a warning (not shown)
}
```

By using an accessor method to mediate property-value assignments, we can develop applications that respond gracefully to runtime problems by anticipating and handling illegal or inappropriate values. But does that mean each and every property access in a program should happen through an accessor method? For example, consider our earlier *getArea( )* method:

```
public function getArea ():Number {
  return width * height;
}
```

Now that we have accessors for the width and height properties, should *getArea( )* be changed as follows?

```
public function getArea ():Number {
  return getWidth() * getHeight();
}
```

The answer depends on the circumstances at hand. Generally speaking, it's quite reasonable to access private properties directly within the class that defines them, so the preceding rewrite of *getArea( )* is not necessarily required nor even recommended. In cases in which speed is a factor, direct property access may be prudent (accessing a property directly is always faster than accessing it through a method). However, when a property's name or datatype is likely to change in the future or when an accessor method provides special services during property access (such as error checking), it pays to use the accessor everywhere, even within the class that defines the property. For example, remember that we modified our earlier *setWidth( )* method to include error checking for invalid data. Whenever we assign the value of `width` within the *Box* class, we still want the benefit of *setWidth( )*'s error checking. That is, although accessing properties directly from within a class conforms to OOP guidelines, it's sensible to use the accessor methods instead.

 If you simply prefer the style of direct property access but still want the benefits of accessor methods, you should consider using Action-Script 2.0's automatic getter and setter methods, discussed later.

Local Variables

We've seen that instance properties are associated with each instance of a class and that class properties are associated with the class itself. Instance and class properties persist as long as the object they're associated with persists. But often you'll need a variable only temporarily. A local variable is a temporary data container used to store a value for the duration of a function or method execution. Local variables can be defined within a function or method only and are normally marked for automatic deletion when the function or method finishes executing (we'll learn the one exception to this rule in the next section, "Nesting Functions in Methods"). To define a local variable in a method, use the *var* statement in the method body. Note that *var* is used for declaring class and instance properties too, but property declarations must be outside of any method definitions; when used within a method, the *var* statement creates a local variable, not a property. For example:

```
function methodName ():returnType {
  var localVariableName:type;
}
```

where *localVariableName* is the identifier (name) for the local variable and *type* is the datatype declaration (optional, but recommended).

A local variable definition can also include an initial value, as follows:

```
var localVariableName:type = value;
```

For example, the following modified version of our earlier *Box.getArea( )* method stores the value of `height * width` in a local variable, area, which it then returns:

```
public function getArea ():Number {
  var area:Number = width * height;
  return area;
}
```

Local variables are used for code clarity and to improve code performance by eliminating repeated method calls or property lookups. For example, in the following method excerpt from a chat application, we display a user's name in a List component (userList) when the user enters a chat room. The user's name is retrieved via the expression *remoteuser.getAttribute( )*. Instead of calling that method repeatedly, we call it once and store the return value in a local variable, username:

```
public function addUser ( ):Void {
  var username:String = remoteuser.getAttribute("username");

  // Use "Guest" as the username if the remoteuser hasn't set a name
  if (username == undefined) {
    username = "Guest";
  }

  // Add the user to the listbox
  userList.addItem(username);
}
```

Consider the alternative approach, which doesn't bother with the local variable username:

```
public function addUser ( ):Void {
  // Use "Guest" as the username if the remoteuser hasn't set a name
  if (remoteuser.getAttribute("username") == undefined) {
    // Add the new user to the listbox
    userList.addItem("Guest");
  } else {
    // Add the new user to the listbox
    userList.addItem(remoteuser.getAttribute("username"));
  }
}
```

The second version (no local variable used) is less readable and requires separate calls to both *userList.addItem( )* and *remoteuser.getAttribute( )*, which is error prone. In the first version (local variable used), the step of adding the username to the List is neatly kept to a single statement and the code is broken into two logical steps: determining the user's name and adding the user's name to the List.

Parameters are also treated as local variables, even though they are not declared with the *var* keyword.

As of Flash Player 6.0.65.0, local variables and function parameters are stored in internal *registers* for quick runtime access (registers are special hardware locations set aside in the computer's CPU rather than its RAM). Hence, when performance is a concern, you should use local variables in favor of repeated object references. For example, instead of:

```
for (var i:Number = 0; i < clipsArray.length; i++) {
  clipsArray[i]._x = i * 10;
  clipsArray[i]._y = i * 10;
  clipsArray[i]._rotation = i * 10;
}
```

It's faster to use:

```
for (var i:Number = 0; i < clipsArray.length; i++) {
  var clip:MovieClip = clipsArray[i];
  clip._x = i * 10;
  clip._y = i * 10;
  clip._rotation = i * 10;
}
```

Note that if you define a local variable of the same name as a property, the local variable hides the property for the entire duration of the method, even before the local variable is defined! To access the property when a local variable of the same name exists, you must qualify it with the this keyword. For example, the following code does not work as expected because it is missing the this keyword. The code assigns the undefined variable power to itself:

```
class Enemy {
  private var power:String = "high";

  public function shoot ():Void {
    trace(power);  // Displays: undefined
                   //(The value of the local variable hides the property
                   // even before the local variable definition!)

    var power:String = power;  // Assigns undefined variable to itself.
  }
}
```

By contrast, the following code works because it uses this.power to access the power instance property (to distinguish it from the local variable of the same name):

```
class Enemy {
  private var power:String = "high";

  public function shoot ():Void {
    trace(this.power);                    // Displays: high
    var power:String = this.power;  // Assigns property to variable
  }
}
```

In order to avoid confusion, you should avoid giving properties and local variables the same name. See "Managing parameter/property name conflicts," earlier in the chapter, for related details.

Nesting Functions in Methods

ActionScript supports *nested functions*, which means that functions can be declared within methods or even within other functions. The following code creates a method, *Box.getArea( )*, that contains a nested function, *multiply( )*. Inside *getArea( )*, the nested function can be invoked as usual. However, like a local variable, a nested function is accessible only to its parent function (the function in which it is declared). Code outside the parent function cannot execute the nested function:

```
class Box {
  private var width:Number;
  private var height:Number;

  public function getArea ():Number {
    return multiply(width, height);

    // Here's the nested function definition.
    // Only the getArea() method can invoke it. Other methods cannot.
    function multiply (a:Number, b:Number):Number {
      return a * b;
    }
  }
}
```

Nested functions are used commonly when assigning callback functions to *setInterval( )* or to objects that support event handler properties, such as *MovieClip*, *Sound*, and *XML* (callback functions are merely functions triggered when a particular event has occurred). For example, the following code shows a simple *TimeTracer* class with a *startTimeDisplay( )* method. The *startTimeDisplay( )* method uses *setInterval( )* to call a nested function, *displayTime( )*, once per second (every 1000 milliseconds). The *displayTime( )* function displays the current time in the Output panel:

```
class TimeTracer {
  public function startTimeDisplay ():Void {
    setInterval(displayTime, 1000);

    // Declare displayTime() as a nested function
    function displayTime ():Void {
      trace(new Date().toString());
    }
  }
}

// Usage:
var tt:TimeTracer = new TimeTracer();
tt.startTimeDisplay();
```

All local variables and parameters defined in a method are available to nested functions, *even after the method finishes executing*! Methods can, hence, use local variables to store data that will be used later by a nested function. For example, to make *displayTime( )* report the time of its first execution, we can store that information in a local variable, begunAt. The *displayTime( )* function can safely access begunAt's value long after the *startTimeDisplay( )* method has completed:

```
class TimeTracer {
  public function startTimeDisplay ():Void {
    // Define the local variable, begunAt.
    var begunAt:String = new Date().toString();

    setInterval(displayTime, 1000);

    function displayTime ():Void {
      // Here, the nested function refers to the local variable begunAt,
      // which is defined in the enclosing method, startTimeDisplay().
      trace("Time now: " + new Date().toString() + ". "
            + "Timer started at: " + begunAt);
    }
  }
}
```

Note that the begunAt variable persists because it is defined in the method outside of *displayTime( )*. If begunAt were declared within *displayTime( )*, its value would be reset each time *displayTime( )* is invoked.

Now let's add a means of stopping the time display. To do so, we must:

1. Store the interval ID returned by *setInterval( )* in a property, timerInterval

2. Add a *stopTimeDisplay( )* method that uses *clearInterval( )* to cancel the periodic calls to *displayTime( )*

3. Invoke *stopTimeDisplay( )* each time *startTimeDisplay( )* is called (thus preventing multiple intervals from running at the same time)

Here's the code:

```
class TimeTracer {
  private var timerInterval:Number;

  public function startTimeDisplay ():Void {
    stopTimeDisplay();

    var begunAt:String = new Date().toString();

    timerInterval = setInterval(displayTime, 1000);

    function displayTime ():Void {
      trace("Time now: " + new Date().toString() + ". "
            + "Timer started at: " + begunAt);
    }
  }
```

```
    public function stopTimeDisplay ():Void {
      clearInterval(timerInterval);
    }
  }
```

When *stopTimeDisplay( )* is called, the interval is halted, and the nested *displayTime( )* function is automatically deleted. Moreover, the local variable begunAt, which was preserved for use by *displayTime( )*, is no longer needed and is therefore also automatically garbage-collected (i.e., deleted).

Accessing the current object from a function nested in a method

A function nested in a method does not have direct access to the current object (the object on which the method was called). However, we can handcraft a hook back to the current object by storing a reference to it in a local variable.

Let's return to our *Box* class to show how a function nested in a method can access the current object via a local variable. We'll give the *Box* class a *debugDimensions( )* method that periodically displays the dimensions of a *Box* instance in the Output panel. The code is similar to *TimeTracer.startTimeDisplay( )*, but this time the nested function, *displayDimensions( )*, needs to display the current *Box* object's width and height. In order to give the *displayDimensions( )* function access to the *Box* object, we store a reference to this in a local variable, boxObj. That variable is accessible every time *displayDimensions( )* runs:

```
    public function debugDimensions ():Void {
      var boxObj:Box = this;

      setInterval(displayDimensions, 1000);

      function displayDimensions ():Void {
        // Access the current object through the local variable boxObj.
        trace("Width: " + boxObj.width + ", Height: " + boxObj.height);
      }
    }
```

Note that if we were feeling tricky, we could bypass the local variable approach altogether and simply pass the current *Box* object (this) to the *displayDimensions( )* function, as shown next. The effect is the same, though the code is perhaps harder to read for less experienced ActionScript programmers. It relies on the fact that *setInterval( )* passes the third argument (and subsequent arguments) to the function specified in the first argument. In this case, this, which contains a reference to the current *Box* object, is passed as the first parameter to *displayDimensions( )*:

```
    public function debugDimensions ():Void {
      // The third argument is passed onto displayDimensions( )
      setInterval(displayDimensions, 1000, this);
      // This function receives the current object (this) as its first argument
      function displayDimensions (boxObj):Void {
        trace("Width: " + boxObj.width + ", Height: " + boxObj.height);
      }
    }
```

The concept of storing the current object in a local variable for use by nested functions is pretty darn important—it enables two-way communication between a method and a callback function defined within that method. Let's look at one more example. This time, we'll create a new *Box* method, *loadDimensions( )*, that loads the dimensions for a *Box* instance from an external XML file. Inside *loadDimensions( )* we create an *XML* object, dimensions_xml. We assign dimensions_xml an *XML. onLoad( )* event handler using a nested function. Then, when the XML data loads, *dimensions_xml.onLoad( )* automatically executes, and we use the loaded XML data to set the current *Box* object's height and width properties. We access the current *Box* object using the local variable boxObj:

```
public function loadDimensions (URL:String):Void {
  // Store a reference to the current box object in boxObj.
  var boxObj:Box = this;

  // Create and prepare the XML object.
  var dimensions_xml:XML = new XML();
  dimensions_xml.ignoreWhite = true;

  // Assign a nested function as the XML object's onLoad() handler.
  // It will be called automatically when the XML file loads.
  dimensions_xml.onLoad = function (success:Boolean):Void {
    if (success) {
      // Assign the newly loaded dimensions to the width and height
      // properties of the Box object that called loadDimensions().
      boxObj.width =
          parseInt(this.firstChild.firstChild.firstChild.nodeValue);
      boxObj.height =
          parseInt(this.firstChild.childNodes[1].firstChild.nodeValue);
    } else {
      // Handle a load error.
      trace("Could not load dimensions from file: " + URL);
    }
  }

  // Load the requested XML file.
  dimensions_xml.load(URL);
}

// Here's a sample XML file, showing the structure expected by loadDimensions().
  <?xml version="1.0"?>
  <DIMENSIONS>
    <WIDTH>8</WIDTH>
    <HEIGHT>9</HEIGHT>
  </DIMENSIONS>
```

The *onLoad( )* handler executes when the XML file is done loading—long after *loadDimensions( )* has finished its own execution. However, even though *loadDimensions( )* has finished executing, the local variable boxObj and even the method parameter URL (which is also a local variable) continue to be available to the nested *onLoad( )* function. If we hadn't stored the current object in a local variable, our callback function wouldn't have had access to the *Box* object, and the width and height properties could not have been set.

Note that the dimensions_xml object is kept alive until its *load( )* operation completes and *onLoad( )* fires. Once *onLoad( )* has executed, if no other references to the dimensions_xml object exists (as in the case is in our example), the interpreter automatically marks the object for deletion, preventing memory waste.

Getter and Setter Methods

Earlier we learned about accessor methods, which are public methods that assign and retrieve the value of a private property. Some developers consider accessor methods cumbersome. They argue that:

```
b.setHeight(4);
```

is more awkward than:

```
b.height = 4;
```

However, in our earlier study, we saw that direct property assignments such as b. height = 4 aren't ideal OOP practice and can lead to invalid property assignments. To bridge the gap between the convenience of property assignment and the safety of accessor methods, ActionScript 2.0 supports "getter" and "setter" methods. Getter and setter methods are accessor-like methods, defined within a class body, that are invoked automatically when a developer tries to get or set a property directly.

To define a getter method, we use the following general syntax:

```
function get propertyName ():returnType {
  statements
}
```

where the get keyword identifies the method as a getter method, *propertyName* is the name of a pseudo-property serviced by the getter method, *returnType* is the datatype returned by the method, and *statements* is zero or more statements executed when the method is invoked (one of which is expected to return the value associated with *propertyName*).

To define a setter method, we use the following general syntax:

```
function set propertyName (newValue:type):Void {
  statements
}
```

where the set keyword identifies the method as a setter method, *propertyName* is the name of a pseudo-property serviced by the setter method, *newValue* receives the value that the caller is requesting be assigned to the pseudo-property, and *statements* is zero or more statements executed when the method is invoked (*statements* is expected to determine and internally store the value associated with *propertyName*). As a developer, you can use the *return* statement alone in a setter method body, but you must not return any value. Setter methods have an automatic return value, discussed later.

Unlike other methods, getter and setter methods cannot be declared with the *private* attribute. An attempt to define a getter or setter as private yields the following error:

```
A member attribute was used incorrectly.
```

Getter and setter methods have a unique, property-access style of being invoked that does not require use of the function call operator, ( ).

 Getter and setter methods are invoked automatically when a programmer tries to access or set a property of the same name using the dot operator.

Therefore, a getter method, *x( )*, on an object, obj, is invoked as:

```
obj.x;
```

rather than:

```
obj.x( );
```

And a setter method, *y( )*, on an object, obj, is invoked as:

```
obj.y = value;
```

rather than:

```
obj.y(value);
```

where *value* is the first (and only) argument passed to *y*.

Getter and setter methods, hence, appear to magically translate property accesses into method calls. For example, if we add a getter method named *height( )* to our *Box* class, then all attempts to retrieve the value of the height property will actually invoke the getter method named *height( )*. The getter method's return value will appear as though it were the value of the height property.

```
// Invokes the getter height( ) and displays
// its return value in the Output panel.
trace(someBox.height);
```

Similarly, if we add a setter method named *height( )* to our *Box* class, attempts to assign the value of the height property invoke the setter method named *height( )*. The value used in the height assignment statement is passed to the setter method, which is expected to store it internally in a private property.

```
// Invokes the setter height( ), which should store 5 internally
someBox.height = 5;
```

With a getter and a setter method named *height( )* defined, the height property becomes an external façade only; it does not exist in the class but can be used as though it did. You can, therefore, think of properties that are backed by getter and setter methods (such as height) as *pseudo-properties*.

It is illegal to create an actual property with the same name as a getter or setter method. Attempts to do so result in the following compile-time error:

```
The same member name may not be repeated more than once.
```

Example 4-2 revises our earlier *Box* class, adding getter and setter methods for the width and height properties. Notice that the values of the width and height pseudo-properties are stored internally in real properties named width_internal and height_internal because we can't use properties named width and height any longer.

Example 4-2. A class with getter and setter methods

```
class Box {
  // Note that width and height are no longer declared as properties
  private var width_internal:Number;
  private var height_internal:Number;

  public function get width ():Number {
    return width_internal;
  }

  public function set width (w:Number):Void {
    width_internal = w;
  }

  public function get height ():Number {
    return height_internal;
  }

  public function set height (h:Number):Void {
    height_internal = h;
  }
}
```

With our getter and setter methods in place, we can now use the width and height pseudo-properties as follows:

```
var b:Box = new Box();
b.width  = 20;      // Calls the width setter.
trace(b.width);     // Calls the width getter. Displays: 20
b.height = 10;      // Calls the height setter.
trace(b.height);    // Calls the height getter. Displays: 10
```

In ActionScript 1.0, getter and setter methods can be created with *Object.addProperty( )*. In fact, ActionScript 2.0's support for getter and setter methods is effectively a wrapper around *Object.addProperty( )* with some minor optimizations.

Example 4-3 shows the equivalent ActionScript 1.0 code for Example 4-2.

Example 4-3. ActionScript 1.0 code to simulate ActionScript 2.0 getter and setter methods

```
_global.Box = function( ){};

_global.Box.prototype.__get__width = function( ) {
  return this.width_internal;
};
_global.Box.prototype.__set__width = function (w) {
  this.width_internal = w;
};

_global.Box.prototype.__get__height = function( ) {
  return this.height_internal;
};
_global.Box.prototype.__set__height = function (h) {
  this.height_internal = h;
};

_global.Box.prototype.addProperty("width",
  Box.prototype.__get__width,
  Box.prototype.__set__width);
_global.Box.prototype.addProperty("height",
  Box.prototype.__get__height,
  Box.prototype.__set__height);
```

When a setter method is called, it always invokes its corresponding getter and returns the getter's return value. This allows a program to use the new value immediately after setting it, perhaps in order to chain method calls. For example, the following code shows a fragment of a fictitious music player application. It uses a setter call to tell the music player which song to play first. It then immediately plays that song by calling *start( )* on the return value of the firstSong assignment.

```
(musicPlayer.firstSong = new Song("lovesong.mp3")).start( )
```

While convenient in some cases, the return-value feature of setters is a deviation from the ECMAScript 4 specification and is, therefore, considered a bug by Macromedia. This buggy behavior imposes limits on getters—specifically, getters should never perform tasks beyond those required to retrieve their internal property value. For example, a getter should not implement a global counter that tracks how many times a property has been accessed. The automatic invocation of the getter by the setter would tarnish the counter's record keeping.

Getter and setter methods can be used both inside and outside of the class block that defines them. For example, we could quite legitimately add the following *getArea( )* method definition to the *Box* class shown in Example 4-2; the direct references to the pseudo-properties width and height are legal and common practice.

```
public function getArea ( ):Number {
  return width * height;
}
```

In fact, getter and setter method usage can even be nested. For example, we could change the preceding *getArea( )* method definition into a getter method definition as follows:

```
public function get area ( ):Number {
  return width * height;
}
```

In that case, we could use pseudo-properties (width, height, and area) to assign a *Box* instance a height and width, and even to retrieve its area:

```
var b:Box = new Box( );
b.width  = 20;
b.height = 10;
trace(b.area);  // Displays: 200
```

Simulating read-only properties

A getter/setter pseudo-property can be made read-only by declaring a getter without declaring a setter.

For example, the area property that we just defined does not have a setter because its value depends on the values of other properties. It doesn't make sense for a user of the class to set the area directly, so we disable assignment by not defining a setter. However, to explain this limitation to users who attempt to set the area property, we could define a do-nothing setter that prints a debug message to the Output panel, as follows:

```
function set area ( ):Void {
  trace("Warning: The area property cannot be set directly.");
}
```

Don't confuse read-only pseudo-properties with private properties (or, for that matter, public properties). A read-only pseudo-property can be read from outside the class but cannot be set. A private property cannot be read or set from outside the class, but a public property can be both read and set from anywhere.

Extra or Missing Arguments

In ActionScript 2.0 (and 1.0), a method can be invoked with more or fewer arguments than its signature specifies. The compiler doesn't complain if you pass the wrong number of arguments. It checks only whether the arguments provided match the specified types. If you pass more arguments than specified, the compiler type checks only as many arguments as are in the method signature. Extra arguments are not (indeed cannot be) type checked automatically by the compiler. Although there is no way to have the compiler warn you if the wrong number of arguments are passed, you can write custom code to do so. For example, the following method, *setCubeDimensions( )*, aborts when passed anything other than three arguments (note the use of the arguments object, which we'll discuss shortly):

```
public function setCubeDimensions (x:Number, y:Number, z:Number):Void {
  // Wrong number of arguments passed, so abort
  if arguments.length != 3 {
    trace ("This function requires exactly 3 arguments.");
    return;
  }
  // Remainder of method not shown...
}
```

When a method is invoked with fewer arguments than it expects, the missing arguments are automatically set to undefined. For example, recall our basic method definition for *Box.setWidth( )*, which specifies one parameter, w:

```
public function setWidth (w:Number):Void {
  width = w;
}
```

The *setWidth( )* method can legally be invoked without arguments as follows:

```
someBox.setWidth( );
```

In this case, someBox.width is set to undefined by the *setWidth( )* method. Methods
should handle the possibility that they may be invoked with fewer arguments than
expected. For example, if we wanted to prevent our *setWidth( )* method from setting
the width property when invoked with no arguments, we could adjust it as follows
(additions shown in bold):

```
public function setWidth (w:Number):Void {
  // If w is undefined, then quit
  if (w == undefined) {
    return;
  }

  // If we got this far, w has a usable value, so proceed normally
  width = w;
}
```

However, we needn't always abort a method simply because arguments are missing.
By anticipating missing arguments, we can effectively provide two flavors of the same
method: one that uses developer-supplied arguments and one that automatically fills
in default values for missing arguments. For example, we could adjust *setWidth( )* as
follows:

```
public function setWidth (w:Number):Void {
  // If w is undefined...
  if (w == undefined) {
    // ...default to 1.
    width = 1;
  } else {
    // ...otherwise, use the supplied value of w.
    width = w;
  }
}
```

We can then invoke *setWidth( )* as either `setWidth( )` or `setWidth(5)`. Java developers will recognize this as ActionScript's (partial) answer to method overloading.

Note that the equality operator (`==`) considers `null` equal to `undefined`. Hence, the invocations, `setWidth( )` and `setWidth(null)` are equivalent. In the former, the developer merely implies that he wishes to omit the value of `w`; in the latter, the developer explicitly specifies that he's not providing a value for `w`. Either way, our redesigned *setWidth( )* method has the same result.

When a method accepts multiple parameters, `null` can be used as a placeholder for missing arguments that precede other arguments. Here, we call a method that expects three arguments (method definition not shown) but we pass the empty placeholder `null` as the first argument:

```
methodThatExpectsThreeArguments (null, 4, 5);
```

Whenever a method is invoked, all the arguments passed in the invocation are available via the `arguments` object. The `arguments` object stores all arguments passed to the method, even when passed more arguments than it expects (i.e., beyond those declared in the method definition). To access any argument, we examine the elements of the `arguments` array, as follows:

```
arguments[n]
```

where *n* is the index of the argument we're accessing. The first argument (the leftmost argument in the method invocation) is stored at index 0 and is referred to as `arguments[0]`. Subsequent arguments are stored in order, proceeding to the right—so, the second argument is `arguments[1]`, the third is `arguments[2]`, and so on. Here's another rewrite of our *setWidth( )* method; it displays the first and second arguments passed to the method:

```
public function setWidth (w:Number):Void {
  trace("Argument 1 is: " + arguments[0]);
  trace("Argument 2 is: " + arguments[1]);
}

// Usage:
someBox.setWidth(15, 25);  // Displays:
                           // Argument 1 is: 15
                           // Argument 2 is: 25
```

From within a method, we can tell how many arguments were passed to the currently executing function by checking the number of elements in `arguments`, as follows:

```
var numArgs:Number = arguments.length;
```

We can easily cycle through all the arguments passed to a method using a *for* loop. Example 4-4 shows a method, *sendMessage( )*, that sends an XML message to a chat server, in the following format:

```
<MESSAGE>
  <ARG>value 1</ARG>
```

```
    <ARG>value 2</ARG>
    ...
    <ARG>value n</ARG>
  </MESSAGE>
```

The *sendMessage( )* method defines no parameters. Instead, it retrieves all its argument values via the arguments object. Any number of arguments can be passed to *sendMessage( )*; each one becomes the content of an <ARG> tag in the XML message sent.

Example 4-4. A method that accepts an unknown number of arguments

```
public function sendMessage ( ):Void {
  // Build the message to send
  var message:String = "<MESSAGE>";

  for (var i:Number = 0; i < arguments.length; i++) {
    message += "<ARG>" + arguments[i] + "</ARG>";
  }

  message += "</MESSAGE>";

  // Display what we're sending in the Output panel
  trace("message sent: \n" + message);

  // Send the message to the server
  socket.send(message);
}
```

As a point of interest, the arguments object also stores:

- A reference to the method currently executing (arguments.callee)
- A reference to the method that called the method currently executing, if any (arguments.caller)

Note that arguments.callee is not the same as this. The latter refers to the object on which the method is invoked, whereas the former is a reference to the current method itself.

For details, see *ActionScript for Flash MX: The Definitive Guide* (O'Reilly).

Constructor Functions (Take 2)

We've done pretty well with our example *Box* class. We've given it methods to invoke and properties to examine and change. Now it's time to return to our *Box* constructor function, which we introduced much earlier in this chapter under "Constructor Functions (Take 1)."

Suppose we want to make every *Box* instance we create start out with a width and height of 1. We need something that can set each new *Box* instance's width and height properties during the instance-creation process. That "something" is our constructor function.

A constructor function is the metaphoric womb of a class; it isn't responsible for creating new instances, but it can be used to initialize each new instance. When we create a new instance of a class using the *new* operator, the class's constructor function runs. Within the constructor function, we can customize the newly created instance by setting its properties or invoking its methods. The instance can then be delivered to the world tailored to the situation at hand—perhaps with width and height properties set to 1 (and big, cute, green eyes).

To define a constructor function, we use the *function* statement within a class body, exactly as we'd define a method. However, a constructor function definition must also observe these rules:

- The constructor function's name must match its class's name exactly (case sensitivity matters).

- The constructor function's definition must not specify a return type (not even *Void*).

- The constructor function must not return a value (the *return* statement is allowed for the sake of exiting the function, provided that no return value is specified).

- The constructor function's definition must not include the *static* attribute, but it can be *public* or *private*.

Here's another look at the *Box* class constructor that we created earlier. Once again, lines 2 and 3 are the (empty) function—the constructor function's body and the rest of the class are omitted from this example:

```
class Box {
  public function Box () {
  }
}
```

 Remember that a constructor's function declaration must not define a return datatype, and the constructor function itself must not return a value. In particular, the constructor function does not return the new instance being created. Creating and returning the new instance is handled automatically by ActionScript as part of the new ClassName( ) operation. Use the constructor function only for initializing property values or performing other instance initialization.

In ActionScript 2.0, a constructor function's sole purpose is to initialize instances. Constructor functions are not mandatory (as they were in ActionScript 1.0). However, because most classes initialize their instances, most classes include a constructor function. As noted earlier, when a class does not define a constructor function explicitly, ActionScript automatically provides a default constructor that takes no parameters and performs no initialization on new instances of the class. Despite this convenience, as a best practice, always include a constructor, even if it is just an empty one. The empty constructor serves as a formal indication that the class design does not require a constructor and should be accompanied by a comment to that effect. For example:

```
class Box {
  // Empty constructor. This class does not require initialization.
  public function Box () {
  }
}
```

 In ActionScript 1.0, a constructor function and a class definition were one in the same. There was no formal *class* statement—classes were created simply by defining a constructor function, as in:

```
// In ActionScript 1.0, this function both
// defines the Box class and serves as
// its constructor function.
function Box (w, h) {
  this.width = w;
  this.height = h;
}
```

Notice that the constructor function can be declared *public* or *private*, just like a normal method. The vast majority of constructor functions are public, but there are specific class designs that require a private constructor (for one example, see Chapter 17). Classes with private constructor functions cannot be instantiated directly. For example, if we supply a private constructor for our *Box* class:

```
class Box {
  private function Box () {
  }
}
```

and then we try to create a *Box* instance:

```
var b:Box = new Box();
```

the compiler generates the following error:

```
The member is private and cannot be accessed.
```

In order to allow instances to be created, a class with a private constructor must provide a class method that creates and returns instances. For example:

```
class Box {
  // Private constructor
  private function Box () {
  }

  // Class method that returns new instances
  public static function getBox ():Box {
    return new Box();
  }
}

// Usage:
var b:Box = Box.getBox();
```

If a class with a private constructor does not provide a public class method that calls the private constructor internally, you cannot instantiate objects of the class. You might use a private constructor in the following situations:

- To create a rough equivalent of a Java-style abstract class (i.e., a class that cannot be instantiated, but must be extended to be used, as discussed in Chapter 8)
- To place limits on when and how a class's instances are created (for example, to prevent a program from creating more than one object from a single class)

While constructors can be declared as *public* or *private*, they cannot be declared *static*. If you specify the *static* attribute in a constructor function definition, the compiler generates the following error:

```
The only attributes allowed for constructor functions are public and private.
```

 Always be sure that the capitalization of a constructor function's name matches its class name exactly. If you change a class's name from *Somename* to *SomeName* but forget to update the constructor function's name to *SomeName( )*, ActionScript will no longer consider the constructor function a constructor, and none of your initialization code will run when instances are created with the *new* operator.

Luckily, the ActionScript compiler warns you as follows when the capitalization of your constructor's name does not match its class name:

```
The member function '[FunctionName]' has a different case from the name of
the class being defined, '[ClassName]', and will not be treated as the class
constructor at runtime.
```

Let's flesh out our basic *Box* constructor so that it assigns 1 to the width and height properties of every new *Box* instance created, as described in the earlier scenario. For clarity, we'll also show the width and height property definitions. By convention (but not by necessity), constructor functions are placed after property definitions but before method definitions. Note also that the constructor declaration does not include a return datatype, as they are prohibited for constructors:

```
class Box {
  private var width:Number;
  private var height:Number;

  public function Box () {
    // Initialize width and height
    width  = 1;
    height = 1;
  }

  // Method definitions typically follow here...
}
```

Now every time we create a new *Box* instance, its width and height are initialized to 1 (otherwise, they'd default to undefined). That's pretty handy, but is also inflexible.

To allow the width and height properties to be customized for each *Box* instance, we add parameters to our constructor function definition:

```
public function Box (w:Number, h:Number) {
  // Initialize width and height, using the
  // values passed to the parameters w and h.
  width  = w;
  height = h;
}
```

A constructor function's parameter values are passed to it via the *new* operator at object-creation time, as follows:

```
new SomeClass(value1, value2,...valuen);
```

where *SomeClass* is the name of the class being instantiated and *value1*, *value2*, ... *valuen* are the values passed to the constructor function. For example, to create a new *Box* instance with an initial width of 2 and height of 3, we'd use:

```
new Box(2, 3);
```

Supplying parameter values to a constructor function is the ActionScript equivalent of genetically predetermining that your baby should be a girl, weigh 7 pounds, and have brown hair.

Constructor functions normally use parameter values to set property values, but parameters can also more generally govern what should happen when an instance is created. For example, the constructor function for a *Chat* class might include a parameter, doConnect, that indicates whether the *Chat* instance should automatically connect to the chat server upon creation:

```
class Chat {
  public function Chat (server:String, port:Number, doConnect:Boolean) {
    if (doConnect) {
      connect(server, port);
    }
  }
}
```

Simulating Multiple Constructor Functions

Unlike Java, ActionScript does not support multiple constructor functions for a single class (referred to as *overloaded constructors* in Java). In Java, a class can initialize an instance differently depending on the number and type of arguments used with the *new* operator. In ActionScript, similar functionality must be implemented manually. Example 4-5, based on our *Box* class, shows one possible way to simulate multiple constructor functions in ActionScript. Flash itself uses an analogous technique to allow *Date* instances to be created from a specific year, month, and day or from a count of milliseconds that have elapsed since January 1, 1970.

In Example 4-5, the *Box* constructor delegates its work to three pseudo-constructor methods, named *boxNoArgs( )*, *boxString( )*, and *boxNumberNumber( )*. Each pseudo-constructor's name indicates the number and datatype of the parameters it accepts (e.g., *boxNumberNumber( )* defines two arguments of type *Number*). Note that in this specific example the pseudo-constructors do not define datatypes for their arguments; this anomaly is discussed in the inline code comments.

If some of the code in Example 4-5 is new to you, look for cross-references to related topics in the code comments.

Example 4-5. Simulating overloaded constructors

```
class Box {
  public var width:Number;
  public var height:Number;

  /**
   * Box constructor. Delegates initialization
   * to boxNoArgs( ), boxString( ), or boxNumberNumber( ).
   */
  public function Box (a1:Object, a2:Object) {
    // As we learned earlier, the arguments object stores the
    // argument values passed to this function.
    // If the constructor was invoked with no arguments, call boxNoArgs( ).
    // If the constructor was invoked with one string argument,
    // call boxString( ). If the constructor was invoked with
    // two numeric arguments, call boxNumberNumber( ).
    if (arguments.length == 0) {
      boxNoArgs( );
    } else if (typeof a1 == "string") {
      // In the following line of code, we'd normally have to cast a1 to the
      // type required by the boxString( ) method's first parameter (in
      // this case, String). However, the ActionScript 2.0 cast operator
      // does not work with the String and Number datatypes, so,
      // unfortunately, we must leave the parameters for boxString( ) and
      // boxNumberNumber( ) untyped. For details on this casting problem,
      // see Chapter 3.
      boxString(a1);
    } else if (typeof a1 == "number" && typeof a2 == "number") {
      // No cast to Number here either; see previous comment.
      boxNumberNumber(a1, a2);
    } else {
      // Display a warning that the method was used improperly.
      trace("Unexpected number of arguments passed to Box constructor.");
    }
  }

  /**
   * No-argument constructor.
   */
  private function boxNoArgs ( ):Void {
    // arguments.caller is a reference to the function that called
    // this function.
```

Example 4-5. Simulating overloaded constructors (continued)

```
    // If this method was not called by the Box constructor, then exit.
    if (arguments.caller != Box) {
      return;
    }
    // Supply a default width and height.
    width  = 1;
    height = 1;
  }

  /**
   * String constructor.
   */
  private function boxString (size):Void {
    // If this method was not called by the Box constructor, then exit.
    if (arguments.caller != Box) {
      return;
    }
    // Set width and height based on a descriptive string.
    if (size == "large") {
      width  = 100;
      height = 100;
    } else if (size == "small") {
      width  = 10;
      height = 10;
    } else {
      trace("Invalid box size specified");
    }
  }

  /**
   * Numeric constructor.
   */
  private function boxNumberNumber (w, h):Void {
    // If this method was not called by the Box constructor, then exit.
    if (arguments.caller != Box) {
      return;
    }
    // Set numeric width and height.
    width  = w;
    height = h;
  }
}

// Usage:
var b1:Box = new Box( );
trace(b1.width);  // Displays: 1

var b2:Box = new Box("large");
trace(b2.width);  // Displays: 100

var b3:Box = new Box(25, 35);
trace(b3.width);  // Displays: 25
```

Using this in Constructor Functions

Within the body of a constructor function, the this keyword refers to the newly created instance. We use this in a constructor function exactly as we use it from within instance methods. For example, the following code uses this to resolve a parameter/property name conflict:

```
public function Box (width:Number, height:Number) {
  // Sets width property (this.width) to value of width parameter (width).
  this.width = width;
  // Sets height property (this.height) to value
  // of height parameter (height).
  this.height = height;
}
```

For details on using this, see the earlier discussion under "Referring to the Current Object with the Keyword this."

Constructor Functions Versus Default Property Values

Earlier in this chapter we learned that an instance property can be assigned a default value provided the value is a compile-time constant expression, such as 10 or "hello world". For example:

```
private var x:Number = 10;
private var msg:String = "hello world";
```

While it's legal to initialize an instance property by assigning it a default value, it's a best practice to perform all instance property initialization in a constructor function. Constructor functions are not limited by the compile-time constant rule, so they can safely calculate property values with arbitrary code such as method calls, conditionals, and loops. Furthermore, by keeping property initialization in constructors, we make our class's initialization code easy to find and maintain.

Completing the Box Class

Throughout this chapter we've studied an example *Box* class. In the real world, our *Box* class might be purely conceptual (i.e., never displayed on screen) or it might have a visual representation. Because most Flash applications are visual, we'll conclude this chapter with a look at how to display *Box* instances on screen.

Not all Flash applications display content on screen in the same way. Each application must decide how the screen is drawn, when it is drawn, and which class or classes contain the drawing code. Here are the major issues to consider when designing an application's display system:

* First decide whether the display elements will render themselves or be rendered by a central class. For example, will the *Box* class provide its own *drawBox( )* method, or will there be a *drawBoxes( )* or *drawScreen( )* method on some other class?

- Decide how often the displayed elements should be updated—either when some event occurs (such as a mouseclick) or repeatedly (as fast as frames are displayed in the Flash Player).

- Decide on the rendering technique. Each visual element in a Flash movie must be displayed in a movie clip. However, movie clips can be placed manually at authoring time or attached with ActionScript at runtime. The content of a movie clip can also be created from scratch using the *MovieClip* Drawing API.

- Decide on a screen refresh strategy. Will each visual element be maintained as a single persistent movie clip that is updated regularly, or will the entire contents of the Stage be cleared and re-created each time the display is updated?

In our example, the *Box* class is responsible for its own screen display. When a box is created, we'll attach an empty movie clip (named `container_mc`) into which we'll draw the box. If the box is resized, we'll redraw the contents of the container clip. To move the box, we'll move its container clip rather than move the box within the clip. This saves us from having to redraw the clip's contents.

Our box display strategy is a runtime-only strategy. Each *Box* instance appears in the Flash Player but can't be placed on the Stage while editing a *.fla* file in the Flash authoring tool. In Chapter 13, we'll see how to create a visual class that can place instances on stage both at runtime and in the Flash authoring tool.

Example 4-6 gives you a final look at the *Box* class in its entirety, complete with screen display code. You should recognize the following items from earlier *Box* class samples:

- The `width` and `height` properties (not pseudo-properties)
- The accessor methods *getWidth( )* and *getHeight( )* (not getter and setter methods)

The following items are completely new to this version of the *Box* class:

- The `container_mc` property, which stores a reference to the movie clip in which we'll draw the box graphic
- The accessor methods *getX( )*, *setX( )*, *getY( )*, and *setY( )*, which retrieve and assign the position of the `container_mc` movie clip
- The *draw( )* method, which draws the box in the `container_mc` movie clip

Finally, the following items have changed in this version of the *Box* class:

- The constructor function takes additional parameters, as follows: x and y specify `container_mc`'s initial horizontal and vertical position, target specifies the movie clip to which `container_mc` will be attached, and depth specifies the depth on which `container_mc` will be attached.
- The *setHeight( )* and *setWidth( )* methods now call *draw( )* after setting the height and width of the box. (Note the flexibility that our accessor methods afford us: we've changed how our class works without changing how it's used.)

The detailed comments will help as you study the code.

Example 4-6. A Box class complete with drawing routines

```
class Box {
  // Box dimensions. Nothing new here.
  private var width:Number;
  private var height:Number;

  // Movie clip to contain visual representation of the box.
  private var container_mc:MovieClip;

  /**
   * Constructor.
   */
  public function Box (w:Number, h:Number,
                       x:Number, y:Number,
                       target:MovieClip, depth:Number) {
    // Create the container clip that will hold Box visuals.
    container_mc = target.createEmptyMovieClip("boxcontainer" + depth,
                                               depth);

    // Initialize size.
    setWidth(w);
    setHeight(h);

    // Initialize position.
    setX(x);
    setY(y);
  }

  /**
   * Accessor to retrieve width. Nothing new here.
   */
  public function getWidth ():Number {
    return width;
  }

  /**
   * Accessor to assign width. This version both assigns the new width
   * property value and redraws the box based on the new width.
   */
  public function setWidth (w:Number):Void {
    width = w;
    draw();
  }

  /**
   * Accessor to retrieve height. Nothing new here.
   */
  public function getHeight ():Number {
    return height;
  }
```

Example 4-6. A Box class complete with drawing routines (continued)

```
/**
 * Accessor to assign height. This version both assigns the new height
 * property value and redraws the box based on the new height.
 */
public function setHeight (h:Number):Void {
  height = h;
  draw( );
}

/**
 * Accessor to retrieve x. For convenience, the x and y coordinates
 * are stored directly on the container movie clip. If numeric accuracy
 * were a concern, we'd store x as a separate Box property so
 * that it wouldn't be rounded by the MovieClip class.
 */
public function getX ():Number {
  return container_mc._x;
}

/**
 * Accessor to assign x.
 */
public function setX (x:Number):Void {
  container_mc._x = x;
}

/**
 * Accessor to retrieve y.
 */
public function getY ():Number {
  return container_mc._y;
}

/**
 * Accessor to assign y.
 */
public function setY (y:Number):Void {
  container_mc._y = y;
}

/**
 * Displays the Box instance on screen. Uses the MovieClip drawing methods
 * to draw lines in container_mc. For more information on the Drawing API,
 * see ActionScript for Flash MX: The Definitive Guide.
 */
public function draw ():Void {
  // Clear the previous box rendering.
  container_mc.clear( );
  // Use a 1-point black line.
  container_mc.lineStyle(1, 0x000000);
  // Position the drawing pen.
  container_mc.moveTo(0, 0);
```

Example 4-6. A Box class complete with drawing routines (continued)

```
        // Start a white fill.
        container_mc.beginFill(0xFFFFFF, 100);
        // Draw the border of the box.
        container_mc.lineTo(width, 0);
        container_mc.lineTo(width, height);
        container_mc.lineTo(0, height);
        container_mc.lineTo(0, 0);
        // Formally stop filling the shape.
        container_mc.endFill( );
    }
}
```

The following code shows how the *Box* class from Example 4-6 could be used on a frame in a Flash document (*.fla*) timeline:

```
    // Create a box 250 x 260 pixels, placed at coordinates
    // (100, 110) in the current movie clip, on depth 1.
    var b:Box = new Box(250, 260, 100, 110, this, 1);
```

After the *Box* instance is created, we can adjust its position and size as follows:

```
    b.setX(400);
    b.setY(400);
    b.setWidth(10);
    b.setHeight(20);

    trace(b.getX( ));       // Displays: 400
    trace(b.getY( ));       // Displays: 400
    trace(b.getWidth( ));   // Displays: 10
    trace(b.getHeight( ));  // Displays: 20
```

Putting Theory into Practice

Code, like art, is never really finished. You should explore your own ideas, even with the simple *Box* class discussed in this chapter. Can you add code that randomly places each *Box* instance on the Stage? Or changes the color of a *Box* instance? What about code that rotates a *Box* instance or animates it along a straight line? Try adding text fields on each box that display its width, height, and area. You could even make the text fields accept user input that can change the size of the *Box*.

You'll gain insight into how to add these kinds of features in the next chapter, which studies an *ImageViewer* class. This chapter covered a tremendous amount of technical ground in a largely theoretical way, so if you are a bit overwhelmed, don't worry. The next chapter covers a concrete implementation to help you apply what you've learned. See you there!

CHAPTER 5

Authoring an ActionScript 2.0 Class

In Chapter 4 we studied the general anatomy of ActionScript 2.0 classes. In this chapter we'll put that theory into practice by authoring a real-world ActionScript 2.0 class named *ImageViewer*. The *ImageViewer* class creates an on-screen rectangular region for displaying a loaded JPEG image. We'll cover designing and coding the class itself, as well as using it in a Flash document.

The *ImageViewer* source files discussed in this chapter are available for download at *http://moock.org/eas2/examples*.

Class Authoring Quick Start

Before we jump into designing the *ImageViewer* class, let's take a brief, high-level look at the minimal steps required to author and use an ActionScript 2.0 class in Flash. Don't worry if some of the concepts in this overview are foreign to you—we'll cover each of them in detail throughout the remainder of this chapter.

To create an ActionScript 2.0 class, follow these general steps:

1. Create a new text file with the *.as* extension using any plain text editor or Flash MX Professional 2004's built-in editor. The *.as* file's name must match the class name exactly (case sensitivity matters).

2. Add the class definition to the *.as* file. For example:

```
class NameOfClass {
  // Class body goes here
}
```

To use an ActionScript 2.0 class in a Flash movie, follow these general steps:

1. Create a *.fla* file with any name, and place it in the same folder as the *.as* file from Step 1 in the preceding procedure.

2. Optionally specify the class's export frame for the *.fla* file via File → Publish Settings → Flash → ActionScript Version → Settings → Export Frame for Classes. This determines when the class loads and when it becomes available in the movie. The export frame is usually set to some frame after your movie's preloader.

3. Use the class as desired throughout the *.fla* file, but after the export frame specified in Step 2 (if any).

4. Export a *.swf* file using one of the following: File → Publish, Control → Test Movie, or File → Export → Export Movie.

The preceding steps apply nicely to small projects in which code reuse and distribution are not factors. For information on managing a group of classes across many applications, see Chapters 9 and 14.

Now let's get started building the *ImageViewer* class.

Designing the ImageViewer Class

Once you get comfortable with the syntax of your first object-oriented language, you'll inevitably realize that the challenge of OOP isn't mastering the syntax, it's designing each application's architecture. As an OOP programmer, you'll face design decisions daily: which classes will make up the application? How will those classes interrelate? What public methods and properties will they expose? What methods and properties must be kept internal? What will all these classes, methods, and properties be named?

Luckily, you won't have to face these questions alone. For years, the OOP community has been cataloging so-called *design patterns*, which describe common solutions to generalized, recurring design problems. We'll see how to apply design patterns to Flash in Part III of this book. Design patterns focus mainly on the interactions among multiple classes. For now, we face a simpler problem: how to design a single, standalone class.

We've already given our *ImageViewer* class a name and a general purpose. Believe it or not, that means a good deal of the design work has already been done. By giving the class a general purpose, we've already determined its responsibilities: loading and displaying an image. Likewise, from the inverse perspective, we've decided that those responsibilities don't belong in other classes. That is, in an application that uses the *ImageViewer* class, other classes won't attempt to load images on their own; instead, they'll instantiate *ImageViewer* instances and use those instances to load images. Thus, just by formulating the *ImageViewer* class's responsibilities, we've shaped how it interacts with other classes, which is an important aspect of any OOP application design. Determining a class's responsibilities necessarily determines, in part, how it fits into a larger structure.

With our *ImageViewer* class's name and purpose settled, we can now establish its detailed functional requirements. Here's a list of functionality that could be required of the *ImageViewer* class:

- Load an image
- Display an image

- Crop an image to a particular rectangular "view region"
- Display a border around the image
- Display image load progress
- Reposition the view region
- Resize the view region
- Pan (reposition) the image within the view region
- Zoom (resize) the image within the view region

From that list, we'll select only what's absolutely required by the current situation, leaving everything else for later. Our approach follows the Extreme Programming rule that you should "never add functionality early" (see *http://www. extremeprogramming.org/rules.html*).

The minimum functionality required to simply get the *ImageViewer* class up and running is:

- Load an image
- Display an image

Let's start with that short list.

From Functional Requirements to Code

Our first step in moving from functional requirements to a completed class is to determine how the *ImageViewer* class will be used by other programmers. For example, what method would a programmer invoke to make an image appear on screen? How about loading an image? Are those two operations implemented as separate methods or as one method? After we've determined how the class should be used by other classes (whether by ourselves or another developer), we can then turn our attention to how it should work (i.e., we can implement the proposed methods). Of course, during implementation we're bound to encounter issues that affect the way the class is used and thus we'll modify our original design.

 The set of public methods and properties exposed by a class is sometimes referred to as the class's *API* (application programming interface). Revision is a natural part of the development cycle, but ideally, the public API doesn't change even when the internal code is revised. The term *refactoring* means to modify the internal code of a program without modifying its external (apparent) behavior. For example, you might refactor a class to make its operation more efficient or to improve upon poor coding practices.

In our example, we're trying to fashion the *ImageViewer* class's API. Traditionally, the term "API" refers to the services provided by an entire library of classes, such as the Java API or the Windows API. However, in current common discussion, the term

"API" is often used to describe functionality made publicly available by anything from a single class to a whole group of classes. A class's API is sometimes also referred to as its *public interface,* not to be confused with the graphical user interface (GUI), nor the interfaces we'll study in Chapter 8.

Recall that our *ImageViewer* class's first functional requirement is to load an image. That operation should be publicly accessible, meaning that code in any class should be able to tell an *ImageViewer* instance to load an image, perhaps multiple times in succession. The network location (URL) of the image to load must be supplied externally. In short, a programmer using an *ImageViewer* instance needs a "load" command, and the *ImageViewer* instance needs a URL from the programmer in order to carry out that command. Sounds like a good candidate for a method! We'll call the "load" command *loadImage( ).* Here's the *loadImage( )* method's basic signature:

```
ImageViewer.loadImage(URL)
```

The method name, *loadImage,* acts as the "verb" to describe the action performed. A method name should be highly comprehensible. Someone reading it in a program's source code should be able to deduce the purpose of the method call without reading copious comments. Well-named methods are effectively self-commenting.

 If you're having trouble naming a method, the real cause may be that your method is trying to do too much. Try splitting the method into multiple methods or restructuring your class, particularly if your method name has the word "and" in it.

The *loadImage( )* method takes one parameter, URL, which specifies the network location of the image to load. The URL parameter must be a string, and the method doesn't return any value. So the complete signature and return type for the method is:

```
ImageViewer.loadImage(URL:String):Void
```

But perhaps we've jumped ahead too quickly. Is a separate *loadImage( )* method required at all? Maybe the URL of the image to load should simply be passed to the *ImageViewer* constructor, as in:

```
var viewer:ImageViewer = new ImageViewer("someImage.jpg");
```

That's more concise than creating an *ImageViewer* instance first and then calling *loadImage( )* on it. But without a *loadImage( )* method, each *ImageViewer* instance can load only one image. If we want *ImageViewer* instances to load multiple images in succession, we need a *loadImage( )* method. Maybe we should implement both the *loadImage( )* method and a constructor parameter URL but make the constructor URL optional. That's an interesting possibility, but it's not strictly required by our current situation. Given that we can easily add the constructor parameter later without affecting our design, we can safely defer the parameter for now. We should record these decisions as part of our class design rationale, either in a formal specification document or simply with comments in the class source code. As you design and implement your classes, be sure to document potential future features under consideration. You should also document features that you've rejected, rather than merely deferred, due to some design limitation. This is particularly true of potential features that have nonobvious drawbacks or limitations. This will help you remember your exact reasons for rejecting the design decision the next time you or someone else revises the code.

Now let's move on to our second functional requirement—to display an image. Displaying an image on screen in the Flash Player necessarily involves at least one movie clip (the one into which the image is loaded). But which movie clip? Should we provide a way to specify an existing clip as the image-holding clip? We could write a *setImageClip( )* method to be invoked before *loadImage( )*, as follows:

```
var viewer:ImageViewer = new ImageViewer();
viewer.setImageClip(someClip_mc);
viewer.loadImage("someImage.jpg");
```

That would work but might also interfere with the content already in the specified clip. For example, if an *ImageViewer* instance attempted to load an image into the main timeline of _level0, the entire contents of the Flash Player would be replaced by the image! Not good. Furthermore, if *setImageClip( )* were used to change the image-holding clip after an image had already been loaded, the *ImageViewer* instance would lose its reference to the original clip. Having lost the clip reference, the *ImageViewer* instance would no longer be able to position, size, or otherwise control the image, nor would it be able to remove the image before loading a different one.

To keep things simple (always keep it simple in the first version!), we want to guarantee a one-to-one association (one image movie clip for each *ImageViewer* instance). Hence, each instance will create a clip to hold the image. This ensures that the clip is empty when we load the image into it and that each instance always loads its image(s) into the same clip. In ActionScript, each movie clip can load only one image at a time.

We've decided that each *ImageViewer* instance will create its own image-holding clip, but we still need to know where to put that clip. That is, we need to be told which existing clip will contain the image-holding clip we create. How about adding a public method, *setTargetClip( )*, that specifies the movie clip and depth on which to put our image-holding clip. Code that uses the *ImageViewer* would look like this:

```
var viewer:ImageViewer = new ImageViewer();
// someClip_mc is the clip that will contain the new image-holding
// clip, and 1 is the depth on which the image-holding clip is created.
viewer.setTargetClip(someClip_mc, 1);
viewer.loadImage("someImage.jpg");
```

Hmm. That feels a bit cumbersome. It shouldn't take two method calls just to load an image. Moreover, we want each *ImageViewer* instance to know its target clip immediately on creation. So let's move the responsibility of setting the target clip to the *ImageViewer* constructor. Anyone creating a new *ImageViewer* instance must provide the target clip and depth as arguments to the constructor, so here is the new constructor signature:

```
ImageViewer(target:MovieClip, depth:Number)
```

Code that uses the *ImageViewer* would now look like this:

```
var viewer:ImageViewer = new ImageViewer(someClip_mc, 1);
viewer.loadImage("someImage.jpg");
```

That code would create the *ImageViewer* instance, which would create a new empty movie clip in someClip_mc at depth 1. It would then load *someImage.jpg* into the empty clip. Once loaded, *someImage.jpg* would automatically appear on screen (assuming someClip_mc were visible at the time).

The signatures and return datatypes of the constructor and *loadImage( )* method in our current class design now look like this (recall that constructor declarations never include a return datatype):

```
ImageViewer(target:MovieClip, depth:Number)
ImageViewer.loadImage(URL:String):Void
```

That looks reasonably sensible. Only one way to find out: let's code it up.

ImageViewer Implementation (Take 1)

Every ActionScript 2.0 class must reside in an external text file with the extension *.as*. Hence, the first step in authoring our *ImageViewer* class is to create a text file named *ImageViewer.as*. If you're working in Flash MX Professional 2004, you can create and edit *ImageViewer.as* using its external-script editor. If you're working in Flash MX 2004 (not the Professional edition), you must use a third-party text editor to create your *.as* text file. Even if you are using Flash MX Professional 2004, you may appreciate the additional features offered by some external editors (such as file management, syntax highlighting, and code hinting).

Popular choices are:

SciTE|Flash
http://www.bomberstudios.com/sciteflash

UltraEdit
http://www.ultraedit.com

Macromedia HomeSite
http://www.macromedia.com/software/homesite

TextPad
http://www.textpad.com

PrimalScript
http://www.sapien.com

Whichever editor you're using, create a new folder on your hard drive named *image-viewer*. We'll place all the files for this tutorial in that folder.

To create the *ImageViewer.as* file using Flash MX Professional 2004, follow these steps:

1. Choose File → New.
2. In the New Document dialog box, on the General tab, for the document Type, choose ActionScript File.
3. Click OK. The script editor launches with an empty file.
4. Choose File → Save As.
5. In the Save As dialog box, specify `ImageViewer.as` as the filename (using upper- and lowercase as shown) and save the file in the *imageviewer* folder you created.

Now let's put a little code into our *ImageViewer.as* file. We know that the name of our class is *ImageViewer*, so we can already sketch out a bare class skeleton. Enter the code from Example 5-1 into your script editor.

Example 5-1. The ImageViewer class skeleton

```
class ImageViewer {
}
```

Notice that the class name, *ImageViewer*, and the filename, *ImageViewer.as*, must match exactly (apart from the *.as* file extension).

 A class's name and the name of the external *.as* text file that contains the class must be identical (apart from the *.as* file extension). Likewise, the file extension must be *.as*. Do not use a text editor that saves extra formatting information, such as in Microsoft Word format. Save the file as plain text. Whenever possible, use Unicode format (UTF-8 encoding). If your editor doesn't support Unicode, use ANSI, ASCII, or Latin 1.

If you named your class *ImageViewer* (with an uppercase "V") but mistakenly named your *.as* file *Imageviewer.as* (with a lowercase "v"), Flash won't be able to find the *ImageViewer* class. In that case, when you attempt to use the *ImageViewer* class, you'll see the following error in the Output panel:

```
The class 'ImageViewer' could not be loaded.
```

Conversely, if you mistakenly named your class *Imageviewer* (with a lowercase "v") but named your *.as* file *ImageViewer.as* (with an uppercase "V"), Flash will find the *ImageViewer.as* file but will complain that it can't find a class in that file that matches the filename. In such a case, when you attempt to use *ImageViewer*, you'll see the following error:

```
The class 'Imageviewer' needs to be defined in a file whose
relative path is 'Imageviewer.as'.
```

If, down the road, you decide to change the class name, you must also change the filename, and vice versa.

Before we put some meat on the bones of our class, you may want to take a minute to customize your editing environment. If you're using Flash MX Professional 2004, you'll probably want to turn on line numbers (View → View Line Numbers) and customize your font styles, code hint timing, and autoindentation rules (Edit → Preferences → ActionScript). You can even tell Flash how to autoformat your code (Edit → Auto Format Options). The autoformat feature itself is accessed via Tools → Auto Format.

Okay, where were we? The class skeleton—right. Your current *ImageViewer.as* file should contain:

```
class ImageViewer {
}
```

Now recall our earlier class design:

```
ImageViewer(target:MovieClip, depth:Number)
ImageViewer.loadImage(URL:String):Void
```

That design shows the basic structure of the *ImageViewer* class's constructor and *loadImage( )* method. Let's fill in those items now. Update your *ImageViewer.as* file to match Example 5-2.

Example 5-2. The ImageViewer class with constructor and loadImage( ) method roughed in

```
class ImageViewer {
  // The constructor function
  public function ImageViewer (target:MovieClip, depth:Number) {
  }

  // The loadImage( ) method
  public function loadImage (URL:String):Void {
  }
}
```

Now that we have our class's constructor and *loadImage( )* method roughed in, we can move on to coding the constructor function body. We decided earlier that the *ImageViewer* class constructor should create an empty movie clip to hold the loaded image. That empty clip should be attached to the target clip at the depth specified, as follows:

```
public function ImageViewer (target:MovieClip, depth:Number) {
  target.createEmptyMovieClip("container_mc" + depth, depth);
}
```

Notice that the empty clip name starts with "container_mc" and ends with the supplied depth. That gives each empty container clip a unique name. For example, if depth is 4, the empty clip's name will be container_mc4. Only one clip can occupy each depth at a given time, and each empty clip's name must be unique (a clip whose name and parent is the same as a preexisting clip is inaccessible via ActionScript). So by generating a unique name based on the specified depth, more than one empty clip can reside in target without conflicts.

We needn't worry if we hadn't thought of this necessity in our original design. For brevity, we skipped some iterations of the typical design process. In a typical first rough pass for the constructor function, many developers probably would have not remembered to create a unique name for each image-holding clip.

In the simplest case, in which you are loading only one image in one *ImageViewer* instance, this wouldn't be a problem. However, once you started creating multiple instances to load multiple images (each in its own clip), you'd have realized the deficiency (a.k.a. bug) in your code and made the necessary adjustments. With practice, you'll learn to anticipate likely design problems.

 In almost all cases, your class design should allow for multiple instances of the same class to coexist peacefully. One exception would be if you define a class that is never instantiated (i.e., implements only class methods and class properties, not instance methods or instance properties). Another exception is the Singleton design pattern discussed in Chapter 17.

In this case, peaceful coexistence means creating movie clips with unique names and putting them on unique depths. Note that, as written, our current code requires the user of the *ImageViewer* class to pass in a unique depth (the code doesn't try to automatically determine a unique depth). Therefore, the user must ensure that the depth passed to the *ImageViewer* constructor does not overwrite an existing asset; document this in the comments for the constructor, as done in Example 5-3.

Moving right along, our constructor is done, so let's implement the *loadImage( )* method so that it loads a JPEG file into the empty clip. The image-loading code looks generally like this:

```
theEmptyClip.loadMovie(URL);
```

Hmm. That brings up a problem: the *loadImage( )* method has no way to access the empty clip created by the constructor. We must alter the constructor so that it stores a reference to the empty clip in an instance property. We'll name that instance property container_mc. Example 5-3 shows the new property and the adjusted constructor function, with additions shown in bold. Update your *ImageViewer.as* file to match Example 5-3 (you don't have to include the comments, but it is a good habit to get into). Now we can use the container_mc property to access the empty clip from within the *loadImage( )* method.

Example 5-3. The ImageViewer class with its new property

```
class ImageViewer {
  // Here's the new property.
  private var container_mc:MovieClip;
```

Example 5-3. The ImageViewer class with its new property (continued)

```
  // The constructor function.
  // The caller is responsible for specifying a unique depth
  // within the target clip.
  public function ImageViewer (target:MovieClip, depth:Number) {
    // Store a reference to the new, empty clip in
    // the container_mc property.
    container_mc = target.createEmptyMovieClip("container_mc" + depth,
                                                 depth);
  }

  public function loadImage (URL:String):Void {
    container_mc.loadMovie(URL);
  }
}
```

Notice that the *loadImage( )* method simply calls Flash's built-in *loadMovie( )* method. When one method simply calls another method, it is known as *wrapping* or creating a *wrapper*; the *loadImage( )* method is said to *wrap* the *loadMovie( )* method. Typically, functions, methods (or even entire classes) are wrapped in order to adapt them to a particular situation. In our case, by wrapping *loadMovie( )* in the *loadImage( )* method, we:

- Make our class more intuitive (*loadImage( )* describes the method's behavior better than *loadMovie( )*)
- Make our class more convenient to use (someViewer.loadImage( ) is more convenient than someViewer.container_mc.loadMovie( ))
- Make our class more flexible and future-proof; we can easily add or change code in the *loadImage( )* method later without affecting the way that the method is used

Example 5-4 shows the completed code for the first version of our *ImageViewer* class with the comments stripped out. Make sure your *ImageViewer.as* file matches the code in Example 5-4.

Example 5-4. The ImageViewer class, version 1

```
class ImageViewer {
  private var container_mc:MovieClip;

  public function ImageViewer (target:MovieClip, depth:Number) {
    container_mc = target.createEmptyMovieClip("container_mc" + depth,
                                                 depth);
  }

  public function loadImage (URL:String):Void {
    container_mc.loadMovie(URL);
  }
}
```

Using ImageViewer in a Movie

Now that our *ImageViewer* class is ready for testing, let's see how to actually use it in a Flash movie! We'll start by obtaining an image file to load, as follows:

1. Find a (nonprogressive format) JPEG image on your system. If you work in an office, ensure that the content of the JPEG you choose is appropriate for the office environment. If you can't find a JPEG image, download one with the completed *ImageViewer* example posted at *http://moock.org/eas2/examples*.

2. Name the JPEG image *picture.jpg* and place it in the same folder as the *Image-Viewer.as* file you created earlier.

Next we'll create a Flash document (.*fla* file) from which we'll publish a Flash movie (.*swf* file) containing an instance of our *ImageViewer* class. For now, we'll place the .*fla* file, .*as* file, .*swf* file, and .*jpg* file all in the same folder, making it easy for each file to access the other files.

> When a .*fla* file and a class file (i.e., an .*as* file with a class definition) reside in the same directory, code in the .*fla* file can refer to the class in the .*as* file directly by name. Hence, the easiest way to use an Action-Script 2.0 class is to place its .*as* file in the same folder as the .*fla* file that uses it. The class will automatically be included in the .*swf* exported from the .*fla* (unless the .*fla* file does not reference the class at all). Unlike ActionScript 1.0, no #include statement is required to incorporate an ActionScript 2.0 class into a .*fla* file.

When reusing classes across many projects, class files should be stored centrally in a location accessible to each project. In Chapters 9 and 14, we'll learn how to structure larger projects that reuse classes.

Now let's create the Flash document that uses the *ImageViewer* class. Follow these steps:

1. In the Flash authoring tool, choose File → New.

2. In the New Document dialog box, on the General tab, for the document Type, choose Flash Document, then click OK.

3. Use File → Save As to save the Flash document as **imageViewer.fla** in the same folder as the *ImageViewer.as* file. (By convention, we name .*fla* files starting with a lowercase letter. The .*fla* file's name need not match the case of the class. Usually, a .*fla* file makes use of multiple classes and its name has no relation to the class names or .*as* filenames.)

4. In *imageViewer.fla*'s main timeline, rename *Layer 1* to **scripts** (we'll place all our code on the *scripts* layer).

We're now ready to use the *ImageViewer* class from within *imageViewer.fla*. Follow these steps to instantiate *ImageViewer* on frame 1 of *imageViewer.fla*'s main timeline:

---

1. Use Window → Development Panels → Actions (F9) to open the Actions panel.

2. Select frame 1 in *imageViewer.fla*'s main timeline.

3. Into the Actions panel, enter the following code:

```
var viewer:ImageViewer = new ImageViewer(this, 1);
viewer.loadImage("picture.jpg");
```

Notice that the *ImageViewer* class is globally available and can be referred to directly by name from any code on any frame, button, or movie clip in *imageViewer.fla*. In fact, if the exported *imageViewer.swf* loads another *.swf* file, that loaded *.swf* can also access the *ImageViewer* class. However, if that loaded *.swf* file also contains a class by the name *ImageViewer*, the loaded *.swf*'s version will not overwrite the *imageViewer.swf* version. For more information on using classes at runtime across multiple *.swf* files, see Chapter 14.

 Through the magic of the Flash compiler, ActionScript 2.0 classes are literally defined on _global, in the style of ActionScript 1.0 classes. To prove it, after defining our *ImageViewer class*, we can execute:

```
trace(typeof _global.ImageViewer);
```

which displays "function" in the Output panel. For details, see "ActionScript 1.0 and 2.0 in Flash Player 6 and 7" in Chapter 1.

Once an ActionScript 2.0 class of a given name is defined, it cannot be redefined by another ActionScript 2.0 class definition. The only way to change a class definition at runtime is to directly overwrite the corresponding global variable, as in:

```
// Replacing the ImageViewer class definition
// with a string disables the ImageViewer class.
_global.ImageViewer = "Goodbye ImageViewer, nice knowing you.";
```

Using an analogous technique, an ActionScript 2.0 class can be overwritten by an ActionScript 1.0 class as follows:

```
_global.ImageViewer = function () {
  // ActionScript 1.0 constructor function body goes here
}
```

Finally, the moment we've been waiting for! Let's export our *imageViewer.swf* file and test it in Flash's Test Movie mode, as follows:

1. Choose Control → Test Movie. The *.swf* file should play, and your image should load and appear.

2. When you're finished marveling at your work, choose File → Close to return to the *imageViewer.fla* file.

You can export *imageViewer.swf* for playback in a web browser using the File → Publish command. However, if you have Flash Player 6 installed in your browser, you'll notice that the *picture.jpg* file doesn't load.

How the Compiler Exports SWF Files

When you export a *.swf* file, the ActionScript 2.0 compiler makes a list of all the classes that the *.swf* requires. Specifically, the list of required classes includes all classes referenced by the *.swf*'s source *.fla* file and all classes that are referenced within those classes. (In our case, the list of required classes is simply *ImageViewer*.) The compiler then searches the filesystem for the corresponding source *.as* files and compiles each source file into the *.swf*, in the form of bytecode that the Flash Player can understand. By default, the compiler searches for *.as* files in the directory that contains the *.fla* file, but it will also search any directories that are listed by the developer in the so-called *document classpath* or *global classpath* (we'll cover classpaths in Chapter 9). Class files that exist on the filesystem but are not required by the *.swf* are not compiled into the *.swf*. And classes that are required but not found cause a compile-time error.

 Even though ActionScript 2.0 is compiled to the same bytecode as ActionScript 1.0 and nearly 100% of ActionScript 2.0 constructs are supported by Flash Player 6, *.swf* files must be exported in Flash Player 6 format to work properly in Flash Player 6. See Chapter 1.

To change *imageViewer.fla*'s export settings to support playback in Flash Player 6, follow these steps:

1. Choose File → Publish Settings.
2. On the Flash tab of the Publish Settings dialog box, select Flash Player 6 as the Version option.
3. Click OK.

Once the version is set to Flash Player 6, any *.swf* file exported from *imageViewer.fla* (via File → Publish, Control → Test Movie, or File → Export → Export Movie) will work in Flash Player 6. ActionScript 2.0 is not supported in Flash Player 5 or older, no matter what the format of the *.swf* file.

Preloading the ImageViewer Class

Wasn't it great to see the *ImageViewer* class in action? But there's a minor problem. Right now the *ImageViewer* class is so tiny you'll hardly notice it loading. However, if it were, say, 50 KB or 100 KB, you'd notice a delay when loading it over a slow connection. By default, all classes load before frame 1 is displayed, causing a delay before a movie can start. If the load time is long enough, a movie will appear broken or hung. Most individual classes won't be large, but in some applications the total size of all classes will exceed 100 KB. Fortunately, Flash lets us specify precisely when a movie's classes are loaded.

Let's change our *imageViewer.fla* file so that the classes it uses aren't loaded until frame 10:

1. Choose File → Publish Settings.
2. In the Publish Settings dialog box, on the Flash tab, next to the ActionScript Version, click Settings.
3. In the ActionScript Settings dialog box, for Export Frame for Classes, enter **10**.
4. Click OK to confirm the ActionScript Settings.
5. Click OK to confirm the Publish Settings.

Now let's add a very basic preloader to our *imageViewer.fla* file so load progress is reported while the *ImageViewer* class loads. When loading is complete, we'll advance the playhead to frame 15 where we'll instantiate *ImageViewer* (as we previously did on frame 1).

First, we'll make the timeline 15 frames long, as follows:

1. In the main timeline of *imageViewer.fla*, select frame 15 of the *scripts* layer.
2. Choose Insert → Timeline → Keyframe (F6).

Next, we'll add a *labels* layer with two frame labels, loading and main. The labels designate the application's loading state and startup point, respectively.

1. Choose Insert → Timeline → Layer.
2. Double-click the new layer's name and change it to **labels**.
3. At frames 4 and 15 of the *labels* layer, add a new keyframe (using Insert → Timeline → Keyframe).
4. With frame 4 of the *labels* layer selected, in the Properties panel, under Frame, change <Frame Label> to **loading**.
5. With frame 15 of the *labels* layer selected, in the Properties panel, under Frame, change <Frame Label> to **main**.

Now we'll add the preloader script to the *scripts* layer:

1. At frame 5 of the *scripts* layer, add a new keyframe (using Insert → Timeline → Keyframe).
2. With frame 5 of the *scripts* layer selected, enter the following code into the Actions panel:

```
if (_framesloaded == _totalframes) {
  gotoAndStop("main");
} else {
  gotoAndPlay("loading");
}
```

Next, we'll move the code that creates our *ImageViewer* instance from frame 1 to frame 15 of the *scripts* layer:

1. Select frame 1 of the *scripts* layer.

2. In the Actions panel, cut (delete using Ctrl-X or Cmd-X) the following code from frame 1:

```
var viewer:ImageViewer = new ImageViewer(this, 1);
viewer.loadImage("picture.jpg");
```

3. With frame 15 of the *scripts* layer selected, paste (using Ctrl-V or Cmd-V) the code you deleted in Step 2 into the Actions panel.

Finally, we'll add a loading message that displays while the *ImageViewer* class loads:

1. With frame 1 of the *scripts* layer selected, enter the following code into the Actions panel:

```
this.createTextField("loadmsg_txt", 0, 200, 200, 0, 0);
loadmsg_txt.autoSize = true;
loadmsg_txt.text = "Loading...Please wait.";
```

2. With frame 15 of the *scripts* layer selected, enter the following code at the end of the Actions panel (after the code entered in Step 2 of the previous procedure):

```
loadmsg_txt.removeTextField( );
```

That's it! Test your movie using Control → Test Movie. Once in Test Movie mode, you can watch a simulated download of your movie by enabling the Bandwidth Profiler (View → Bandwidth Profiler) and then choosing View → Simulate Download. Because our class is so small, you may have to select a very slow download speed to see the preloading message. To change the download speed, choose View → Download Settings.

ImageViewer Implementation (Take 2)

Now that we have a working, albeit simple, version of the *ImageViewer* class, we can add more features to it. As we do so, we'll take care not the change the public API of the class. For example, at this stage we shouldn't change the *loadImage( )* method's name to *loadAndDisplayImage( )*. Nor should we change the order or datatype of the parameters for the constructor or the *loadImage( )* method.

However, adding to the *ImageViewer* class's API is acceptable and normal. Changing its private methods or properties is also acceptable because such changes do not affect external code. However, changing the class's public API is dangerous and considered bad form because it forces corresponding rewrites in all code that uses the class.

 During your internal development stages (alpha and beta), API changes are relatively common. But once a class is released to the world, its public API should remain fixed.

Any changes to the public API should preferably be accompanied by documentation and a change in the class's major version number. Additions to the public API (i.e., new methods) need not require a major version change because they won't break existing code.

We've completed the first two features (loading and displaying an image) from our list of possible functional requirements shown earlier under "Designing the ImageViewer Class." Let's move on to the third and fourth requirements: cropping the image and giving it a border.

Flash doesn't have any built-in means of altering a bitmap once it's loaded. Hence, we can't literally crop our loaded image. Instead, we must apply a mask to it, which hides unwanted areas of the image from view. To mask our image, we'll first create an empty movie clip, then draw a filled square in it, then apply that square as a mask over the image-holding clip. We'll add parameters to the *ImageViewer* constructor to specify the size of the mask and the position of the cropped image.

At this stage of development, we've made the design decision to add two parameters to the constructor function to control cropping. Doesn't this undermine our earlier goal of a stable public API? Not necessarily. First of all, we haven't released any code publicly, so no one else is using our class yet. Second, to ensure backward compatibility, we can allow the constructor to assume sensible default values even if the new arguments are omitted when calling the constructor.

To create our border, we'll create a movie clip, then draw a square outline in it. We'll place the border clip visually on top of the image. We'll retrieve the thickness and color of the border from parameters that we'll add to the *ImageViewer* constructor. Again, we've made the design decision to specify the border thickness and color at the time the object is instantiated. Another option would be to create a new method through which these could be set. The latter option gives the caller the flexibility to change those settings even after the object has been created.

To accommodate our border and mask clips, we'll redesign the structure of our on-screen assets. Previously, we created a single movie clip, container_mc, into which we loaded an image.

 For the sake of brevity and clarity, when I say "the movie clip container_mc," I really mean "the movie clip referenced by the instance property container_mc." The name of the clip itself is technically container_mc*depth* (where *depth* is the depth on which the clip resides). But the instance property is named container_mc.

Here's the original clip-creation code:

```
container_mc = target.createEmptyMovieClip("container_mc" + depth, depth);
```

This time we'll use container_mc merely as a holder for three movie clips: the mask clip (mask_mc), the border clip (border_mc), and a new image-holding clip (image_mc). We'll put the image_mc clip on the bottom (at depth 0 in container_mc), the mask_mc clip in the middle (at depth 1), and the border_mc clip on top (at depth 2), as shown in Figure 5-1.

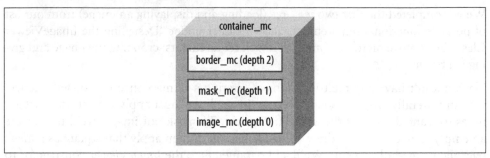

Figure 5-1. ImageViewer movie clip structure

The question is, within the *ImageViewer* class, when should we create the border, mask, image, and container clips? In the first version of the *ImageViewer* class, we created the container_mc clip in the constructor function. We could theoretically take the same approach now (i.e., create the border, mask, and image clips in the constructor). But instead, in this version of the *ImageViewer* class, we'll define internal (private) methods to handle the creation of the various clips. Splitting out the work into separate methods has the following benefits:

- It makes the code more intelligible.
- It simplifies the testing process (testing each method individually is easier than testing a large block of code that performs many operations).
- It allows assets to be created and re-created independently (e.g., the border on an image can change without reloading the image).
- It allows asset-creation operations to be modified or overridden independently (e.g., a new border-creation routine can be coded without disturbing other code).

Thus, we've made this design decision to increase our class's flexibility and maintainability.

Table 5-1 lists the new clip-creation methods, all of which are declared *private*.

Table 5-1. The ImageViewer class's new instance methods that create movie clips

Method name	Method description
buildViewer( )	Invokes individual methods to create the container, image, mask, and border clips
createMainContainer( )	Creates the container_mc clip
createImageClip( )	Creates the image_mc clip
createImageClipMask( )	Creates the mask_mc clip
createBorder( )	Creates the border_mc clip

Now that our clip-creation operations are separated into methods, we need to add properties that provide those methods with the following information:

- A reference to the target clip to which `container_mc` should be attached
- A list of depths indicating the visual stacking order of the container, image, mask, and border clips
- The style (line weight and color) of the border around the image

Table 5-2 lists the *ImageViewer* class's complete set of instance and class properties, all of which are declared *private*.

The properties indicated as class properties define a single value that all *ImageViewer* instances reference. Instance properties pertain separately to each instance.

Table 5-2. The ImageViewer class's instance and class properties

Property name	Type	Property description
container_mc	Instance	A reference to the main container clip, which contains all movie clips used by each *ImageViewer* instance
target_mc	Instance	A reference to the clip that will contain the container_mc clip, as specified by the *ImageViewer* constructor
containerDepth	Instance	The depth on which container_mc is created in target_mc, as specified by the *ImageViewer* constructor
imageDepth	Class	The depth on which image_mc is created in container_mc
maskDepth	Class	The depth on which mask_mc is created in container_mc
borderDepth	Class	The depth on which border_mc is created in container_mc
borderThickness	Instance	The thickness, in pixels, of the border around the image_mc clip
borderColor	Instance	The integer RGB color of the border around the image_mc clip

The final change to our *ImageViewer* class comes in the constructor function, which must define new parameters to support the new methods and properties of the class. We must define parameters to specify:

- The position of the image (x and y)
- The size of the mask over the image (w and h)
- The style of the border around the image (borderThickness and borderColor)

In addition to these new parameters, we'll keep our original target and depth parameters, so the *ImageViewer* constructor signature is now:

```
ImageViewer(target:MovieClip, depth:Number, x:Number, y:Number,
            w:Number, h:Number, borderThickness:Number, borderColor:Number)
```

ImageViewer (Take 2), Design Summary

With the constructor redesign finished, the changes for version 2 of our *ImageViewer* class are complete.

Here's the final class design for this version. It repeats information from tables 5-1 and 5-2 in order to show how you might represent a class during the design phase of a project, perhaps before you've actually produced any code:

Constructor
```
ImageViewer(target:MovieClip, depth:Number, x:Number, y:Number,
            w:Number, h:Number, borderThickness:Number, borderColor:Number)
```
Private properties
```
container_mc
target_mc
containerDepth
imageDepth
maskDepth
borderDepth
borderThickness
borderColor
```
Public properties
None
Private methods
buildViewer(x:Number, y:Number, w:Number, h:Number)
createMainContainer(x:Number, y:Number)
createImageClip( )
createImageClipMask(w:Number, h:Number)
createBorder(w:Number, h:Number)
Public methods
loadImage(URL:String)

ImageViewer Implementation (Take 2)

Example 5-5 shows the actual code for the *ImageViewer* class, version 2. Study the comments carefully for code explanations. If some of the specific ActionScript techniques are new to you (e.g., drawing lines or masking movie clips), consult an ActionScript language reference such as *ActionScript for Flash MX: The Definitive Guide* (O'Reilly).

Example 5-5. The ImageViewer class, take 2

```
// ImageViewer class, Version 2
class ImageViewer {
  // Movie clip references
  private var container_mc:MovieClip;
  private var target_mc:MovieClip;

  // Movie clip depths
  private var containerDepth:Number;
  private static var imageDepth:Number  = 0;
  private static var maskDepth:Number   = 1;
```

Example 5-5. The ImageViewer class, take 2 (continued)

```
private static var borderDepth:Number = 2;

// Border style
private var borderThickness:Number;
private var borderColor:Number;

// Constructor
public function ImageViewer (target:MovieClip,
                            depth:Number,
                            x:Number,
                            y:Number,
                            w:Number,
                            h:Number,
                            borderThickness:Number,
                            borderColor:Number) {
  // Assign property values.
  target_mc = target;
  containerDepth = depth;
  this.borderThickness = borderThickness;
  this.borderColor = borderColor;

  // Set up the visual assets for this ImageViewer.
  buildViewer(x, y, w, h);
}

// Creates the clips to hold the image, mask, and border.
// This method subcontracts all its work out to individual
// clip-creation methods.
private function buildViewer (x:Number,
                             y:Number,
                             w:Number,
                             h:Number):Void {
    createMainContainer(x, y);
    createImageClip();
    createImageClipMask(w, h);
    createBorder(w, h);
}

// Creates the container that holds all the assets
private function createMainContainer (x:Number, y:Number):Void {
  container_mc =
    target_mc.createEmptyMovieClip("container_mc" + containerDepth,
                                    containerDepth);
  // Position the container clip.
  container_mc._x = x;
  container_mc._y = y;
}

// Creates the clip into which the image is actually loaded
private function createImageClip ():Void {
  container_mc.createEmptyMovieClip("image_mc", imageDepth);
}
```

Example 5-5. The ImageViewer class, take 2 (continued)

```
// Creates the mask over the image
private function createImageClipMask (w:Number,
                                      h:Number):Void {
  // Create the mask only if a valid width and height are specified.
  if (!(w > 0 && h > 0)) {
    return;
  }

  // In the container, create a clip to act as the mask over the image.
  container_mc.createEmptyMovieClip("mask_mc", maskDepth);

  // Draw a rectangle in the mask.
  container_mc.mask_mc.moveTo(0, 0);
  container_mc.mask_mc.beginFill(0x0000FF);  // Use blue for debugging
  container_mc.mask_mc.lineTo(w, 0);
  container_mc.mask_mc.lineTo(w, h);
  container_mc.mask_mc.lineTo(0, h);
  container_mc.mask_mc.lineTo(0, 0);
  container_mc.mask_mc.endFill( );

  // Hide the mask (it will still function as a mask when invisible).
  // To see the mask during debugging, comment out the next line.
  container_mc.mask_mc._visible = false;

  // Notice that we don't apply the mask yet. We must do that
  // after the image starts loading, otherwise the loading of
  // the image will remove the mask.
}

// Creates the border around the image
private function createBorder (w:Number,
                               h:Number):Void {
  // Create the border only if a valid width and height are specified.
  if (!(w > 0 && h > 0)) {
    return;
  }

  // In the container, create a clip to hold the border around the image.
  container_mc.createEmptyMovieClip("border_mc", borderDepth);

  // Draw a rectangular outline in the border clip, with the
  // specified dimensions and color.
  container_mc.border_mc.lineStyle(borderThickness, borderColor);
  container_mc.border_mc.moveTo(0, 0);
  container_mc.border_mc.lineTo(w, 0);
  container_mc.border_mc.lineTo(w, h);
  container_mc.border_mc.lineTo(0, h);
  container_mc.border_mc.lineTo(0, 0);
}

// Loads the image
```

Example 5-5. The ImageViewer class, take 2 (continued)

```
  public function loadImage (URL:String):Void {
    // Load the JPEG file into the image_mc clip.
    container_mc.image_mc.loadMovie(URL);

    // Here comes an ugly hack. We'll clean this up in Example 5-6
    // when we add proper preloading support in Version 3.
    // After one frame passes, the image load will have started,
    // at which point we safely apply the mask to the image_mc clip.
    container_mc.onEnterFrame = function ():Void {
      this.image_mc.setMask(this.mask_mc);
      delete this.onEnterFrame;
    }
  }
}
```

Using ImageViewer (Take 2)

Now that our *ImageViewer* class can crop an image and add a border to it, let's put ourselves in the position of a developer who's using the class (not creating and maintaining it). When we used the first version of the *ImageViewer* class, we placed the following code on frame 15 of *imageViewer.fla*:

```
  var viewer:ImageViewer = new ImageViewer(this, 1);
  viewer.loadImage("picture.jpg");
```

ImageViewer version 2 added two new features comprising quite a lot of code. However, none of the public API defined by *ImageViewer* version 1 changed in version 2; version 2 made additions only to that API. The *loadImage( )* method changed internally, but its external usage did not change at all. Likewise, the constructor function changed internally, but externally it only added parameters. It retains the target and depth parameters from version 1 and adds six new parameters: x, y, w, h, borderThickness, and borderColor. Hence, users of *ImageViewer* version 1 can easily update *imageViewer.fla* to use *ImageViewer* version 2's new features, as follows:

1. Replace the old *ImageViewer.as* file with the new one.

2. Change the code on frame 15 of *imageViewer.fla* to include the six new parameters expected by the *ImageViewer* constructor. For example:

```
  var viewer:ImageViewer = new ImageViewer(this, 1, 100, 100,
                                      250, 250, 10, 0xCE9A3C);
  viewer.loadImage("picture.jpg");
```

Now let's consider what would happen if we upgraded from *ImageViewer* version 1 to version 2 without changing any code in *imageViewer.fla*. (For the sake of this scenario, let's presume that version 2 contains performance enhancements that have prompted us to upgrade.) We'd replace our *ImageViewer.as* file, as in the previous Step 1, but we'd skip Step 2, leaving the following code on frame 15:

```
  var viewer:ImageViewer = new ImageViewer(this, 1);
  viewer.loadImage("picture.jpg");
```

How would *ImageViewer* version 2 respond to being constructed with only two parameters? Fortunately, very well. Version 2 specifically safeguards against missing parameters. The *createImageClipMask( )* and *createBorder( )* methods create the mask and border clips only if a useful width and height are supplied, as shown in this excerpt from Example 5-5:

```
if (!(w > 0 && h > 0)) {
  return;
}
```

Thus, when no width and height are supplied to the constructor, *ImageViewer* version 2's behavior matches *ImageViewer* version 1's behavior exactly.

> After a class is formally released, upgrading to a new version should not break code that uses the old version. Changes to the class itself should not force changes to code that merely uses the class. One way to achieve this is for the new class to assume reasonable default behavior if some arguments are not supplied.

ImageViewer Implementation (Take 3)

Let's review the potential functional requirements for the *ImageViewer* class:

- Load an image
- Display an image
- Crop an image to a particular rectangular "view region"
- Display a border around the image
- Display image load progress
- Reposition the view region
- Resize the view region
- Pan (reposition) the image within the view region
- Zoom (resize) the image within the view region

So far, we've successfully implemented the first four items. In the next version of the *ImageViewer* class, we'll add the fifth feature: display image load progress. We'll leave the remaining items unimplemented until the situation specifically requires them. (Plot spoiler: in Chapter 7 we'll return to the *ImageViewer* class to add two more features.)

To implement load-progress display for our *ImageViewer* class, we'll use the *MovieClipLoader* class, which was added to Flash Player 7 after a heartfelt petition to Macromedia for improved preloading support (curious readers can view the petition at *http://moock.org/blog/archives/000010.html*).

Our load-progress implementation involves these main changes to the *ImageViewer* class:

- Add two new properties:

  imageLoader
    holds a *MovieClipLoader* instance

  statusDepth
    indicates the depth of a load-progress text field

- Modify the *ImageViewer* constructor to first create a *MovieClipLoader* instance and then register the *ImageViewer* instance to receive events from it.

- Modify the *loadImage( )* method to:
  - Load the JPEG file using *MovieClipLoader* instead of *loadMovie( )*
  - Create a text field in which to display load progress

- Add three methods—*onLoadProgress( )*, *onLoadInit( )*, and *onLoadError( )*—to handle *MovieClipLoader* events.

The preceding design changes might seem like a pretty big leap given that we're adding only one feature (image load progress). Take heart. The code required to add preloading support might seem fairly complex if you're new to it, but luckily, preloading code doesn't vary much from situation to situation. Once you've implemented preloading support a few times, you'll be able to add it to your own classes in one fell swoop, as we've done here.

Let's look at each of the preceding changes in turn. First, here's the code for the new imageLoader and statusDepth properties:

```
private var imageLoader:MovieClipLoader;
private static var statusDepth:Number = 3;
```

Next, here's the modified *ImageViewer* constructor (additions shown in bold):

```
public function ImageViewer (target:MovieClip,
                             depth:Number,
                             x:Number,
                             y:Number,
                             w:Number,
                             h:Number,
                             borderThickness:Number,
                             borderColor:Number) {
  // Assign property values.
  target_mc = target;
  containerDepth = depth;
  this.borderThickness = borderThickness;
  this.borderColor = borderColor;

  // Create the MovieClipLoader instance and store it in
  // the new imageLoader property.
  imageLoader = new MovieClipLoader();
```

```
        // Register this ImageViewer instance to receive events
        // from the MovieClipLoader instance.
        imageLoader.addListener(this);

        // Set up the visual assets for this ImageViewer.
        buildViewer(x, y, w, h);
    }
```

Here's the revised *loadImage( )* method. Note that even though the entire contents of the method have changed, the method's usage is unaltered, so the class's public API is not affected:

```
    public function loadImage (URL:String):Void {
        // Use the MovieClipLoader instance to load the image. This line replaces
        // the previous loadMovie( ) call.
        imageLoader.loadClip(URL, container_mc.image_mc);

        // Create a load-status text field to show the user load progress.
        container_mc.createTextField("loadStatus_txt", statusDepth, 0, 0, 0, 0);
        container_mc.loadStatus_txt.background = true;
        container_mc.loadStatus_txt.border = true;
        container_mc.loadStatus_txt.setNewTextFormat(new TextFormat(
                                        "Arial, Helvetica, _sans",
                                        10, borderColor, false,
                                        false, false, null, null,
                                        "right"));
        container_mc.loadStatus_txt.autoSize = "left";

        // Position the load-status text field.
        container_mc.loadStatus_txt._y = 3;
        container_mc.loadStatus_txt._x = 3;

        // Indicate that the image is loading.
        container_mc.loadStatus_txt.text = "LOADING";

    }
```

Finally, Example 5-6 shows the three methods that handle image loading events: *onLoadProgress( )*, *onLoadInit( )*, and *onLoadError( )*. The *onLoadProgress( )* method fires automatically when a portion of the image has arrived. The *onLoadInit( )* method fires automatically once the image has loaded completely and the image_mc's _width and _height properties have been initialized. The *onLoadError( )* method fires automatically when a load error such as "File not found" occurs.

The *MovieClipLoader* class also provides the *onLoadStart( )* and *onLoadComplete( )* events, which are not required by our *ImageViewer* class. For details, see Flash's Help under ActionScript Dictionary → M → MovieClipLoader.

Example 5-6. Image loading event handlers added to version 3 of the ImageViewer class

```
    public function onLoadProgress (target:MovieClip,
                            bytesLoaded:Number,
                            bytesTotal:Number):Void {
```

Example 5-6. Image loading event handlers added to version 3 of the ImageViewer class (continued)

```
    // Display load progress in the on-screen text field.
    // Divide bytesLoaded and bytesTotal by 1024 to get kilobytes.
    container_mc.loadStatus_txt.text = "LOADING: "
        + Math.floor(bytesLoaded / 1024)
        + "/" + Math.floor(bytesTotal / 1024) + " KB";
  }

  public function onLoadInit (target:MovieClip):Void {
    // Remove the loading message.
    container_mc.loadStatus_txt.removeTextField();

    // Apply the mask to the loaded image. This cleanly replaces the
    // onEnterFrame() hack from version 2's loadImage() method in Example 5-5.
    container_mc.image_mc.setMask(container_mc.mask_mc);
  }

  public function onLoadError (target:MovieClip, errorCode:String):Void {
    // Depending on the value of errorCode, display an appropriate
    // error message in the on-screen text field.
    if (errorCode == "URLNotFound") {
      container_mc.loadStatus_txt.text = "ERROR: File not found.";
    } else if (errorCode == "LoadNeverCompleted") {
      container_mc.loadStatus_txt.text = "ERROR: Load failed.";
    } else {
      // Catch-all to handle possible future error codes.
      container_mc.loadStatus_txt.text = "Load error: " + errorCode;
    }
  }
}
```

Version 3 of our *ImageViewer* class is nearly complete. However, we have one more issue to account for: cleaning up after each *ImageViewer* instance before it's deleted.

Deleting a Class's Resources

In programming, the fun's not over until you've put your proverbial toys away. Each instance of our *ImageViewer* class creates movie clip instances that persist in the Flash Player until they are explicitly removed, even if the *ImageViewer* instance that created them is, itself, deleted! For example, the following code creates an *ImageViewer* instance, loads an image, and then deletes the *ImageViewer* instance:

```
    var viewer:ImageViewer = new ImageViewer(this, 1, 100, 100,
                                             250, 250, 10, 0xCE9A3C);
    viewer.loadImage("picture.jpg");
    delete viewer;
```

After the code executes—despite the statement delete viewer;—the *picture.jpg* loads and appears on screen. Why? Because the clips created by the *ImageViewer* instance were not removed before the variable viewer was deleted.

Leaving movie clips on stage is not the only way the *ImageViewer* class orphans resources. Under certain circumstances, an *ImageViewer* instance can also abandon *itself* in the *MovieClipLoader* listener list. Recall that when an *ImageViewer* instance is constructed, it registers itself as an imageLoader listener using imageLoader.addListener(this). As a result, each *ImageViewer* instance is stored in its own imageLoader's list of listener objects. After this line of code executes:

```
var viewer:ImageViewer = new ImageViewer(this, 1);
```

there are actually two references to the *ImageViewer* instance: one in viewer and the other in viewer.imageLoader's list of listener objects. If the viewer instance is deleted during a load operation, the instance in viewer.imageLoader's listener list will live on.

Of course, you might naturally expect that deleting viewer would also delete viewer.imageLoader and, consequently, viewer.imageLoader's list of listener objects. In general, that would be true, but the *MovieClipLoader* class presents a special case: after a *MovieClipLoader* instance starts a *loadClip( )* operation, the instance (along with its list of listener objects) is kept alive internally by the Flash Player until either the operation completes or the movie clip targeted by the load operation is removed. For example, in the following code, the mcl instance is kept in memory until *level1.swf* has finished loading into box:

```
var mcl:MovieClipLoader = new MovieClipLoader();
mcl.loadClip("level1.swf", box);
delete mcl;
```

Hence, even though we can successfully delete all external references to an *ImageViewer* instance, the instance may still exist internally in its own imageLoader's listener list!

Each *ImageViewer* instance, therefore, should clean up its resources before it is deleted. We perform the cleanup in a custom method: *destroy( )*. The *destroy( )* method takes no parameters and must be invoked before an *ImageViewer* instance is deleted. The source code for *destroy( )* is simple but also critical and imperative. It removes the *ImageViewer* instance from the imageLoader's listener list and deletes the hierarchy of movie clips that display the image on screen (thus halting any load in progress):

```
public function destroy ():Void {
  // Cancel load event notifications
  imageLoader.removeListener(this);
  // Remove movie clips from Stage (removing container_mc removes subclips)
  container_mc.removeMovieClip();
}
```

Now, to delete any *ImageViewer* instance, we first invoke *destroy()*, as follows:

```
// Clean up the instance's resources
viewer.destroy();
// Delete the instance
delete viewer;
```

Incidentally, the name "destroy" is arbitrary. We could have synonymously used "die," "kill," or "remove" with the same effect.

Finally, it's worth noting that the imageLoader listener list issue is not a particularly unique situation. Any time an object is registered as a listener of another object, it must be unregistered before being deleted. Example 5-7 shows the danger of not unregistering an object before deleting it.

Example 5-7. A lost listener

```
var obj:Object = new Object( );
obj.onMouseDown = function ( ):Void {
  trace("The mouse was pressed.");
}
Mouse.addListener(obj);
delete obj;
```

Try the following:

1. Place the Example 5-7 code on frame 1 of a movie.

2. Run the movie in Test Movie mode (Control → Test Movie).

3. Click the Stage.

You should see "The mouse was pressed." appear in the Output panel, even though the object obj was deleted! The reference to the object in the variable obj may have been deleted, but another reference continues to exist in the *Mouse* object's list of listener objects. To safely delete the object obj, first unregister it as a *Mouse* listener, as follows:

```
Mouse.removeListener(obj);
delete obj;
```

 This section discussed one specific case in which an object reference might inadvertently persist after deleting an instance of a class. Failure to free up resources results in memory waste, which over time could hinder performance or cause an application to fail. When you write a class, you should include a cleanup routine that a programmer can call before deleting an instance. Think carefully about which resources need to be freed. Don't simply avoid deleting instances as a way to avoid orphaning resources. You should delete instances when they are no longer needed and make sure that you free all resources before doing so. Remember: anything your code creates, it should also eventually destroy.

The Final ImageViewer Code

Example 5-8 shows the final code for version 3 of the *ImageViewer* class. Update your code in *ImageViewer.as* to match the example. For usage instructions, refer to the earlier section "Using ImageViewer (Take 2)" (nothing was added to the class's public API between version 2 and version 3, so its use has not changed). If you have any trouble getting things running properly, you can download finished source files for all three versions of the *ImageViewer* example from *http://moock.org/eas2/ examples.*

 The download progress for a loading image will not display when the image is loaded off a local hard disk. To test your *imageViewer.swf*, be sure to post your images to a web server and play the movie in a web browser.

We'll return to the *ImageViewer* class again in Chapter 7.

Example 5-8 uses the JavaDoc commenting style to document the class's methods and constructor function. In Java, when comments are formatted according to Java-Doc conventions, automatic HTML documentation can be generated from a class source file. Unfortunately, at the time of this writing, Flash does not support Java-Doc directly, but a third-party tool or Flash itself could conceivably add support in the future. Either way, the JavaDoc style is a common, easy-to-follow convention that can greatly improve source code readability. For reference, the JavaDoc conventions used in Example 5-8 are:

@author
   The author(s) of the class

@version
   The version of the class

@param
   A method or constructor parameter name and purpose

For more information on JavaDoc, see:

> *http://java.sun.com/j2se/javadoc*
> *http://java.sun.com/j2se/javadoc/writingdoccomments*
> *http://java.sun.com/j2se/1.4.2/docs/tooldocs/windows/javadoc.html#javadoctags*

Example 5-8 shows our *ImageViewer* class to date.

Example 5-8. The ImageViewer class, version 3

```
/**
 * ImageViewer, Version 3.
 * An on-screen rectangular region for displaying a loaded image.
 * Updates at: http://moock.org/eas2/examples/
 *
 * @author: Colin Moock
 * @version: 3.0.0
 */
class ImageViewer {
  // The movie clip that will contain all ImageViewer assets
  private var container_mc:MovieClip;
```

Example 5-8. The ImageViewer class, version 3 (continued)

```
// The movie clip to which container_mc will be attached
private var target_mc:MovieClip;

// Depths for visual assets
private var containerDepth:Number;
private static var imageDepth:Number = 0;
private static var maskDepth:Number = 1;
private static var borderDepth:Number = 2;
private static var statusDepth:Number = 3;

// The thickness of the border around the image
private var borderThickness:Number;
// The color of the border around the image
private var borderColor:Number;

// The MovieClipLoader instance used to load the image
private var imageLoader:MovieClipLoader;

/**
 * ImageViewer Constructor
 *
 * @param    target           The movie clip to which the
 *                            ImageViewer will be attached.
 * @param    depth            The depth in target on which to
 *                             attach the viewer.
 * @param    x                The horizontal position of the viewer.
 * @param    y                The vertical position of the viewer.
 * @param    w                The width of the viewer, in pixels.
 * @param    h                The height of the viewer, in pixels.
 * @param    borderThickness  The thickness of the image border.
 * @param    borderColor      The color of the image border.
 *
 */
public function ImageViewer (target:MovieClip,
                             depth:Number,
                             x:Number,
                             y:Number,
                             w:Number,
                             h:Number,
                             borderThickness:Number,
                             borderColor:Number) {
  // Assign property values
  target_mc = target;
  containerDepth = depth;
  this.borderThickness = borderThickness;
  this.borderColor = borderColor;
  imageLoader = new MovieClipLoader();

  // Register this instance to receive events
  // from the imageLoader instance
  imageLoader.addListener(this);
```

Example 5-8. The ImageViewer class, version 3 (continued)

```
    // Set up the visual assets for this ImageViewer
    buildViewer(x, y, w, h);
  }

  /**
   * Creates the on-screen assets for this ImageViewer.
   * The movie clip hierarchy is:
   *  [d]: container_mc
   *         2: border_mc
   *         1: mask_mc (masks image_mc)
   *         0: image_mc
   * where [d] is the user-supplied depth passed to the constructor.
   *
   * @param   x   The horizontal position of the viewer.
   * @param   y   The vertical position of the viewer.
   * @param   w   The width of the viewer, in pixels.
   * @param   h   The height of the viewer, in pixels.
   */
  private function buildViewer (x:Number,
                                y:Number,
                                w:Number,
                                h:Number):Void {
    // Create the clips to hold the image, mask, and border
    createMainContainer(x, y);
    createImageClip();
    createImageClipMask(w, h);
    createBorder(w, h);
  }

  /**
   * Creates a movie clip, container_mc, to contain
   * the ImageViewer visual assets.
   *
   * @param   x   The horizontal position of the
   *             container_mc movie clip.
   * @param   y   The vertical position of the
   *             container_mc movie clip.
   */
  private function createMainContainer (x:Number, y:Number):Void {
    container_mc = target_mc.createEmptyMovieClip(
                                    "container_mc" + containerDepth,
                                    containerDepth);
    container_mc._x = x;
    container_mc._y = y;
  }

  /**
   * Creates the clip into which the image is actually loaded
   */
  private function createImageClip ():Void {
    container_mc.createEmptyMovieClip("image_mc", imageDepth);
  }
```

Example 5-8. The ImageViewer class, version 3 (continued)

```
/**
 * Creates the mask over the image. Note that this method does
 * not actually apply the mask to the image clip because a clip's
 * mask is lost when new content is loaded into it. Hence, the mask
 * is applied from onLoadInit( ).
 *
 * @param   w   The width of the mask, in pixels.
 * @param   h   The height of the mask, in pixels.
 */
private function createImageClipMask (w:Number,
                                      h:Number):Void {
  // Create the mask only if a valid width and height are specified
  if (!(w > 0 && h > 0)) {
    return;
  }

  // In the container, create a clip to act as the mask over the image
  container_mc.createEmptyMovieClip("mask_mc", maskDepth);

  // Draw a rectangle in the mask
  container_mc.mask_mc.moveTo(0, 0);
  container_mc.mask_mc.beginFill(0x0000FF);   // Use blue for debugging
  container_mc.mask_mc.lineTo(w, 0);
  container_mc.mask_mc.lineTo(w, h);
  container_mc.mask_mc.lineTo(0, h);
  container_mc.mask_mc.lineTo(0, 0);
  container_mc.mask_mc.endFill( );

  // Hide the mask (it will still function as a mask when invisible)
  container_mc.mask_mc._visible = false;
}

/**
 * Creates the border around the image.
 *
 * @param   w       The width of the border, in pixels.
 * @param   h       The height of the border, in pixels.
 */
private function createBorder (w:Number,
                               h:Number):Void {
  // Create the border only if a valid width and height are specified.
  if (!(w > 0 && h > 0)) {
    return;
  }

  // In the container, create a clip to hold the border around the image
  container_mc.createEmptyMovieClip("border_mc", borderDepth);

  // Draw a rectangular outline in the border clip, with the
  // specified dimensions and color
  container_mc.border_mc.lineStyle(borderThickness, borderColor);
  container_mc.border_mc.moveTo(0, 0);
```

Example 5-8. The ImageViewer class, version 3 (continued)

```
    container_mc.border_mc.lineTo(w, 0);
    container_mc.border_mc.lineTo(w, h);
    container_mc.border_mc.lineTo(0, h);
    container_mc.border_mc.lineTo(0, 0);
  }

  /**
   * Loads a JPEG file into the image viewer.
   *
   * @param   URL   The local or remote address of the image to load.
   */
  public function loadImage (URL:String):Void {
    imageLoader.loadClip(URL, container_mc.image_mc);

    // Create a load-status text field to show the user load progress
    container_mc.createTextField("loadStatus_txt", statusDepth, 0, 0, 0, 0);
    container_mc.loadStatus_txt.background = true;
    container_mc.loadStatus_txt.border = true;
    container_mc.loadStatus_txt.setNewTextFormat(new TextFormat(
                                        "Arial, Helvetica, _sans",
                                        10, borderColor, false,
                                        false, false, null, null,
                                        "right"));
    container_mc.loadStatus_txt.autoSize = "left";

    // Position the load-status text field
    container_mc.loadStatus_txt._y = 3;
    container_mc.loadStatus_txt._x = 3;

    // Indicate that the image is loading
    container_mc.loadStatus_txt.text = "LOADING";
  }

  /**
   * MovieClipLoader handler. Triggered by imageLoader when data arrives.
   *
   * @param   target        A reference to the movie clip for which
   *                         progress is being reported.
   * @param   bytesLoaded   The number of bytes of target
   *                         that have loaded so far.
   * @param   bytesTotal    The total size of target, in bytes.
   */
  public function onLoadProgress (target:MovieClip,
                                  bytesLoaded:Number,
                                  bytesTotal:Number):Void {
    container_mc.loadStatus_txt.text = "LOADING: "
        + Math.floor(bytesLoaded / 1024)
        + "/" + Math.floor(bytesTotal / 1024) + " KB";
  }

  /**
   * MovieClipLoader handler. Triggered by imageLoader when loading is done.
   *
```

Example 5-8. The ImageViewer class, version 3 (continued)

```
  * @param    target    A reference to the movie clip for which
  *                      loading has finished.
  */
 public function onLoadInit (target:MovieClip):Void {
   // Remove the loading message
   container_mc.loadStatus_txt.removeTextField();

   // Apply the mask to the loaded image
   container_mc.image_mc.setMask(container_mc.mask_mc);
 }

/**
 * MovieClipLoader handler. Triggered by imageLoader when loading fails.
 *
 *
 * @param    target    A reference to the movie clip for which
 *                      loading failed.
 * @param    errorCode    A string stating the cause of the load failure.
 */
 public function onLoadError (target:MovieClip, errorCode:String):Void {
   if (errorCode == "URLNotFound") {
     container_mc.loadStatus_txt.text = "ERROR: File not found.";
   } else if (errorCode == "LoadNeverCompleted") {
     container_mc.loadStatus_txt.text = "ERROR: Load failed.";
   } else {
     // Catch-all to handle possible future error codes
     container_mc.loadStatus_txt.text = "Load error: " + errorCode;
   }
 }

/**
 * Must be called before the ImageViewer instance is deleted.
 * Gives the instance a chance to destroy any resources it has created.
 */
 public function destroy ():Void {
   // Cancel load event notifications
   imageLoader.removeListener(this);
   // Remove movie clips from the Stage
   container_mc.removeMovieClip();
 }
}
```

Back to the Classroom

It was great to get our hands dirty in this chapter. We really started to see how an application (or at least part of an application) can be conceived and realized with OOP. Now it's time to return to some theory. In the next chapter, we'll learn how to set up an *inheritance* relationship, one kind of relationship between two or more classes. Then we'll get back to the hands-on stuff in Chapter 7.

CHAPTER 6
Inheritance

In OOP, inheritance is a formal relationship between two or more classes, wherein one class borrows (or *inherits*) the property and method definitions of another class. In the practical, technical sense, inheritance simply lets one class make use of the code in another class.

But the term *inheritance* implies much more than code reuse. Inheritance is as much an intellectual tool as it is a technical tool. It lets programmers conceptualize a group of classes in hierarchical terms. In biology, inheritance is a genetic process through which one living creature passes on traits to another. You are said to have inherited your mother's eyes or your father's nose, even though you don't look exactly like either of your parents. In OOP, inheritance has a similar connotation. It lets a class look and feel in many ways like another class, while adding its own unique features.

We'll consider the benefits of, and alternatives to, inheritance near the end of this chapter, under "The Theory of Inheritance." But first, we need to study the syntax and general use of inheritance.

A Primer on Inheritance

Let's consider a very simple, abstract example to get a feel for how inheritance works (we'll get into practical applications once we cover the basic syntax). Here's a class named *A*, with a single method, *x( )*, and a single property, p:

```
class A {
  public var p:Number = 10;

  public function x ():Void {
    trace("Method x() was called.");
  }
}
```

As usual, we can create an instance of class *A*, invoke method *x( )*, and access property p like this:

```
var aInstance:A = new A( );
aInstance.x( );      // Displays: Method x( ) was called.
trace(aInstance.p);  // Displays: 10
```

Nothing new so far. Now let's add a second class, *B*, that inherits method *x( )* and property p from class *A*. To set up the inheritance relationship between *A* and *B*, we use the *extends* keyword to indicate that class *B* inherits class *A*'s method and property definitions:

```
class B extends A {
  // No methods or properties defined.
}
```

ActionScript 1.0 offered two ways to establish inheritance. Here's the official technique:

```
function Class A ( ) { ... }
function Class B ( ) { ... }
ClassB.prototype = new Class A( );
```

Here's the undocumented technique:

```
function Class A ( ) { ... }
function Class B ( ) { ... }
ClassB.prototype.__proto__ = ClassA.prototype;
```

To learn the difference between these approaches, consult Chapter 12 of *ActionScript for Flash MX: The Definitive Guide* (O'Reilly), which covers the topic in depth.

Don't confuse extending a class with augmenting or enhancing a class's features. When class B extends class A, no changes whatsoever are made to class A. Contrast this with a case in which we add a new method to a dynamic class such as *MovieClip*. The latter is simply enhancing an existing class and has nothing to do with inheritance.

Now here's the neat part about extending a class. Because class *B* extends (inherits from) class *A*, instances of *B* can automatically use the method *x( )* and the property p (even though class *B* does not define that method or property directly):

```
var bInstance:B = new B( );
bInstance.x( );      // Displays: Method x( ) was called.
trace(bInstance.p);  // Displays: 10
```

When bInstance.x( ) is invoked, the interpreter checks class *B* for a method named *x( )*. The interpreter does not find method *x( )* defined in class *B*; so it checks *B*'s *superclass* (i.e., the class that *B* extends), class *A*, for the method. There, the interpreter finds *x( )* and invokes it on bInstance.

Notice that class *B* does not define any methods or properties of its own. In practice, there isn't much point in defining a class that doesn't add anything to the class it extends; therefore, doing so is usually discouraged. Normally, class *B* would define its own methods and/or properties in addition to inheriting *A*'s methods and properties. That is, a subclass is really a superset of the features available in its superclass (the subclass has everything available in the superclass and more). Accordingly, here is a more realistic version of class *B*, which inherits method *x( )* and property p from class *A*, and also defines its own method, *y( )*:

```
class B extends A {
  public function y ():Void {
    trace("Method y() was called.");
  }
}
```

Now instances of *B* can use all the methods and properties of both *B* and its superclass, *A*:

```
var bInstance:B = new B();
// Invoke inherited method, defined by class A.
bInstance.x();         // Displays: Method x() was called.
// Invoke method defined by class B.
bInstance.y();         // Displays: Method y() was called.
// Access inherited property.
trace(bInstance.p);  // Displays: 10
```

Thus, class *B* is said to *specialize* class *A*. It uses the features of class *A* as a base on which to build, adding its own features or even—as we'll see later—overriding *A*'s features with versions modified for its own needs. Accordingly, in an inheritance relationship between two classes, the extended class (in our case, class *A*) is called the *base class*, and the class that does the extending (in our case, class *B*) is called the *derived class*. However, the terms "base class" and "derived class" have several synonyms, including *superclass* and *subclass*, *parent* and *child*, and *type* and *subtype*.

Inheritance can (and often does) involve many more than two classes. For example, even though class *B* inherits from class *A*, class *B* can act as a base class for another class. The following code shows a third class, *C*, that extends class *B* and also defines a new method, *z( )*. Class *C* can use all the methods and properties defined by itself, its superclass (*B*), or its superclass's superclass (*A*):

```
class C extends B {
  public function z ():Void {
    trace("Method z() was called.");
  }
}
```

```
// Usage:
var cInstance:C = new C();
// Invoke method inherited from A.
cInstance.x();  // Displays: Method x() was called.
// Invoke method inherited from B.
cInstance.y();  // Displays: Method y() was called.
// Invoke method defined by C.
cInstance.z();  // Displays: Method z() was called.
// Access property inherited from A.
trace(cInstance.p);  // Displays: 10
```

Furthermore, a single superclass can have any number of subclasses (however, a superclass has no way of knowing which subclasses extend it). The following code adds a fourth class, *D*, to our example. Like class *B*, class *D* inherits directly from

class *A*. Class *D* can use the methods and properties defined by itself and by its
superclass, *A*.

```
class D extends A {
  public function w ():Void {
    trace("Method w() was called.");
  }
}
```

With four classes now in our example, we've built up what's known as an *inheritance
tree* or *class hierarchy*. Figure 6-1 shows that hierarchy visually. Note that a single
subclass can't have more than one direct superclass, but its superclass can have a
superclass, allowing the hierarchy to continue ad nauseum.

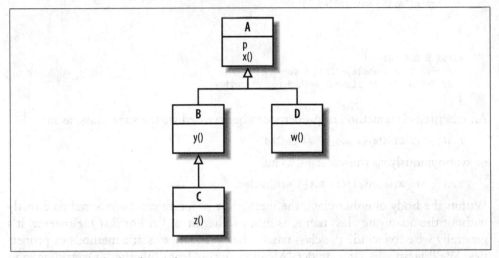

Figure 6-1. Example class hierarchy

All OOP applications can be depicted with a class diagram such as the one shown in
Figure 6-1. In fact, many developers start their work by creating a class diagram
before moving to code. Class diagrams can be informal, drawn according to a developer's personal iconography, or formal, drawn according to a diagramming specification such as Unified Modeling Language (UML) (see *http://www.uml.org*).

 gModeler, an online Flash application written by Grant Skinner, creates class diagrams from which code and documentation can be
exported. See *http://www.gmodeler.com*.

Just as we design our own class hierarchies for our OOP applications, ActionScript
also organizes its built-in classes according to a hierarchy. In fact, every class in
ActionScript (both built-in and custom) inherits directly or indirectly from the root
of the built-in hierarchy: *Object*. The *Object* class defines some very basic methods

that all classes can use. For example, any class can use the *Object.toString( )* method, which returns a string representation of an object.

Class Method and Class Property Inheritance

A subclass inherits its superclass's *instance* methods and properties, plus its *class* methods and properties (i.e., those defined with the *static* attribute). For example, in the following code, we define a static method, *s( )*, in the class *A*. The method *s( )* is inherited by *A*'s subclass, *B*.

```
class A {
  public static function s ():Void {
    trace("A.s() was called.");
  }
}

class B extends A {
  // For this example, class B does not
  // define any of its own methods or properties.
}
```

An inherited class method or property can be accessed via the superclass, as in:

```
A.s();  // Displays: A.s() was called.
```

or synonymously via the subclass, as in:

```
B.s();  // Also displays: A.s() was called.
```

Within the body of either class, the method or property can be referred to directly without the qualifying class name, as in *s( )* rather than *A.s( )* or *B.s( )*. However, it's generally wise to include the class name when referring to static methods or properties. We'll learn why later, under "Member Access from Inherited, Overriding, and Overridden Instance Methods."

 The class methods and properties of some built-in classes (e.g., *Math*) are not inherited by their subclasses. The cause and workaround for this problem are discussed later in this chapter under "Subclassing Built-in Classes."

Note that a bug in ActionScript 2.0 prevents access to inherited static properties before the superclass that defines the property is used in a script. For details, see "Subclasses and class properties" in Chapter 4.

Subclasses as Subtypes

Recall from Chapter 3 that every class effectively defines a custom datatype. Correspondingly, a subclass is considered a *subtype* of its superclass. But the term *"subtype"* is not just figurative; it means literally that an instance of the subtype can

---

be used anywhere its superclass's type is expected. For example, if we create a variable, aInstance, whose type is class *A*, as follows:

```
var aInstance:A;
```

we can then legally assign that variable an instance of any subclass of class *A*:

```
aInstance = new B( );  // No problem.
```

 A variable typed to a given class can legally store instances of any subclasses of that class.

The preceding assignment works because the compiler knows that any instance of class *B* has (through inheritance) all the methods and properties defined by class *A*. However, the reverse is not true. We cannot assign an instance of *A* to a variable whose datatype is *B*:

```
var bInstance:B = new A( );  // Error.
```

That assignment does not work because the compiler cannot guarantee that an instance of class *A* will have the methods and properties defined by class *B*. Hence, the compiler generates a type mismatch error:

```
Type mismatch in assignment statement. Found A where B is required.
```

We'll return to this topic later in this chapter when we study polymorphism. For a full discussion of type mismatches, again see Chapter 3.

An OOP Chat Example

Now that we're familiar with the basic syntax of inheritance, let's take a high-level look at how inheritance can be used in a real application. Consider a chat application that defines a class, *ChatRoom*, which handles communication among a group of users. The *ChatRoom* class defines methods for displaying and sending chat messages and for managing a list of users in the room. Table 6-1 shows the *ChatRoom* class's property and methods.

Table 6-1. ChatRoom class's property and methods

Method or property name	Purpose
userList	Property storing a reference to the on-screen *List* component that displays users in the room.
displayMessage( )	Displays an incoming user message in a text field.
sendMessage( )	Sends an outgoing message to other users.
onAddUser( )	Adds the new user to the userList. Invoked when a user joins the room.
onRemoveUser( )	Removes the departed user from the userList. Invoked when a user leaves the room.
onUserChangeName( )	Changes the user's name in the userList. Invoked when a user's name changes.

Now suppose that our chat application has multiple room types: some rooms are regular chats and some are "avatar chats." In the avatar chat rooms, each user in the room is represented by a little cartoon character (an "avatar") that can be positioned on screen. When a user in an avatar chat room sends a message to other users, other users see the message both in the normal chat text field and in a cartoon speech bubble next to the sender's avatar. (If you've never seen an avatar chat before, you'll find one example at *http://moock.org/unity/uchatavatar*.)

To implement our new avatar chat room, we could (but never should!) copy all of the code from *ChatRoom* into a new class, *AvatarChatRoom*, and then add the avatar-specific features to that new class. Of course, from then on, any time the code in *ChatRoom* changed, we'd have to copy the changes to *AvatarChatRoom* by hand. Across an entire application, that kind of copy-and-paste code maintenance becomes unmanageable in a hurry and should be avoided at all costs. Instead of copying the code from *ChatRoom* to *AvatarChatRoom*, we simply make *AvatarChatRoom* a subclass of *ChatRoom*. After all, a regular chat room already does most of what an avatar chat room does; the avatar chat room just has the extra responsibility of managing the cartoon representation of each user.

The *AvatarChatRoom* class uses some of the *ChatRoom* class's methods as-is, just as our simple class *B* used class *A*'s *x( )* method. For example, to send a message, *AvatarChatRoom* uses *ChatRoom.sendMessage( )* directly. For other tasks (e.g., positioning avatars), the *AvatarChatRoom* defines its own methods, just as class *B* added the method *y( )*. But for still other tasks (e.g., displaying a message), the *AvatarChatRoom* needs behavior that differs somewhat from an existing *ChatRoom* method. For example, when a user's message is received, the *AvatarChatRoom* class must show the message in a text bubble next to the user's avatar (in addition to displaying it in the "incoming messages" text field, as does the *ChatRoom* class). That means the *AvatarChatRoom* class must change what happens when the *displayMessage( )* method executes. Known as *overriding*, changing the behavior of a method is the topic of the next section in this chapter.

Table 6-2 shows the *AvatarChatRoom*'s properties and methods, indicating which members are inherited, which are new, and which are overridden. For another prolonged inheritance example, see Chapter 7.

Table 6-2. AvatarChatRoom class's methods and properties

Method or property name	Inheritance relationship	Original behavior	Behavior added by *AvatarChatRoom* class
userList	Inherited property	Stores a reference to the on-screen *List* component that displays users in the room	None
avatars	Property added by subclass	Not applicable	Stores a list of *Avatar* instances displayed on screen

Table 6-2. AvatarChatRoom class's methods and properties (continued)

Method or property name	Inheritance relationship	Original behavior	Behavior added by *AvatarChatRoom* class
displayMessage( )	Overridden method	Displays an incoming user message in a text field	Also displays a message bubble next to the user's avatar
sendMessage( )	Inherited method	Sends an outgoing message to other users	None
onAddUser( )	Overridden method	Adds the new user to the userList	Also displays a new avatar on the screen
onRemoveUser( )	Overridden method	Removes the departed user from the userList	Also removes the user's avatar on the screen
onUserChangeName( )	Overridden method	Changes the user's name in the userList	Also changes the name displayed under an avatar
onUserChangePosition( )	Method added by subclass	Not applicable	Positions the user's avatar on screen

Example 6-1 shows the skeletal code for the *ChatRoom* and *AvatarChatRoom* classes. The class properties and implementation details of each class's methods are omitted, allowing us to focus our attention directly on the inheritance structure. In place of method implementations, we use the *trace( )* function to display a message describing the method's behavior in the Output panel.

Example 6-1. An inheritance example using ChatRoom and AvatarChatRoom

```
// This code must be placed in an external file named ChatRoom.as
class ChatRoom {
  // mx.controls is the package path for the built-in List component.
  // See Chapter 9 for details on packages.
  private var userList:mx.controls.List;

  // Declare the five public methods of the ChatRoom class.
  public function displayMessage (userID:String, msg:String):Void {
    trace("Displaying chat message in chat text field.");
  }

  public function sendMessage (msg:String):Void {
    trace("Sending chat message.");
  }

  public function onAddUser (userID:String):Void {
    trace("Adding user to userList.");
  }

  public function onRemoveUser (userID:String):Void {
    trace("Removing user from userList.");
  }

  public function onUserChangeName (userID:String, newName:String):Void {
    trace("Changing name in userList.");
```

```
  }
}
// This code must be placed in an external file named AvatarChatRoom.as
class AvatarChatRoom extends ChatRoom {
  private var avatars:Array;

  // Override four of the methods of the ChatRoom class,
  // excluding sendMessage( ).
  public function displayMessage (userID:String, msg:String):Void {
    // AvatarRoom.displayMessage( ) also invokes ChatRoom.displayMessage( ).
    super.displayMessage(userID, msg);
    trace("Displaying message in avatar text bubble.");
  }

  public function onAddUser (userID:String):Void {
    // AvatarRoom.onAddUser( ) also invokes ChatRoom.onAddUser( ).
    super.onAddUser(userID);
    trace("Creating avatar for new user.");
  }

  public function onRemoveUser (userID:String):Void {
    // AvatarRoom.onRemoveUser( ) also invokes ChatRoom.onRemoveUser( ).
    super.onRemoveUser(userID)
    trace("Removing avatar for user.");
  }

  public function onUserChangeName (userID:String, newName:String):Void {
    // AvatarRoom.onUserChangeName( ) also
    // invokes ChatRoom.onUserChangeName( ).
    super.onUserChangeName(userID, newName);
    trace("Changing name on avatar.");
  }

  // Declare a new method not present in the ChatRoom class.
  public function onUserChangePosition (userID:String,
                                        newX:Number, newY:Number):Void {
    trace("Repositioning avatar.");
  }
}
```

You should notice that the code in Example 6-1 declares five methods of the *ChatRoom* class. The *AvatarChatRoom* class likewise declares five methods, four of which override methods in the *ChatRoom* class plus *onUserChangePosition( )*, which is new. Let's take a closer look at overriding, its use and implications.

Overriding Methods and Properties

In our study of inheritance so far, we've covered *reuse*, in which a subclass uses its superclass's methods and properties, and *extension*, in which a subclass adds its own methods and properties. We'll now turn to *redefinition*, in which a subclass provides an alternative version of a method or property in its superclass. (Bear in mind that reuse, extension, and redefinition are not mutually exclusive. A subclass might employ all three techniques in regard to the superclass's members.) Redefinition lets us customize an existing class for a specific purpose by augmenting, constraining, or even nullifying one or more of its original behaviors. Redefining a method or property is known technically as *overriding* that method or property.

ActionScript allows any of a class's members (that is, static properties, instance properties, static methods, and instance methods) to be redefined. We'll take a look at the most typical kind of redefinition first: overriding instance methods.

Overriding Instance Methods

To override a superclass's instance method, we simply supply an instance method definition of the same name in the subclass. For example, in the following code, in which B is a subclass of A, the method $B.x()$ overrides the method $A.x()$:

```
class A {
  // Declare an instance method in the superclass
  public function x ():Void {
    trace("A.x() was called.");
  }
}

// Class B is a subclass of class A
class B extends A {
  // Override the superclass's method of the same name
  public function x ():Void {
    trace("B.x() was called.");
  }
}
```

When $x()$ is invoked on an instance of class A, the interpreter uses A's definition of the method. But when $x()$ is invoked on an instance of class B, the interpreter uses B's definition of the method instead of class A's definition:

```
var aInstance:A = new A();
aInstance.x();  // Displays: A.x() was called.

var bInstance:B = new B();
bInstance.x();  // Displays: B.x() was called.
```

Let's consider a more applied example. Suppose we're building a geometry simulation that depicts rectangles and squares. To handle the rectangles, we create a *Rectangle* class, as follows:

```
// This code must be placed in an external file named Rectangle.as
class Rectangle {
  private var w:Number = 0;
  private var h:Number = 0;
```

```
  public function setSize (newW:Number, newH:Number):Void {
    w = newW;
    h = newH;
  }

  public function getArea ():Number {
    return w * h;
  }
}
```

To handle squares, we could create a completely unrelated *Square* class. But a square is really just a rectangle with sides of equal width and height. To exploit that similarity, we'll create a *Square* class that extends *Rectangle* but alters the *setSize( )* method to prevent w and h from being set unless newW equals newH. The constraint applies only to squares, not to rectangles in general, so it doesn't belong in the *Rectangle* class.

Here's the *Square* class, showing the overridden *setSize( )* method:

```
// This code must be placed in an external file named Square.as
class Square extends Rectangle {
  public function setSize (newW:Number, newH:Number):Void {
    // Here's the constraint introduced by the Square class.
    if (newW == newH) {
      w = newW;
      h = newH;
    }
  }
}
```

A real-world version of *Square.setSize( )* might accept only one argument for the side length, instead of accepting two potentially different parameters. This eliminates the need to check whether the sides are equal (although we still want to check that the side length is a positive number). For example:

```
public function setSize (sideLength:Number):Void {
  if (sideLength > 0) {
    w = sideLength;
    h = sideLength;
  }
}
```

However, our current focus is adding constraints to a method without changing the method's signature, so we'll stick with our newW and newH parameters for the sake of this example.

When *setSize( )* is invoked on a *Square* or *Rectangle* instance, the interpreter uses the version of the method that matches the actual class of the instance.

When an instance method is invoked on an object, the interpreter first searches for the instance method defined on the class used to instantiate the object.

For example, in the following code, we invoke *setSize( )* on a *Rectangle* instance. The interpreter knows that the instance's class is *Rectangle*, so it invokes *Rectangle. setSize( )*:

```
var r:Rectangle = new Rectangle();
r.setSize(4,5);
trace (r.getArea());  // Displays: 20
```

By contrast, in the following code, we invoke *setSize( )* on a *Square* instance. This time the interpreter knows that the instance's class is *Square*, so it invokes *Square. setSize( )*, not *Rectangle.setSize( )*:

```
var s:Square = new Square();
s.setSize(4,5);
trace (s.getArea());  // Displays: 0 (The setSize() method prevented the
                      //            illegal property assignment.)
```

In the preceding code, the output of *s.getArea( )*—0—indicates that values of w and h were not set properly by the call to *s.setSize( )*; the *Square.setSize( )* method sets w and h only when newW and newH are equal.

But what if the declared datatype doesn't match the type of instance stored in a variable?

 Even if the datatype of s is declared as *Rectangle*, because it stores a *Square* instance, the interpreter uses the version of the method from the instance's actual class (namely *Square*).

Consider this example:

```
// Datatype is declared as Rectangle...
var s:Rectangle = new Square();
s.setSize(4,5);
// ...but Square.setSize() was still used!
trace (s.getArea());  // Displays: 0
```

Similarly, even if the instance s were cast to the *Rectangle* class, the interpreter would still use the version of the method from the instance's actual class (which, again, is *Square*):

```
var s:Square = new Square();
// Instance s is cast to Rectangle.
Rectangle(s).setSize(4,5);
// ...but Square.setSize() was still used.
trace (s.getArea());  // Displays: 0
```

In all cases, instance method calls on an object remain true to that object's actual class!

Notice also that a cast does not change the class of the object. A cast only instructs the compiler and interpreter to treat an object as though it were of a specified type. For more information on casting, see "Casting" in Chapter 3.

Invoking an Overridden Instance Method

When a subclass overrides an instance method, the superclass's version of the method is not lost. It remains accessible to instances of the subclass via the *super* operator, which can invoke an overridden method as follows:

```
super.methodName(arg1, arg2, ...argn);
```

where *methodName* is the name of the overridden method to invoke, and *arg1*, *arg2*, *... argn* are the arguments to pass to that method. (We'll learn more about other uses of *super* later in this chapter.)

Let's see how to use *super* to invoke a method of the superclass that is overridden. So far, our *Square.setSize( )* method needlessly duplicates the code in the *Rectangle. setSize( )* method. The *Rectangle* version is:

```
public function setSize (newW:Number, newH:Number):Void {
  w = newW;
  h = newH;
}
```

The *Square* version of *setSize( )* merely adds an *if* statement:

```
public function setSize (newW:Number, newH:Number):Void {
  if (newW == newH) {
    w = newW;
    h = newH;
  }
}
```

To avoid the duplication of setting w and h in both methods, we can use *super*, as shown in this revised version of *Square.setSize( )*:

```
public function setSize (newW:Number, newH:Number):Void {
  if (newW == newH) {
    // Invoke the superclass's setSize() method, in this case
    // Rectangle.setSize(), on the current instance.
    super.setSize(newW, newH);
  }
}
```

The revised *Square.setSize( )* method checks if newW and newH are equal; if they are, it invokes *Rectangle.setSize( )* on the current instance. The *Rectangle.setSize( )* method takes care of setting w and h.

The *setSize( )* method example shows how a subclass can override a method to constrain its behavior. A subclass can also override a method to augment its behavior. For example, we might create *ScreenRectangle*, a subclass of *Rectangle* that draws a rectangle to the screen. The subclass in the following code adds a *draw( )* method and augments *setSize( )*. The *ScreenRectangle.setSize( )* method retains the behavior of the overridden *Rectangle.setSize( )* but adds a call to *draw( )*, so the rectangle changes size on screen whenever *setSize()* is invoked. Here's the code:

```
class ScreenRectangle extends Rectangle {
```

```
  public function setSize (newW:Number, newH:Number):Void {
    // Call Rectangle.setSize().
    super.setSize(newW, newH);

    // Now render the rectangle on screen.
    draw();
  }

  public function draw ():Void {
    // Screen-rendering code goes here.
    // For example rendering code, see Example 4-6.
  }
}
```

Finally, overriding can be used to nullify the behavior of a method. The technique is straightforward: the subclass's version of the overridden method simply does nothing. For example, the following code shows a subclass named *ReadOnlyRectangle* that disables the *Rectangle.setSize( )* method, preventing an instance from changing size:

```
class ReadOnlyRectangle extends Rectangle {
  // This effectively disables the setSize() method
  // for instances of the ReadOnlyRectangle class.
  public function setSize (newW:Number, newH:Number):Void {
    // Do nothing.
  }
}
```

Nullifying a method is legal but, in most cases, not considered good OOP practice. Generally speaking, every subclass should support the methods of its superclass(es). That way, external code can safely use the superclass's methods on instances of the subclass (as we'll see later, treating unlike objects alike is an important part of *polymorphism*).

Overriding Class Methods

We saw earlier how to override instance methods of a superclass. To override a superclass's class method (i.e., a method declared with the *static* attribute), we simply add a *static* method definition of the same name in the subclass. For example, in the following code, the *static* method *B.m( )* overrides the *static* method *A.m( )*:

```
class A {
  public static function m ():Void {
    trace("A.m() was called.");
  }
}

class B extends A {
  public static function m ():Void {
    trace("B.m() was called.");
  }
}
```

When invoking a class method, whether or not overridden, you should provide the class name as part of the method invocation. For example, to invoke *B*'s version of *m( )*, you should use *B.m( )*, and to invoke *A*'s version of *m( )*, you should use *A.m( )*. For example:

```
A.m();    // Displays: A.m( ) was called
B.m();    // Displays: B.m( ) was called
m( );     // Avoid this unqualified method call
```

In fact, if you are accessing the method from code outside the class, you must include the class name. However, from within the class that defines the method, you can legally refer to the method without the qualifying class name (e.g., *m( )* instead of *B. m( )*). This practice, while legal, is not recommended. We'll learn why under "Member Access from Inherited and Overridden Class Methods" later in this chapter.

You may wonder what happens if you declare a nonstatic method in a subclass in an attempt to overwrite a static method of the same name defined in the superclass. Consider this code example:

```
class A {
  // The static keyword defines a class method
  public static function m ():Void {
    trace("A.m( ) was called.");
  }
}

class B extends A {
  // Note the omission of the static keyword, so this is an instance method
  public function m ():Void {
    trace("B.m( ) was called.");
  }
}
```

The preceding code effectively defines a new instance method, *m( )*, for instances of class *B*, but it has no effect on the class method of the same name defined in class *A*. Therefore, the method the interpreter invokes depends on which object is used in the invocation. For example, in the following code, you might be surprised by the results of invoking *B.m( )*:

```
A.m();    // Displays: A.m( ) was called
B.m( );   // Displays: Error! The property being referenced does
          // not have the static attribute.
```

In the preceding code, because there is no class method (i.e., static method) named *m( )* defined on the class *B*, invoking *B.m( )* actually causes a compile-time error. The *m( )* method in class *B* is declared as an instance method, so it must be invoked on an instance as follows:

```
bInstance:B = new B( );
bInstance.m();   // Displays: B.m( ) was called
```

You wouldn't ordinarily define class methods (i.e., static methods) and instance methods (i.e., nonstatic methods) of the same name. Therefore, in the preceding example, if your invocation of *B.m( )* causes an error, you probably just forgot the *static* attribute when defining the *m( )* method within the *B* class.

Note that the *super* operator cannot be used to invoke a superclass's version of a class method from within the subclass version. The keyword *super* can be used only in instance methods and constructor functions. To access the superclass's version of a class method, reference the superclass in the method invocation, as in:

```
SomeSuperClass.someOverriddenMethod( );
```

Overriding Properties

Just as instance and class methods can be overridden, so can instance and class properties. To override a superclass's property, we add a property definition of the same name in the subclass. For example, in the following code, for instances of class *B*, the instance property B.p overrides the instance property A.p:

```
class A {
  public var p:Number = 10;
}

class B extends A {
  public var p:Number = 15;
}
```

Remember that overriding a property using a subclass declaration has no effect on instances of the superclass. Therefore, all instances of class *A* have an initial value of 10 for the property p. However, because p is overridden in the subclass, all instances of class *B* have an initial value of 15 for the property p:

```
var aInstance:A = new A( );
trace(aInstance.p);  // Displays: 10

var bInstance:B = new B( );
trace(bInstance.p);  // Displays: 15
```

Any kind of property can override any other kind of property. That is, an instance property can override an instance property or a class property; a class property can override a class property or an instance property. However, we're sure to instigate mass confusion if we override an instance property with a class property or vice versa.

 For the sake of code clarity, you should override instance properties with only other instance properties, and override class properties with only other class properties.

The preceding example overrode a superclass's instance property with an instance property in the subclass. Similarly, here's an example of overriding a superclass's class property (declared *static*) with a class property in the subclass:

```
class A {
  // Create a class property, s
  public static var s:Number = 20;
}

class B extends A {
  // Override the class property, s
  public static var s:Number = 25;
}
```

When a class property is overridden, it is not lost and can still be accessed via the superclass. For example:

```
class A {
  public static var s:Number = 20;
}

class B extends A {
  public static var s:Number = 25;

  public function showS () {
    // Show the subclass version of s.
    trace("B.s is: " + B.s);

    // Show the superclass version of s.
    trace("A.s is: " + A.s);
  }
}

// Usage:
var bInstance:B = new B();
bInstance.showS();  // Displays:
                    // B.s is: 25
                    // A.s is: 20
```

Note, however, that the *super* keyword, which we used earlier to access an overridden instance method, cannot be used to reference an overridden class property. For example, if in *B.shows()* we change the statement:

```
trace("A.s is: " + A.s);
```

to:

```
trace("A.s is: " + super.s);
```

the resulting output is:

```
A.s is: undefined
```

The preceding use of *super* causes the following error when Check Syntax (Tools → Check Syntax) is performed on class *B* in Flash MX Professional 2004's script editor:

Unfortunately, due to a bug in Flash MX 2004, the compiler does not generate the same compile-time error when the class is used in a *.fla* file.

Unlike a class property, an instance property that is overridden does not continue to exist independently. Rather, a single instance property with a single value exists for each instance of the overriding subclass. For example, in the following code, class *A* defines a property, p, that is overridden by class *B*. An instance of class *B* maintains a single value for the property p, despite whether p is assigned by methods in the superclass or the subclass.

```
class A {
  public var p:Number;

  public function setTo20 ():Void {
    p = 20;
  }
}

class B extends A {
  public var p:Number;

  public function setTo10 ():Void {
    p = 10;
  }
}

// Usage example:
var bInstance:B = new B();

// Use superclass method to set p.
bInstance.setTo20();
trace(bInstance.p); // Displays: 20

// Use subclass method to set p.
bInstance.setTo10();
trace(bInstance.p); // Displays: 10
```

This single-property-value behavior contrasts with Java, in which the subclass maintains a memory slot both for its own definition of the overridden property and for its superclass's definition. In Java, the equivalent code would output:

```
0
10
```

because, in Java, invoking bInstance.setTo20() would modify the superclass version of the property p, not the subclass version because *setTo20()* is defined in the superclass despite being invoked on a subclass instance. In ActionScript, no such separation exists. Even when *A.setTo20()* is invoked via the keyword *super*, the property affected is still the single property p. The following code demonstrates. It adds a new method, *callSetTo20()* to class *B* (class *A* remains unchanged):

```
class B extends A {
  public var p:Number;

  public function setTo10 ():Void {
    p = 10;
  }

  public function callSetTo20 ():Void {
    super.setTo20();
  }
}

// Usage example:
var bInstance:B = new B();

// Use superclass method to set p.
bInstance.setTo20();
trace(bInstance.p); // Displays: 20

// Use subclass method to set p.
bInstance.setTo10();
trace(bInstance.p); // Displays: 10

// Use superclass method through super to set p.
bInstance.callSetTo20();
trace(bInstance.p); // Displays: 20 (not 10, the previous value)
```

Again, in Java, the last line of the equivalent code would yield 10, not 20, because calling bInstance.callSetTo20( ) sets the superclass's version of the property p, not the subclass's version. Java displays the value of the subclass's version of the property, which would be 10. For comparison, Example 6-2 lists the Java code for classes *A* and *B*.

Example 6-2. Overridden property access in Java

```
public class A {
  public int p;

  public void setTo20 () {
    p = 20;
  }
}

public class B extends A {
  public int p;

  public void setTo10 () {
    p = 10;
  }

  public void callSetTo20 () {
    super.setTo20();
    // Check superclass value for p, after setting it.
```

Example 6-2. Overridden property access in Java (continued)

```
    System.out.println("Superclass version of p is: " + super.p);
  }

  public static void main (String [] args) {
    B b = new B( );
    // This line affects the superclass version of p.
    b.setTo20( );
    // The subclass version is not affected.
    System.out.println("Subclass version of p is: " + b.p);

    // This line affects the subclass version of p.
    b.setTo10( );
    // The subclass version is affected.
    System.out.println("Subclass version of p is: " + b.p);

    // This line affects the superclass version of p.
    b.callSetTo20( );
    // The subclass version is not affected.
    System.out.println("Subclass version of p is: " + b.p);
  }
}

// Output:
Subclass version of p is: 0
Subclass version of p is: 10
Superclass version of p is: 20
Subclass version of p is: 10
```

The super keyword and overridden property access

In ActionScript 2.0, we cannot use *super* to retrieve the value of an overridden instance property because, as we just learned, instance properties that are overridden do not continue to exist independently.

However, strangely enough, if an overridden instance property is initialized in the superclass body (outside of a method or the constructor), then that initial value is permanently accessible via *super*:

```
class A {
  // Initialize the property p to 10.
  public var p:Number = 10;
}

class B extends A {
  public var p:Number = 15;

  public function showP ( ):Void {
    // Show the value of p.
    trace("p is: " + p);

    // Modify the value of p, then show the modified value.
    p = 5;
```

```
        trace("p is: " + p);

        // Show the initial value of p, assigned by
        // the superclass. This will yield 10 even though p has
        // been modified on the current object.
        trace("super.p is: " + super.p);
    }
}

// Usage:
var bInstance:B = new B( );
bInstance.showP( );  // Displays:
                     // p is: 15
                     // p is: 5
                     // super.p is: 10
```

This uncommon *super* behavior is caused by the compiler's automatic conversion of ActionScript 2.0 code to ActionScript 1.0 code (which is a necessary evil guaranteeing that most ActionScript 2.0 code will work in Flash Player 6). The behavior may be changed in future versions of the language. You should, therefore, avoid using it.

Member Access from Inherited, Overriding, and Overridden Instance Methods

We've now seen how to override instance methods, static methods, instance properties, and static properties. We've also seen how to invoke overridden instance methods. With all these overridden methods and properties afoot, we're forced to consider some tricky scope questions. For example, from within an instance method that overrides another instance method, what properties and methods are accessible? What about from within the overridden version of the method? What if the properties and methods being accessed are, themselves, overridden?

Before we can answer these questions, we need a short lesson on how the compiler resolves *unqualified member references*. To *qualify* a reference is to include explicitly the object or class to which the property or method pertains.

Therefore, an unqualified member reference is any mention of a property or method that does not explicitly include the name of an object or class. For example, this is an unqualified reference to the method *x( )*:

```
x( )
```

By contrast, this reference to *x( )* is qualified because it specifies the object on which *x( )* should be invoked (this, the current object):

```
this.x( )
```

Here is an unqualified reference to the property p:

```
p
```

By contrast, this reference to the property p is qualified because it specifies the class on which p is defined (*A*):

```
A.p
```

 When a class is compiled, if the compiler encounters an unqualified member reference, it deduces the object or class to which the member pertains and permanently adds that object or class to the reference.

That is, at compile time, all unqualified member references are permanently converted to qualified member references of the form:

```
objectName.memberName
```

or

```
ClassName.memberName
```

If you don't specify an object or class when referring to a member in your source code, the compiler will supply the object or class it thinks is correct. The compiler chooses the "correct" object or class based on the name of the member and the compile-time context in which the member reference occurs.

For example, in the following class, *A*, we define one instance property (instanceProp) and one class property (classProp). We make unqualified references to those properties in the methods *getClassProp( )* and *getInstanceProp( )*:

```
class A {
  public static var classProp:Number = 0;
  public var instanceProp:Number = 1;

  public function getClassProp ():Number {
    return classProp;
  }

  public function getInstanceProp ():Number {
    return instanceProp;
  }
}
```

After compilation, the interpreter effectively treats the code as follows (note the addition of A. and this., shown in bold):

```
class A {
  public static var classProp:Number = 0;
  public var instanceProp:Number = 1;

  public function getClassProp ():Number {
    return A.classProp;
  }

  public function getInstanceProp ():Number {
    return this.instanceProp;
```

```
            }
        }
```

The compiler knows that classProp should be treated as A.classProp because the classProp property is defined as *static*. Likewise, the compiler knows that instanceProp should be treated as this.instanceProp because the instanceProp property has no *static* attribute, so it must be an instance property accessed via the current object (i.e., this).

It's not uncommon or even bad form to use unqualified member references. Most of the time, the compiler's automatic resolution of those references is intuitive. However, as we'll see next, when members are accessed from overridden and inherited methods, the compiler's behavior is less obvious. Therefore, to avoid adding confusion to an already complex situation, it's wise to fully qualify all member references when using inherited or overridden methods.

Now that we understand how the compiler resolves unqualified member references, let's consider the three possible member access scenarios:

• Member access from an inherited instance method
• Member access from an overriding instance method
• Member access from an overridden instance method invoked via *super*

In the preceding scenarios, we'll explore what happens when each of the following members are accessed:

• An instance method defined in the subclass
• An inherited instance method
• An overridden instance method
• An instance property defined by the subclass
• An inherited instance property
• An overridden instance property
• A class property defined by the subclass
• An inherited class property
• An overridden class property
• A class method defined by the subclass
• An inherited class method
• An overridden class method

We'll also point out tricky cases in which unqualified member resolution can lead to potentially surprising results. You don't need to memorize all the behaviors now, but it is a good idea to skim the next pages to better understand scope issues. If you learn to recognize whether you are, say, accessing an inherited class property from an overridden class method, you can refer back to this chapter for the necessary details on scope resolution.

Member access from an inherited instance method

As we learned earlier, an inherited instance method is an instance method defined in the superclass but used by the subclass. For example, in the following code, class *B* inherits the method *methOfA( )* from class *A*:

```
class A {
  public function methOfA ():Void {
  }
}
class B extends A {
}
```

An instance of *B* can invoke *methOfA( )* as follows:

```
var bInstance:B = new B();
bInstance.methOfA();
```

Table 6-3 describes what happens when bInstance invokes *methOfA( )* and *methOfA( )* accesses various methods and properties.

Table 6-3. Member access from an inherited instance method

Member accessed	Example	Notes

Instance method of subclass	`class A {`
	`  public function methOfA():Void {`
	`    methOfB();  // Error!`
	`  }`
	`}`
	
	`class B extends A {`
	`  public function methOfB():Void {`
	`  }`
	`}`
		Compile-time error. Methods of a superclass can't refer to methods defined only on a subclass, and Class *A* does not define *methOfB( )*, so the reference is illegal.

Inherited instance method (defined in superclass)	`class A {`
	`  public function methOfA():Void {`
	`    // Executes otherMethOfA()`
	`    otherMethOfA();`
	`  }`
	`  public function otherMethOfA():Void {`
	`  }`
	`}`
	
	`class B extends A {`
	`}`
	
	`// Usage`
	`var bInstance:B = new B();`
	`bInstance.methOfA();    // Executes properly`
		One method of a class can call another method of the same class, even when invoked via an instance of a subclass.

Table 6-3. Member access from an inherited instance method (continued)

Member accessed	Example	Notes
Overridden instance method (defined in both superclass and subclass)	```class A {
  public function methOfA ():Void {
    // Executes B's version of overriddenMeth( ) if
    // invoked on an instance of class B.
    // Executes A's version of overriddenMeth( ) if
    // invoked on an instance of class A.
    overriddenMeth( );
  }
  public function overriddenMeth( ):Void {
  }
}

class B extends A {
  public function overriddenMeth( ):Void {
  }
}

// Usage
var aInstance:A = new A( );
var bInstance:B = new B( );
// Invokes A's version of overriddenMeth( ).
aInstance.methOfA( );
// Invokes B's version of overriddenMeth( ).
bInstance.methOfA( );``` | The version of the overridden method executed depends on the class of the instance on which the method is invoked. |
| Instance property of subclass | ```class A {
  public function methOfA( ):Void {
    trace(propOfB); // Error!
  }
}

class B extends A {
  public var propOfB:Number = 1;
}``` | Compile-time error. Methods of a superclass can't refer to properties defined only on a subclass, and class A does not define propOfB, so the reference is illegal. |
| Inherited instance property (defined in superclass) | ```class A {
  public var propOfA:Number = 2;
  public function methOfA( ):Void {
    trace(propOfA);   // Displays: 2
  }
}

class B extends A {
}``` | A method of the superclass, such as *methOfA( )*, can access properties of the superclass, such as propOfA. |

Table 6-3. Member access from an inherited instance method (continued)

Member accessed	Example	Notes
| Overridden instance property (defined in both superclass and subclass) | ```
class A {
  public var overriddenProp:Number = 3;
  public function methOfA( ):Void {
    trace(overriddenProp);
  }
}

class B extends A {
  public var overriddenProp:Number = 4;
}

// Usage
var aInstance:A = new A( );
var bInstance:B = new B( );
aInstance.methOfA( );  // Displays: 3
bInstance.methOfA( );  // Displays: 4
``` | Even though the property is accessed in class *A*, when *methOfA( )* is invoked on an instance of *B*, the subclass's value of the overridden property (4, not 3) appears because bInstance can store only one value in overriddenProp. (In Java, calls to *methOfA( )* would always display 3.) |
| Class method of subclass, unqualified reference[a] | ```
class A {
  public function methOfA( ):Void {
    classMethOfB( );  // Error!
  }
}

class B extends A {
  public static function classMethOfB( ):Void {
  }
}
``` | Compile-time error. Class *A* does not define *classMethOfB( )*, and methods of a superclass can't resolve unqualified references to class methods of a subclass, so the reference is illegal. |
| Class method of subclass, qualified reference[a] | ```
class A {
  public function methOfA( ):Void {
    B.classMethOfB( );  // Executes properly
  }
}

class B extends A {
  public static function classMethOfB( ):Void {
  }
}
``` | *B.classMethOfB( )* is a qualified reference, so the compiler knows to look on class *B* for this class method (this is true for all classes, independent of whether *B* is a subclass of *A*). |
| Inherited class method (defined in superclass)[a] | ```
class A {
  public static function classMethOfA( ):Void {
  }
  public function methOfA( ):Void {
    // Executes A.classMethOfA( )
    classMethOfA( );
  }
}

class B extends A {
}

// Usage
var bInstance:B = new B( );
bInstance.methOfA( ); // Invokes A.classMethOfA( )
``` | At compile time, unqualified references to class methods are resolved relative to the current class. So *classMethOfA( )* resolves to *A.classMethOfA( )*. *A.classMethOfA( )* executes even when invoked from an instance of subclass *B*. |

Table 6-3. Member access from an inherited instance method (continued)

Member accessed	Example	Notes
| Overridden class method (defined in both superclass and subclass)[a] | ```
class A {
  public static function overriddenClassMeth():Void {
  }
  public function methOfA():Void {
    // Executes A.overriddenClassMeth()
    overriddenClassMeth();
  }
}

class B extends A {
  public static function overriddenClassMeth():Void {
  }
}

// Usage—compare also with preceding example
var bInstance:B = new B();
// Invokes A.overriddenClassMeth()
bInstance.methOfA();
``` | At compile time, unqualified references to class methods are resolved relative to the current class. From within class A, overriddenClassMeth() is converted to A. overriddenClassMeth(). Class A can invoke B's version using the qualified reference B. overriddenClassMeth(). |

[a] The same access rules apply to class properties as to class methods.

Member access from an overriding instance method

An instance method in a subclass that overrides an instance method in a superclass is known as an *overriding instance method*. For example, in the following code, the method *over( )* in class *B* overrides the method of the same name in class *A*:

```
class A {
  public function over ():Void {
  }
}
class B extends A {
  public function over ():Void {
  }
}
```

An instance of *B* can invoke *B*'s version of *over( )* as follows:

```
var bInstance:B = new B();
bInstance.over();
```

Table 6-4 describes what happens when bInstance invokes the overriding instance method *over( )*, and *over( )* subsequently accesses various methods and properties. Pay special attention to the Notes column, which highlights differences between member access in an overriding method and member access from an inherited method (as covered in Table 6-3).

In general terms, inherited and overridden methods have the scope of the superclass (where they are defined), whereas overriding methods have the scope of the subclass (where they are defined).
```

Table 6-4. Member access from an overriding instance method

Member accessed	Example	Notes
Instance method of subclass	```class A { public function over ():Void { } } class B extends A { public function methOfB():Void { } public function over ():Void { methOfB(); // Executes B.methOfB() } }```	Methods defined within a subclass can access each other, even when one is an overriding method. So, the overriding method, *B.over( )*, can execute *B. methOfB( )*. Compare with Table 6-3, in which invoking an instance method of a subclass from an *inherited* method yields an error.
Inherited instance method (defined in superclass)	```class A { public function over ():Void { } public function otherMethOfA():Void { } } class B extends A { public function over ():Void { // Invokes otherMethOfA( ) otherMethOfA(); } }```	As in Table 6-3, any method of the subclass (*B*), even an overriding method, can access a method defined in the superclass (*A*).
Overridden instance method (defined in both superclass and subclass)	```class A { public function over ():Void { } public function over2 ():Void { } } class B extends A { public function over ():Void { // Invokes B.over2( ) not A.over2( ) over2(); } public function over2 ():Void { } }```	As in all cases, the compiler attempts to resolve unqualified references within the subclass before looking to the superclass. In this case, the overriding *over( )* method invokes *over2( )*, another overriding method in the same subclass.
Instance property of subclass	```class A { public function over ():Void { } } class B extends A { public var propOfB:Number = 1; public function over ():Void { trace(propOfB); // Displays: 1 } }```	Methods defined within a subclass can access properties defined in the same subclass. So, the overriding method, *B.over( )*, can access propOfB. Compare with Table 6-3, in which accessing an instance property of a subclass from an *inherited* method yields an error.

Table 6-4. Member access from an overriding instance method (continued)

Member accessed	Example	Notes
Inherited instance property (defined in superclass)	```class A { public var propOfA:Number = 2; public function over ():Void { } } class B extends A { public function over ():Void { trace(propOfA); // Displays: 2 } }```	Methods defined within a subclass, even overriding methods, can access properties defined in the superclass. So, the overriding method, *B.over( )*, can access propOfA.
Overridden instance property (defined in both superclass and subclass)	```class A { public var overriddenProp:Number = 3; public function over ():Void { } } class B extends A { public var overriddenProp:Number = 4; public function over ():Void { trace(overriddenProp); // Displays: 4 } }```	The subclass method displays the subclass's value of the overridden property (4, not 3). Because bInstance stores only one value in overriddenProp, the overriding method has no access to the superclass's overridden property value.
Class method of subclass, unqualified reference[a]	```class A { public function over ():Void { } } class B extends A { public static function classMethOfB( ):Void { } public function over ():Void { classMethOfB( ); // Invokes B.classMethOfB( ) } }```	At compile time, unqualified references to class methods are resolved relative to the current class (*classMethOfB( )*, is resolved to *B.classMethOfB( )*, which exists). Compare with Table 6-3, in which an unqualified reference to a static method from within an *inherited* method (defined in the superclass) yields an error.
Class method of subclass, qualified reference[a]	```class A { public function over ():Void { } } class B extends A { public static function classMethOfB( ):Void { } public function over ():Void { B.classMethOfB( ); // Executes properly } }```	*B.classMethOfB( )* is a qualified reference, so the compiler knows to look on class *B* for the class method (this is true for all classes even in the case of overriding methods).

Table 6-4. Member access from an overriding instance method (continued)

Member accessed	Example	Notes
| Inherited class method (defined in superclass)[a] | ```
class A {
  public static function classMethOfA():Void {
  }
  public function over ():Void {
  }
}

class B extends A {
  public function over ():Void {
    classMethOfA();  // Invokes A.classMethOfA()
  }
}
``` | At compile time, unqualified references to class methods are resolved relative to the current class. So *classMethOfA()* resolves *B.classMethOfA()*. Although, subclass *B* doesn't directly define *classMethOfA()*, that reference succeeds because an inherited class method can be accessed via any subclass, so *B.classMethOfA()* and *A.classMethOfA()* work the same in this case. |
| Overridden class method (defined in both superclass and subclass)[a] | ```
class A {
  public static function overriddenClassMeth():
Void {
  }
  public function over ():Void {
    // Invokes A.overriddenClassMeth()
    overriddenClassMeth();
  }
}

class B extends A {
  public static function overriddenClassMeth():
Void {
  }
  public function over ():Void {
    // Invokes B.overriddenClassMeth()
    overriddenClassMeth();
  }
}

// Usage:
var aInstance:A = new A();
var bInstance:B = new B();
// Invokes A's version of overriddenClassMeth()
aInstance.over();
// Invokes B's version of overriddenClassMeth()
bInstance.over();
``` | At compile time, unqualified references to class methods are resolved relative to the current class. So in *B*'s version of *over()*, *overriddenClassMeth()* resolves to *B.overriddenClassMeth()*. To invoke *A*'s version of the method, use the qualified reference *A. overriddenClassMeth()*.<br><br>Notice that when an unqualified reference is used, the version of the method invoked is that of the class that contains the method call. |

[a] The same access rules apply to class properties as to class methods.

Member access from an overridden method invoked via super

A method in a superclass that is overridden by a method in a subclass is known as an *overridden instance method*. As we learned earlier, an overridden instance method can be invoked via the keyword *super*. For example, in the following code, the overridden method, *over()*, in class *A* is invoked via *super* from the overriding method of the same name in class *B*:

```
class A {
```

```
    public function over ():Void {
    }
}
class B extends A {
    public function over ():Void {
        super.over();
    }
}
```

Note the difference between using an inherited method versus calling an overridden method via *super*. In the former case, the subclass does not define the method but rather implicitly executes the method inherited from the superclass. In the latter case, the subclass's overriding method must use *super* to explicitly call the overridden superclass method.

In the following code, we invoke the *over( )* method on an instance of B. Without looking at the class definitions we can't tell that it invokes *A.over( )* via *super* behind the scenes. In fact, in a properly designed object-oriented application, the internal implementation should be of no concern to the external code calling the class.

```
    var bInstance:B = new B();
    bInstance.over();
```

Member access from an overridden method is the same as from an inherited method, as shown in Table 6-3. The following code shows you the syntactical difference between overridden method access and inherited method access. Despite the difference in code, the Notes column in Table 6-3 pertains verbatim to member access from overridden methods. See also the earlier sections "Overriding Properties" and "Overriding Instance Methods."

Here, we invoke the overridden method, *over( )*, via *super*, which in turn invokes *otherMethOfA( )*:

```
    class A {
     public function over ():Void {
      // Executes otherMethOfA( )
      otherMethOfA();
     }
     public function otherMethOfA():Void {
     }
    }

    class B extends A {
     public function over ():Void {
      // Executes A's version of over()
      super.over();
     }
    }
    // Usage:
    var bInstance:B = new B();
    bInstance.over();
```

Here, we invoke the inherited method, *methOfA( )*, which in turn invokes *otherMethOfA( )*:

```
// ==== Inherited method access ====
class A {
 public function methOfA():Void {
  // Executes otherMethOfA()
  otherMethOfA();
 }
 public function otherMethOfA():Void {
 }
}

class B extends A {
}

// Usage:
var bInstance:B = new B();
bInstance.methOfA();
```

The complexity of overridden member access in Tables 6-3 and 6-4 is, in itself, a warning to the developer not to override methods lightly.

 Always use caution when overriding members. Excessive overriding can lead to unmanageable, confusing source code. If you can't easily predict the runtime results of your code's overridden member access, you should simplify your code.

Now that we've learned how member access works in inherited and overridden instance methods, let's see how it works in inherited and overridden class methods.

Member Access from Inherited and Overridden Class Methods

Compared to instance method member access, member access from class methods is quite restricted. A class method cannot use the keyword *super* to refer to members of a superclass. Neither can it refer to instance properties or instance methods.

 A class method, whether overridden or not, is allowed to access other class methods and class properties only.

However, even within these restrictions, member access from a class method has the potential to be confusing. For clarity of code (and your own sanity), you should always refer to class methods and class properties through a fully qualified class reference (e.g., *SomeClass.someMethod( )*, not *someMethod( )*).

The potential for confusion lies once again in the compiler's automatic resolution of unqualified member references. Let's take a walk through this bramble, starting with a class, *A*, that defines a single class method, *m( )*, and a single class property, p.

```
class A {
  public static var p:String = "Hello there";
  public static function m ():Void {
    trace(p);
  }
}
```

As we learned earlier, at compile time, unqualified *static* member references (such as p) are resolved to qualified references of the form:

ClassName.memberName

where *ClassName* is the name of the class that contains the member reference and *memberName* is the name of the member.

Hence, when the compiler compiles the preceding code for class *A*, it resolves the unqualified property p in method *m( )* to the qualified reference: A.p. Once the compiler's work is done, the bytecode for method *m( )* effectively reads:

```
public static function m ():Void {
  trace(A.p);
}
```

Therefore, when we invoke *m( )* through *A*:

```
A.m( );
```

it displays the value of A.p, namely:

```
Hello there
```

So far, so good. Now suppose class *B* extends class *A*, adding no properties or methods of its own:

```
class B extends A {
}
```

When we invoke *m( )* through *B*:

```
B.m( );
```

it likewise displays the value of A.p, namely:

```
Hello there
```

Why? Because class *A* was compiled exactly as before, and the unqualified reference p in the method *m( )*was resolved to A.p.

 Invoking *m( )* through *B* at runtime has no impact on what has already happened at compile time.

Now things get interesting. Let's override the class property p in class *B*:

```
class B extends A {
  public static var p:String = "Goodbye";
}
```

Once again, we invoke *m( )* through *B*:

```
B.m( );
```

and the output is *again*:

```
Hello there
```

What's going on here? Our class *B* now defines its own property, p. And the method *m( )* was invoked through *B*. So we might think the property reference to p in the method *m( )* should yield the value of B.p ("Goodbye") rather than the value of A.p ("Hello there"). As tempting as that line of thinking is, we'd be wrong. It's worth repeating: invoking *m( )* through *B* at *runtime* has no impact on what has already happened at *compile time*. The compile-time conversion of p to A.p is permanent, and it happens regardless of our creation of B.p and our invocation of *m( )* through *B*. While we may think that our code ambiguously reads:

```
public static function m ():Void {
  trace(p);
}
```

To the interpreter, it reads, unambiguously as:

```
public static function m ():Void {
  trace(A.p);
}
```

Despite our best efforts, we cannot convince the interpreter that we mean B.p when we refer to the unqualified property p from within a static method of *A*. (You should be starting to see why qualified references to static members are so much clearer than unqualified references.)

We're almost out of the bramble.

Suppose we now override both the class method *m()* and the class property p in *B*:

```
class B extends A {
  public static var p:String = "The property B.p";
  public static function m ():Void {
    trace(p);
  }
}
```

At compile time, the reference in *B.m( )* to p resolves to: B.p. So this time if we invoke *m( )* through *B*:

```
B.m( );
```

we're invoking *B*'s version of the method, so the output is:

```
Goodbye
```

And if we invoke *m( )* through *A*:

```
A.m( );
```

we're invoking *A*'s version of the method, so the output is:

```
Hello there
```

Finally, we have what we wanted. Each class method displays the class property defined within its class.

 The moral of the story is "Always qualify your static member references."

Hopefully this little journey through the bramble will help us avoid similar thorns in our code.

Best Practices for Overriding

So far, our consideration of overriding in ActionScript 2.0 has been limited to "like members." That is, we've seen how an instance method can override another instance method or how a class property can override another class property. But we haven't discussed what happens when, say, an instance property overrides a class method. We've specifically avoided this topic, because even though ActionScript 2.0 allows a property to override a method, doing so is atrocious OOP form.

In fact, ActionScript does not prevent any kind of overriding. If a member in a subclass has the same name as a member in its superclass, the subclass's version overrides the superclass version. If the two members are both methods, they can have any number of parameters, any types of parameters, any return type, or any access level (*public* or *private*). If one member is a class member, the other can be an instance member. If one member is a property, the other can be a method. As long as the names of the members match, the override is legal. This extremely lenient behavior is a departure from the ECMA specification and should not be relied on.

For guidance on what constitutes best practices for overriding, we'll start with Java's rules. Note that, in Java, "properties" are called "variables," and for technical reasons, only instance methods are said to "override" each other. Variables and class methods are said to "hide" (not "override") each other. However, to maintain our ActionScript perspective in the following discussion, we'll use ActionScript's terminology even though we're describing Java's rules.

In Java, a legal override of a method must obey these rules:

- Both methods must be instance methods, or both methods must be class methods. An instance method cannot override a class method and vice versa.
- Both methods must have the same name.
- Both methods must have the same number of parameters. (ActionScript 2.0 developers must sometimes ignore this rule; see the later explanation.)

- The parameters of both methods must have the same datatypes. (ActionScript 2.0 developers must sometimes ignore this rule; see the later explanation.)
- Both methods must have the same return type.
- The overriding method must be at least as accessible as the overridden method (that is, the overriding method can't be *private* if the overridden method is *public*).

In Java, an instance property can override an instance property or a class property. The reverse is also true—a class property can override an instance property or a class property. However, as noted earlier, it's clearest to override instance properties only with other instance properties and class properties only with other class properties.

Table 6-5 summarizes Java's member overriding rules. When programming in ActionScript, it's wise to follow them, with one exception: in ActionScript, it is legitimate to change the number, datatype(s), and order of parameters for a method when overriding it. The method doing the overriding might need to offer different parameters in order to handle a specialized situation. In Java, defining a subclass method with the same name as a superclass method, but with a different number, datatype(s), or order of parameters constitutes a method *overload*, not a method *override*. That is, in Java, rather than obscuring the superclass's method, the subclass's version of the method coexists with the superclass's version. ActionScript does not support overloading, so the incongruent-parameter override is considered acceptable.

Table 6-5. Overriding members in Java

Member overridden	Overriding member is an instance method	Overriding member is a class method	Overriding member is an instance property	Overriding member is a class property
Instance method	Legal, with restrictions listed earlier	Illegal	Coexistence[a]	Coexistence[a]
Class method	Illegal	Legal, with restrictions listed earlier	Coexistence[a]	Coexistence[a]
Instance property	Coexistence[a]	Coexistence[a]	Legal	Legal
Class property	Coexistence[a]	Coexistence[a]	Legal	Legal

[a] In Java, there is effectively no override because the property and method of the same name can coexist. ActionScript does not allow a property and a method in the same class to have the same name. This form of member overriding should be avoided in ActionScript.

Constructor Functions in Subclasses

Now that we've studied the behavior of properties in relation to inheritance, let's turn our attention to constructors, which we first discussed in Chapter 4.

A constructor function initializes the instances of a class by:

- Calling methods that perform setup tasks
- Setting properties on the object being created

When a class is extended, the subclass can define a constructor function of its own. A subclass constructor is expected to:

- Perform setup tasks related to the subclass
- Set properties defined by the subclass
- Invoke the superclass constructor (sometimes called the *superconstructor*)

In all inheritance relationships, setup and property initialization relating to the superclass occur in the superclass constructor, not in the subclass constructor.

 A subclass constructor function, if specified, is formally required to invoke its superclass constructor, via the keyword *super*, as the first statement in the function. If no such invocation is provided, the compiler adds a no-argument superclass constructor call automatically.

For example, here is a simple subclass function definition:

```
class A {
  public function A () {
  }
}

class B extends A {
  // Subclass constructor
  public function B () {
    // Invoke superclass's constructor function explicitly
    super();
  }
}
```

The following two constructor function definitions are functionally synonymous. In the first case, we provide a call to *super( )* explicitly; in the second case, the compiler provides the call to *super( )* implicitly:

```
public function B () {
  // Invoke superclass's constructor function explicitly.
  super();
}

public function B () {
  // No constructor call. The compiler provides one implicitly.
}
```

In general, it's good form to always provide a call to *super( )* in a subclass constructor, even if that call has no arguments. If you intentionally omit the call to *super( )*, be sure to add a comment explaining why; otherwise, it may look as if you simply forgot it.

If a subclass does not define a constructor function at all, the compiler automatically creates one and adds a call to *super( )* as its only statement. Hence, the following two definitions of the class *B* are functionally identical; the first is an explicit version of what the compiler creates automatically in the second:

```
// Explicitly provide constructor
class B extends A {
  // Declare a constructor explicitly
  public function B () {
    // Invoke superclass's constructor function explicitly
    super();
  }
}

// Let compiler create default constructor automatically
class B extends A {
}
```

Invoking *super( )* anywhere but as the first statement of a subclass constructor function causes the following error:

```
The superconstructor must be called first in the constructor body.
```

Furthermore, *super( )* must not be used twice in a constructor function. (Using *super( )* twice also yields the preceding error message because the second use is not the constructor's first statement.)

Restricting *super( )* to the first line of a constructor function has the following benefits:

- Prevents methods from being called on an object that has not yet been initialized.
- Prevents property access on an object that has not yet been initialized.
- Prevents property assignments in the superclass constructor from overwriting property assignments in the subclass constructor.
- Guarantees that constructors in a class hierarchy execute from the top down. For example, if class *C* extends *B* which extends *A*, then when a new *C* instance is created, *A*'s constructor runs first, then *B*'s, then *C*'s.

> Don't confuse the two forms of the *super* operator. The first form, *super( )*, invokes a superclass's constructor function. The second form, *super.methodName( )*, invokes a superclass's method. The first form is allowed only as the first statement of a constructor function. The second form is allowed anywhere in a constructor function or instance method and can be used multiple times.

A subclass constructor function can (and often does) define different parameters than its superclass counterpart. This technique allows a subclass to alter the way its superclass instantiates objects. For example, suppose a *Rectangle* class defines a constructor with width and height parameters. A *Square* subclass could provide its own constructor that defines a single side parameter (squares have the same width and height, so specifying both is redundant). Example 6-3 shows the code.

Example 6-3. The Rectangle and Square constructors

```
class Rectangle {
  private var w:Number = 0;
  private var h:Number = 0;

  // Rectangle constructor
  public function Rectangle (width:Number, height:Number) {
    setSize(width, height);
  }

  public function setSize (newW:Number, newH:Number):Void {
    w = newW;
    h = newH;
  }

  public function getArea ():Number {
    return w * h;
  }
}

class Square extends Rectangle {
  // Square constructor
  public function Square (side:Number) {
    // Pass the side parameter onto the Rectangle constructor.
    super(side, side);
  }

  // Earlier in this chapter, we implemented the Square.setSize() method
  // with two parameters (newH and newW). This time we'll streamline
  // the method, allowing only a single parameter to be passed.
  public function setSize (side:Number):Void {
    super.setSize(side, side);
  }
}
```

When defining a subclass's constructor function, be careful not to unintentionally disable the behavior of a superclass's constructor. In the following example, the *ColoredBall* class erroneously defines a constructor function that doesn't supply necessary information to its superclass's constructor function:

```
class Ball {
  private var r:Number;
  public function Ball (radius:Number) {
    r = radius;
  }
}

class ColoredBall extends Ball {
  private var c:Number;
```

```
// Here's the problematic constructor...
public function ColoredBall (color:Number) {
    // OOPs! No call to super( ), so all ColoredBalls
    // will start with no radius!
    c = color;
  }
}
```

Wait a minute. Doesn't the compiler automatically supply the call to *super( )*? Yes, it does; however, the implicit call to *super( )* doesn't include the necessary radius parameter.

As written, the *ColoredBall* constructor does not allow us to create a *ColoredBall* instance with an initial radius defined. Therefore, the *ColoredBall* constructor must not call only *super( )*, but it must also accept radius as a parameter and pass it on to the superclass constructor. Here's the corrected version of *ColoredBall*, which preserves the *Ball* constructor's behavior:

```
class ColoredBall extends Ball {
  private var c:Number;

  // All fixed up...
  public function ColoredBall (radius:Number, color:Number) {
    super(radius);
    c = color;
  }
}
```

Notice that, as a matter of good form, we list the superclass's constructor arguments first (in this case, the radius), then the additional subclass constructor arguments (in this case, the color).

Extraneous Superclass Constructor Invocation in Flash Player 6

Due to the historical architecture of ActionScript 1.0, in Flash Player 6–format *.swf* files, a class's constructor function executes needlessly once for each of its subclasses. For example, the following code shows two simple classes, *A* and *B*. Class *A*'s constructor reports a message to the Output panel when it runs. Class *B* does nothing but extend class *A*.

```
class A {
  public function A () {
    trace("A's constructor was executed.");
  }
}

class B extends A {
}
```

Class *A* has one subclass, *B*; hence, in a Flash Player 6–format *.swf* file, class *A*'s constructor executes once, needlessly, even if no instance of *A* or *B* is ever created. For example, if the following code appears in a *.fla* file, then *A*'s constructor will run:

```
var bInstance:B;
```

Extraneous constructor executions can perform unwanted tasks, such as attaching a movie clip or incrementing an instance counter. To prevent unwanted code execution, use a parameter that indicates that the constructor is being called intentionally. For example:

```
class A {
  public function A (doConstruct:Boolean) {
    if (doConstruct) {
      // Normal constructor code goes here.
    }
  }
}

class B extends A {
  public function B () {
    // Pass true to the constructor to tell it to perform initialization.
    super(true);
  }
}
```

This problem does not affect Flash Player 7–format *.swf* files that use ActionScript 2.0. For much more information, see Chapter 12 of *ActionScript for Flash MX: The Definitive Guide* (O'Reilly).

Subclassing Built-in Classes

Just as we can create subclasses of our own custom classes, we can also create subclasses of ActionScript's built-in classes, allowing us to implement specialized functionality based on an existing ActionScript class. For example, suppose we wanted to implement a *timediff( )* method that would return the amount of time, in milliseconds, between two *Date* instances. We could put *timediff( )* on a *Date* subclass named *DateDeluxe*, as follows:

```
class DateDeluxe extends Date {

  public function DateDeluxe (year:Number, month:Number, date:Number,
                             hour:Number, min:Number,
                             sec:Number, ms:Number) {
    super(year, month, date, hour, min, sec, ms);
  }

  public function timediff (d:Date):Number {
    return Math.abs(this.getTime() - d.getTime());
  }
}
```

Notice that the *DateDeluxe* class must provide a constructor function that forwards arguments to the *Date* class constructor. Here's how we'd use the new *DateDeluxe* class:

```
// Make a DateDeluxe instance
var d1:DateDeluxe = new DateDeluxe( );

// Waste some time...
for (var i:Number = 0; i < 10000; i++) {
  // Dum dee dum...
}

// Make another DateDeluxe instance
var d2:DateDeluxe = new DateDeluxe( );

// Show the elapsed time between d1 and d2
trace(d1.timediff(d2));
```

As attractive as the *DateDeluxe* example is, not all built-in ActionScript classes can be subclassed, due to various implementation factors. For example, the *TextField* class cannot be subclassed because there's no way to create a *TextField* subclass instance via *MovieClip.createTextField( )*; that method creates instances only of the *TextField* class and cannot be instructed to create an instance of a *TextField* subclass. (Instance of *TextField* cannot be created via new TextField( ).)

Similarly, the *XML* class cannot be subclassed in many situations because it provides no way to specify the class to use when creating child nodes (which are instances of *XMLNode*).

To circumvent the general problem of extending a nonextendable built-in class, you should use *composition* instead of inheritance. We'll study composition later in this chapter, but briefly, composition involves storing an instance of a class in a property and forwarding method and property access to that instance. Example 6-4 uses composition to create a *TextFieldDeluxe* class that stores a *TextField* instance in a property named tf. The *TextFieldDeluxe* class adds hypertext links to any text assigned to the htmlText property. An ActionScript 2.0 setter method, *htmlText( )*, intercepts the property assignment before forwarding it on to the tf instance. The code shows only part of the class, giving you enough to understand how the method and property forwarding aspects work. The remainder of the class (not shown) would be implemented in the same way.

Example 6-4. Creating a subclass using composition

```
class TextFieldDeluxe {
  private var tf:TextField;

  public function TextFieldDeluxe (target:MovieClip, name:String,
                      depth:Number, x:Number, y:Number,
                      w:Number, h:Number) {
    target.createTextField(name, depth, x, y, w, h);
```

Example 6-4. Creating a subclass using composition (continued)

```
    tf = target[name];
  }

  public static function addLinks (s:String):String {
    // The real implementation of link insertion is not shown here.
    // Instead, we just add some text to the string, as a proof of concept.
    return s + "[LINK ADDED HERE]";
  }

  public function set htmlText (s:String):Void {
    tf.htmlText = TextFieldDeluxe.addLinks(s);
  }

  public function get htmlText ():String {
    return tf.htmlText;
  }

  public function addListener (listener:Object):Boolean {
    return tf.addListener(listener);
  }

  public function getDepth ():Number {
    return tf.getDepth();
  }

  // ...Remainder of class not shown
}
```

Here's how we'd use the *TextFieldDeluxe* class:

```
    var tfd:TextFieldDeluxe = new TextFieldDeluxe(someClip_mc, "theField", 1,
                                    20, 20, 400, 200);
    // Text field displays: Hello world[LINK ADDED HERE]
    tfd.htmlText = "Hello world";
    trace(tfd.getDepth());        // Output panel displays: 1
```

Built-in Classes that Store Function Libraries

Some built-in ActionScript classes are simply collections of class methods and class properties—the *Math*, *Key*, *Mouse*, *Selection*, and *Stage* classes exist merely to store related functions and variables (e.g., *Math.random( )* and Key.ENTER). Rather than subclassing these classes, also known as *static function libraries*, you should distribute your own static function libraries separately. For example, rather than adding a *factorial( )* method to a subclass of the *Math* class, you should create a custom class, say *AdvancedMath*, to hold your *factorial( )* method. The *AdvancedMath* class need not (indeed, should not) be related to the *Math* class via inheritance.

Augmenting Built-in Classes and Objects

In the previous section we learned how to subclass a built-in class. New properties and methods can also be added directly to an existing built-in class, without subclassing it. However, the technique uses an old-school ActionScript 1.0 hack, is heavy-handed, and requires that we break the important OOP precept that warns us to keep method and property definitions contained within a class definition. Nevertheless, it does work and can be convenient if used sparingly and prudently.

Here's the general syntax for adding a new method to a built-in class at runtime:

```
ClassName.prototype.methodName = function (param1, param2, ...paramn) {
  statements
};
```

Here's the general syntax for adding a new property to a built-in class at runtime:

```
ClassName.prototype.propertyName = value;
```

For example, the following code adds a new method, *isEmpty( )*, to the built-in *String* class. The *isEmpty( )* method returns true when a string has no characters in it; otherwise, false:

```
String.prototype.isEmpty = function () {
  return (this == "") ? true : false;
};

// Usage example:
var s1:String = "Hello World";
var s2:String = "";

trace(s1.isEmpty());  // Displays: false
trace(s2.isEmpty());  // Displays: true
```

However, the previous code example—and this entire technique—has a problem: the newly defined method or property isn't added until runtime; therefore, the compiler has no idea that the new member exists and will generate an error if it is used with typed data. For example, the code in the preceding example creates two typed variables, s1 and s2, so the code yields this error:

```
There is no method with the name 'isEmpty'.
```

To avoid this problem, we're forced into a nasty, hacked solution. We inform the compiler that we've defined a *String.isEmpty( )* method by adding it to the *String* class's intrinsic class definition, found in the location listed next. In each of the following file paths, substitute your operating-system user-account name for *USER* and your Flash language code for *LANGUAGE CODE* (the *LANGUAGE CODE* for English is "en"):

Built-in *String* intrinsic class definition on Windows (this folder is a hidden folder on some computers):

c:\Documents and Settings\USER\Local Settings\Application Data\Macromedia\ Flash MX 2004\LANGUAGE CODE\Configuration\Classes\String.as

---

Built-in *String* intrinsic class definition on Mac:

HD:/Users/USER/Library/Application Support/Macromedia/Flash MX 2004/ LANGUAGE CODE/Configuration/Classes/String.as

Here's an excerpt from a modified version of the *String.as* intrinsic class definition. It shows only the new method and doesn't show the rest of the intrinsic class definition:

```
//*************************************************************************
// ActionScript Standard Library
// String object
//*************************************************************************

intrinsic class String
{
    // We add this line to the file so that the compiler
    // knows about our new isEmpty( ) method
    function isEmpty( ):Boolean;
}
```

The *String.as* fix itself has a problem: it must be implemented on every computer that uses the *String.isEmpty( )* method. That is, if you fix the *String.as* file on your work computer and then take your work home, you'll have to fix it on your home computer too. This makes the source code distribution for any application that uses *String.isEmpty( )* very awkward, particularly if more than one application on your system requires changes to the *String.as* file! Hence, as mentioned earlier, you should use this technique only when absolutely necessary, and you should be particularly hesitant to use it if you plan on distributing your code among a team or to the public. In fact, if you're convinced you regularly need to add new methods and properties to built-in classes, you may simply want to use ActionScript 1.0 or perhaps not declare datatypes in your ActionScript 2.0 code. In ActionScript 2.0, you should avoid the practice unless you are working with old code.

 The compiler does not generate errors when new methods or properties are accessed on the following built-in classes: *Array*, *ContextMenu*, *ContextMenuItem*, *Function*, *FunctionArguments* (a.k.a. the *Arguments* object), *LoadVars*, *MovieClip*, *Object*, and *TextField*. Those classes are all defined as *dynamic*, which allows new methods and properties to be added to their instances without errors.

The Theory of Inheritance

So far this chapter has focused mainly on the practical details of using inheritance in ActionScript 2.0. But the theory of why and when to use inheritance in OOP runs much deeper than the technical implementation. Before we conclude, let's consider some basic theoretical principles, bearing in mind that a few pages is hardly enough room to do the topic justice. For a much more thorough consideration of inheritance theory, see *Using Inheritance Well* (*http://archive.eiffel.com/doc/manuals/ technology/oosc/inheritance-design/page.html*), an online excerpt from Bertrand Meyer's illuminating work *Object-Oriented Software Construction* (Prentice Hall).

Why Inheritance?

Superficially, the obvious benefit of inheritance is code reuse. Inheritance lets us separate a core feature set from customized versions of that feature set. Code for the core is stored in a superclass while code for the customizations is kept neatly in a subclass. Furthermore, more than one subclass can extend the superclass, allowing multiple customized versions of a particular feature set to exist simultaneously. If the implementation of a feature in the superclass changes, all subclasses automatically inherit the change.

But inheritance also lets us express the architecture of an application in hierarchical terms that mirror the real world and the human psyche. For example, in the real world, we consider plants different from animals, but we categorize both as living things. We consider cars different from planes, but we see both as vehicles. Correspondingly, in a human resources application, we might have an *Employee* superclass with *Manager*, *CEO*, and *Worker* subclasses. Or, in a banking application, we might create a *BankAccount* superclass with *CheckingAccount* and *SavingsAccount* subclasses. These are canonical examples of one variety of inheritance sometimes called *subtype inheritance*, in which the application's class hierarchy is designed to model a real-world situation (a.k.a. the *domain* or *problem domain*).

However, while the *Employee* and *BankAccount* examples make attractive demonstrations of inheritance, not all inheritance reflects the real world. In fact, overemphasizing real-world modeling can lead to miscomprehension of inheritance and its subsequent misuse. For example, given a *Person* class, we might be tempted to create *Female* and *Male* subclasses. These are logical categories in the real world, but if the application using those classes were, say, a school's reporting system, we'd be forced to create *MaleStudent* and *FemaleStudent* classes just to preserve the real-world hierarchy. In our program, male students do not define any operations differently from female students and, therefore, should be used identically. Hence, the real-world hierarchy in this case conflicts with our application's hierarchy. If we need gender information, perhaps simply for statistics, we're better off creating a single *Student* class and simply adding a gender property to the *Person* class. As tempting as it may be, we should avoid creating inheritance structures based solely on the real world rather than the needs of your software.

Finally, in addition to code reuse and logical hierarchy, inheritance allows instances of different subtypes to be used where a single type is expected. Known as *polymorphism*, this important benefit warrants a discussion all its own.

Polymorphism and Dynamic Binding

Polymorphism is a feature of all truly object-oriented languages, wherein an instance of a subclass can be used anywhere an instance of its superclass is expected. The word *polymorphism* itself means literally "many forms"—each single object can be treated as an instance of its own class or as an instance of any of its superclasses.

Polymorphism's partner is *dynamic binding*, which guarantees that a method invoked on an object will trigger the behavior defined by that object's actual class (no matter what the type of the data container in which the object resides).

 Don't confuse dynamic binding, which occurs at runtime, with static type checking, which occurs at compile time. Dynamic binding takes into consideration the class of the instance stored in a variable, whereas static type checking does the opposite—it ignores the datatype of the data and considers only the declared datatype of the variable.

Let's see an example at work, and then we'll reconcile this new information with what we learned earlier in Chapter 3 regarding type checking and type casting.

The canonical example of polymorphism and dynamic binding is a graphics application that displays shapes. The application defines a *Shape* class with an unimplemented *draw()* method:

```
class Shape {
  public function draw ():Void {
    // No implementation. In other languages, draw() would be
    // declared with the abstract attribute, which syntactically
    // forces subclasses of Shape to provide an implementation.
  }
}
```

The *Shape* class has several subclasses—a *Circle* class, a *Rectangle* class, and a *Triangle* class, each of which provides its own definition for the *draw()* method:

```
class Circle extends Shape {
  public function draw ():Void {
    // Code to draw a Circle on screen, not shown...
  }
}

class Rectangle extends Shape {
  public function draw ():Void {
    // Code to draw a Rectangle on screen, not shown...
  }
}

class Triangle extends Shape {
  public function draw ():Void {
    // Code to draw a Triangle on screen, not shown...
  }
}
```

The application stores many different *Circle*, *Rectangle*, and *Triangle* instances in an array named shapes. The shapes array could be created by the user or generated internally. For this example, we'll populate it with 10 random shapes:

```
var rand:Number;
var shapes:Array = new Array();
```

```
for (var i:Number = 0; i < 10; i++) {
  // Retrieve a random integer from 0 to 2
  rand = Math.floor(Math.random( ) * 3);
  if (rand == 0) {
    shapes[i] = new Circle( );
  } else if (rand == 1) {
    shapes[i] = new Rectangle( );
  } else if (rand == 2) {
    shapes[i] = new Triangle( );
  }
}
```

When it comes time to update the screen, the application runs through its shapes array, invoking *draw( )* on each element without knowing (or caring) whether the element contains a *Circle*, *Rectangle*, or *Triangle* instance:

```
for (var i:Number = 0; i < shapes.length; i++) {
  shapes[i].draw( );
}
```

In the preceding loop, *dynamic binding* is the runtime process by which each invocation of *draw( )* is associated with the appropriate implementation of that method. That is, if the instance is a *Circle*, the interpreter invokes *Circle.draw( )*; if it's a *Rectangle*, the interpreter invokes *Rectangle.draw( )*; and if it's a *Triangle*, the interpreter invokes *Triangle.draw( )*. Importantly, the class of each instance in shapes is not known at compile time. The random shapes array is generated at runtime, so the appropriate version of *draw( )* to invoke can be determined only at runtime. Hence, dynamic binding is often called *late binding*: the method call is *bound* to a particular implementation "late" (i.e., at runtime).

You might ask how this dynamic binding example differs from the code example under "Casting" in Chapter 3, reproduced here for your convenience:

```
var ship:EnemyShip = theEnemyManager.getClosestShip( );
if (ship instanceof Bomber) {
  Bomber(ship).bomb( );                // Cast to Bomber
} else if (ship instanceof Cruiser) {
  Cruiser(ship).evade( );              // Cast to Cruiser
} else if (ship instanceof Fighter) {
  Fighter(ship).callReinforcements( ); // Cast to Fighter
  Fighter(ship).fire( );               // Cast to Fighter
}
```

The preceding code checks ship's datatype using the *instanceof* operator and then casts it to the *Bomber*, *Cruiser*, or *Fighter* class before invoking a method, such as *bomb( )*, *evade( )*, or *fire( )*. So why doesn't our shapes example check the class of each array element or perform any type casting?

Well, for one thing, the compiler doesn't perform type checking on array elements accessed with the [ ] operator. So let's take the array access out of the equation and simplify the situation as follows:

```
var someShape:Shape = new Circle( );
someShape.draw( );       // Invokes Circle.draw( ) not Shape.draw( )
```

In this case, the compiler checks the datatype of the someShape variable, namely *Shape*, and confirms that the *Shape* class defines *draw( )*. However, at runtime, thanks to dynamic binding, the call to shape.draw( ) invokes *Circle.draw( )* instead of *Shape.draw( )*. (The *draw( )* method happens to be declared on the *Circle* class, but if it weren't, *Circle* would still inherit *draw( )* from the *Shape* class.)

In contrast, the *bomb( )*, *evade( )*, and *fire( )* methods are not declared in the *EnemyShip* class. Those methods are declared only in the *Bomber*, *Cruiser*, and *Fighter* subclasses, so our *EnemyShip* example needs to perform casting to prevent compiler errors and manual type checking (using *instanceof*) to prevent runtime errors. So our *Shape* example is simplified by the fact that the superclass defines a method named *draw( )*, which is common to all its subclasses.

> Dynamic binding means that the runtime interpreter ignores the datatype of the container and instead considers the class of the data in the container. In this case, the interpreter ignores the *Shape.draw( )* method in the superclass and instead uses the overriding subclass version, *Circle.draw( )*, because shape holds a *Circle* instance despite being declared with the *Shape* datatype.

To bring the discussion full circle, let's revisit our *Ball* and *Basketball* example, also from Chapter 3:

```
var ball1:Ball = new Basketball( ); // Legal, so far...
if (ball1 instanceof Basketball) {  // Include manual runtime type checking
  Basketball(ball1).inflate( );     // Downcast prevents compiler error!
}
```

Here we see again the advantage of late binding. The manual downcast to the *Basketball* type is purely for the compiler's benefit. However, dynamic binding ensures that the *Basketball.inflate( )* method is invoked because the interpreter recognizes that ball1 stores an instance of type *Basketball* even though the variable's datatype is *Ball*. What if we store a *Ball* instance instead of a *Basketball* instance in ball1? See the following code snippet (changes shown in bold):

```
var ball1:Ball = new Ball( );       // Store a Ball instance
if (ball1 instanceof Basketball) {  // Include manual type checking
  Basketball(ball1).inflate( );     // Cast to Basketball type
}
```

In this case, the manual runtime type checking (the *if* statement) prevents the interpreter from executing Basketball(ball1).inflate( ). See that! Manual type checking works! But let's remove the type checking and try again:

```
var ball1:Ball = new Ball();        // Store a Ball instance
Basketball(ball1).inflate();        // This cast is a "lie"
```

Here, the cast to the *Basketball* type is a "lie." The attempt to invoke *inflate( )* fails at runtime because the cast to *Basketball* fails and, hence, returns null. The interpreter can't invoke *inflate( )* (or any other method) on null.

The key benefit of dynamic binding and polymorphism is containment of changes to code. Polymorphism lets one part of an application remain fixed even when another changes. For example, let's consider how we'd handle the random list of shapes if polymorphism didn't exist. First, we'd have to use unique names for each version of *draw( )*:

```
class Circle extends Shape {
  public function drawCircle ( ):Void {
    // Code to draw a Circle on screen, not shown...
  }
}

class Rectangle extends Shape {
  public function drawRectangle ( ):Void {
    // Code to draw a Rectangle on screen, not shown...
  }
}

class Triangle extends Shape {
  public function drawTriangle ( ):Void {
    // Code to draw a Triangle on screen, not shown...
  }
}
```

Then we'd have to check the class of each shape element manually and invoke the appropriate draw method, as follows:

```
for (var i:Number = 0; i < shapes.length; i++) {
  if (shapes[i] instanceof Circle) {
    shapes[i].drawCircle();
  } else if (shapes[i] instanceof Rectangle) {
    shapes[i].drawRectangle ();
  } else if (shapes[i] instanceof Triangle) {
    shapes[i].drawTriangle();
  }
}
```

That's already more work. But imagine what would happen if we added 20 new kinds of shapes. For each one, we'd have to update and recompile the code in the preceding examples. In a polymorphic world, we don't have to touch the code that invokes *draw( )* on each *Shape* instance. As long as each *Shape* subclass supplies its own valid definition for *draw( )*, our application will "just work" without other changes.

Polymorphism not only lets programmers collaborate more easily, but it allows them to use and expand on a code library without requiring access to the library's source code. Some argue that polymorphism is OOP's greatest contribution to computer science.

Inheritance Versus Composition

In this chapter, we focused most of our attention on one type of interobject relationship: inheritance. But inheritance isn't the only game in town. *Composition*, an alternative form of interobject relationship, often rivals inheritance as an OOP design technique. In composition, one class (the *front end class*) stores an instance of another class (the *back end class*) in an instance property. The front end class delegates work to the back end class by invoking methods on that instance. Here's the basic approach, shown in code:

```
// The back end class is analogous to the superclass in inheritance.
class BackEnd {
  public function doSomething () {
  }
}

// The front end class is analogous to the subclass in inheritance.
class FrontEnd {
  // An instance of the back end class is stored in
  // a private instance property, in this case called be.
  private var be:BackEnd;

  // The constructor creates the instance of the back end class.
  public function FrontEnd () {
    be = new BackEnd();
  }

  // This method delegates work to BackEnd.doSomething().
  public function doSomething () {
    be.doSomething();
  }
}
```

Notice that the *FrontEnd* class does not extend the *BackEnd* class. Composition does not require or use its own special syntax, as inheritance does. Furthermore, the front end class may use a subset of the methods of the back end class, or it may use all of them, or it may add its own unrelated methods. The method names in the front end class might match those exactly in the back end class, or they might be completely different. The front end class can constrain, extend, or redefine the back end class's features, just like a subclass in inheritance, as briefly outlined earlier in Example 6-4.

Example 6-3 showed how, using inheritance, a *Square* class could constrain the behavior of a *Rectangle* class. Example 6-5 shows how that same class relationship can be implemented with composition instead of inheritance. In Example 6-5, notice that the *Rectangle* class is unchanged. But this time, the *Square* class does not extend *Rectangle*. Instead, it defines a property, r, that contains a *Rectangle* instance. All operations on r are filtered through *Square*'s public methods. The *Square* class forwards, or *delegates*, method calls to r.

Example 6-5. An example composition relationship

```
// The Rectangle class is unchanged from Example 6-3.
class Rectangle {
  private var w:Number = 0;
  private var h:Number = 0;

  public function Rectangle (width:Number, height:Number) {
    setSize(width, height);
  }

  public function setSize (newW:Number, newH:Number):Void {
    w = newW;
    h = newH;
  }

  public function getArea ():Number {
    return w * h;
  }
}

// Here's the new Square class.
// Compare with the version under "Invoking an Overridden Instance Method."
class Square {
  private var r:Rectangle;

  public function Square (side:Number) {
    r = new Rectangle(side, side);
  }

  // Note that we use our earlier version of Square.setSize( ), which defines
  // two parameters, newW and newH. We stick to the original implementation
  // for the sake of direct comparison, rather than implementing a more
  // elegant version, which would define a single sideLength parameter only.
  public function setSize (newW:Number, newH:Number):Void {
    if (newW == newH) {
      r.setSize(newW, newH);
    }
  }

  public function getArea ():Number {
    return r.getArea( );
  }
}
```

Is-A, Has-A, and Uses-A

In OOP parlance, an inheritance relationship is known colloquially as an "Is-A" relationship because, from a datatype perspective, the subclass can be seen literally as being an instance of the superclass (i.e., the subclass can be used wherever the superclass is expected). In our earlier polymorphic example, a *Circle* "Is-A" *Shape* because the *Circle* class inherits from the *Shape* class and can be used anywhere a *Shape* is used.

A composition relationship is known as a "Has-A" relationship because the front end class stores an instance of the back end class (e.g., a *ChessBoard* "Has-A" *Tile*). The "Has-A" relationship should not be confused with the "Uses-A" relationship, in which a class instantiates an object of another class but does not store it in an instance property. In a "Uses-A" relationship, the class uses the object and throws it away. For example, a *Circle* might store its numeric color in a property, col ("Has-A"), but then use a *Color* object temporarily to actually set that color on screen ("Uses-A").

In Example 6-5, our *Square* class "Has-A" *Rectangle* instance and adds restrictions to it that effectively turn it into a *Square*. In the case of *Square* and *Rectangle*, the "Is-A" relationship seems natural, but the "Has-A" relationship can also be used. Which begs the question: which relationship is best?

When to use composition over inheritance

Example 6-5 raises a serious design question. How do you choose between composition and inheritance? In general, it's fairly easy to spot a situation in which inheritance is inappropriate. An *AlertDialog* instance in an application "has an" OK button, but an *AlertDialog* instance, itself, "isn't an" OK button. However, spotting a situation in which composition is inappropriate is trickier, because any time you can use inheritance to establish the relationship between two classes, you could use composition instead. If both techniques work in the same situation, how can you tell which is the best option?

If you're new to OOP, you may be surprised to hear that composition is often favored over inheritance as an application design strategy. In fact, some of the best-known OOP design theoreticians explicitly advocate composition over inheritance (see *Design Patterns*, published by Addison-Wesley). Hence, conventional wisdom tells us to at least consider composition as an option even when inheritance seems obvious. That said, here are some general guidelines to consider when deciding whether to use inheritance or composition:

- If a parent class needs to be used where a child class is expected (i.e., if you want to take advantage of polymorphism), consider using inheritance.
- If a class just needs the services of another class, you consider a composition relationship.
- If a class you're designing behaves very much like an existing class, consider an inheritance relationship.

For more advice on choosing between composition and inheritance, read Bill Venner's excellent JavaWorld article, archived at his site: *http://www.artima.com/ designtechniques/compoinh.html*. Mr. Venner offers compelling evidence that, generally speaking:

- Changing code that uses composition has fewer consequences than changing code that uses inheritance.
- Code based on inheritance generally executes faster than code based on composition. (This is potentially important in ActionScript, which executes far more slowly than Java.)

In ActionScript, the composition versus inheritance debate most frequently appears when using the *MovieClip* class. The debate is over whether one should subclass the *MovieClip* class or store a *MovieClip* instance as a property of another class. Both approaches are acceptable, though *MovieClip* inheritance is more complicated and requires use of a Library symbol in a *.fla* file. For an example of *MovieClip* composition, see Chapter 5, in which the *ImageViewer* class uses a *MovieClip* to display an image on screen. For an example of *MovieClip* inheritance, see Chapter 13. When working with the *MovieClip* class, the preceding guidelines can help you determine whether to use inheritance or composition.

Using composition to shed an old habit

Because ActionScript 1.0 leniently allowed properties to be added to any object of any class, some Flash developers grew accustomed to forming marriages of convenience between completely unrelated objects. For example, in order to load the coordinates for a "circle" movie clip, some developers would marry an *XML* instance with a *MovieClip* instance, as follows:

```
// *** ActionScript 1.0 code ***

// Create an XML instance.
var coords = new XML();

// Store a reference to circle_mc directly on the
// coords instance, in a property named mc.
coords.mc = circle_mc;

// When the coordinates data loads, use the XML instance's
// mc property to transfer the loaded data to the circle_mc movie clip.
coords.onLoad = function ():Void {
  this.mc._x = parseInt(this.firstChild...);  // XML node access not shown
  this.mc._y = parseInt(this.firstChild...);  // XML node access not shown
};

// Load the coordinates data.
coords.load("circleCoords.xml");
```

We can correctly argue that the preceding ActionScript 1.0 practice contributes to:

- Unreliable, ungeneralized application architecture
- Spaghetti code that is a tangle of special cases
- Code that is difficult to follow, extend, and change

However, in ActionScript 2.0, there's a more practical problem: the previous code won't compile. In ActionScript 2.0, it's illegal to add properties to a class unless the class is *dynamic*, which the *XML* class is not. The rules of ActionScript 2.0 are designed to help programmers avoid such pitfalls.

An impulsive response to the situation would be: "Fine, what's the easiest way I can circumvent ActionScript 2.0's strictness and add my property to the *XML* instance?" That kind of thinking might lead to subclassing *XML* and adding the mc property to the subclass as follows:

```
class CoordsXML extends XML{
  private var mc:MovieClip;

  public function CoordsXML (mc:MovieClip, URL:String) {
    this.mc = mc;
    load(URL);
  }

  public function onLoad(success:Boolean):Void {
    mc._x = parseInt(firstChild...);  // XML node access not shown
    mc._y = parseInt(firstChild...);  // XML node access not shown
  }
}
```

Extending *XML* as shown technically works, but here we must return to our inheritance versus composition question. Is the relationship we need simply a case of using the *XML* object to load data (composition) or do we really need a new kind of *XML* object (inheritance)? It's not very natural to claim that an *XML* subclass that arbitrarily stores a reference to a movie clip really "Is-A" kind of *XML*. We don't need a new breed of *XML* here; we merely need to use *XML* to load some data. Hence, the situation calls for more of a "Has-A," or even simply a "Uses-A," relationship. After all, we're trying to represent a circle here. The means of transfer (the *XML*) and the means of display (the *MovieClip*) are mere implementation details. That is, if we want a circle on screen, then we should make a *Circle* class. The *Circle* class should deal with loading data and providing a draw-to-screen method. How that actually happens is left up to the *Circle* class.

In the next example, the *Circle* class uses an *XML* instance to load data and a *MovieClip* instance to draw to the screen. These two instances are stored as *Circle* properties, as follows:

```
class Circle {
  var coordsLoader:XML;
  var mc:MovieClip;

  public function Circle (target:MovieClip,
                          symbolID:String,
                          name:String,
                          depth:Number) {
    mc = target.attachMovie(symbolID, name, depth);
```

```
      coordsLoader = new XML();
    }

    public function loadCoords (URL:String):Void {
      var clip:MovieClip = this.mc;

      coordsLoader.onLoad = function (success:Boolean):Void {
        if (success) {
          clip._x = parseInt(this.firstChild...); // XML node access not shown
          clip._y = parseInt(this.firstChild...); // XML node access not shown
        } else {
          // Handle a load error
          trace("Could not load coords from file: " + URL);
        }
      };

      coordsLoader.load(URL);
    }
  }
```

With access to both instances, the *Circle* class can happily transfer loaded coordinates from the XML file to the movie clip. Not only is this composition relationship more natural, but it lets us easily change the implementation details later without breaking any code that uses the *Circle* class. For example, we could change the *XML* instance to a *LoadVars* instance without affecting any external code that invokes *Circle.loadCoords()*.

Note that a *Circle* instance doesn't really have to store the *XML* instance in the coordsLoader property. Instead, the *Circle.loadCoords()* method could store the *XML* instance in a local variable (in other words, we could define a "Uses-A" relationship rather than a "Has-A" relationship). The latter technique works but has a higher performance cost because the *XML* instance has to be constructed anew every time *loadCoords()* is invoked.

Abstract and Final Classes Not Supported

Many OOP designs require the use of a so-called *abstract class*. An abstract class is any class that defines one or more *abstract methods*—methods that have a signature and a return type but no implementation (i.e., no code in the method body). A class that wishes to extend an abstract class must implement all of the superclass's abstract methods; otherwise, a compile-time error occurs. All subclasses of an abstract class effectively promise to provide some real code to do a job the abstract class only describes in theory.

Abstract classes are a common, important part of polymorphic designs. For example, in our earlier discussion of polymorphism, we studied a *Shape* class with *Circle*, *Rectangle*, and *Triangle* subclasses. Traditionally, the *Shape* class's *draw()* method would be defined as an abstract method, guaranteeing that:

- Each *Shape* subclass provides a means of drawing itself to the screen
- External code can safely call *draw( )* on any *Shape* subclass (the compiler will not let a class extend *Shape* without implementing *draw( )*)

Unfortunately, ActionScript 2.0 does not yet support abstract classes or abstract methods. Instead of defining an abstract method in ActionScript, we simply define a method with no code in its body. It's left up to the programmer (not the compiler) to ensure that the subclasses of a would-be abstract class implement the appropriate method(s).

In contrast to an *abstract method*, which must be implemented by a subclass, a *final method* is a method that must not be implemented by a subclass; otherwise, a compile-time error occurs. Final methods are used to prevent programmers from creating subclasses that accidentally introduce problems into the behavior of a superclass or intentionally sabotage a superclass. Like abstract methods, this useful OOP feature is not part of ActionScript 2.0 for Flash Player 7, but may be implemented in the future.

Let's Try Inheritance

We have studied a lot of theory in this chapter. When you're ready to see how inheritance feels in the real world, move on to the next chapter, where the *ImageViewer* class is extended.

Authoring an ActionScript 2.0 Subclass

In the preceding chapter, we learned the principles of inheritance in ActionScript 2.0. In this chapter, we'll study an applied inheritance example, *ImageViewerDeluxe*. The *ImageViewerDeluxe* class is a subclass of the *ImageViewer* class that we created in Chapter 5. You'll need the files from that chapter for this tutorial (see Example 5-8 and "Using ImageViewer (Take 2)"), or you can download them from *http://moock. org/eas2/examples*. The *ImageViewerDeluxe* source files discussed in this chapter are available from the same URL.

Extending ImageViewer's Capabilities

Recall from Chapter 5 the list of possible functional requirements for our *ImageViewer* class:

- Load an image
- Display an image
- Crop an image to a particular rectangular "view region"
- Display a border around the image
- Display image load progress
- Reposition the view region
- Resize the view region
- Pan (reposition) the image within the view region
- Zoom (resize) the image within the view region

The *ImageViewer* class already implements the first five requirements, but it stops there. In the *ImageViewerDeluxe* class, we'll add the next two items on the list: the abilities to reposition and resize the viewer. It's important to note that those features could easily have been added directly to the *ImageViewer* class. For the sake of this example, we'll presume that we don't have access to the *ImageViewer* source code, perhaps because it's a commercial component that isn't open source. In other words, in this case we're using inheritance out of faux necessity, not because it necessarily provides the best design. This often happens when working with standard class libraries and components. In Part III, we'll study more complex interclass relationships, in which inheritance is a matter of choice rather than circumstance.

The ImageViewerDeluxe Skeleton

The bare bones of any subclass requires:

- A class declaration that defines the inheritance relationship
- A constructor that invokes the superclass constructor with the expected arguments

Hence, our *ImageViewerDeluxe* class starts out with the skeleton shown in Example 7-1. Refer to Example 5-8 for the *ImageViewer* class definition.

Example 7-1. The ImageViewerDeluxe class skeleton

```
/**
 * The ImageViewerDeluxe class skeleton
 */
class ImageViewerDeluxe extends ImageViewer {
  public function ImageViewerDeluxe (target:MovieClip,
                                     depth:Number,
                                     x:Number,
                                     y:Number,
                                     w:Number,
                                     h:Number,
                                     borderThickness:Number,
                                     borderColor:Number) {
    // Invoke the ImageViewer constructor from Example 5-8
    super(target, depth, x, y, w, h, borderThickness, borderColor);
  }
}
```

Our *ImageViewerDeluxe* class does not alter the way an *ImageViewer* instance is constructed. It merely preserves the *ImageViewer* class constructor's behavior by accepting the same arguments as the *ImageViewer* constructor and forwarding them to it via *super( )*.

To create the *ImageViewerDeluxe.as* class file using Flash MX Professional 2004, follow these steps:

1. Choose File → New.
2. In the New Document dialog box, on the General tab, for Type, choose Action-Script File.
3. Click OK. The script editor launches with an empty file.
4. Copy the code from Example 7-1 into the script editor.
5. Choose File → Save As.

---

6. In the Save As dialog box, specify `ImageViewerDeluxe.as` as the filename (which is case sensitive), and save the file in the *imageviewer* folder that you created in Chapter 5.

Already, our *ImageViewerDeluxe* class is ready for use. Instances of the *ImageViewerDeluxe* class have all the *ImageViewer* class's methods and can be used anywhere *ImageViewer* instances are used.

Adding setPosition( ) and setSize( ) Methods

Now let's give the *ImageViewerDeluxe* class its new features: the abilities to reposition and resize the viewer. We'll implement two new methods to support these features:

setPosition( )
> Changes the location of the viewer by assigning the (x, y) coordinates of the viewer's main container movie clip

setSize( )
> Changes the size of the viewer by re-creating the mask and border over the image movie clip (i.e., by recropping the image)

Here's the *setPosition( )* method:

```
public function setPosition (x:Number, y:Number):Void {
  container_mc._x = x;
  container_mc._y = y;
}
```

The *setPosition( )* method is declared *public*, allowing it to be accessed from any code inside or outside the *ImageViewerDeluxe* class. The body of *setPosition( )* uses the good old-fashioned _x and _y properties of the *MovieClip* class to position the image viewer on screen. Notice that code in the *ImageViewerDeluxe* class has direct access to the container_mc property. As we learned in Chapter 6, a subclass can access all of its superclass's properties and methods, even those declared *private*.

Here's the *setSize( )* method, which resizes the image viewer by recropping the image:

```
public function setSize (w:Number, h:Number):Void {
  createImageClipMask(w, h);
  createBorder(w, h);
  container_mc.image_mc.setMask(container_mc.mask_mc);
}
```

To resize our image viewer on screen, we first re-create its mask:

```
createImageClipMask(w, h)
```

then we re-create its border:

```
createBorder(w, h)
```

and finally, we reassign the new mask movie clip (mask_mc) as a mask over the image movie clip (image_mc):

```
container_mc.image_mc.setMask(container_mc.mask_mc);
```

The *setSize( )* method gives a good sense of the convenience and logic of OOP. Every class offers a set of services; other classes can use those services to build new functionality. In *setSize( )*, most of the work involves simply invoking methods that already exist in the *ImageViewer* class.

Example 7-2 shows the updated code for the *ImageViewerDeluxe* class. Enter the new code, shown in bold, into your *ImageViewerDeluxe.as* file.

Example 7-2. The ImageViewerDeluxe class with reposition and resize features

```
/**
 * An ImageViewer subclass that adds reposition and resize features
 */
class ImageViewerDeluxe extends ImageViewer {
  public function ImageViewerDeluxe (target:MovieClip,
                                     depth:Number,
                                     x:Number,
                                     y:Number,
                                     w:Number,
                                     h:Number,
                                     borderThickness:Number,
                                     borderColor:Number) {

    super(target, depth, x, y, w, h, borderThickness, borderColor);
  }

  public function setPosition (x:Number, y:Number):Void {
    container_mc._x = x;
    container_mc._y = y;
  }

  public function setSize (w:Number, h:Number):Void {
    createImageClipMask(w, h);
    createBorder(w, h);
    container_mc.image_mc.setMask(container_mc.mask_mc);
  }
}
```

Autosizing the Image Viewer

Well, that was so easy we may as well have a little more fun. Now that our *ImageViewerDeluxe* class supports resizing, let's add the ability to automatically resize the viewer to fit the size of any loaded image.

To set the size of the viewer when an image loads, we'll override the *ImageViewer* class's *onLoadInit( )* method. From the *ImageViewerDeluxe* version of the method, we'll check the size of the loaded image and then use our handy new *setSize( )*

---

method to resize the viewer to those dimensions. We'll also use *super( )* to invoke the overridden version of *onLoadInit( )* so that the original behavior of the method is preserved. Here is the absolute quick-and-dirtiest way to add the new autosize feature:

```
public function onLoadInit (target:MovieClip):Void {
  super.onLoadInit(target);
  setSize(container_mc.image_mc._width, container_mc.image_mc._height);
}
```

Admittedly, that code works, but it's inflexible. For starters, every *ImageViewerDeluxe* instance created will resize itself when it loads an image. That should be optional, not mandatory. Furthermore, as we saw when we implemented *setSize( )*, it often pays to break up functionality into discrete methods, each of which can be accessed selectively by users of the class. Let's reexamine the autosize feature to see how it can be broken up.

First, we want the autosize feature to be optional, so we need a new Boolean property, showFullImage, which indicates whether the viewer should autosize (true) or not (false). The showFullImage property should be *private*, and should be set and retrieved via accessor methods: *getShowFullImage( )* and *setShowFullImage( )*.

Next, it's likely that an *ImageViewerDeluxe* user would want to use our autosize feature even after an image loads. For example, an interface might provide a button to reveal the entire image. Given that we're building autosize functionality already, it's sensible to offer this feature in a separate method: *scaleViewerToImage( )*.

Finally, consider what the *scaleViewerToImage( )* method does: it checks the width and height of the image in the viewer and sets the viewer's size to those dimensions. Checking the width and height of the image in the viewer is useful in and of itself. For example, if the viewer is used as part of a dynamic interface that automatically adjusts itself to the viewer's size, the creator of that interface will need some way to retrieve the viewer's dimensions. Hence, we should create public methods that return the width and height of the image in the viewer: *getImageWidth( )* and *getImageHeight( )*.

Let's see how this all plays out in code.

First, here's our showFullImage property definition. The property defaults to false (don't autosize).

```
private var showFullImage:Boolean = false;
```

Next, here are the accessor methods for showFullImage:

```
public function setShowFullImage(show:Boolean):Void {
  showFullImage = show;
}

public function getShowFullImage():Boolean {
  return showFullImage;
}
```

The *getImageWidth( )* and *getImageHeight( )* methods are equally simple. They simply return the _width and _height of the image_mc movie clip. Recall that container_mc is an instance property defined by the *ImageViewer* class and that image_mc is a movie clip—nested within container_mc—that contains the current loaded image.

```
public function getImageWidth ():Number {
  return container_mc.image_mc._width;
}

public function getImageHeight ():Number {
  return container_mc.image_mc._height;
}
```

Finally, here's the *scaleViewerToImage( )* method. It uses *getImageWidth( )* and *getImageHeight( )* to determine the new size of the viewer.

```
public function scaleViewerToImage ():Void {
  setSize(getImageWidth(), getImageHeight());
}
```

Now we can return to our *onLoadInit( )* method, where the viewer does its autosizing. Recall what the quick-and-dirty version looked like:

```
public function onLoadInit (target:MovieClip):Void {
  super.onLoadInit(target);
  setSize(container_mc.image_mc._width, container_mc.image_mc._height);
}
```

Here's the revised version, which autosizes only if the viewer's autosize feature is turned on (i.e., if showFullImage is true):

```
public function onLoadInit (target:MovieClip):Void {
  super.onLoadInit(target);
  if (showFullImage) {
    scaleViewerToImage( );
  }
}
```

Notice how compact and readable the method is now that the autosize functionality is separated into distinct methods. The autosize feature is now optional, and we've exposed new methods to retrieve the image dimensions and arbitrarily resize the viewer to fit the image it's displaying. Great stuff!

 It's easy to get carried away with adding new features. In most real-world cases, features should be added only to satisfy some specific requirement. The wisdom of the Extreme Programming methodology applies here: never add functionality early.

More functionality means more code complexity, which translates into more development and maintenance time. In our autosize example, we posed scenarios that made extra functionality a requirement. If the real-world case had no such requirement, breaking our autosize feature up into separate methods would not have been wise.

Example 7-3 shows the final code for the *ImageViewerDeluxe* class. Update your code in *ImageViewerDeluxe.as* to match the example (changes from Example 7-2 shown in bold).

Example 7-3. The ImageViewerDeluxe class, final version

```
/**
 * An ImageViewer that can be repositioned and resized after it is created
 */
class ImageViewerDeluxe extends ImageViewer {

  // Flag indicating whether the viewer should be
  // scaled to match the size of the image.
  private var showFullImage:Boolean = false;

  public function ImageViewerDeluxe (target:MovieClip,
                                     depth:Number,
                                     x:Number,
                                     y:Number,
                                     w:Number,
                                     h:Number,
                                     borderThickness:Number,
                                     borderColor:Number) {

    super(target, depth, x, y, w, h, borderThickness, borderColor);
  }

  /**
   * Sets the position of the viewer.
   *
   * @param   x       The new horizontal position of the viewer.
   * @param   y       The new vertical position of the viewer.
   */
  public function setPosition (x:Number, y:Number):Void {
    container_mc._x = x;
    container_mc._y = y;
  }

  /**
   * Sets the size of the viewer (i.e., adjusts the
   * border and mask size).
   *
   * @param   w       The new width of the viewer, in pixels.
   * @param   h       The new height of the viewer, in pixels.
   */
  public function setSize (w:Number, h:Number):Void {
    createImageClipMask(w, h);
    createBorder(w, h);
    container_mc.image_mc.setMask(container_mc.mask_mc);
  }

  /**
   * Returns the width of the clip that contains the image.
   */
```

Example 7-3. The ImageViewerDeluxe class, final version (continued)

```
public function getImageWidth ():Number {
  return container_mc.image_mc._width;
}

/**
 * Returns the height of the clip that contains the image.
 */
public function getImageHeight ():Number {
  return container_mc.image_mc._height;
}

/**
 * Set flag indicating whether the entire image should be
 * displayed or the image should be cropped to fit the viewer.
 *
 * @param    show    A flag indicating whether the viewer should be
 *                   scaled to match the size of the image.
 */
public function setShowFullImage(show:Boolean):Void {
  showFullImage = show;
}

/**
 * Returns flag indicating whether the entire image should be
 * displayed or the image should be cropped to fit the viewer.
 */
public function getShowFullImage():Boolean {
  return showFullImage;
}

/**
 * Adjusts the size of the viewer so that the entire
 * image is visible.
 */
public function scaleViewerToImage ():Void {
  setSize(getImageWidth(), getImageHeight());
}

/**
 * MovieClipLoader handler. Triggered by imageLoader when loading is done.
 * Overrides ImageViewer.onLoadInit(), adding autosizing feature.
 */
public function onLoadInit (target:MovieClip):Void {
  super.onLoadInit(target);

  if (showFullImage) {
    scaleViewerToImage();
  }
}
}
```

Using ImageViewerDeluxe

To try out the new *ImageViewerDeluxe* class, follow these steps:

1. In Flash MX 2004 or Flash MX Professional 2004, open the *imageViewer.fla* we created in Chapter 5.
2. Use Window → Development Panels → Actions (F9) to open the Actions panel.
3. In *imageViewer.fla*'s main timeline, select frame 15.
4. Delete all existing code from the Actions panel in that frame.
5. Into the Actions panel, enter the following code:

   ```
   var viewer:ImageViewerDeluxe = new ImageViewerDeluxe(this, 1, 20,
                                            10, 0, 0, 3, 0xFF0000);
   viewer.setShowFullImage(true);
   viewer.loadImage("picture.jpg");
   loadmsg_txt.removeTextField(); // Removes the loading message (see frame 1).
   ```

6. Choose Control → Test Movie. The *.swf* file should play, and your image should load and appear with a red border. The viewer should size itself to reveal the entire image.

If you have any trouble using the class, compare your work with the finished example files available at *http://moock.org/eas2/examples*.

> As with the *ImageViewer* class, the *ImageViewerDeluxe* class does not display download progress for a loading image when the image is loaded off a local hard disk. To test the preloader, be sure to post your images to a web server, and play the movie in a web browser.

Moving Right Along

The *ImageViewerDeluxe* class from this chapter showed us how inheritance can work in a real application. Now that we've explored classes and inheritance in both theory and practice, we've covered most skills needed in typical OOP Flash development. However, we still have a few concepts left to consider over the next few chapters—namely, interfaces (abstract datatypes), packages (containers for classes), and exceptions (errors you can add to your programs). These last three theoretical topics will prepare you for Parts II and III, which present many more applied OOP examples and scenarios.

CHAPTER 8

Interfaces

An *interface* is an ActionScript 2.0 language construct used to define a new datatype, much as a class defines a datatype. However, whereas a class both defines a datatype and provides the implementation for it, an interface defines a datatype in abstract terms only; an interface provides no implementation for the datatype. That is, a class doesn't just declare a bunch of methods and properties, it also supplies concrete behavior—the method bodies and property values that make the class actually do something. An interface, instead of providing its own implementation, is adopted by one or more classes that agree to provide the implementation. A class that provides an implementation for an interface belongs both to its own datatype and to the datatype defined by the interface. As a member of multiple datatypes, the class can then play multiple roles in an application.

 Don't confuse the term *interface*, as discussed in this chapter, with other uses of the word. In this chapter, "interface" refers to an Action-Script 2.0 language construct, not a graphical user interface (GUI) or the public API of a class, sometimes also called an interface in general OOP theory.

Unless you're familiar with interfaces already, theoretical descriptions of them can be hard to follow, so lets dive right into an example.

The Case for Interfaces

Suppose we're creating an order-form application with a class, *OrderProcessor*, that manages the order-filling process. If a customer makes a mistake while filling in the order form, the *OrderProcessor* class signals an error by broadcasting an event, *OrderProcessorEvent*. Many classes may want to respond to the event—one class, *OrderUI*, may want to display an error message on screen; another class, *OrderChat*, may want to alert a live support technician; and yet another class, *StatsTracker*, may want to log the problem to a database for statistics tracking. To respond to the *OrderProcessorEvent*, each class defines an *onOrderError( )* method. When the event occurs, the *OrderProcessor* class invokes each class's *onOrderError( )* method automatically.

That all seems logical enough so far, but what happens if one of the error-event-handling classes fails to define *onOrderError( )*? The event will occur, but the negligent class won't respond. We must guarantee that every class that signs up to receive *OrderProcessor* events actually defines the *onOrderError( )* method.

To make that guarantee, we limit the type of objects that can register to receive events from *OrderProcessor*. Specifically, if an object wants to receive events from *OrderProcessor*, it must be an instance of the *OrderListener* class or an instance of one of *OrderListener*'s subclasses. The *OrderListener* class itself implements the *onOrderError( )* method in a generic way:

```
class OrderListener {
  public function onOrderError ():Void {
    // Generic implementation of onOrderError(), not shown...
  }
}
```

Any class that wishes to receive events from *OrderProcessor* extends *OrderListener* and overrides *OrderListener.onOrderError( )*, providing some specialized behavior. For example, the following class, *StatsTracker*, extends *OrderListener* and overrides *onOrderError( )*, providing database-specific behavior:

```
class StatsTracker extends OrderListener {
  // Override OrderListener.onOrderError().
  public function onOrderError () {
    // Send problem report to database. Code not shown...
  }
}
```

Back in the *OrderProcessor* class (the class that broadcasts events), we define a method, *addListener( )*, that registers an object to receive events. Only instances of the *OrderListener* datatype (including its subclasses) can be passed to *addListener( )*:

```
class OrderProcessor {
  public function addListener (ol:OrderListener):Boolean {
    // Code here should register ol to receive OrderProcessor events,
    // and return a Boolean value indicating whether registration
    // succeeded (code not shown).
  }
}
```

If an object passed to *addListener( )* is not of type *OrderListener* (which also includes instances of any one of its subclasses), the compiler generates a type mismatch error. If the object belongs to an *OrderListener* subclass that doesn't implement *onOrderError( )*, at least the generic *OrderListener.onOrderError( )* will execute.

Sounds reasonable, right? Almost. But there's a problem. What if a class wishing to receive events from *OrderProcessor* already extends another class? For example, suppose the *OrderUI* class extends *MovieClip*:

```
class OrderUI extends MovieClip {
    public function onOrderError () {
      // Display problem report on screen, not shown...
    }
}
```

In ActionScript, a single class cannot extend more than one class. The *OrderUI* class already extends *MovieClip,* so it can't extend *OrderListener*. Hence, instances of *OrderUI* can't register to receive events from *OrderProcessor*. What we really need in this situation is a way to indicate that *OrderUI* instances actually belong to two datatypes: *OrderUI* and *OrderListener*.

Enter...interfaces!

Interfaces and Multidatatype Classes

Earlier, we created the *OrderListener* datatype by defining an *OrderListener* class. That approach forces every *OrderProcessor* event consumer to be an instance of either *OrderListener* or an *OrderListener* subclass. To loosen that restriction, we can create the *OrderListener* datatype by defining an *OrderListener* interface rather than an *OrderListener* class. That way, any class can agree to provide an implementation for *OrderListener* while still inheriting from any other class. Let's see how this works.

Syntactically, an interface is simply a list of methods. For example, the following code creates an interface named *OrderListener* that contains a single method, *onOrderError( )*:

```
interface OrderListener {
    function onOrderError();
}
```

Classes use the *implements* keyword to enter into an agreement with an interface, promising to define the methods it contains. For example, to indicate that the *OrderUI* class agrees to define the method *onOrderError( )* (defined by the *OrderListener* interface), we use this code (note the portion in bold):

```
class OrderUI extends MovieClip implements OrderListener {
    public function onOrderError () {
      // Display problem report on screen, not shown...
    }
}
```

Instead of extending the *OrderListener* class, the *OrderUI* class extends *MovieClip* and implements the *OrderListener* interface. Because *OrderUI* implements *OrderListener*, it can be used anywhere the *OrderListener* datatype is required. Instances of *OrderUI* now belong to two datatypes: *OrderUI* and *OrderListener*.

Thus, despite the fact that *OrderUI* extends *MovieClip*, *OrderUI* instances still belong to the *OrderListener* type and can be passed safely to *OrderProcessor. addListener( )* (Wow, Ron, that's amazing! It's a pasta maker *and* a juicer!)

If *OrderUI* didn't define a method named *onOrderError( )*, the compiler would generate the following error:

```
The class must implement method 'onOrderError' from interface
'OrderListener'.
```

Compiler errors are the key to the entire interface system. They guarantee that a class lives up to its implementation promises, which allows external code to use it with the confidence that it will behave as required. That confidence is particularly important when designing an application that will be extended by another developer or used by third parties.

Now that we have a general idea of what interfaces are and how they're used, let's get down to some nitty-gritty syntax details.

 The hypothetical order application just discussed is one example of the *delegation event model*, which is covered in detail in Chapter 19.

Interface Syntax and Use

Recall that an interface is a construct used to define a new datatype without implementing any of the methods supported by the datatype.

To create an interface in ActionScript 2.0, we use the *interface* keyword, using the following syntax:

```
interface SomeName {
  function method1 (param1:datatype,...paramn:datatype):returnType;
  function method2 (param1:datatype,...paramn:datatype):returnType;
  ...
  function methodn (param1:datatype,...paramn:datatype):returnType;
}
```

where *SomeName* is the name of the interface, *method1*, ...*methodn* are the methods defined by the interface, *param1:datatype*, ...*paramn:datatype* are the parameters of the methods, and *returnType* is the datatype of each method's return value.

 In interfaces, method declarations do not (and must not) include curly braces. The following method declaration causes a compile-time error in an interface because it includes curly braces:

```
function method1 (param:datatype):returnType {
}
```

The errors generated are:

```
Function bodies are not permitted in interfaces.
This statement is not permitted in an interface definition.
```

All methods declared in an interface must be *public*; hence, by convention, the attribute *public* (which is the default) is omitted from method definitions in an interface. Property definitions are not allowed in ActionScript 2.0 interfaces; neither can interface definitions be nested (this contrasts with Java's interfaces, in which constant definitions are allowed and interfaces can be nested). As with ActionScript 2.0 classes, each interface must be defined in its own *.as* file, whose name must exactly match the name of the interface (case sensitivity matters).

Let's briefly review the three types of *.as* files we've covered so far:

Class files
> Contain the method and property definitions for each class. They start with the *class* keyword. (See Chapter 4.)

Intrinsic files
> Contain method signatures strictly for the purpose of satisfying the compiler's type checking. They start with the *intrinsic* keyword. (See Chapter 4.)

Interface files
> Contain a list of methods to be implemented but not the implementations themselves. They start with the *interface* keyword.

A class that wishes to adopt an interface's datatype must agree to implement that interface's methods. To form such an agreement, the class uses the *implements* keyword, which has the following syntax:

```
class SomeName implements SomeInterface {
}
```

where *SomeName* is the name of the class that promises to implement the needed methods, and *SomeInterface* is the name of the interface (as defined using the *interface* keyword in an external *.as* file). The *SomeName* class is said to "implement the *SomeInterface* interface." Note that *implements* must always come after any *extends* clause that might also be present. Furthermore, if you specify a class instead of an interface after the *implements* keyword, the compiler generates this error:

```
A class may not implement a class, only interfaces.
```

The class *SomeName* must implement all methods defined by *SomeInterface*, otherwise a compile-time error such as the following occurs:

```
The class must implement method 'methodname' from interface 'SomeInterface'.
```

The implementing class's method definitions must match the interface's method definitions exactly, including number of parameters, parameter types, and return type. If any of those aspects differs between the interface and the implementing class, the compiler generates the following error:

```
The implementation of the interface method doesn't match its definition.
```

In theory, when a class implements a method from an interface, it should be able to define the method as either a class method (i.e., *static*) or an instance method. Unfortunately, a bug in ActionScript 2.0 prevents a class from using the *static* attribute when implementing a method defined by an interface. Due to the bug, a method defined by an interface cannot be implemented as a class method. If the method in the implementing class must be a class method, then it should not be listed in the interface at all.

A class can legally implement more than one interface by separating interface names with commas, as follows:

```
class SomeName implements SomeInterface, SomeOtherInterface {
}
```

in which case, the class *SomeName* belongs to all three of the following datatypes: *SomeName*, *SomeInterface*, and *SomeOtherInterface*. If a class implements two interfaces that define a method by the same name, but with different signatures, the following error occurs:

```
Multiple implemented interfaces contain same method with different types.
```

If, on the other hand, a class implements two interfaces that define a method by the same name and with the exact same signature, no error occurs. The real question is whether the class can provide the services required by both interfaces within a single method definition. In most cases, the answer is no.

 Once an interface has been implemented by one or more classes, adding new methods to it will cause compile-time errors in those implementing classes (because the classes won't define the new methods)! Hence, you should think carefully about the methods you want in an interface during the design phase and be sure you're confident in your application's design before you commit it to code.

If a class declares that it implements an interface, but that interface cannot be found by the compiler, the following error occurs (notice that the compiler misleadingly refers to the interface as a class!):

```
The class 'InterfaceName' could not be loaded.
```

Interface Naming Conventions

Like classes, interfaces should be named with an initial capital letter so they're easy to identify as datatypes. Interfaces used for event handling typically take the form *SomeClass*Listener, where *SomeClass* is the name of the class broadcasting the events. For example, in Chapter 19, we'll create a class named *Randomizer* that broadcasts events. Classes wishing to process *Randomizer* events must implement *RandomizerListener*.

Most other interfaces are named after the additional ability they describe. For example, suppose an application contains a series of classes that represent visual objects. Some of the objects can be repositioned; others cannot. In our design, objects that can be repositioned must implement an interface named *Moveable*. Here is a theoretical *ProductIcon* class that implements *Moveable*:

```
class ProductIcon implements Moveable {
  public function getPosition ():Position {
  }
  public function setPosition (pos:Position):Void {
  }
}
```

The interface name, *Moveable*, indicates the specific capability that the interface adds to a class. An object might be a piece of clipart or a block of text, but if it implements *Moveable*, we know it can be repositioned. Other similar names might be *Storable*, *Killable*, or *Serializable*. Some developers also preface interface names with an I, as in *IMoveable*, *IKillable*, and *ISerializable*.

Interface Inheritance

As with classes, an interface can use the *extends* keyword to inherit from another interface. For example, the following code shows an interface, *IntA*, that extends another interface, *IntB*. In this setup, interface *IntB* is known as the *subinterface,* and interface *IntA* is known as the *superinterface*.

```
interface IntA {
  function methodA ():Void;
}
interface IntB extends A {
  function methodB ():Void;
}
```

Classes that implement interface *IntB* must provide definitions for both *methodA( )* and *methodB( )*. Interface inheritance lets us define a type hierarchy much as we would with class inheritance, but without accompanying method implementations.

Unlike Java, ActionScript 2.0 interfaces do not support multiple interface inheritance; that is, an interface cannot extend more than one other interface.

Marker Interfaces

Interfaces need not contain any methods at all to be useful. Occasionally, empty interfaces, called *marker interfaces*, are used to "mark" (designate) a class as having some feature. Requirements for the *marked classes* (i.e., classes implementing a marker interface) are provided by the documentation for the marker interface.

For example, our earlier *OrderProcessor* class used the *OrderListener* interface to ensure that the appropriate event methods are defined on any object wishing to receive event notifications.

Now consider a similar but more complex situation—a web-based email application that contains three classes: *MessageComposer*, *MessageSender*, and *MessageReceiver*. Each class wants to broadcast its own events. The event-handling methods required of every event-receiving object are defined in the following corresponding interfaces: *MessageComposerListener*, *MessageSenderListener*, and *MessageReceiverListener*. In the email application, because more than one class broadcasts events, it's sensible to define a general class, *EventListenerList*, to manage objects that receive events (known as *event-consumer objects*). Each of the *MessageComposer*, *MessageSender*, and *MessageReceiver* classes uses an *EventListenerList* instance to manage event-consumer objects. For example, when a *MessageComposer* instance wants to add a new event-consumer object to its *EventListenerList*, it passes that object to *EventListenerList.addListener()*, as follows:

```
listenerList.addListener(consumerObject);
```

Can you spot the problem? The event-consumer objects for each of the event-producing classes belong to different datatypes! A consumer object for the *MessageComposer* class belongs to the *MessageComposerListener* datatype, while a consumer object for the *MessageSender* class belongs to the *MessageSenderListener* datatype. The *addListener()* method can accept only one type of consumer object as an argument, but it needs to be used with multiple datatypes.

Solution? Make all event-consumer objects homogeneous by creating a marker interface, *EventListener*. The three listener interfaces in the mail application extend *EventListener*. The *addListener()* method then accepts consumer objects of type *EventListener*. Hence, different types of event-consumer objects (specifically, subtypes of *EventListener*) can be passed to the method. The method definition for *addListener()* follows (note the use of the marker interface, *EventListener*, shown in bold):

```
public function addListener (l:EventListener):Boolean {
  // Search for the specified event consumer.
  // listeners is an array of event-consumer objects.
  var len:Number = listeners.length;
  for (var i:Number = len; --i >= 0; ) {
    if (listeners[i] == l) {
      // The new event consumer is already in the list, so quit.
      return false;
    }
  }

  // The new listener is not already in the list, so add it.
  listeners.push(l);
  return true;
}
```

Note that we could have solved the problem alternatively by allowing any object to be used as an event consumer object, as follows:

```
public function addListener (l:Object):Boolean {
```

That works in the technical sense but does nothing to suggest to the developer that event-consumer objects must implement one of the application's event-listener interfaces. By forcing event-consumer objects to implement the marker interface, *EventListener*, the application guides the developer to the documentation for that interface. The documentation should describe the application's general event architecture, helping the developer understand how to properly handle events. This system is a native part of Java. We'll return to it in Chapter 19.

Multiple Type Inheritance with Interfaces

In our earlier order-form example, we learned that a class can inherit from another class while also belonging to a separate datatype defined by an interface. Our earlier *OrderUI* class inherited from *MovieClip* but also belonged to the *OrderListener* datatype because it implemented the *OrderListener* interface. That architectural pattern is one of the more common and powerful uses of interfaces—one in which a class belongs to multiple datatypes without inheriting from multiple classes. Let's take a closer look at this pattern with a new example (source code available at: *http://moock.org/eas2/examples*).

Suppose we're creating an application that stores objects on disk, either via a server-side script or a *SharedObject* instance. Each stored object is responsible for providing a method, *serialize( )*, that returns a string representation of the object. The string representation can be used to reconstitute the object from scratch. For example, a *Rectangle* class with width and height properties might provide a *serialize( )* method that returns the string "width=w|height=h" (where w and h are the values of the width and height properties). Later, the string "width=w|height=h" is retrieved and used to create a new *Rectangle* instance of the original size. To keep things simple for this example, we'll presume that every object must store only property names and values and that no property values are, themselves, objects that would need serialization.

When the time comes to save the state of our application, the *StorageManager* class performs the following tasks:

• Gathers objects for storage
• Converts each object to a string (via *serialize( )*)
• Transfers the objects to disk

In order to guarantee that every stored object can be serialized (i.e., converted to a string), the *StorageManager* class rejects any instances of classes that do not belong to the *Serializable* datatype. The *Serializable* datatype is defined by the interface *Serializable*, which contains a single method, *serialize( )*, as follows:

```
interface Serializable {
  function serialize( ):String;
}
```

Classes that support serialization as described are said to "implement *Serializable*." To handle generic serialization cases, in which property names and values are retrieved and converted to strings, we create a class, *Serializer*, which implements *Serializable*. The *Serializer* class has the following methods:

setSerializationProps( )
> Specifies which properties of the object, as specified by *setSerializationObj( )*, to serialize, as an array

setSerializationObj( )
> Specifies which object to serialize

setRecordSeparator( )
> Specifies the string to use as a separator between properties

serialize( )
> Returns a string representing the object

Here's the class listing for *Serializer*:

```
class Serializer implements Serializable {
  private var serializationProps:Array;
  private var serializationObj:Serializable;
  private var recordSeparator:String;

  public function Serializer () {
    setSerializationObj(this);
  }

  public function setSerializationProps (props:Array):Void {
    serializationProps = props;
  }

  public function setSerializationObj (obj:Serializable):Void {
    serializationObj = obj;
  }

  public function setRecordSeparator (rs:String):Void {
    recordSeparator = rs;
  }

  public function serialize ():String {
    var s:String = "";
    for (var i:Number = serializationProps.length; --i >= 0; ) {
      s += serializationProps[i]
         + "=" + String(serializationObj[serializationProps[i]]);
      if (i > 0) {
        s += recordSeparator;
      }
    }
    return s;
  }
}
```

To use the *Serializer* class's serialization services, a class can simply extend *Serializer*. By extending *Serializer* directly, the extending class inherits both the *Serializable* interface and the *Serializer* class's implementation of that interface.

 It is common to define a class that implements a particular interface and then extend that class (i.e., create subclasses that use it). Subclassing in this way allows you to separate a datatype's interface from its implementation. The subclasses use the implementation via inheritance but other, unrelated classes can still choose to implement the interface directly, supplying their own custom behavior.

For example, the following code shows a *Point* class that defines x and y properties, which need to be serialized. The *Point* class extends *Serializer*, allowing it to use *Serializer*'s services directly.

```
// The Point class
class Point extends Serializer {
  private var x:Number;
  private var y:Number;

  public function Point (x:Number, y:Number) {
    super( );

    setRecordSeparator(",");
    setSerializationProps(["x", "y"]);

    this.x = x;
    this.y = y;
  }
}
```

Code that wishes to save a *Point* instance to disk simply calls *serialize( )* on that instance, as follows:

```
var p:Point = new Point(5, 6);
trace(p.serialize( ));  // Displays: y=6,x=5
```

Note that the *Point* class does not implement *Serializable* directly. It extends *Serializer*, which in turn implements *Serializable*.

The *Point* class does not extend any other class, so it's free to extend *Serializer*. However, if a class wants to use *Serializer* but already extends another class, it must use composition instead of inheritance. That is, rather than extending *Serializer*, the class implements *Serializable* directly, stores a *Serializer* object in an instance property, and forwards *serialize()* method calls to that object. For example, here's a *Rectangle* class that extends a *Shape* class but uses *Serializer* via composition (refer specifically to the sections in bold):

```
// The Shape superclass
class Shape {
  private var target:MovieClip;
```

```
    private var depth:Number;

    public function Shape (t:MovieClip, d:Number) {
      target = t;
      depth = d;
    }
  }

  // The Rectangle subclass implements Serializable directly
  class Rectangle extends Shape implements Serializable {
    private var width:Number = 0;
    private var height:Number = 0;
    private var serializer:Serializer;

    public function Rectangle (t:MovieClip, d:Number) {
      super(t, d);
      // Here is where the composition takes place
      serializer = new Serializer();
      serializer.setRecordSeparator("|");
      serializer.setSerializationProps(["height", "width"]);
      serializer.setSerializationObj(this);
    }

    public function setSize (w:Number, h:Number):Void {
      width = w;
      height = h;
    }

    public function getArea ():Number {
      return width * height;
    }

    public function draw ():Void {
      var container_mc:MovieClip = target.createEmptyMovieClip("rect"
                                                              + depth,
                                                              depth);
      container_mc.clear();
      container_mc.lineStyle(1, 0x000000);
      container_mc.moveTo(0, 0);
      container_mc.beginFill(0xFFFFFF, 100);
      container_mc.lineTo(width, 0);
      container_mc.lineTo(width, height);
      container_mc.lineTo(0, height);
      container_mc.lineTo(0, 0);
      container_mc.endFill();
    }

    public function serialize ():String {
      // Here is where the Rectangle class forwards the serialize()
      // invocation to the Serializer instance stored in serializer
      return serializer.serialize();
    }
  }
}
```

As with the *Point* class, code that wishes to store a *Rectangle* instance simply invokes *serialize( )* on that instance. Through composition, the invocation is forwarded to the *Serializer* instance stored by the *Rectangle* class. Here is an example of its use:

```
var r:Rectangle = new Rectangle(this, 1);
r.setSize(10, 20);
trace(r.serialize( ));  // Displays: width=10|height=20
```

If a class would rather implement its own custom *serialize( )* method instead of using the generic one provided by *Serializer*, then the class should simply implement the *Serializable* interface directly, providing the *serialize( )* method definition and body itself.

Separating the *Serializable* datatype's interface from its implementation allows any class to flexibly choose from among the following options when providing an implementation for the *serialize( )* method:

- Extend *Serializer*
- Use *Serializer* via composition
- Provide its own *serialize( )* method directly

If the class does not already extend another class, it can extend *Serializer* (this option means the least work). If the class already extends another class, it can still use *Serializer* via composition (this option is the most flexible). Finally, if the class needs its own special serialization routine, it can implement *Serializable* directly (this option means the most work but may be required by the situation at hand).

This flexibility led Sun to formally recommend that, in a Java application, any class that is expected to be subclassed should be an implementation of an interface. As such, it can be subclassed directly, or it can be used via composition by a class that inherits from another class. Sun's recommendation is also sensible for large-scale ActionScript applications.

Figure 8-1 shows the generic structure of a datatype whose implementation can be used via either inheritance or composition.

Figure 8-2 shows the structure of the specific *Serializable*, *Point*, and *Rectangle* example.

Up Next, Packages

Interfaces are an important application development tool, because they promote flexible class architectures in the context of a statically typed language. They solve the problem of implementing classes that belong to multiple datatypes without introducing the complexities of multiple class inheritance.

Next we'll study another valuable ActionScript 2.0 tool, *packages*, which are used to organize classes (and interfaces) into logical groups.

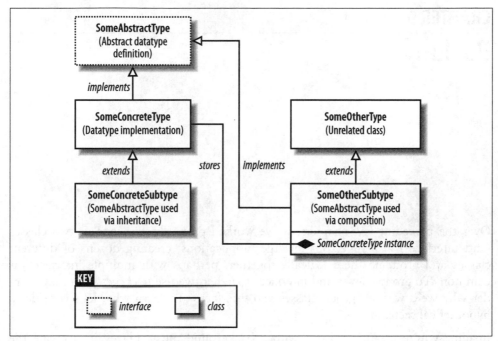

Figure 8-1. Multiple datatype inheritance via interfaces

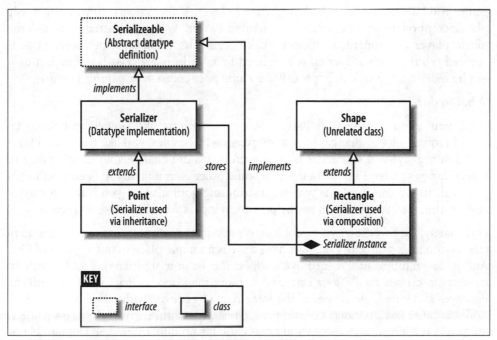

Figure 8-2. Multiple datatype inheritance Serializable example

CHAPTER 9

Packages

Over the preceding few chapters, we've worked primarily with one or two classes (and interfaces) at a time. But in larger applications, creating dozens of different classes and grouping them logically together, perhaps with multiple interfaces, is common. To group classes and interfaces together, we use *packages*. You may wonder why we'd want to group classes and interfaces. To learn why, let's consider a hypothetical scenario.

Imagine you're creating a game with a background music player. You create the game in-house, but you use a third-party component for the music player. In the game, you have a class for the player, named *Player*. Unbeknownst to you, the music player component also defines a class named *Player*! When you attempt to use the music player component, it doesn't work because its version of the *Player* class is ignored (your game's *Player* class is defined first, and once a class is defined, it cannot be redefined). This conflict is called a *namespace collision* or *naming conflict*.

What to do?

Well, you could rename your *Player* class to something like *GamePlayer*, but that would require a lot of changes to your existing code. Besides, you like the name *Player* and don't really want to change it. And even if you did change your class's name to *GamePlayer*, you have no guarantee that some other component you need won't conflict with it. Or conversely, if you are distributing your classes, you have no way of anticipating the class names in use by other developers who might use your code.

Fortunately, *packages* solve your problem. A package is a unique place to put a group of classes, much as a directory on your hard drive is a unique place to put a group of files. And just as multiple files named *index.html* can exist in more than one folder without conflicts, a class named *Player* can exist in more than one package without conflicts. Packages allow multiple classes of the same name to coexist without namespace collisions, because each package constitutes a *namespace* within which the class name is unique. A namespace is a set of names that contains no duplicates. The Domain Name System (DNS) defines a namespace in which registrants can reserve a domain name, such as *moock.org*, without fear that someone else might use the same name.

Package Syntax

Every package has a name that describes the classes it contains. By convention, package names do not use initial caps but might use mixed case, such as *greatUtils*. This helps distinguish them from classes, which by convention start with a capital letter. For example, a package that contains classes for a game might be named *game*, while a package that contains general utilities might be named *tools*, and a library of visual classes might be named *graphics*. Delaying, for a moment, the discussion of how to create a package, let's see how the classes within an existing package are accessed.

To refer to a specific class within a package, we use the dot operator, as follows:

```
packagename.ClassName
```

For example, in the following code, the names *game*, *tools*, and *graphics* are package names and the names *Player*, *Randomizer*, and *Vector2D* are class names:

```
game.Player
tools.Randomizer
graphics.Vector2D
```

Packages can be nested to form a hierarchy; that is, a package can contain another package. For example, the *game* package might contain a *vehicles* package that contains a *SpaceShip* class. When referring to a class in a nested package, separate each package name with the dot operator. For example:

```
game.vehicles.SpaceShip
```

By nesting packages, we can organize our classes into discrete subcategories within a larger category, which again prevents naming conflicts. For example, a traffic simulation application and a driving game may both want to use the *vehicles* namespace. To do so without naming conflicts, each application must nest *vehicles* within the larger application namespace:

```
trafficsimulator.vehicles
game.vehicles
```

On a more general level, two companies may both want to use the *game* namespace for the creation of games. Namespaces, therefore, often include the name of the organization producing the classes they contain, as in:

```
somecompany.game.vehicles
```

As we'll learn later, under "Package Naming Conventions," many organizations use their domain name as a namespace, because it is guaranteed to be unique.

Flash's own v2 component classes are categorized in hierarchical packages. For example, the classes for general user interface components such as List, Button, RadioButton, and ComboBox are contained by the *mx.controls* package. Classes related to the individual List component are stored in a nested package, *mx.controls.listclasses*. And components that act as application containers, such as Window and ScrollPane, are stored in the *mx.containers* package. Notice that a package can contain both classes and other packages, much as a file folder can contain both files and other folders.

A reference to a class that includes its complete package name is known as a *fully qualified reference*. By contrast, an *unqualified reference* includes just the class name. For example, *SpaceShip* is an unqualified reference, while *game.vehicles.SpaceShip* is a fully qualified reference.

Prior to discussing packages, we've used unqualified references when creating instances of classes and specifying the datatypes of variables, parameters, and return types. For example, if the class *SpaceShip* were not in a package, we would use the following syntax to create a *SpaceShip* instance and store it in a typed variable:

```
var ship:SpaceShip = new SpaceShip();
```

However, if a class is in a package, we must use a fully qualified reference when creating instances of the class and specifying the datatypes of variables, parameters, and return types. Therefore, if the *SpaceShip* class were in the package *game.vehicles*, we would use fully qualified references, such as:

```
var ship:game.vehicles.SpaceShip = new game.vehicles.SpaceShip();
```

Similarly, when *SpaceShip* is not in a package, we specify the return type of a method using :SpaceShip, as in:

```
public function getClosestShip ():SpaceShip {
  // Method body not shown...
}
```

However, if the *SpaceShip* class is in a package, such as *game.vehicles*, we must declare the fully qualified path. So the preceding example becomes:

```
public function getClosestShip ():game.vehicles.SpaceShip {
  // Method body not shown...
}
```

We haven't talked yet about how to define the *SpaceShip* class or put it in the *vehicles* or *game.vehicles* package. Regardless, you'll notice that using fully qualified class references becomes tedious in a hurry. The following code requires more typing and takes longer to read than its nonpackage counterpart:

```
var ship:game.vehicles.SpaceShip = new game.vehicles.SpaceShip();
```

To make life easier, ActionScript 2.0 provides the *import* statement, covered next.

The import Statement

The *import* statement lets us use an unqualified class reference as an alias (shorthand) for a fully qualified class reference. The basic syntax of *import* is:

```
import packagename.ClassName;
```

After the *import* statement appears in a script or class, every unqualified reference to *ClassName* is automatically converted to the fully qualified reference, *packagename.ClassName*. For example, after issuing the following *import* statement:

```
import game.vehicles.SpaceShip;
```

the compiler will subsequently treat the unqualified reference *SpaceShip* as though it were literally *game.vehicles.SpaceShip*.

Hence, the earlier assignment statement:

```
var ship:game.vehicles.SpaceShip = new game.vehicles.SpaceShip();
```

can be shortened to:

```
import game.vehicles.SpaceShip;
var ship:SpaceShip = new SpaceShip();
```

Because of the *import* statement, the compiler knows we mean *game.vehicles.* *SpaceShip* when we specify the unqualified class name *SpaceShip*. The *import* statement doesn't allow us to specify an identifier to use in place of the fully qualified reference; the alias name is always the name of the class, excluding the package name(s). Don't try something like this (it won't work):

```
import spaceAlias = game.vehicles.SpaceShip;  // Won't work!
```

Importing an Entire Package

The earlier *import* statement:

```
import game.vehicles.SpaceShip;
```

imports only the *SpaceShip* class, not other classes in the package. To import all the classes in a package, use the wildcard character, *, as follows:

```
import packagename.*;
```

This wildcard syntax lets us refer to any class in *packagename* by its unqualified name rather than its fully qualified name (i.e., *packagename.ClassName*).

For example, suppose the *geometry* package contains three classes *Circle*, *Triangle*, and *Rectangle*. Rather than importing each class individually, as follows:

```
import geometry.Circle;
import geometry.Triangle;
import geometry.Rectangle;
```

we can simply use:

```
import geometry.*;
```

After that statement has been issued, we can then refer to *Circle*, *Triangle*, and *Rectangle*, without including the package name, *geometry*.

If we use package wildcards to import two classes with the same name but from different packages, we again encounter a namespace collision. To access the ambiguous classes, we must use their fully qualified class names. For example, suppose we're writing an application that uses the classes *game.vehicles.Ship* and *ordering.* *Ship*. The application imports all classes in *game.vehicles* and in *ordering*:

```
import game.vehicles.*;
import ordering.*;
```

When we attempt to access the *Ship* class without qualification, the class that was imported first (*game.vehicles.Ship*) is used:

```
var s:Ship = new Ship( );  // Creates a new game.vehicles.Ship
```

The only way to create an *ordering.Ship* instance is to use a fully qualified reference, as in:

```
var s:ordering.Ship = new ordering.Ship( );
```

To avoid confusion, we should use fully qualified names for all references to *Ship*. However, attempting to import two classes of the same name directly, as in:

```
import game.vehicles.Ship;
import ordering.Ship;
```

yields this error:

```
The class 'ordering.Ship' cannot be imported because its leaf name is
already being resolved to imported class 'game.vehicles.Ship'.
```

The solution is to not import either *Ship* class and use only fully qualified references to access *game.vehicles.Ship* and *ordering.Ship*.

Note that wildcard imports work with only one package at a time. There is no way to import an entire hierarchy of packages. We must import the classes of each package individually. For example, to import the classes in *game.vehicles*, *game.logic*, and *game.data*, we must use:

```
import game.vehicles.*;
import game.logic.*;
import game.data.*;
```

not:

```
import game.*;
```

The statement import game.* imports only the classes contained by the *game* package; it does not import any classes in subpackages of *game*.

 Don't confuse the *import* statement with the #include directive! The two are completely unrelated. The #include directive copies external code into the current script, whereas *import* merely establishes an unqualified class name (e.g., *SpaceShip*) as an alias for a fully qualified class name (e.g., *game.vehicles.SpaceShip*). The *import* statement pertains only to classes stored in packages. Imported classes are compiled into a movie only if they are actually referenced in it. Included code, by contrast, is compiled into the movie whether it is needed or not, so be frugal with your #include directives.

Package Naming Conventions

Earlier we posed a scenario in which a game and a music component each defined unrelated classes named *Player*. We learned how packages could fix this problem by providing a unique, fully qualified identifier for each class. For example:

```
musiccomponent.Player
game.Player
```

But this merely trades one problem for another. We still need a way to prevent one application's *game.Player* class from conflicting with another application's *game. Player* class. In other words, just as two class names can conflict, two package names can conflict. To avoid package or class naming conflicts you should use the convention of placing all your classes and packages in a package named after your organization's domain name. For example, classes and subpackages created by Acme Corp., whose domain name is *acme.com*, would be stored in the package:

```
com.acme
```

Notice that com precedes acme (the package name is the reverse of the domain name).

Thus, a *game.Player* class created by Acme and a *game.Player* class created by, say, Nintendo, could be stored safely in the following unique packages:

```
com.acme.game.Player
com.nintendo.game.Player
```

Domain names are guaranteed to be unique by the system of authorized top-level-domain (TLD) registrars; thus, starting your package names with your organization's domain name avoids name conflicts with code developed by other organizations.

Naming conflicts remain a possibility within a large organization. So large organizations should adopt the convention of, say, including another identifier, such as the department name or project in the package hierarchy. Nintendo's GameCube division might use a package name such as:

```
com.nintendo.gamecube.game.Player
```

Notice that the first part of the package name, *com.nintendo.gamecube*, goes from the general (*com*) to the specific (*.nintendo* and *.gamecube*). Then the package name switches gears from the organization and department names to a name dependent on the purpose, in this case *.game*. Here are two more example package names from my own software, Unity. Unity is a multiuser application development kit, on top of which many different applications can be built. The following packages contain classes for the applications Tic Tac Toe and Avatar Chat:

```
org.moock.unity.tictactoe
org.moock.unity.avatarchat
```

Notice that, again, both package names start with the general domain name (*org. moock*), then specify the general purpose (*.unity*), then specify the particular purpose (an application written for the Unity platform).

Defining Packages

Defining a package for a class requires two general steps:

1. Create a directory structure whose name identically matches the package hierarchy.
2. Specify the package name when defining the class.

Note that there is no such thing as a package file, per se. A package is a concept based on placing a given class's *.as* file in the appropriate folder.

For example, to place the class *Player* in the package *com.yourdomain.game*, we'd follow these steps:

1. Create a new directory named *com*.
2. Create a new directory inside *com* named *yourdomain*.
3. Create a new directory inside *yourdomain* named *game*.
4. Create a text file, *Player.as*, in the directory */com/yourdomain/game/*.
5. In *Player.as*, add the following code:

```
class com.yourdomain.game.Player {
  // Class body not shown...
}
```

 The class declaration must use the fully qualified class name, in this case *com.yourdomain.game.Player*, indicating to the compiler that the package for the *Player* class is *com.yourdomain.game*.

If any part of the package or class name does not match the actual names of the system directories and *.as* file, the compiler generates an error (case sensitivity matters!). For example, if the letter "e" were missing in the word "game" in our class definition:

```
// Oops! Missing the "e" in "game"!
class com.yourdomain.gam.Player {
  // Class body not shown...
}
```

the compiler would generate the error:

```
The class 'com.yourdomain.gam.Player' needs to be defined in a
file whose relative path is 'com\yourdomain\gam\Player.as'.
```

In our generic game example, we put all the game-related classes in a package named *game*. We might also define a subpackage named *vehicle* to hold the classes that implement all the vehicles, including *SpaceShip* and its subclasses (perhaps *Fighter*, *Bomber*, and *Cruiser*). Furthermore, the *SpaceShip* class might have a superclass named *Vehicle* that also resides in the *vehicles* package. It's not uncommon for a package and a class to have the same name (except the package name is lowercase and the class name is uppercase). For example, in Chapter 17, we'll create a class named *Logger* and place it in a package named *logger*. The fully qualified class reference is:

```
logger.Logger
```

Here, we can see the capitalization conventions for packages and classes really pay off. At a glance, we know that *logger* is the package because it starts with a lowercase "l" and that *Logger* is the class because it starts with a capital "L."

Note that the package path for our example *SpaceShip* class is:

```
game.vehicles.SpaceShip
```

not

```
game.vehicles.Vehicle.SpaceShip
```

That is, don't attempt to include the superclass name in the fully qualified name for a subclass. A package names tells the compiler where to find the subclass's *.as* file and has no bearing on the subclass's inheritance relationship to the superclass (which is established via *extends*).

Package Access and the Classpath

In order for a *.fla* file to access a class in a package, the root directory of the package must reside within the *classpath*. The classpath is simply the list of directories (paths) on your hard drive in which the compiler looks for classes. Entries in the classpath can be added globally for all documents (the *global classpath*) or on a per-*.fla* file basis (a *document classpath*).

By default, the global classpath includes the following directories:

- The current directory, usually represented by a period (.)—i.e., the directory in which the *.fla* resides

- The *Classes* directory, *$(LocalData)/Classes*—that is, the *Classes* directory in the user configuration directory for the Flash MX 2004 or Flash MX Professional 2004 application

The *Classes* directory is found in one of the following locations, depending on your operating system. In each of the following paths, substitute your operating system user account name for *USER* and your Flash language code for LANGUAGE_CODE, which is "en" for English:

Windows 2000, Windows XP

C:\Documents and Settings\USER\Local Settings\Application Data\Macromedia\Flash MX 2004\LANGUAGE_CODE\Configuration\Classes

Note that the *Local Settings* folder is hidden by default but can be revealed in Windows Explorer using Tools → Folder Options → View → Advanced Settings → Files and Folders → Hidden Files and Folders → Show Hidden Files and Folders.

Windows 98

    C:\Windows\Application Data\Macromedia\Flash MX 2004\LANGUAGE_CODE\Config-uration\Classes or C:\Windows\Profiles\USER\Application Data\Macromedia\Flash MX 2004\LANGUAGE_CODE\Configuration\Classes

Macintosh OS X

    Hard Drive/Users/USER/Library/Application Support/Macromedia/Flash MX 2004/LANGUAGE_CODE/Configuration/Classes

Because the default global classpath includes the current directory (.), every *.fla* file can access classes in the same directory as the *.fla* itself. Similarly, every *.fla* file can access classes in the */Configuration/Classes* directory. You should not remove either of those directories from the global classpath.

Furthermore, if the root directory of a package resides in either the same directory as the *.fla* file or in the */Configuration/Classes* directory, then the classes in that package are accessible to the *.fla* file.

For example, suppose that, on Windows XP, we create a document, *game.fla* and place it in the directory *c:\data\projects\fungame*. Then we create a class, *com.yourdomain.game.Player* and place its class file in: *c:\data\projects\fungame\com\yourdomain\game\Player.as*. Because *game.fla* and the root of the *Player* class's package reside in the same directory, *game.fla* finds the *Player* class successfully.

```
// Given this directory setup, game.fla can access the Player class
C:\data\projects\fungame\game.fla
C:\data\projects\fungame\com\yourdomain\game\Player.as
```

Likewise, if the class file for *com.yourdomain.game.Player* resides in the */Configuration/Classes* directory, then *game.fla* (and, indeed, any *.fla* file) will find the *Player* class successfully.

```
// Given this directory setup, game.fla can access the Player class
C:\data\projects\fungame\game.fla
C:\Documents and Settings\USER\Local Settings\Application Data\
Macromedia\Flash MX 2004\LANGUAGE_CODE\Configuration\Classes\com\yourdomain
\game\Player.as
```

If *Player.as* is not found in either of those locations, the compiler generates the following error:

```
The class 'com.yourdomain.game.Player' could not be loaded.
```

 It's not a good idea to store your class files in the */Configuration/Classes* directory. That directory can easily be confused with a similarly named directory in Flash's application folder, and it is awkward to include in routine data backups. You should store your class files with the rest of your project data (images, videos, sounds, *.fla* files, etc.). Classes used across multiple projects should be stored in a central location, such as *c:/data/actionscript*.

Adding a New Directory to the Classpath

If we want to store our *Player.as* class file in a directory other than the two included by default in the global classpath (and */Configuration/Classes*), we have to add the package root directory to either the global classpath or the document classpath (i.e., the classpath specified by *game.fla* itself). For example, suppose we were to place *Player.as* here:

```
C:\data\actionscript\com\yourdomain\game\Player.as
```

To give all *.fla* files access to the *Player* class, we'd add the directory *C:\data\actionscript* to the global classpath, as follows:

1. Select Edit → Preferences → ActionScript → Language → ActionScript 2.0 Settings.
2. Under Classpath, click the plus sign (+) to add a new classpath entry. A blank entry appears.
3. In the classpath entry, type **C:\data\actionscript**. (Or use the crosshair button to browse to that directory.)
4. Click OK to accept the ActionScript 2.0 settings.
5. Click OK to accept the new preferences.

Alternatively, if we were using the *Player* class only in *game.fla*, we could give *game.fla* individual access to the *Player* class by adding the directory *C:\data\actionscript* to *game.fla*'s own classpath, like this:

1. Open *game.fla* in Flash MX 2004.
2. Select File → Publish Settings → Flash → ActionScript 2.0 Settings.
3. Follow Steps 2–5 in the preceding procedure.

 When more than one project uses the same classes, it's sensible to store them in a central location. For information on storing classes centrally, see Chapter 14.

Classpath entries can also be specified using relative paths, such as ./ for the directory that contains the *.fla* file, ../ for one directory up from the *.fla* file, ../../ for two directories up, and so on. For example, if your *.fla* file is stored in this location:

```
C:\data\projects\fungame\movie\game.fla
```

and the classes used by *game.fla* are stored in this location:

```
C:\data\projects\fungame\classes
```

you can grant *game.fla* access to the classes in the *classes* directory by specifying the following relative classpath:

```
../classes
```

Relative classpaths are useful when sharing files across disparate filesystems or operating systems, as is common when working with a team or using version control software.

Simulating Packages in ActionScript 1.0

ActionScript 1.0 did not have formal support for packages, but we can simulate packages in ActionScript 1.0 by creating a unique global object and defining all classes on it. (In fact, that's exactly what the ActionScript 2.0 compiler does behind the scenes.)

For example, the following code creates an object, com, and then creates a property of that object, yourdomain:

```
if (_global.com == undefined) {
  _global.com = new Object();
}
if (_global.com.yourdomain == undefined) {
  _global.com.yourdomain = new Object();
}
```

To create a class, *Box*, in the simulated package, *com.yourdomain*, we'd use this ActionScript 1.0 code:

```
com.yourdomain.Box = function () {
  // class body
}
```

Here's a convenient function, *AsSetupPackage( )*, that you can use to create a simulated package for your own ActionScript 1.0 classes:

```
_global.AsSetupPackage = function (path) {
  var a = path.split('.');
  var o = _global;
  for (var i = 0; i < a.length; i++) {
    var name = a[i];
    if (o[name] == undefined) {
      o[name] = new Object();
    }
    o = o[name];
  }
}

// Usage:
AsSetupPackage("com.yourdomain");
```

Just a Little More Theory

In Parts II and III, we'll see packages used in plenty of practical examples. But before we move on to those situations, we must first conclude our study of ActionScript 2.0's conceptual principles. Last up is the tool, *exceptions*, which is used to generate and respond to program errors, as we'll see in the final chapter in Part I.

Exceptions

Throughout this book, we've encountered plenty of compile-time errors—errors reported in the Output panel when a movie is exported. If a compile-time error occurs in an ActionScript 2.0 program, compilation fails and Flash won't generate a *.swf* file to execute. But not all ActionScript errors occur at compile time. Some errors don't occur until runtime, and they may not cause the program to fail completely. For example, suppose we attempt to load an XML file from disk, but the file is not found. If the movie is running in Test Movie mode, the failed load causes the Output panel to display an error message—but the movie continues to run. The following code demonstrates:

```
// If the specified file doesn't exist...
var xmlDoc:XML = new XML( );
xmlDoc.load("http://www.somenonexistentsite.com/someNonExistentFile.xml");

// ...the Output panel displays:
Error opening URL
"http://www.somenonexistentsite.com/someNonExistentFile.xml"
```

In an ideal world, we'd like to be able to recover from nonfatal error conditions such as a file-not-found. We'd like to tell the user there was a problem loading the file and perhaps display the problematic filename.

Unfortunately, in ActionScript there are precious few built-in runtime errors and, what's worse, there's no standard error-handling mechanism for dealing with the errors that do occur at runtime—at least, not for the errors that are generated by ActionScript itself. Most errors in ActionScript occur in the form of custom error codes and return values. For example, a method might return the value -1, `false`, or `null` to indicate that some operation failed. This requires us to write different, individualized code for each kind of error generated by ActionScript.

Luckily, the situation is not so bleak for our own code. As of Flash Player 7, we can write code that generates standardized errors via the *throw* statement. We handle those errors via the *try/catch/finally* statement. (The *throw* and *try/catch/finally* statement syntax and behavior are borrowed from Java and C++.)

The vast majority of ActionScript 2.0 is backward compatible with Flash Player 6. However, the exception-handling features discussed in this chapter require Flash Player 7 to work. Hence, outside this chapter, code examples in this book do not use exception handling. This allows nearly all examples to run cheerfully in Flash Player 6.

The Exception-Handling Cycle

To learn how to dispatch and respond to errors in our own programs, we'll return to the *Box* class example from Chapter 4. Recall that in the *Box* class, we defined a *setWidth( )* method to set the width property of a *Box* instance. The *setWidth( )* method checks whether a new width is within legal range before changing the width property of the *Box* instance. If the new width specified is not valid, no change is made, and the method signals a problem by returning the value false. The relevant *Box* class code follows. (Note that the *Box* class code in this example is incomplete; for now we're concentrating only on the portions of the class that deal with setting the width property.)

```
class Box {
  private var width:Number;

  public function setWidth (w:Number):Boolean {
    if ((isNaN(w) || w == null) || (w <= 0 || w > Number.MAX_VALUE)) {
      // Invalid data, so quit.
      return false;
    }
    width = w;
    return true;
  }
}
```

When *setWidth( )* returns the value false, it does so to indicate an error condition. Code that invokes the *setWidth( )* method is expected to check *setWidth( )*'s return value and respond gracefully if there's a problem (i.e., if *setWidth( )* returns false).

Let's now revise the *setWidth( )* method so that it generates an *exception*, a standard form of error supported directly by ActionScript 2.0. Error dispatch and recovery with exceptions works in much the same way as the preceding *setWidth( )* method; when a problem occurs, an error is signaled, and some error-recovery code is expected to handle it.

To generate an exception (i.e., signal an error) in our code, we use the *throw* statement, which takes the following form:

```
throw expression
```

where *expression* is a data value that describes the unusual or problematic situation. Using *throw* to signal an error is known as "throwing an exception." ActionScript allows any value to act as the *expression* of a *throw* statement. For example, the *expression* value could be the string literal "Something went wrong!" or it could be a numeric error code. However, the best practice is for *expression* to be an instance of the *Error* class (or an instance of a subclass of *Error*).

The *Error* class, introduced as a built-in class in Flash Player 7, is a standard class for representing error conditions. Instances of the *Error* class represent an error (a.k.a. an *exception*) in a program.

 The *Error* class defines two public properties, name and message, used to describe the error. The *Error* class also defines a single method, *toString( )*, which returns the value of message or, if message is not defined, returns the string "Error."

Here's one way to write *setWidth( )* so that it generates an exception with a *throw* statement when an invalid width is received:

```
public function setWidth (w:Number):Void {
  if ((isNaN(w) || w == null) || (w <= 0 || w > Number.MAX_VALUE)) {
    throw new Error("Invalid width specified.");
  }
  width = w;
}
```

When the *throw* statement executes, program control is immediately transferred to a special section of code that knows how to deal with the problem (we'll discuss this shortly). In official terms, the code that deals with the problem is said to *handle the exception*.

In our revised *setWidth( )* method, when the value of w is illegal, we use *throw* to halt the method, and we pass a new *Error* object out of the method to the section of code (not yet shown) that will handle the problem:

```
throw new Error("Invalid width specified.");
```

We also supply a description of the problem—"Invalid width specified"—as an argument to the *Error* constructor. The code block that handles the exception (again, not yet shown) uses the *Error* instance to diagnose what went wrong. Notice that *setWidth( )* no longer returns a Boolean success or failure value. If the method encounters a problem, it uses the *throw* statement to both quit and signal a failure. Otherwise, it completes normally and we can rest assured that it performed its job successfully.

Now that our *setWidth( )* method includes the *throw* statement (i.e., now that it might generate an exception), we must adjust the way we invoke it. Previously, we would have used the return value of *setWidth( )* to determine what to do in the event of a problem:

```
var b:Box = new Box( );
var someWidth:Number = -10;

// Check setWidth( )'s return value...
```

```
if (b.setWidth(someWidth)) {
  // ...setWidth( ) returned true, so no problems; proceed as planned.
  trace("Width set successfully.");
} else {
  // ...setWidth( ) returned false! ERROR! Invalid data. Display a warning.
  trace("An error occurred.");
}
```

But now, when invoking the new exception-based version of our method, we don't
bother checking the return value of *setWidth( )*. Instead, we set up a code branch
using the formal *try/catch/finally* statement instead of an *if/else* statement. Here's
how the new version looks:

```
var b:Box = new Box( );
var someWidth:Number = -10;

try {
  b.setWidth(someWidth);
  // If we get this far, no exception occurred; proceed as planned.
  trace("Width set successfully.");
} catch (e:Error) {
  // ERROR! Invalid data. Display a warning.
  trace("An error occurred: " + e.message);
}
```

Let's study the preceding code in closer detail. The *try* keyword tells the interpreter
that we're about to execute some code that might generate an exception:

```
try {
  // Code here might cause an exception.
}
```

In this case, the code we're executing is *setWidth( )*:

```
try {
  b.setWidth(someWidth);
  // If we get this far, no exception occurred; proceed as planned.
  trace("Width set successfully.");
}
```

The *catch* block handles exceptions generated by the *try* block. That is, the code in
the *catch* block executes if, and only if, code in the *try* block generates an exception:

```
} catch (e:Error) {
  // ERROR! Invalid data. Display a warning.
  trace("An error occurred: " + e.message);
}
```

When we invoke b.setWidth( ) within the *try* block, if *setWidth( )*'s *throw* statement
doesn't execute (i.e., if no error occurs), then the subsequent statements in the *try*
block execute normally and the program skips the *catch* block entirely. But if
setWidth( ) throws an exception, the program immediately skips to and executes the
catch block.

Notice, therefore, the typical structure:

- Code in a *try* clause invokes a function that might throw an exception.
- Code in the invoked function throws an exception using the *throw* statement if an error occurs.
- Control returns either to the *try* block (if no error is thrown) or the *catch* block (if an error is thrown). The *catch* block deals with any errors that occur in the *try* block.

When the *catch* block is executed, it receives the *expression* of the *throw* statement as a parameter. In our present example, within the *catch* block, the parameter e stores the *Error* instance created by the *throw* statement in the *Box.setWidth( )* method:

```
// Here's the throw statement, excerpted from setWidth( ).
throw new Error("Invalid width specified.");
```

We can use that *Error* instance to help diagnose the problem. The string passed to the *Error* constructor is available via the message property of the *Error* instance. In our example *catch* statement, we simply display the *Error* instance's message in the Output panel, as follows:

```
trace("An error occurred: " + e.message);
```

The *Error* class's *toString( )* method, which is called automatically when an instance is used in a string context, returns the value of the message property. Hence, in a string context, e and e.message are equivalent. For example, the following two statements are synonymous:

```
trace("An error occurred: " + e.message);
trace("An error occurred: " + e);
```

We'll use them interchangeably throughout this chapter.

Note that the parameter listed in a *catch* block should not need to be declared as a variable before being used. However, due to a bug in version 7.0 of the Flash MX 2004 authoring tool, the compiler (incorrectly) generates an error when a *catch* block parameter is referenced without first being declared. For example, in version 7.0 of Flash MX 2004, the following code:

```
public function someMethod ( ):Void {
  try {
    throw new Error("Some error message.");
  } catch (e:Error) {
    // Respond to the error.
    trace("An error occurred: " + e);
  }
}
```

(incorrectly) generates the following error:

```
There is no property with the name 'e'.
```

This bug is fixed in the Flash MX 2004 updater, available at: *http://macromedia.com/ support/flash/downloads.html*. (To work around the bug without installing the updater, simply declare the parameter e as a variable.)

Metaphorically, the code that detects a problem throws an exception (passes an *Error* object) to the *catch* block, which receives it as a parameter (*catches* it).

Incidentally, the *try* block can throw an error directly. For example, in the following code, the *catch* block is executed when x divided by y is the numeric value NaN (as is the case when both x and y are 0):

```
var x:Number = 0;
var y:Number = 0;
var e:Error;  // Declare e as parameter to avoid compiler bug
try {
  if (isNaN(x/y)) {
    throw new Error("Quotient is NaN.");
  } else {
    trace ("Result is " + String(x/y));
  }
} catch (e:Error) {
  trace("Error: " + e.message);
}
```

In the preceding example, you might think that attempting to divide by 0 (when y is 0) would cause ActionScript itself to throw a "Division by zero" exception, but no such luck. ActionScript doesn't throw exceptions. It is up to the developer to check for error conditions and invoke *throw* as desired. Furthermore, in Action-Script, dividing anything other than 0 by 0 yields Infinity (for positive numerators) or -Infinity (for negative numerators).

Whatever the case, it's more common for *try* blocks to invoke methods that throw exceptions than for a *try* block to include a *throw* statement directly. Later, under "Exception Bubbling," we'll learn more about how errors are transferred from methods to enclosing *try* blocks. For now, you can simply rely on the rules in the following tip.

Within a *try* block, if a statement executes, you can safely trust that all preceding statements have executed successfully. If code in a *try* block (or a method invoked in the *try* block) throws an error, the remaining statements in the *try* block are skipped and the statements in the *catch* block are executed. If no exception is thrown, the *try* block completes and execution resumes with the statements immediately following the *try/catch/finally* statement.

To find out what happens if the error is never caught (or, synonymously, never *trapped*), see "Uncaught Exceptions," later in this chapter.

Handling Multiple Types of Exceptions

Our first exception example was overly simplistic. What happens if our method generates more than one kind of error? Are they all sent to the same *catch* block? Well, that's up to the developer; they certainly could be, but it's more typical and better practice for different kinds of errors to be handled by separate *catch* blocks. Let's examine why.

Suppose we wanted a finer-grained set of error messages in our *setWidth( )* method: one for general invalid data, one for too small a width, and one for too large a width. Our revised *setWidth( )* method might look like this:

```
public function setWidth (w:Number):Void {
  if (isNaN(w) || w == null) {
    throw new Error("Illegal Box dimension specified.");
  } else if (w <= 0) {
    throw new Error("Box dimensions must be greater than 0.");
  } else if (w > Number.MAX_VALUE) {
    throw new Error("Box dimensions must be less than Number.MAX_VALUE.");
  }
  width = w;
}
```

To handle the three possible error messages in our new *setWidth( )* message, we might be tempted to code our *try/catch/finally* statement as follows:

```
try {
  b.setWidth(someWidth);
  // If we get this far, no exception occurred; proceed as planned.
  trace("Width set successfully.");
} catch (e:Error) {
  switch (e.message) {
    case "Illegal Box dimension specified.":
    trace("An error occurred: " + e.message);
    trace("Please specify a valid dimension.");
    break;

    case "Box dimensions must be greater than 0.":
    trace("An error occurred: " + e.message);
    trace("Please specify a larger value.");
    break;

    case "Box dimensions must be less than Number.MAX_VALUE.":
    trace("An error occurred: " + e.message);
    trace("Please specify a smaller value.");
    break;
  }
}
```

Admittedly, that code does work, but it's fraught with problems. First, and most serious, the errors are distinguished from one another only by the text in a string that is hidden within the *Box* class. Each time we want to check the type of an error, we have to look inside the *Box* class and find the message string. Using the string for error identification across multiple methods and classes is highly prone to human error and makes our code difficult to maintain. Second, the *switch* statement itself is barely more readable than our original, *if/else* statement (the one we used before we added exceptions to the *setWidth( )* method). We're not much farther ahead than we would be if we had used, say, numeric error codes instead of formal exceptions.

Fortunately, there's a formal (and elegant) way to handle multiple exception types. Each *try* block can have any number of supporting *catch* blocks. When an exception is thrown in a *try* block that has multiple *catch* blocks, the interpreter executes the *catch* block whose parameter's datatype matches the datatype of the value originally thrown. The datatypes of the *catch* parameter and thrown value are considered a match if they are identical or if the *catch* parameter type is a superclass of the thrown value's type.

Here's the general syntax of a *try* statement with multiple *catch* blocks:

```
try {
  // Code that might generate an exception.
} catch (e:ErrorType1) {
  // Error-handling code for ErrorType1.
} catch (e:ErrorType2) {
  // Error-handling code for ErrorType2.
} catch (e:ErrorTypen) {
  // Error-handling code for ErrorTypen.
}
```

If a *throw* statement in the preceding *try* block were to throw an expression of type *ErrorType1*, then the first *catch* block would be executed. For example, the following code causes the first *catch* block to execute:

```
throw new ErrorType1( );
```

If a *throw* statement were to pass an expression of type *ErrorType2*, then the second *catch* clause would be executed, and so on. As we learned earlier, in ActionScript the *throw* statement expression can belong to any datatype. However, as an OOP best practice, we should throw only instances of the *Error* class or one of its subclasses (this best practice follows Java, where *throw* can be used only with *Throwable* and its subclasses).

If we want to throw multiple kinds of exceptions in an application, we should define an *Error* subclass for each kind of exception. It is up to you as the developer to decide what level of granularity you require (i.e., to what degree you need to differentiate among different error conditions). However, don't confuse the following discussion of how to implement granularity in error handling as an insistence that you must implement such granularity.

Determining Exception Type Granularity

Should you define an *Error* subclass for each error condition? Typically, no, you won't need that level of granularity because in many cases multiple error conditions can be treated in the same way. If you don't need to differentiate among multiple error conditions, you can group them together under a single custom *Error* subclass. For example, you might define a single *Error* subclass named *InvalidInputException* to handle a wide range of input problems.

That said, you should define a separate *Error* subclass for each error condition that you want to distinguish from other possible conditions. To help you understand when you should create a new subclass for a given error condition and to demonstrate how to group multiple conditions into a single subclass, let's return to our familiar *Box* class.

Earlier we generated three exceptions from the *Box.setWidth( )* method: one for general invalid data, one for too small a width, and one for too large a width. All three *Box*-related exceptions used the generic *Error* class. Here's the code again:

```
public function setWidth (w:Number):Void {
  if (isNaN(w) || w == null) {
    throw new Error("Illegal Box dimension specified.");
  } else if (w <= 0) {
    throw new Error("Box dimensions must be greater than 0.");
  } else if (w > Number.MAX_VALUE) {
    throw new Error("Box dimensions must be less than Number.MAX_VALUE.");
  }
  width = w;
}
```

In the preceding code, to differentiate *Box* exceptions from all other exceptions in our application, we use the *Error* class's message property, which, as we just learned, made our exceptions awkward to use and prone to human error. A better way to set *Box*-related data errors apart from other errors in our application is to define a custom *Error* subclass, *BoxDimensionException*, as follows:

```
// Code in BoxDimensionException.as:
class BoxDimensionException extends Error {
  public var message:String = "Illegal Box dimension specified.";
}
```

With our *BoxDimensionException* class in place, our *Box.setWidth( )* method can throw its very own type of error, as follows:

```
public function setWidth (w:Number):Void {
  if (isNaN(w) || w == null) {
    // Throw a BoxDimensionException instead of an Error.
    throw new BoxDimensionException();
  } else if (w <= 0) {
    throw new BoxDimensionException();
  } else if (w > Number.MAX_VALUE) {
    throw new BoxDimensionException();
```

```
    }
    width = w;
}
```

Notice that the preceding method definition throws the same error type (*BoxDimensionException*) for all three *Box*-related error conditions. As developers of the *Box* class, we now face the crux of the error granularity issue. We must decide not only how distinguishable we want *Box* error messages to be from other application errors, but also how distinguishable we want those errors to be from one another. We have the following options:

Option 1: use a single Box error class.
  Leave the preceding *setWidth( )* method definition as-is. As we'll see shortly, this option lets us distinguish *Box* errors from other generic errors in the program, but it does not help us distinguish internally among the three varieties of *Box*-related errors (invalid data, too small a width, and too large a width).

Option 2: simplify code, but still use a single Box error class.
  Refactor the *setWidth( )* method to check for all three error conditions using a single *if* statement. This option is the same as the previous option, but uses cleaner code.

Option 3: use debugging messages to distinguish among errors.
  Add configurable debugging messages to the *BoxDimensionException* class. This option adds slightly more granularity than the previous two options but only for the sake of the developer and only during debugging.

Option 4: create a custom exception class for each error condition.
  Create two custom *BoxDimensionException* subclasses, *BoxUnderZeroException* and *BoxOverflowException*. This option provides the most granularity—it lets a program respond independently to the three varieties of *Box*-related errors using formal branching logic.

Let's consider the preceding options in turn.

Using a single custom exception type

Our first option is to accept the preceding *setWidth( )* definition, which throws the same error type (*BoxDimensionException*) for all three *Box*-related error conditions. Because the method uses *BoxDimensionException* and not *Error* to throw exceptions, *Box* exceptions are already distinguishable from other generic exceptions. Users of the *setWidth( )* method can use code such as the following to discriminate between *Box*-related errors and other generic errors:

```
var b:Box = new Box( );
var someWidth:Number = -10;

try {
  // This call to setWidth( ) will generate a BoxDimensionException.
  b.setWidth(someWidth);
```

```
   // Other statements in this try block might generate other generic errors.
   // For demonstration purposes, we'll throw a generic error directly.
   throw new Error("A generic error.");
} catch (e:BoxDimensionException) {
   // Handle Box dimension errors here.
   trace("An error occurred: " + e.message);
   trace("Please specify a valid dimension.");
} catch (e:Error) {
   // Handle all other errors here.
   trace("An error occurred: " + e.message);
}
```

For many applications, the level of error granularity provided by *BoxDimensionException* is enough. In such a case, we should at least refactor the *setWidth( )* method so that it doesn't contain redundant code (throwing the *BoxDimensionException* three times). Here's the refactored code (which was option 2 in our earlier list):

```
public function setWidth (w:Number):Void {
   if ((isNaN(w) || w == null) || (w <= 0) || (w > Number.MAX_VALUE)) {
      throw new BoxDimensionException( );
   }
   width = w;
}
```

Using configurable debugging messages

Now let's turn to option 3 (adding configurable debugging messages to the *BoxDimensionException* class). Options 1 and 2 let us distinguish a *Box* exception from other exceptions in the application but didn't help us distinguish, say, an overflow exception from a less-than-zero exception. If we feel that it's difficult to debug a *Box* dimension problem without knowing whether a box is too big or too small, we can adjust the *BoxDimensionException* class so that it accepts an optional description (the equivalent of a proverbial "note to self"). Here's the adjusted *BoxDimensionException* class:

```
class BoxDimensionException extends Error {
   // The default error message still stands.
   public var message:String = "Illegal Box dimension specified.";

   // Provide a constructor that allows a custom message to be supplied.
   public function BoxDimensionException (boxErrMsg:String) {
      super(boxErrMsg);
   }
}
```

To make use of our adjusted *BoxDimensionException* class in *setWidth( )*, we revert to our *setWidth( )* code used in option 1 and add debugging error messages, as follows:

```
public function setWidth (w:Number):Void {
   if (isNaN(w) || w == null) {
      // The default error message is fine in this case,
```

```
      // so don't bother specifying a custom error message.
      throw new BoxDimensionException();
    } else if (w <= 0) {
      // Here's the custom "too small" error message.
      throw new BoxDimensionException("Box dimensions must "
                                     + "be greater than 0.");
    } else if (w > Number.MAX_VALUE) {
      // Here's the custom "too big" error message.
      throw new BoxDimensionException("Box dimensions must be less "
                                      + "than Number.MAX_VALUE.");
    }
    width = w;
  }
```

Now that *setWidth( )* supplies custom error messages, we'll have an easier time debugging a *Box* problem because we'll know more information when the error occurs. Our use of the *setWidth( )* method has not changed, but we're better informed when something goes wrong, as shown next:

```
var b:Box = new Box();
var someWidth:Number = -10;

try {
  b.setWidth(someWidth);
} catch (e:BoxDimensionException) {
  // Handle Box dimension errors here.
  // In this case, the helpful debugging output is:
  //    An error occurred: Box dimensions must be greater than 0.
  trace("An error occurred: " + e.message);
} catch (e:Error) {
  // Handle all other errors here.
  trace("An error occurred: " + e.message);
}
```

Multiple custom BoxDimensionException subclasses

Option 3 (adding configurable debugging messages to the *BoxDimensionException* class) helped us investigate a problem in our code during development, but it doesn't help the program take independent action to recover from individual *Box* errors. To allow the program to execute independent code branches based on the type of *Box* error thrown, we need custom *BoxDimensionException* subclasses (option 4).

> If you want a program to differentiate among error conditions, implement a separate *Error* subclass for each one. Don't rely on the Error.message property alone to implement program branching logic. If your custom *Error* subclass defines a constructor that accepts an error string, you should use that string only for debugging, not for branching logic.

To allow our program to independently differentiate among the *Box* class's three error conditions, we create three custom exception types by creating three *Error* subclasses: *BoxDimensionException*, *BoxUnderZeroException*, and *BoxOverflowException*. In our case, the *BoxDimensionException* class extends *Error* directly. The *BoxUnderZeroException* and *BoxOverflowException* classes both extend *BoxDimensionException* because we want to differentiate these specific error types from a more general invalid dimension exception. Hence, the datatype hierarchy is shown in Figure 10-1.

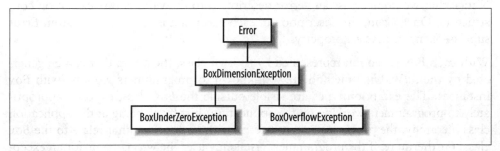

Figure 10-1. The custom exception class hierarchy

Here's the source code for our three *Box Error* subclasses:

```
// Code in BoxDimensionException.as:
class BoxDimensionException extends Error {
  public var message:String = "Illegal Box dimension specified.";
}

// Code in BoxUnderZeroException.as:
class BoxUnderZeroException extends BoxDimensionException {
  public var message:String = "Box dimensions must be greater than 0.";
}

// Code in BoxOverflowException.as:
class BoxOverflowException extends BoxDimensionException {
  public var message:String = "Box dimensions must be less "
                            + "than Number.MAX_VALUE.";
}
```

Each class specifies the value of its message property directly and does not allow it to be customized on a per-use basis. Truth be told, now that we're dealing with class-based errors instead of string-based errors, the message property is completely secondary. What matters is the datatype of the exception generated by the *throw* statement. When catching any of the preceding *Box* exceptions, our program will use the exception's datatype (not the message property) to distinguish between the three kinds of exceptions.

Now that we have three exception types, let's update our *setWidth( )* method to throw those types. Here's the code:

```
public function setWidth (w:Number):Void {
  if (isNaN(w) || w == null) {
    throw new BoxDimensionException();
  } else if (w <= 0) {
```

```
        throw new BoxUnderZeroException();
    } else if (w > Number.MAX_VALUE) {
        throw new BoxOverflowException();
    }
    width = w;
}
```

Notice that we do not pass any error description to the various *Box* exception constructors. Once again, the description of each exception is set by each custom *Error*
subclass using its `message` property.

With each *Box* exception represented by its own class, the errors that can be generated by the *setWidth( )* method are well-known to programmers working with *Box*
instances. The exception types are visible outside the *Box* class, exposed appropriately to programmers working on the application. Just by glancing at the application
class hierarchy, the programmer can determine the exceptions that relate to the *Box*
class. Furthermore, if the programmer mistakenly uses the wrong name for an exception, the compiler generates a datatype error.

Now let's see how to add branching logic to our code based on the types of exceptions that can be generated by *Box.setWidth( )*. Pay close attention to the datatype of
each *catch* block parameter:

```
var b:Box = new Box();
var someWidth:Number = -10;

try {
    b.setWidth(someWidth);
} catch (e:BoxOverflowException) {
    // Handle overflow.
    trace("An error occurred: " + e.message);
    trace("Please specify a smaller value.");
} catch (e:BoxUnderZeroException) {
    // Handle under zero.
    trace("An error occurred: " + e.message);
    trace("Please specify a larger value.");
} catch (e:BoxDimensionException) {
    // Handle general dimension errors.
    trace("An error occurred: " + e.message);
    trace("Please specify a valid dimension.");
}
```

In the preceding code, if the *setWidth( )* method generates a *BoxOverflowException*,
the first *catch* block executes. If *setWidth( )* generates a *BoxUnderZeroException*, the
second *catch* block executes. And if *setWidth( )* generates a *BoxDimensionException*,
the third *catch* block executes. Notice that the error datatypes in the *catch* blocks
progress from specific to general. When an exception is thrown, the *catch* block executed is the first one that matches the datatype of the exception.

Hence, if we changed the datatype of the first *catch* block parameter to
BoxDimensionException, the first catch block would execute for all three kinds of

exceptions! (Remember, *BoxDimensionException* is the superclass of both *BoxUnderZeroException* and *BoxOverflowException*, so they are considered matches for the *BoxDimensionException* datatype.) In fact, we could prevent all of the *catch* blocks from executing simply by adding a new first *catch* block with a parameter datatype of *Error*:

```
try {
  b.setWidth(someWidth);
} catch (e:Error) {
  // Handle all errors. No other catch blocks will ever execute.
  trace("An error occurred:" + e.message);
  trace("The first catch block handled the error.");
} catch (e:BoxOverflowException) {
  // Handle overflow.
  trace("An error occurred: " + e.message);
  trace("Please specify a smaller value.");
} catch (e:BoxUnderZeroException) {
  // Handle under zero.
  trace("An error occurred: " + e.message);
  trace("Please specify a larger value.");
} catch (e:BoxDimensionException) {
  // Handle general dimension errors.
  trace("An error occurred: " + e.message);
  trace("Please specify a valid dimension.");
}
```

Obviously, the addition of the first *catch* clause in the preceding code is self-defeating, but it does illustrate the hierarchical nature of exception handling. By placing a very generic *catch* block at the beginning of the catch list, we can handle all errors in a single location. Conversely, by placing a very generic *catch* block at the *end* of the catch list, we can provide a general safety net that handles any errors not caught by earlier *catch* blocks. For example, in the following code, the final *catch* block executes only if the *try* block generates an exception that doesn't belong to the *BoxOverflowException*, *BoxUnderZeroException*, or *BoxDimensionException* datatypes:

```
try {
  b.setWidth(someWidth);
} catch (e:BoxOverflowException) {
  // Handle overflow.
  trace("An error occurred: " + e.message);
  trace("Please specify a smaller value.");
} catch (e:BoxUnderZeroException) {
  // Handle under zero.
  trace("An error occurred: " + e.message);
  trace("Please specify a larger value.");
} catch (e:BoxDimensionException) {
  // Handle general dimension errors.
  trace("An error occurred: " + e.message);
  trace("Please specify a valid dimension.");
} catch (e:Error) {
  // Handle any errors that don't qualify as BoxDimensionException errors.
}
```

Remember, error granularity is a choice. In option 4 we created a custom *Error* subclass for each variety of exception generated by the *Box* class. This approach gives our program the greatest ability to respond independently to different types of errors. But such flexibility is not necessarily required in many situations. Let the needs of your program's logic dictate how granular you make your errors.

In the first release of the Flash MX 2004 authoring tool, a bug prevents *catch* statements from executing when the *catch* parameter datatype refers to a class that has been imported via the *import* statement. For example, in the following code, the *catch* statement never executes because *SomeCustomError* is imported:

```
import somePackage.SomeCustomError;
try {
  throw new SomeCustomError( );
} catch(e:SomeCustomError) {
  // This code should execute but it does not
  // if the movie is compiled with version 7.0
  // of the Flash MX 2004 authoring tool.
  trace("Caught: " + e);
}
```

To work around the problem, we can include the full package name when specifying a custom error class as a *catch* block parameter. For example:

```
import somePackage.SomeCustomError;
try {
  throw new SomeCustomError( );
} catch(e:somePackage.SomeCustomError) {
  // Now that the package name is included, this code runs.
  trace("Caught: " + e);
}
```

This bug is fixed in the Flash MX 2004 updater, available at:

http://macromedia.com/support/flash/downloads.html

Exception Bubbling

Earlier we learned that exceptions in a *try* block can be thrown either directly or as the result of a method call. In reality, an exception can be thrown anywhere in an ActionScript program, even on a frame in a timeline! Given that an exception can be thrown anywhere, how does the ActionScript interpreter find the corresponding *catch* block to handle it? And what if no *catch* block exists? These mysteries are resolved through the magic of *exception bubbling*. Let's follow along a bubbly ride with the ActionScript interpreter as it encounters a *throw* statement in a program. During the following dramatization, the interpreter's musing are shown in code comments.

When a *throw* statement executes, the interpreter immediately stops normal program flow and looks for an enclosing *try* block. For example, here's a *throw* statement:

```
// INTERPRETER: Hmm. A throw statement.
// Is there an enclosing try block for it?
throw new Error("Something went wrong");
```

If the *throw* statement is enclosed in a *try* block, the interpreter next tries to find a *catch* block whose parameter's datatype matches the datatype of the value thrown (in the present case, *Error*):

```
// INTERPRETER: Great, I found a try block. Is there a matching catch block?
try {
  throw new Error("Something went wrong");
}
```

If a matching *catch* block is found, the interpreter transfers program control to that block:

```
try {
  throw new Error("Something went wrong");
// INTERPRETER: Found a catch block whose parameter datatype is Error!
//              The hunt's over. I'll execute this catch block now...
} catch (e:Error) {
  // Handle problems...
}
```

But if a matching *catch* block cannot be found or if the *throw* statement did not appear within a *try* block in the first place, then the interpreter checks whether the *throw* statement occurred within a method or function. If the *throw* statement occurred in a method or function, the interpreter searches for a *try* block around the code that invoked the method or function. The following code demonstrates how the interpreter reacts when, within a method, it encounters a *throw* statement that has no enclosing *try* block:

```
public function doSomething ():Void {
  // INTERPRETER: Hmm. No try block here. I'll check who called this method.
  throw new Error("Something went wrong");
}
```

If the code that invoked the method or function is enclosed in a *try* block, the interpreter looks for a matching *catch* block there and, if it finds a match, executes it. The following code demonstrates an exception thrown out of a method and caught where the method is invoked (i.e., one level up the *call stack*).

```
class ErrorDemo {
  public function doSomething ():Void {
    // INTERPRETER: Hmm. No try block here.
    // I'll check who called this method.
    trace("About to throw an exception from doSomething() method.");
    throw new Error("Something went wrong");
  }

  public static function startApp ():Void {
```

```
  // INTERPRETER: Aha, here's who called doSomething(). And here's
  //              an enclosing try block with a catch block whose
  //              parameter datatype is Error! My work's done. catch
  //              block, please execute now...
  try {
    var demo:ErrorDemo = new ErrorDemo();
    demo.doSomething();
  } catch (e:Error) {
    // Handle problems...
    trace("Exception caught in startApp(), thrown by doSomething().");
  }
  }
}
```

 The *call stack* is the list of functions and methods currently being executed by the interpreter at any given point in a program. The list
includes the functions and methods in the reverse order from which
they were called, from top to bottom. When a function is immediately
below another function in the call stack, then the lower function was
invoked by the higher. The lowest function in the call stack is the
function currently executing.

You can use the Flash debugger to view the call stack for the current movie, as described
in the Flash authoring tool online Help, under ActionScript Reference Guide → Debugging. Note, however, that the Flash debugger displays the currently executing function
visually on top rather than on the bottom. That is, the visual display of the call stack in
the Flash debugger is the reverse of the call stack discussed in the preceding note. Ultimately, the distinction is arbitrary—the glass is half full or it's half empty; the stack
works top down or bottom up, depending on your point of view.

In the preceding code, an exception thrown by a method was caught by a *try/catch*
block enclosing the method call statement. However, if no *try* block is found around
the function or method caller, the interpreter searches up the entire call stack for a
try block with a matching *catch* block. The following code shows a method throwing an error that is caught two levels up the call stack:

```
class ErrorDemo {
  public function doSomething ():Void {
    // INTERPRETER: Hmm. No try block here.
    // I'll check who called this method.
    trace("About to throw an exception from doSomething() method.");
    throw new Error("Something went wrong");
  }

  public static function startApp ():Void {
    // INTERPRETER: Aha, here's who called doSomething(). But still
    //              no try block here. I'll check who called this method.
    var demo:ErrorDemo = new ErrorDemo();
    demo.doSomething();
  }
}
```

```
// Meanwhile, elsewhere in the program...
// INTERPRETER: Aha! Found a try block that has a catch block whose
//              parameter's datatype is Error! My work's done. catch block,
//              please execute now...
try {
  ErrorDemo.startApp( );
} catch (e:Error) {
  // Handle problems...
  trace("Exception caught where Error.startApp( ) was invoked.");
}
```

Notice that the interpreter finds the *try/catch* block despite the fact that it surrounds not the error-throwing method, nor the caller of the error-throwing method, but the caller of the method that called the error-throwing method!

Uncaught Exceptions

We've seen a number of scenarios in which we've caught (trapped) various errors. But what happens if the interpreter never finds a *catch* block that can handle the thrown exception? If no eligible *catch* block is found anywhere in the call stack, then the interpreter:

- Sends the value of the thrown *Error* object's message property to the Output panel (or simply sends the thrown expression itself if it wasn't an *Error* object)
- Aborts execution of all code currently remaining in the call stack (including frame scripts and callback functions such as a *setInterval( )* callback)

Execution of the program then resumes normally. For example, if an uncaught exception occurs on frame 1, layer 1 of a movie, the code on frame 2 executes normally. In fact, code on frame 1, layer 2 will also execute normally. For frame-based code, only the specific frame script that generated the uncaught exception is aborted.

The following code demonstrates a method that throws an error that is never caught:

```
class ErrorDemo {
  public function doSomething ( ):Void {
    // INTERPRETER: Hmm. No try block here.
    // I'll check who called this method.
    throw new Error("Something went wrong");
  }

  public static function startApp ( ):Void {
    // INTERPRETER: Aha, here's who called doSomething( ). But still
    // no try block here. I'll check who called this method.
    doSomething( );
  }
}

// Meanwhile, elsewhere in the program...
```

```
// INTERPRETER: Hmm. Well, I searched all the way to the top, and still
//              no try block. I'll send "Something went wrong" to the Output
//              panel. Maybe the programmer will know what to do.
ErrorDemo.startApp( );
```

As we've just seen, because exceptions bubble up the call stack, it's not necessary for a method to catch its own exceptions. And it's not even necessary for the caller of a method to catch its exceptions. The exception can legally be caught at any level in the call stack. Any method can delegate exception handling to the code that calls it. That said, it's bad form and harmful to a program to throw an exception and then never catch it. You should always catch exceptions or, having encountered an uncaught exception, revise your code so that the exception isn't thrown in the first place.

Unfortunately, there's no way in ActionScript to tell the compiler to force a program to catch its own exceptions. As we'll learn later, ActionScript does not support Java-style *checked exceptions*, which are exceptions that must be caught in order for a program to compile. In Java terminology, all exceptions in ActionScript are unchecked.

The finally Block

So far, we've discussed only the *try* and *catch* blocks in the *try/catch/finally* statement. As we've seen, a *try* block contains code that might throw an exception, and a *catch* block executes code in response to a thrown exception. The *finally* block, by comparison, always executes, whether or not code in the *try* block throws an exception.

The *finally* block is placed once (and only once) as the last block in a *try/catch/finally* statement. For example:

```
try {
  // Statements
} catch (e:ErrorType1) {
  // Handle ErrorType1 exceptions.
} catch (e:ErrorTypen) {
  // Handle ErrorTypen exceptions.
} finally {
  // This code always executes, no matter how the try block exits.
}
```

Misplacing the *finally* block causes a compile-time error.

In the preceding code, the *finally* block executes in one of the four circumstances:

- Immediately after the *try* block completes without errors
- Immediately after a *catch* block handles an exception generated in the *try* block
- Immediately before an uncaught exception bubbles up
- Immediately before a *return*, *continue*, or *break* statement transfers control out of the *try* or *catch* blocks (but see the bug described under "A Nested Exception Bug," later in this chapter)

The *finally* block of a *try/catch/finally* statement typically contains cleanup code that must execute whether or not an exception occurs in the corresponding *try* block. For example, suppose we're creating a space shooter game and we define a class, *SpaceShip*, to represent spaceships in the game. The *SpaceShip* class has a method, *attackEnemy( )* that performs the following tasks:

- Sets the spaceship's current target
- Fires on that target
- Clears the current target (i.e., sets the *SpaceShip*'s currentTarget property to null)

In our hypothetical application, we'll assume that the first two of the preceding tasks might generate an exception. Further, we'll assume that the *attackEnemy( )* method doesn't handle those exceptions itself; instead, it passes them up to the calling method. But whether or not an exception is generated, the *attackEnemy( )* method must set the currentTarget property to null.

Here's what the *attackEnemy( )* method would look like if we coded it with a *catch* statement (i.e., without using *finally*):

```
public function attackEnemy (enemy:SpaceShip):Void {
  try {
    setCurrentTarget(enemy);
    fireOnCurrentTarget( );
  } catch (e:Error) {
    // Clear the current target if an exception occurs.
    setCurrentTarget(null);
    // Pass the exception up to the calling method.
    throw e;
  }
  // Clear the current target if no exception occurs.
  setCurrentTarget(null);
}
```

Notice that we must duplicate the statement, setCurrentTarget(null). We place it both in the *catch* block and after the *try/catch* statement, guaranteeing that it will run whether or not there's an exception in the *try* block. But duplicating the statement is error prone. In the preceding method, a programmer could have easily forgotten to clear the current target after the *try/catch* block.

If we change our strategy by clearing the current target in a *finally* block, we remove the redundancy in the preceding code:

```
public function attackEnemy (enemy:SpaceShip):Void {
  try {
    setCurrentTarget(enemy);
    fireOnCurrentTarget( );
  } finally {
    setCurrentTarget(null);
  }
}
```

In the revised version, the *finally* block clears the current target whether there's an exception or not. Because both situations are handled, we no longer have any need for a *catch* block; we can simply let the exception bubble up to the calling method automatically.

You might be wondering why we need the *finally* block at all. That is, why not just use the following code?

```
// This code might look decent, but there's a problem. Can you spot it?
public function attackEnemy (enemy:SpaceShip):Void {
  setCurrentTarget(enemy);
  fireOnCurrentTarget();
  setCurrentTarget(null);
}
```

Remember that when an exception is thrown, program control is transferred to the nearest suitable *catch* block in the call stack. Hence, if *fireOnCurrentTarget( )* throws an exception, control transfers out of *attackEnemy( )*, never to return, and setCurrentTarget(null) would never execute. By using a *finally* block, we guarantee that setCurrentTarget(null) executes before the exception bubbles up.

The *attackEnemy( )* method example reflects the most common use of *finally* in multithreaded languages like Java, where a program can have multiple sections of code executing simultaneously. In Java, the following general structure is common-place—it guards against the possibility that an object busy with a task might be inappropriately altered by another object during the execution of that task:

```
// Set a state indicating this object's current task.
// External objects should check this object's state
// before accessing or manipulating this object.
doingSomething = true;
try {
  // Perform the task.
  doSomething();
} finally {
  // Unset the "in-task" state (whether or not
  // the task generated an exception).
  doingSomething = false;
}
```

In ActionScript, the preceding state-management code is effectively unnecessary because the language is single-threaded, so no external object will ever attempt to alter the state of an object while it is busy executing a method. Hence, *finally* is used much more rarely in ActionScript than it is in multithreaded languages. However, it can still be used for organizational purposes, to contain code that performs cleanup duties after other code has executed.

Nested Exceptions

So far we've used only single-level *try/catch/finally* statements, but exception-handling logic can also be nested. A *try/catch/finally* statement can appear inside the *try*, *catch*, or *finally* block of another *try/catch/finally* statement. This hierarchical nesting allows any block in a *try/catch/finally* statement to execute code that might, itself, throw an error.

For example, suppose we were writing a multiuser, web-based message board system. We define a core class for the application (called *BulletinBoard*), another class that manages the user interface (called *GUIManager*), and another class that represents a user on the board (called *User*). We give *BulletinBoard* a method, *populateUserList( )*, which displays the list of current active users. The *populateUserList( )* method splits its work into two stages: first it retrieves a List component from the application's *GUIManager* instance, then it populates that List with users from a supplied array of *User* instances. These two stages can both potentially generate an exception, so a nested *try/catch/finally* structure is used in the *populateUserList( )* method. Let's take a closer look at this nested structure.

During the first stage of *populateUserList( )*, if the List component isn't available, a *UserListNotFound* exception is thrown by the *GUIManager*. The *UserListNotFound* exception is caught by the outer *try/catch/finally* statement.

If, on the other hand, the List component is available, the *populateUserList( )* method proceeds with stage two, during which a loop populates the List component with users from the supplied array. For each iteration through the loop, if the current user's ID cannot be found, the *User.getID( )* method throws a *UserIdNotSet* exception. The *UserIdNotSet* exception is caught by the nested *try/catch/finally* statement.

Here's the code (we won't work closely with components until Chapter 12, so if some of this code looks new to you, try returning to it once you're finished reading that chapter):

```
public function populateUserList (users:Array):Void {
  try {
    // Start stage 1...get the List.
    // If getUserList() throws an exception, the outer catch executes.
    var ulist:List = getGUIManager().getUserList();
    // Start stage 2...populate the List.
    for (var i:Number = 0; i < users.length; i++) {
      try {
        var thisUser:User = User(users[i]);
        // If getID() throws an exception, the nested catch executes.
        ulist.addItem(thisUser.getName(), thisUser.getID());
      } catch (e:UserIdNotSet) {
        trace(e);
        log.warn(e);
        continue;  // Skip this user.
      }
```

```
    }
  } catch (e:UserListNotFound) {
    trace(e);
    log.warn(e);
  }
}
```

Now that we've had a look at a specific nested exception example, let's consider how nested exceptions are handled in general.

If an exception occurs in a *try* block that is nested within another *try* block, and the inner *try* block has a *catch* block that can handle the exception, then the inner *catch* block is executed and the program resumes at the end of the inner *try/catch/finally* statement.

```
try {
  try {
    // Exception occurs here.
    throw new Error("Test error");
  } catch (e:Error) {
    // Exception is handled here.
    trace(e);  // Displays: Test error
  }
  // The program resumes here.
} catch (e:Error) {
  // Handle exceptions generated by the outer try block.
}
```

If, on the other hand, an exception occurs in a *try* block that is nested within another *try* block, but the inner *try* block does not have a *catch* block that can handle the exception, then the exception bubbles up to the outer *try/catch/finally* statement (and, if necessary, up the call stack) until a suitable *catch* block is found or the exception is not caught. If the exception is caught somewhere in the call stack, the program resumes at the end of the *try/catch/finally* statement that handled the exception. Note that in the following code example (and subsequent examples), the hypothetical error datatype *SomeSpecificError* is a placeholder used to force the thrown exception to not be caught. In order to test the code example in your own code, you'd have to create a subclass of *Error* called *SomeSpecificError*.

```
try {
  try {
    // Exception occurs here.
    throw new Error("Test error");
  } catch (e:SomeSpecificError) {
    // Exception is not handled here.
    trace(e);  // Never executes because the types don't match.
  }
} catch (e:Error) {
  // Exception is handled here.
  trace(e);  // Displays: Test error
}
// The program resumes here, immediately after the outer catch block
// has handled the exception.
```

If an exception occurs in a *try* block that is nested within a *catch* block, and the inner *try* block does not have a *catch* block that can handle the exception, then the search for a matching *catch* block begins outside the outer *try/catch/finally* statement:

```
try {
  // Outer exception occurs here.
  throw new Error("Test error 1");
} catch (e:Error) {
  // Outer exception handled here.
  trace(e);  // Displays: Test error 1
  try {
    // Inner exception occurs here.
    throw new Error("Test error 2");
  } catch (e:SomeSpecificError) {
    // Inner exception is not handled here.
    trace(e);  // Never executes because the types don't match.
  }
}
// The search for a matching catch block for the inner exception starts here.
```

Last, if an exception occurs in a *try* block that is nested within a *finally* block, but a prior exception is already in the process of bubbling up the call stack, then the new exception is handled before the prior exception continues to bubble up.

```
// This method throws an exception in a finally block.
public function throwTwoExceptions ():Void {
  try {
    // Outer exception occurs here. Because there is no catch block for this
    // try block, the outer exception starts to bubble up,
    // out of this method.
    throw new Error("Test error 1");
  } finally {
    try {
      // Inner exception occurs here. The inner exception is
      // handled before the outer exception actually bubbles up.
      throw new Error("Test error 2");
    } catch (e:Error) {
      // Inner exception is handled here.
      trace("Internal catch: " + e);
    }
  }
}

// Elsewhere, within another method that calls the preceding method.
try {
  throwTwoExceptions();
} catch (e:Error) {
  // The outer exception, which has bubbled up from throwTwoExceptions(),
  // is handled here.
  trace("External catch: " + e);
}

// Output (notice that the inner exception is caught first):
Internal catch: Test error 2
External catch: Test error 1
```

If, in the preceding example, the exception thrown in the *finally* block had never been caught, then the interpreter would have sent it to the Output panel and aborted all other code in the call stack. As a result, the original, outer exception would have been discarded along with all code in the call stack. The following code demonstrates the preceding principle. It throws an uncaught exception from a *finally* statement. As a result, the exception thrown by the outer *try* block is discarded. To test the code, you can run it directly on a frame in the timeline.

```
try {
  // Outer exception occurs here.
  throw new Error("Test error 1");
} finally {
  try {
    // Inner exception occurs here.
    throw new Error("Test error 2");
  } catch (e:SomeSpecificError) {
    // Inner exception is not handled here.
    trace("internal catch: " + e); // Never executes because
                                   // the types don't match.
  }
}
// The search for a matching catch block for the inner exception starts
// here. If no match is ever found, then the Output panel displays
// "Test error 2", and the bubbling of the outer exception is aborted.
```

The preceding code demonstrates the effect of an uncaught exception in one scenario, but once again, it's not appropriate to allow an exception to go uncaught. In the preceding case, we should either catch the exception or revise our code so that the exception isn't thrown in the first place.

A Nested Exception Bug

Earlier we learned that *finally* executes no matter what happens in a *try* block. In theory, that *should* be true. However, a bug in Flash Player 7 prevents *finally* from executing when a nested *try/catch/finally* statement returns from a function, as shown in the following code:

```
function nestedFinallyBugDemo ():Void {
  try {
    try {
      throw new Error("Test error");
    } finally {
      trace("Inner finally block.");
      return;
    }
  } finally {
    trace("Outer finally block.");  // Due to a bug in Flash Player 7,
                                    // this line never executes.
  }
}
nestedFinallyBugDemo();
```

```
  // Displays:
  Inner finally block.
```

The need for this structure is rare, so you probably won't encounter the bug, and Macromedia may very well fix it in Flash Player 8 if not an interim version of Flash Player 7.

Control Flow Changes in try/catch/finally

As we've seen throughout this chapter, the *throw* statement changes the flow of a program. When the interpreter encounters a *throw* statement, it immediately stops what it's doing and transfers program control to eligible *catch* and *finally* blocks. However, it is also quite legal for those *catch* and *finally* blocks to change program flow again via *return* (in the case of a method or function) or *break* or *continue* (in the case of a loop). Furthermore, a *return*, *break*, or *continue* statement can also appear in a *try* block.

To learn the rules of flow changes in the *try/catch/finally* statement, let's look at how the *return* statement affects program flow in a *try*, *catch*, and *finally* block. The following code examples contain a method, *changeFlow( )* that demonstrates a control flow in various hypothetical situations. Note that, in all cases, the behavior of the *changeFlow( )* method would be the same if it were a standalone function.

Example 10-1 shows a *return* statement in a *try* block, placed before an error is thrown. In this case, the method returns normally, and no error is ever thrown or handled. However, before the method returns, the *finally* block is executed. Note that you're unlikely to see code exactly like Example 10-1 in the real world. In most applied cases, the *return* statement would occur in a conditional statement and execute in response to some specific condition in the program.

Example 10-1. Using return in try, before throw

```
function changeFlow ( ):Void {
  try {
    return;
    throw new Error("Test error.");
  } catch (e:Error) {
    trace("Caught: " + e);
  } finally {
    trace("Finally executed.");
  }
  trace("Last line of method.");
}

// Output when changeFlow( ) is invoked:
Finally executed.
```

Example 10-2 shows a *return* statement in a *try* block, placed after an error is thrown. In this case, the *return* statement is never executed because an error is thrown before it is reached. Once the error is caught and the *try/catch/finally* completes, execution resumes after the *try/catch/finally* statement, and the method exits at the end of the method body. Again, Example 10-2 demonstrates a principle but is atypical of real-world code, which would normally throw the error based on some condition.

Example 10-2. Using return in try, after throw

```
function changeFlow ():Void {
  try {
    throw new Error("Test error.");
    return;
  } catch (e:Error) {
    trace("Caught: " + e);
  } finally {
    trace("Finally executed.");
  }
  trace("Last line of method.");
}

// Output when changeFlow( ) is invoked:
Caught: Test error.
Finally executed.
Last line of method.
```

Example 10-3 shows a *return* statement in a *catch* block. In this case, the *return* statement executes when the work of error handling is done, and the code after the *try/catch/finally* statement never executes. However, as usual, before the method returns, the *finally* block is executed. Unlike Examples 10-1 and 10-2, this code is typical of a real-world scenario in which a method is aborted due to the occurrence of an error.

Example 10-3. Using return in catch

```
function changeFlow ():Void {
  try {
    throw new Error("Test error.");
  } catch (e:Error) {
    trace("Caught: " + e);
    return;
  } finally {
    trace("Finally executed.");
  }
  trace("Last line of method.");
}

// Output when changeFlow( ) is invoked:
Caught: Test error.
Finally executed.
```

Last, Example 10-4 shows a *return* statement in a *finally* block. In this case, the *return* statement executes when the *finally* block executes (as we learned earlier, a *finally* block executes when its corresponding *try* block completes in one of the following ways: without errors, with an error that was caught, with an error that was not caught, or due to a *return*, *break*, or *continue* statement). Notice that the *return* statement in Example 10-4 prevents any code in the method beyond the *try/catch/finally* statement from executing. You might use a similar technique to quit out of a method after invoking a block of code, whether or not that code throws an exception. In such a case, you'd typically surround the entire *try/catch/finally* block in a conditional statement (otherwise the remainder of the method would never execute!).

Example 10-4. Using return in finally

```
function changeFlow ():Void {
  try {
    throw new Error("Test error.");
  } catch (e:Error) {
    trace("Caught: " + e);
  } finally {
    trace("Finally executed.");
    return;
  }
  trace("Last line of method.");  // Not executed.
}

// Output when changeFlow( ) is invoked:
Caught: Test error.
Finally executed.
```

If a *return* statement occurs in a *finally* block after a *return* has already been issued in the corresponding *try* block, then the *return* in the *finally* block replaces the *return* already in progress.

Limitations of Exception Handling in ActionScript 2.0

As you use exceptions in your code, you should be aware of the following exception-handling limitations in ActionScript 2.0.

No Checked Exceptions

In ActionScript 2.0, if a method throws an exception, it's up to the programmer to know about it in advance and handle it appropriately. Nothing you write in your code can force you or anyone else to handle an exception. The compiler will make no complaints if an exception is not handled. (Of course, an uncaught exception can cause code to be aborted at runtime, as discussed earlier under "Uncaught Exceptions")

Exceptions are, hence, harder to work with in ActionScript than in languages that support compile-time errors for uncaught exceptions. In Java, for example, an exception can be either checked (a compile-time error occurs if the exception is not handled) or unchecked (no compile-time error occurs if the exception is not handled).

In Java, the declaration for a method that throws a checked exception explicitly includes the exception in the method header. Here's a Java method declaration that explicitly states the type of exception the method can throw (in this case the method can throw exceptions of type *IOException*):

```
public void someMethod( ) throws IOException {
}
```

Upon reading the preceding method declaration, the programmer immediately knows she must handle *IOExceptions* when invoking the method. If the programmer invokes the method without catching or rethrowing the exception, Java will produce an error and the program will not compile. This strictness forces programmers to dutifully deal with exceptions, leading to less time debugging exception-related errors. ActionScript doesn't support the *throws* clause in method declarations.

No Built-in Exceptions

We saw earlier that Flash doesn't throw an exception when a developer attempts an illegal operation, such as dividing by zero. Neither the class library built into the Flash Player nor the Flash MX 2004 v2 components throw exceptions. The only exceptions generated in Flash are those thrown by custom-written programs. This exception-less environment leads to two problems. First, Flash must relay all error information to the programmer using unwieldy error codes or return values. Second (and much worse), Flash often fails silently when a runtime error occurs. Silent errors are very difficult to track down. In the future, as versions of the Flash Player that support exception handling are adopted, it is likely that ActionScript will generate more built-in exceptions.

Exception Performance Issues

In programming languages that do not support exceptions, programmers often use error codes to represent error conditions. That is, if a method or function encounters an error, it returns a message or code describing the problem and expects the caller to know how to interpret that code. While more awkward than exceptions in many situations, this older, grassroots style of signaling an error in a program is actually faster than throwing an exception.

For this reason, even with exceptions supported in ActionScript, returned error codes are sometimes still a good technique for error handling, primarily in situations that are highly performance intensive. Both exception handling and error codes are useful and can be used together in different parts of the same program, depending upon the performance needs of different parts of your code.

But before you get excited about speed improvements and swear off exceptions for life, be aware that in most programs, no human-perceivable improvement in speed results from using error codes instead of exceptions. But in situations in which every last bit of performance makes a difference to the program, it may be necessary to forego exceptions in favor of faster error codes.

The speed test in Example 10-5 compares the amount of time it takes to throw and catch 1000 exceptions with the amount of time it takes to handle a return value of false 1000 times. On average, throwing an exception takes approximately three times as long as handling the return value. However, on my aging Pentium III 700 MHz Windows test machine, the entire process of throwing 1000 exceptions took a mere 187 milliseconds (compared to 57 milliseconds to handle the false return values). In most programs, this potential 130-millisecond savings will be irrelevant. In the vast majority of cases, the benefits of clean exception-based code far outweigh the performance costs.

Example 10-5. Exception handling benchmark test

```
// The class file, in ExceptionPerformanceTest.as.
class ExceptionPerformanceTest {
  public function test1 ():Void {
    throw new CustomException();
  }

  public function test2 ():Boolean {
    return false;
  }
}

// The exception class in CustomException.as.
class CustomException extends Error {
  public var message:String = "This is the error message.";
}

// The test code, in ExceptionPerformanceTest.fla.
var ept:ExceptionPerformanceTest = new ExceptionPerformanceTest();

var count1:Number = 0;
var count2:Number = 0;

var start1:Number = getTimer();
for (var i:Number = 0; i < 1000; i++) {
  try {
    ept.test1();
  } catch (e:Error) {
    count1++;
  }
}
var elapsed1 = getTimer() - start1;

var start2:Number = getTimer();
```

Example 10-5. Exception handling benchmark test (continued)

```
for (var i:Number = 0; i < 1000; i++) {
  if (!ept.test2()) {
    count2++;
  }
}
var elapsed2 = getTimer() - start2;

trace(elapsed1);  // On my Pentium III 700, displays: 187
trace(elapsed2);  // On my Pentium III 700, displays: 57
```

From Concepts to Code

We've come to the end of Part I and finished our study of ActionScript 2.0 OOP theory. If you've read and understood everything up to this point (or at least most of it), you now have the conceptual foundation required to create object-oriented Flash applications. From here on out, you simply need to build practical experience on top of that foundation. Parts II and III of this book will help you do just that. In Part II, we'll study application frameworks, visual programming, and code distribution. In Part III, we'll explore several widely accepted solutions to specific architectural problems in object-oriented programming.

Application Development

Part II teaches you how to structure entire applications with ActionScript 2.0. You'll learn best practices for setting up and architecting an object-oriented project, plus how user interface components and movie clips fit into a well-structured Flash application. You'll also see how to share code with other developers and use code libraries developed by others. All this will help you build more scalable, extensible, stable applications.

An OOP Application Framework

Flash is notoriously open-ended. If there are several of ways to skin a cat, there are even more ways to build a Flash application. Flash's flexibility can cause confusion for developers, especially when they're building their first application. This chapter's goal is to overcome that confusion by providing one explicit example of how to structure an OOP Flash application. By no means is the example presented here the only way to create a Flash application, but it is certainly a legitimate, reusable approach that makes a good foundation for any OOP project. We'll consider the example in the abstract sense first, not in reference to any particular application. Our framework could be applied to anything from an email application to a video game. In the next chapter, we'll see how to apply our generic framework to a real-world situation—a currency conversion application.

The application framework described in this chapter derives from a Java mentality more than, say, a Microsoft Visual Basic style. That is, our application will be a pure OOP application, in which everything happens in classes and the *.fla* file is used only to load classes and provide component linkage. Not every application in Flash needs to be pure OOP. Flash also fully supports drag-and-drop visual development, a la Visual Basic. Visual development practices involve placing components on stage manually at authoring time and setting component properties and data bindings via panels in the Flash authoring tool. These practices are beyond the scope of this book but are covered in detail in Flash's online Help. In particular, see Help → Using Components, and if you're using Flash MX Professional 2004, see Help → Using Flash → Working with Screens. For a visual developer's introduction to Flash application development, see *Building a Google Search Application with Macromedia Flash MX Professional*, at *http://www.macromedia.com/devnet/mx/flash/articles/google_search.html*.

The example files discussed in this chapter are available for download at *http://moock.org/eas2/examples*.

The Basic Directory Structure

Before we start creating content, let's lay out the basic directory structure for our application.

Follow these steps:

1. Create a directory named *AppName* on your hard drive. The *AppName* directory will contain everything in our project, including source code and final output. In a real project, you'd use your application's actual name instead of *AppName*.

2. In the *AppName* directory, create a subdirectory named *deploy*. The *deploy* directory will contain the final, compiled application, ready for posting to a web site or other distribution medium.

3. In the *AppName* directory, create a subdirectory named *source*. The *source* directory will contain all source code for the application, including classes (*.as* files) and Flash documents (*.fla* files).

Your application directory structure should look like this:

```
AppName/
    deploy/
    source/
```

In our example application, we have no external assets such as sounds, text copy (Word documents, etc.), or artwork (e.g., scans, Photoshop files, or Illustrator files). In a more complex scenario, we'd create an *AppName/assets* folder to contain those external files.

The Flash Document (.fla file)

Every Flash application must include at least one Flash document (*.fla* file). The Flash document is the source file from which a Flash movie (*.swf* file) is exported. The Flash movie is what's actually displayed in the Flash Player (i.e., the Flash runtime environment). Many Flash applications are broken down into multiple *.swf* files that are loaded individually at runtime. For example, one *.swf* file might be a single level in a video game, whereas another *.swf* file might be a self-contained animation or the "Contact Us" section of a web site. Even in these multiple–*.swf* file scenarios, there's always a single, base *.swf* file on which the rest of the application is built. Sometimes, the base *.swf* file simply acts as an empty container, used only to display load progress for the rest of the application. At the other extreme, the entire application resides in the base *.swf* file directly, and no external *.swf* files are loaded.

Our basic application framework falls into the last category—it includes a single *.swf* file only and, hence, requires only one *.fla* file. However, our application framework does not preclude the use of other *.swf* files down the road that might contain different sections of a web site, different stages in a form or quiz, or different levels in a video game.

To create our application's main *.fla* file, follow these steps:

1. In the Flash authoring tool, choose File → New.

2. In the New Document dialog box, on the General tab, for Type, choose Flash Document, then click OK.

3. Use File → Save As to save the Flash document as *AppName.fla* in the *AppName/ source* directory.

We'll return to the *.fla* file in a moment. Right now, let's move on to our application's classes.

The Classes

Because we're building a pure OOP application, all of our application's content is created by its classes. In Flash, most applications are visual and include graphical user interfaces. Hence, the classes of an OOP Flash application typically create and manage user interface components. But in our example, we'll include only two sample classes. For now, our focus is the generic structure of our framework, so neither class creates any visuals or performs any specific practical task. To emphasize the generic nature of our framework, we'll name our classes *A* and *B*. (In Chapter 12, we'll see how to create components and manage a user interface based on the present skeletal framework.)

An OOP application can have any number of classes, but only one of them is used to start the application in motion. In our example, class *A* starts the application. Class *A* has a class method, generically named *main( )*. By convention, the *main( )* method contains an application's startup code. In an actual application, class *A* would be replaced by a specific class whose *main( )* method performs a specific startup duty. For example, in a quiz application, the primary class might be *Quiz*, and the *main( )* method might initialize the quiz and display the quiz's first question. In a chat application, the primary class might be *ChatClient*, and the *main( )* method might connect to the server. In both cases, the remainder of the application cascades from that first invocation of *main( )*. For example, an answer to question 1 would cause question 2 to appear, or a successful connection to the server would cause a chat interface to appear.

For the sake of our example framework, we'll consider *A*'s startup task to be simply creating an instance of *B*.

Our use of the class method named *main( )* follows Java's methodology exactly. But in Flash, the *main( )* method is an optional convention. In Java, it is a requirement of the language. In Java, *main( )* is invoked automatically, whereas in Flash, you must manually call *main( )* from, say, the first frame of the timeline following the application's preloader.

We'll store our classes in the package *com.somedomain*. In your application, you should change *com.somedomain* to match your web site's domain name. For example, I create all my classes under the package *org.moock* because my domain name is *moock.org*.

To create the directories for the *com.somedomain* package, follow these steps:

1. In the *AppName/source* directory, create a subdirectory named *com*.

2. In the *AppName/source/com* directory, create a subdirectory named *somedomain*.

To create class *A*, follow these steps if you're using Flash MX Professional 2004. If you're using Flash MX 2004 (standard edition), use an external text editor to create the *.as* class file following similar steps:

1. In Flash MX Professional 2004, choose File → New.

2. In the New Document dialog box, on the General tab, for Type, choose Action-Script File.

3. Click OK. The script editor launches with an empty file.

4. Enter the following code into the script editor:

```
import com.somedomain.B;

class com.somedomain.A {
  private static var bInstance:B;
  public function A () {
    // In this example, class A's constructor is not used.
  }
  public static function main ():Void {
    trace("Starting application.");
    bInstance = new B();
  }
}
```

5. Choose File → Save As.

6. In the Save As dialog box, specify **A.as** as the filename, and save the file in the directory: *AppName/source/com/somedomain*.

Similarly, to create class *B*, use Flash MX Professional 2004 or an external text editor to create the *B.as* file in the *AppName/source/com/somedomain* folder with the following content:

```
class com.somedomain.B {
  public function B () {
    trace("An instance of class B was constructed.");
  }
}
```

Notice that in our example framework we store the files for our class hierarchy under the *AppName/source* subdirectory. That's a reasonable place to store the files, but it's not mandatory. The class files could theoretically go anywhere. As long as the directory in which they reside is added to the global or document classpath, the classes will be accessible to timeline code and other ActionScript classes. For information on classpaths, see "Package Access and the Classpath" in Chapter 9. For information on storing classes in a central repository, see Chapter 14.

The Document Timeline

We've now created two classes (*A* and *B*) and a Flash document that will use them (*AppName.fla*). Let's see exactly how *AppName.fla* loads the classes and invokes the class method *A.main( )*, which starts our application.

In Chapter 2, we learned that the fundamental metaphor of a Flash document is the timeline, which can be used to create animations like a filmstrip. When used for animation, the frames in the timeline are displayed in rapid linear succession by the Flash Player. However, the timeline can also be used to create a series of application states, in which specific frames correspond to specific states and frames are displayed according to the application's logic, not linearly (according to the passing of time).

In our example application framework, we'll use the timeline of *AppName.fla* to create two basic application states: *loading* and *main*. Each state is implemented by pausing the playhead in a corresponding labeled frame. On the frame labeled *loading*, we display a loading message while our application's classes load. On the frame labeled *main*, we invoke *A.main( )*, which starts the application.

Using frames as application states is a common practice for creating Flash applications (both OOP and non-OOP). While the practice definitely works and is widespread, it can also be awkward to work with and generally feels unfamiliar to programmers coming from other languages. To address this situation, Flash MX Professional 2004 introduces a Visual Basic–style forms-based development feature called Screens, which is not covered in this book. For information on developing applications with Screens, see Help → Using Flash → Working with Screens (Flash Professional only).

To load our *A* and *B* classes, we'll follow these general steps:

1. Specify the export frame for classes in the movie.
2. Add the labeled state frames *loading* and *main* to *AppName.fla*'s timeline.
3. Add code that displays a loading message while the movie loads.

The specific procedures for those three steps are listed next. If you've already read Chapter 5 you'll have seen some of these procedures before.

To specify the export frame for classes in the movie, follow these steps:

1. Open *AppName.fla* in the Flash authoring tool
2. Choose File → Publish Settings.
3. In the Publish Settings dialog box, on the Flash tab, next to the ActionScript Version, click Settings.

4. In the ActionScript Settings dialog box, for the Export Frame for Classes option, enter **10**. The choice of frame 10 is arbitrary, but the specified frame must come after the code that displays the loading message (i.e., after the preloader).

5. Click OK to confirm the ActionScript settings.

6. Click OK to confirm the publish settings.

To add the labeled state frames *loading* and *main* to *AppName.fla*'s timeline, follow these steps:

1. In *AppName.fla*'s main timeline, double-click *Layer 1* and rename it to **scripts**. We'll place all our code on the *scripts* layer. As a best practice, you should keep all your timeline code in the *scripts* layer, which should be the topmost layer in your timeline. The *scripts* layer should contain only scripts, not movie clips or other content. Some developers call the layer *actions* instead of *scripts*, but the premise is the same.

2. In the main timeline of *AppName.fla*, select frame 15 of the *scripts* layer.

3. Choose Insert → Timeline → Keyframe (F6).

4. Choose Insert → Timeline → Layer.

5. Double-click the new layer's name and change it to **labels**.

6. At frames 4 and 15 of the *labels* layer, add a new keyframe (Insert → Timeline → Keyframe or F6). Just as the *scripts* layer holds all our scripts, the *labels* layer is used exclusively to hold frame labels. Frame labels are a convenient, human-friendly way to refer to frames instead of referring to frames by number.

7. With frame 4 of the *labels* layer selected, in the Properties panel, under Frame, change <Frame Label> to **loading**.

8. With frame 15 of the *labels* layer selected, in the Properties panel, under Frame, change <Frame Label> to **main**.

Next, follow these steps to add code that displays a loading message while the movie loads:

1. At frame 5 of the *scripts* layer, add a new keyframe (Insert → Timeline → Keyframe or F6).

2. With frame 5 of the *scripts* layer selected, enter the following code into the Actions panel (F9):

```
if (_framesloaded == _totalframes) {
  gotoAndStop("main");
} else {
  gotoAndPlay("loading");
}
```

3. With frame 1 of the *scripts* layer selected, enter the following code into the Actions panel:

```
this.createTextField("loadmsg_txt", 0, 200, 200, 0, 0);
loadmsg_txt.autoSize = true;
loadmsg_txt.text = "Loading...Please wait.";
```

4. With frame 15 of the *scripts* layer selected, enter the following code into the Actions panel:

```
loadmsg_txt.removeTextField( );
```

We've now provided the basic timeline structure that loads our application's classes. All that's left is to start the application by invoking *A.main( )*. We do that on the frame labeled *main* in *AppName.fla*. Add the following code to the end of the script on frame 15 (i.e., just below `loadmsg_txt.removeTextField( );`):

```
import com.somedomain.A;
A.main( );
```

In theory, that will be the last change we ever make to *AppName.fla*, unless we want to include components, sounds, or custom graphics. Any code in our application will reside in a class that's referenced either directly by *A.main( )* or indirectly by a class referenced in *A.main( )*. We won't place any more code in *AppName.fla*.

Our application is complete. We now need to test that everything works. To do that, we need to export a *.swf* file and run it in the Flash Player.

The Exported Flash Movie (.swf file)

Our application is now ready for testing and—assuming all goes well—deployment. To specify the directory in which to create *AppName.swf*, follow these steps:

1. With *AppName.fla* open, choose File → Publish Settings → Formats.
2. Under the File heading, for Flash (*.swf*), enter **../deploy/AppName.swf**.
3. Click OK.
4. To test our application in the Flash authoring tool's Test Movie mode, select Control → Test Movie. Testing a movie actually creates *AppName.swf* in the *AppName/deploy* directory and immediately loads it into a debugging version of the Flash Player.

For our application, we'll export to Flash Player 7 format (the default in Flash MX 2004), but you could also export to Flash Player 6 format if you expect your visitors to be using that version of the Flash Player. For information on setting the movie format and ActionScript version, see "ActionScript 1.0 and 2.0 in Flash Player 6 and 7" in Chapter 1.

If your application is working, you should see the following appear in the Output panel:

```
Starting application.
An instance of class B was constructed.
```

If the preceding messages don't appear in the Output panel, try comparing your source files to the ones posted at *http://moock.org/eas2/examples*.

When everything works in Test Movie mode, publish an HTML page that includes the movie, ready for posting to a web site as follows:

---

1. With *AppName.fla* open, choose File → Publish Settings → Formats.
2. Under the File heading, for HTML (*.html*), enter `../deploy/AppName.html`.
3. Click Publish.
4. Click OK.
5. Test locally by opening *AppName.html* in your web browser.
6. When the local testing proves successful, upload the *.html* and *.swf* files to your web server.
7. Test in your browser from the remote site by browsing to the URL where you uploaded the *.html* file. Note that the package location and author-time folder structure do not matter once you upload your files to the server. Packages and classpaths matter only at compile time. Furthermore, you can upload the *.html* and *.swf* wherever you like on your server, but in our example, the two files must reside in the same web server folder.

It's a good idea to test in all supported versions of the Flash Player in all target web browsers on all target platforms throughout the lifetime of a project. If you wait until the end of the project to test in various browsers, you might discover serious problems that would have been easier to fix if they had been caught earlier.

For detailed information on exporting and publishing Flash movies, see Help → Using Flash → Publishing.

Projects in Flash MX Professional 2004

To help manage the files in a large application, Flash MX Professional 2004 supports the concept of *projects*. A project is a group of related files that can be managed via the Project panel in the Flash MX Professional 2004 authoring tool. The Project panel resembles a file explorer and offers the following features:

- Authoring tool integration with source control applications such as Microsoft Visual SourceSafe
- Easy access to related source files
- One-click application publishing, even while editing class files

A discussion of using the Projects feature is outside the scope of this book. For details on Flash projects, see Help → Using Flash → Working with Projects (Flash Professional only).

Let's See It in Action!

Although this chapter may have felt quite conceptual, it lays very important groundwork for OOP development and for many of the examples in the remainder of this book. In the next chapter, we'll put some meat on the bones of our application framework by building a currency conversion application.

Using Components with ActionScript 2.0

In Chapter 11, we learned how to structure a basic OOP application in ActionScript 2.0. In this chapter, we'll see how to create a GUI application based on that structure. As usual, you can download the sample files discussed in this chapter from *http://moock.org/eas2/examples*.

Currency Converter Application Overview

Our example GUI application is a simple currency converter. Figure 12-1 shows the components used in our currency converter interface (Button, ComboBox, Label, TextArea, and TextInput). The user must specify an amount in Canadian dollars, select a currency type from the drop-down list, and click the Convert button to determine the equivalent amount in the selected currency. The result is displayed on screen.

Figure 12-1. The currency converter application

We'll place the assets for our application in the following directory structure, which mirrors the structure we used in Chapter 11. Note that the *deploy* and *source* folders are both subdirectories of *CurrencyConverter* and that *org/moock/tools* is a subdirectory of the *source* folder:

```
CurrencyConverter/
  deploy/
```

```
source/
    org/
        moock/
            tools/
```

Our application's main Flash document is named *CurrencyConverter.fla*. It resides in *CurrencyConverter/source*. To create the *CurrencyConverter.fla* file, we'll copy the file *AppName.fla* (which we created in Chapter 11) to the *CurrencyConverter/source* directory, and rename the file to *CurrencyConverter.fla*. That gives *CurrencyConverter.fla* the basic structure it needs, including a class preloader on frames 2 and 3 and a frame labeled *main*, on which we'll start the application.

Our application's only class is *CurrencyConverter*. It is stored in an external *.as* class file named *CurrencyConverter.as*, which resides in *CurrencyConverter/source/org/moock/ tools*. Our exported application (a Flash movie) is named *CurrencyConverter.swf*. It resides in *CurrencyConverter/deploy*.

Now let's take a closer look at each of these parts of our application.

Preparing the Flash Document

Our *CurrencyConverter* class instantiates all the components needed for our application at runtime. Even though we create instances of components at runtime, Flash requires us to add the components to the *CurrencyConverter.fla*'s Library during authoring. Unfortunately, Flash does not allow us to simply drag the required components from the Flash Components panel to *CurrencyConverter.fla*'s Library. Instead, to add a component to the Library, we must drag an instance of it to the Stage. Although component instances can be left on the Stage of a *.fla* file, that development style is not our current focus. So we'll delete the instances from the Stage; however, Flash leaves a copy of the underlying component in the Library (which was our original goal).

Adding Components to the Document

Here are the steps to follow to add the Button component to *CurrencyConverter.fla*'s Library. To add the ComboBox, Label, TextArea, and TextInput components to the Library, follow the same steps, choosing the appropriate component instead of Button.

1. With *CurrencyConverter.fla* open in the Flash authoring tool, select Window → Development Panels → Components.

2. In the Components panel, in the folder named UI Components, click and drag the Button component to the Stage. The Button component appears in the Library.

3. Select and delete the Button instance from the Stage.

If we were working in a brand new *.fla* file, our components would now be ready for runtime instantiation. However, recall that we're working with the basic Flash document we created in Chapter 11, which exports its classes at frame 10 and displays a preloading message while those classes load. Because of this preloading structure, our components would not currently work if we attempted to use them! We need to integrate the components into our preloading structure.

 When a document's ActionScript 2.0 classes are exported on a frame later than frame 1, components will not work in that document unless they are loaded *after* the class export frame!

To load our components after frame 10, we must set them to not export on frame 1, and then we must place a dummy instance of each component on stage after frame 10. The dummy instance is not used; it merely forces the component to load.

Here are the steps we follow to prevent the Button component from being exported on frame 1. To prevent the remaining components from being exported on frame 1, follow the same steps, choosing the appropriate component instead of Button.

1. Select the Button component in the Library.
2. From the Library's pop-up Options menu in the top-right corner of the panel, select Linkage.
3. In the Linkage Properties dialog box, under Linkage, uncheck the Export in First Frame checkbox.
4. Click OK.

When a component's Export in First Frame option is unchecked, the component is not compiled with the movie unless an instance of the component is placed on the document's timeline. The component loads at the frame on which an instance of it is placed. But the component initialization process requires a movie's ActionScript 2.0 classes to be available *before* the component is exported. Hence, in our *CurrencyConverter.fla* document, we'll place an instance of each of our components on frame 12, two frames after our document's ActionScript 2.0 classes are exported. To store the dummy component instances, we'll create a new timeline layer and keyframe, as follows:

1. Select Insert → Timeline → Layer.
2. Double-click the new layer and rename it **load components**.
3. Select frame 12 in the *load components* layer.
4. Select Insert → Timeline → Keyframe.
5. Select frame 13 in the *load components* layer.
6. Select Insert → Timeline → Keyframe. This second keyframe prevents the dummy component instances from showing up in our application. We need them only for loading; the *CurrencyConverter* class handles the actual creation of component instances in our application.

With our component-loading keyframe prepared, we can now place a dummy instance of each component on our document's timeline, as follows:

1. Select frame 12 in the *load components* layer.

2. From the Library, drag an instance of each component to the Stage.

3. Optionally use the Component Inspector panel (Window → Development Panels → Component Inspector) to add dummy text to each component instance indicating that it is not used, as shown in Figure 12-2. Consult Flash's online help for instructions on setting component parameters via the Component Inspector.

Figure 12-2 shows how our document's timeline and Stage look with frame 12 of the *load components* layer selected.

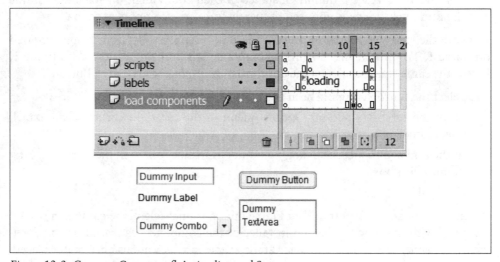

Figure 12-2. CurrencyConverter.fla's timeline and Stage

Starting the Application

In Chapter 11, we saw how to start an OOP application by invoking the *main( )* method of the application's primary class (i.e., the class and method that we design to be the program launch point). We'll start our currency converter by invoking *main( )* on our application's primary (indeed, only) class, *CurrencyConverter*. The *main( )* call comes on frame 15 of the *scripts* layer in *CurrencyConverter.fla*'s timeline, after our classes and components have been preloaded. Here's the code:

```
import org.moock.tools.CurrencyConverter;
CurrencyConverter.main(this, 0, 150, 100);
```

Notice that the *import* statement allows us, in the future, to refer to the *CurrencyConverter* class by its name without typing its fully qualified package path. As implied by the preceding code, our class's *main( )* method expects four parameters: the movie clip to hold the currency converter (this) and the depth, horizontal position, and vertical position—0, 150 and 100, respectively—at which to display the converter within the clip.

Our *CurrencyConverter.fla* file is now ready. We can now turn our attention to the class that creates and manages the currency converter application itself, *CurrencyConverter*.

The CurrencyConverter Class

The *CurrencyConverter* class's three main duties are to:

- Provide a method that starts the application (*main( )*)
- Create the application interface
- Respond to user input

Before we examine the specific code required to perform those duties, you should skim the entire class listing, presented in Example 12-1. For now, you don't need to read the code too carefully; we'll study it in detail over the remainder of this chapter.

Example 12-1. The CurrencyConverter class

```
// Import the package containing the Flash UI components we're using.
import mx.controls.*;

// Define the CurrencyConverter class, and include the package path.
class org.moock.tools.CurrencyConverter {
  // Hardcode the exchange rates for this example.
  private static var rateUS:Number = 1.3205;  // Rate for US dollar
  private static var rateUK:Number = 2.1996;  // Rate for pound sterling
  private static var rateEU:Number = 1.5600;  // Rate for euro

  // The container for all UI elements
  private var converter_mc:MovieClip;

  // The user interface components
  private var input:TextInput;          // Text field for original amount
  private var currencyPicker:ComboBox;  // Currency selection menu
  private var result:TextArea;          // Text field for conversion output

  /**
   * CurrencyConverter Constructor
   *
   * @param    target   The movie clip to which
   *                     converter_mc will be attached.
   * @param    depth    The depth, in target, on which to
   *                     attach converter_mc.
   * @param    x        The horizontal position of converter_mc.
   * @param    y        The vertical position of converter_mc.
   */
  public function CurrencyConverter (target:MovieClip, depth:Number,
```

Example 12-1. The CurrencyConverter class (continued)

```
                               x:Number, y:Number) {
    buildConverter(target, depth, x, y);
  }

  /**
   * Creates the user interface for the currency converter
   * and defines the events for that interface.
   */
  public function buildConverter (target:MovieClip, depth:Number,
                                  x:Number, y:Number):Void {
    // Store a reference to the current object for use by nested functions.
    var thisConverter:CurrencyConverter = this;

    // Make a container movie clip to hold the converter's UI.
    converter_mc = target.createEmptyMovieClip("converter", depth);
    converter_mc._x = x;
    converter_mc._y = y;

    // Create the title.
    var title:Label = converter_mc.createClassObject(Label, "title", 0);
    title.autoSize = "left";
    title.text = "Canadian Currency Converter";
    title.setStyle("color", 0x770000);
    title.setStyle("fontSize", 16);

    // Create the instructions.
    var instructions:Label = converter_mc.createClassObject(Label,
                                                      "instructions",
                                                      1);
    instructions.autoSize = "left";
    instructions.text = "Enter Amount in Canadian Dollars";
    instructions.move(instructions.x, title.y + title.height + 5);

    // Create an input text field to receive the amount to convert.
    input = converter_mc.createClassObject(TextInput, "input", 2);
    input.setSize(200, 25);
    input.move(input.x, instructions.y + instructions.height);
    input.restrict = "0-9.";
    // Handle this component's enter event using a generic listener object.
    var enterHandler:Object = new Object();
    enterHandler.enter = function (e:Object):Void {
      thisConverter.convert();
    }
    input.addEventListener("enter", enterHandler);

    // Create the currency selector ComboBox.
    currencyPicker = converter_mc.createClassObject(ComboBox, "picker", 3);
    currencyPicker.setSize(200, currencyPicker.height);
    currencyPicker.move(currencyPicker.x, input.y + input.height + 10);
    currencyPicker.dataProvider = [
                      {label:"Select Target Currency", data:null},
                      {label:"Canadian to U.S. Dollar", data:"US"},
```

Example 12-1. The CurrencyConverter class (continued)

```
                    {label:"Canadian to UK Pound Sterling", data:"UK"},
                    {label:"Canadian to EURO", data:"EU"}]);

  // Create the Convert button.
  var convertButton:Button = converter_mc.createClassObject(Button,
                                                    "convertButton",
                                                    4);
  convertButton.move(currencyPicker.x + currencyPicker.width + 5,
                    currencyPicker.y);
  convertButton.label = "Convert!";
  // Handle this component's events using a handler function.
  // As discussed later under "Handling Component Events," this technique
  // is discouraged by Macromedia.
  convertButton.clickHandler = function (e:Object):Void {
    thisConverter.convert();
  };

  // Create the result output field.
  result = converter_mc.createClassObject(TextArea, "result", 5);
  result.setSize(200, 25);
  result.move(result.x, currencyPicker.y + currencyPicker.height + 10);
  result.editable = false;
}

/**
 * Converts a user-supplied quantity from Canadian dollars to
 * the selected currency.
 */
public function convert ():Void {
  var convertedAmount:Number;
  var origAmount:Number = parseFloat(input.text);
  if (!isNaN(origAmount)) {
    if (currencyPicker.selectedItem.data != null) {
      switch (currencyPicker.selectedItem.data) {
        case "US":
          convertedAmount = origAmount / CurrencyConverter.rateUS;
          break;
        case "UK":
          convertedAmount = origAmount / CurrencyConverter.rateUK;
          break;
        case "EU":
          convertedAmount = origAmount / CurrencyConverter.rateEU;
          break;
      }
      result.text = "Result: " + convertedAmount;
    } else {
      result.text = "Please select a currency.";
    }
  } else {
    result.text = "Original amount is not valid.";
  }
}
```

Example 12-1. The CurrencyConverter class (continued)

```
// Program point of entry
public static function main (target:MovieClip, depth:Number,
                             x:Number, y:Number):Void {
  var converter:CurrencyConverter = new CurrencyConverter(target, depth,
                                                          x, y);
}
}
```

Importing the Components' Package

Our *CurrencyConverter* class makes many references to various component classes (*Button*, *CombBox*, *Label*, etc.). The component classes we need reside in the package *mx.controls*. Throughout our *CurrencyConverter* class, we could refer to the components by their fully qualified names, such as *mx.controls.Button* or *mx.controls. ComboBox*. That obviously gets tedious, so prior to defining our *CurrencyConverter* class, we import the entire *mx.controls* package, as follows:

```
import mx.controls.*;
```

Once the *mx.controls* package is imported, we can refer to a component class such as *Button* without specifying its full package name. Note that not all component classes reside in the *mx.controls* package. For example, the classes for containers such as *Window* and *ScrollPane* reside in the *mx.containers* package. To determine the package for a component class, consult its entry in Flash's built-in Components Dictionary (Help → Using Components → Components Dictionary).

For complete details on packages and the *import* statement, see Chapter 9.

CurrencyConverter Properties

Our *CurrencyConverter* class defines two general categories of properties: class properties that specify the exchange rates for various currencies and instance properties that store references to some of the components in our user interface:

```
// The exchange rate properties
private static var rateUS:Number = 1.3205;  // Rate for US dollar
private static var rateUK:Number = 2.1996;  // Rate for Pound Sterling
private static var rateEU:Number = 1.5600;  // Rate for euro

// The container for all UI elements
private var converter_mc:MovieClip;

// The user interface components
private var input:TextInput;                // Text field for original amount
private var currencyPicker:ComboBox;        // Currency selection menu
private var result:TextArea;                // Text field for conversion output
```

For the sake of this example, the exchange rates in our application are permanently set in class properties. In a real currency converter, they'd most likely be retrieved at runtime from a dynamic, server-side source, as described in *Flash Remoting: The Definitive Guide* by Tom Muck (O'Reilly).

Notice that not all of our user interface components are stored in instance properties. After creation, some components (e.g., the Label components) need not be used again and, hence, are not stored in instance properties. When creating a component, we store a reference to it only if another method in the class needs to manipulate it later in the application.

The main( ) method

The currency converter application's startup method is *CurrencyConverter.main( )*:

```
public static function main (target:MovieClip, depth:Number,
                            x:Number, y:Number):Void {
  var converter:CurrencyConverter = new CurrencyConverter(target, depth,
                                        x, y);
}
```

The *main( )* method is a class method (i.e., declared *static*) because it is invoked once for the entire application and is not associated with a particular instance. The *main( )* method uses a common Java convention to set things in motion: it creates an instance of the application's primary class, *CurrencyConverter*, and stores that instance in a local variable, converter. The instance manages the remainder of the application either by itself or, in larger applications, by creating and interacting with other classes. Notice that the application's primary class, *CurrencyConverter*, is also the class that defines the *main( )* method. In fact, the *CurrencyConverter* class creates an instance of itself! This structure is both legitimate and common.

As we saw previously, *CurrencyConverter.main( )* is invoked from the frame labeled *main* following the preloader. When the *main( )* method exits, the local converter variable goes out of scope (i.e., no longer exists), and the reference to the *CurrencyConverter* instance in it is automatically deleted. However, the application continues to run because the movie clip and other components created by *CurrencyConverter* continue to exist on stage, even after *main( )* exits. Physical assets on stage (e.g., movie clips and text fields) that are created at runtime exist until they are explicitly removed (or the clip in which they reside is removed), even if they are not stored in variables or properties.

As we'll see later, the *CurrencyConverter* instance created by *main( )* is kept alive in the scope chain of the *buildConverter( )* method. The movie clip and components created by *buildConverter( )* retain a reference back to the *CurrencyConverter* instance via the scope chain. Without that reference, our application wouldn't be able to respond to component events.

The Class Constructor

The *CurrencyConverter* class constructor is straightforward. It simply invokes *buildConverter( )*, which creates our application's user interface:

```
public function CurrencyConverter (target:MovieClip, depth:Number,
                                   x:Number, y:Number) {
  buildConverter(target, depth, x, y);
}
```

Notice that, like the *main( )* method, the constructor passes on its arguments to another section of the program—in this case the *buildConverter( )* method, which uses the arguments to create the application's interface.

Creating the User Interface

As we've just learned, the currency converter interface is created by the *buildConverter( )* method. To create the interface, *buildConverter( )* instantiates user interface components and defines event handlers that dictate the interface's behavior.

You should already have skimmed the full listing for *buildConverter( )* earlier in Example 12-1. Now let's study the method line by line.

The first line of code in *buildConverter( )* may be unfamiliar to some programmers—it stores a reference to the current object in a local variable named thisConverter:

```
var thisConverter:CurrencyConverter = this;
```

Storing the current object in a local variable adds it to the *buildConverter( )* method's scope chain. This not only allows the current object to be accessed by nested functions, but it keeps the current object alive for as long as those nested functions exist. As we'll see shortly, the event handlers in our application are implemented as nested functions; they use the thisConverter variable to access the current *CurrencyConverter* instance. For general information on this technique, see "Nesting Functions in Methods" in Chapter 4 and "Handling Component Events" later in this chapter.

The interface container

Now we can move on to creating interface elements. First, we must create a container movie clip to which all our components are placed. We give the clip an instance name of converter and place it inside the specified target clip at the specified depth. Recall that the target and depth are supplied to the *main( )* method in *CurrencyConverter.fla*, which passes them on to the *CurrencyConverter* constructor, which in turn passes them to *buildConverter( )*.

```
converter_mc = target.createEmptyMovieClip("converter", depth);
```

Placing our application's components in a single movie clip container makes them easy to manipulate as a group. For example, to move the entire group of components, we can simply set the _x and _y properties of the container clip:

```
converter_mc._x = x;
converter_mc._y = y;
```

Again, the values x and y were originally supplied to the *main( )* method on frame 15 of *CurrencyConverter.fla*.

Notice that our main container clip is stored in the instance property converter_mc. Storing the clip in a property allows it to be accessed outside the *buildConverter( )* clip, for the purpose of, say, repositioning it or deleting it. In our case, we do not reposition or delete the main container, so we could, in theory, store it in a local variable instead of a property. In this case, however, we store it in the instance property converter_mc simply to make the class easier to enhance in the future.

The title Label component

Now that our container movie clip is prepared, we can put our components into it. We start by giving our application a title using a Label component, which is used to display a single line of text on screen.

The following code creates a Label component named title inside converter_mc and places it on depth 0:

```
var title:Label = converter_mc.createClassObject(Label, "title", 0);
```

All components in our application are created with the *UIObject* class's *createClassObject( )* method. Its three parameters specify:

- The class of component to create
- The instance name of the component
- The depth of the component inside its parent movie clip or component

The *createClassObject( )* method returns a reference to the newly created component. In the case of our title instance, we store that reference in a local variable named title. We use a local variable in this case because we have no need to access the title instance later. If, elsewhere in our application, we needed access to the title component, we'd store it in an instance property instead of a local variable.

Note that the instance name, "title" is used by convention for clarity, but we never use that name in our code. In our application, we refer to components via variables and properties only. In this case, we refer to the title instance by the variable name title—not by its instance name (which happens to be the same as the variable name). By convention, most of our component instance names match the variable or property name in which they are stored. However, nothing requires the instance name and the variable or property name to match; only the variable or property name matters to our application (the instance name is ignored).

Now take a closer look at the code we use to create the title instance:

```
converter_mc.createClassObject(Label, "title", 0);
```

Notice that we invoke *createClassObject( )* on converter_mc, which is a *MovieClip* instance, despite the fact that the *MovieClip* class does not define a *createClassObject( )* method! We can use *createClassObject( )* on *MovieClip* instances because that method is added to the *MovieClip* class at runtime by the v2 component architecture (along with various other methods). Adding a new method or new property to a class at runtime works only when the recipient class is declared *dynamic*, as is the built-in *MovieClip* class.

Because we're accessing *createClassObject( )* through *MovieClip*, we also don't need to worry that it returns an object of type *UIObject*, not type *Label* as required by our title variable. In theory, the following line of code should generate a type mismatch error because *createClassObject( )* returns a *UIObject*, but title's datatype is *Label*:

```
var title:Label = converter_mc.createClassObject(Label, "title", 0);
```

However, no error occurs because type checking is not performed on methods that are added to a class dynamically at runtime. When invoking *createClassObject( )* on a component, to prevent a compiler error, you *must* cast the return value to the type of object you are creating. For example, here we cast the return of *createClassObject( )* to the *Label* type, as is required if converter_mc holds a component instance instead of a *MovieClip* instance:

```
var title:Label = Label(converter_mc.createClassObject(Label, "title", 0));
```

Now that our application's title instance has been created, we can adjust its display properties, as follows:

```
title.autoSize = "left";              // Make the label resize automatically
title.text = "Canadian Currency Converter";  // Set the text to display
title.setStyle("color", 0x770000);    // Set the text color
title.setStyle("fontSize", 16);       // Set the text size
```

For more information on setting the style of a single component or all the components in an application, see Help → Using Components → Customizing Components → Using Styles to Customize Component Color and Text.

The instructions Label component

To create the instructions for our application, we'll use another Label component similar to the application title created earlier. We store this Label instance in a local variable named instructions:

```
var instructions:Label = converter_mc.createClassObject(Label,
                                                "instructions", 1);
instructions.autoSize = "left";
instructions.text = "Enter Amount in Canadian Dollars";
instructions.move(instructions.x, title.y + title.height + 5);
```

The last line of the preceding code places the instructions Label 5 pixels below the title Label.

Components can be positioned only with the *move( )* method. Attempts to set a component's read-only x and y properties fail silently. Note that components support the properties x, y, width, and height (without an underscore). However, *MovieClip* instances support the properties _x and _y, _width, and _height (with an underscore).

The *move( )* method expects a new x coordinate as its first parameter and a new y coordinate as its second parameter. To leave the instructions instance's horizontal location unchanged, we specify its existing horizontal location (instructions.x) as the first argument to *move( )*. The instructions instance's vertical location is calculated as the vertical position of the title instance, plus the title instance's height, plus a 5-pixel buffer.

The input TextInput component

With the title and instructions completed, we can move on to components that accept user input. Our first input component is a TextInput instance, which lets a user enter a single line of text (in this case, an amount in Canadian dollars):

```
input = converter_mc.createClassObject(TextInput, "input", 2);
input.setSize(200, 25);
input.move(input.x, instructions.y + instructions.height);
input.restrict = "0-9.";
```

We use *setSize( )* to make our TextInput component 200 x 25 pixels.

Components can be resized only with *setSize( )*. Attempts to set a component's read-only width and height properties fail silently.

We use the restrict property to prevent the user from entering anything other than numbers or a decimal point character. Negative values and dollar signs are not allowed.

Next, we define what happens when the Enter key (or Return key) is pressed while the TextInput component instance has keyboard focus. When Enter is pressed, we want to convert the user-supplied value to the chosen currency. Conversion is performed by the *CurrencyConverter.convert( )* method. To invoke that method when Enter is pressed, we register an *event listener object* to receive events from the TextInput instance. In this case, the event listener object is simply an instance of the generic *Object* class:

```
var enterHandler:Object = new Object();
```

On the generic *Object* instance, we define an *enter( )* method that is invoked automatically by input (our TextInput instance) when the Enter key is pressed:

```
enterHandler.enter = function (e:Object):Void {
  thisConverter.convert();
}
```

Notice that the *enter( )* method accesses the current *CurrencyConverter* instance via the thisConverter variable we defined earlier. That variable is accessible to the nested *enterHandler.enter( )* method for as long as the input instance exists.

Finally, we register the generic *Object* instance to receive events from input, specifying "enter" as the type of event the instance is interested in receiving:

```
input.addEventListener("enter", enterHandler);
```

Although it's perfectly legitimate to use a generic *Object* instance to handle events, in more complex applications, an event listener object may well be an instance of a separate class. However, when a single event from a single user interface component generates a single response (as in our present case), it is also possible to handle the event with an *event handler function* rather than a generic *Object* instance. Later, we'll use an event handler function to handle events from our application's Convert button. We'll also learn why Macromedia discourages the use of event handler functions. In the specific case of *TextInput.enter( )*, however, we're forced to use a listener object due to a bug in the *TextInput* class that prevents its event handler functions from working properly.

The currencyPicker ComboBox component

Our application already has a place for the user to enter a dollar amount. Next, we add the drop-down menu (a ComboBox component) that lets the user pick a currency to which to convert. The ComboBox instance is stored in the currencyPicker property and is created, sized, and positioned exactly like previous components in the application:

```
currencyPicker = converter_mc.createClassObject(ComboBox, "picker", 3);
currencyPicker.setSize(200, currencyPicker.height);
currencyPicker.move(currencyPicker.x, input.y + input.height + 10);
```

To populate our currencyPicker component with choices, we set its dataProvider property to an array whose elements are generic objects with label and data properties. The value of each object's label property is displayed on screen as an option in the drop-down list. The value of each object's data property is used later by the *convert( )* method to determine which currency was selected by the user.

```
currencyPicker.dataProvider = [
                  {label:"Select Target Currency", data:null},
                  {label:"Canadian to U.S. Dollar", data:"US"},
                  {label:"Canadian to UK Pound Sterling", data:"UK"},
                  {label:"Canadian to EURO", data:"EU"}];
```

We chose this implementation to separate the application's display layer from its data layer (which might retrieve conversion rates from a server-side application). An alternative, less flexible implementation might embed the currency conversion rates directly in the data property of each ComboBox item.

The convertButton Button component

We've already seen that the user can convert a value simply by pressing the Enter key while typing in the input text field. We'll now add an explicit Convert button to the application for users who prefer not to use the Enter key.

The convertButton component is an instance of the *mx.controls.Button* component class, not to be confused with the native *Button* class that represents instances of *Button* symbols in a movie. Because we imported the *mx.controls.* package earlier, the compiler knows to treat unqualified references to *Button* as references to the *mx.controls.Button* class.

To create and position the convertButton component, we use now-familiar techniques:

```
// Create the Convert button.
var convertButton:Button = converter_mc.createClassObject(Button,
                                                          "convertButton",
                                                          4);
convertButton.move(currencyPicker.x + currencyPicker.width + 5,
                   currencyPicker.y);
```

To specify the text on convertButton, we assign a string to its label property:

```
convertButton.label = "Convert!";
```

Finally, we must define what happens when convertButton is clicked. To do so, we assign an event handler function to convertButton's clickHandler property, as follows:

```
convertButton.clickHandler = function (e:Object):Void {
  // Invoke convert( ) on the current CurrencyConverter instance
  // when convertButton is clicked.
  thisConverter.convert( );
};
```

The preceding code demonstrates one way to handle component events. It defines an anonymous function that is executed automatically when convertButton is clicked. The property name, clickHandler, specifies the event to handle, in this case the *click* event. To define an event handler for a different event, we'd define an *event*Handler property where *event* is the name of the event. For example, to handle the List component's *change* event or *scroll* events, we'd assign a function to the changeHandler or scrollHandler property.

Because the anonymous function is nested inside the *buildConverter( )* method, it has access to *buildConverter( )*'s local variables via the scope chain. Hence, convertButton can reference the current *CurrencyConverter* instance via the local variable thisConverter. We use that reference to invoke the *convert( )* method.

We've now seen two different ways to handle events from components. For guidance on which to use in various situations, see "Handling Component Events," later in this chapter.

The result TextArea component

Our interface is almost complete. We have a TextInput component that accepts a dollar amount from the user, a ComboBox component that lets the user pick a currency, and a button that triggers the conversion. All we need now is a TextArea component in which to display currency conversion results. TextArea components are used to display one or more lines of text on screen within a bordered, adjustable rectangle.

Here's the code that creates, sizes, and positions our TextArea component:

```
result = converter_mc.createClassObject(TextArea, "result", 5);
result.setSize(200, 25);
result.move(result.x, currencyPicker.y + currencyPicker.height + 10);
```

To prevent the user from changing the contents of the result TextArea component, we set its editable property to false (by default, TextArea component instances are editable):

```
result.editable = false;
```

And that concludes the *buildConverter( )* method. Let's move on to the *convert( )* method, which performs currency conversion.

Converting Currency Based on User Input

In the preceding section, we created the user interface for our currency converter application. We specified that when the Convert button is clicked or when the user presses the Enter key while entering a number, the *convert( )* method should be invoked. The *convert( )* method converts a user-supplied value to a specific currency and displays the result on screen. It also displays error messages. The code in *convert( )* provides a good example of how components are accessed and manipulated in a typical ActionScript 2.0 OOP application. Here's a reminder of the full code listing for *convert( )*:

```
public function convert ():Void {
  var convertedAmount:Number;
  var origAmount:Number = parseFloat(input.text);
  if (!isNaN(origAmount)) {
    if (currencyPicker.selectedItem.data != null) {
      switch (currencyPicker.selectedItem.data) {
        case "US":
          convertedAmount = origAmount / CurrencyConverter.rateUS;
          break;
        case "UK":
          convertedAmount = origAmount / CurrencyConverter.rateUK;
          break;
        case "EU":
```

```
            convertedAmount = origAmount / CurrencyConverter.rateEU;
        break;
      }
      result.text = "Result: " + convertedAmount;
    } else {
      result.text = "Please select a currency.";
    }
  } else {
    result.text = "Original amount is not valid.";
  }
}
```

Our first task in *convert( )* is to create two local variables: convertedAmount, which stores the postconversion value, and origAmount, which stores the user-supplied value. The value of origAmount is retrieved from the input component's text property, which stores the user input as a *String*. We convert that *String* to a *Number* using the built-in *parseFloat( )* function:

```
var convertedAmount:Number;
var origAmount:Number = parseFloat(input.text);
```

But the input.text property might be empty, or it might not be valid (that is, it might contain a nonmathematical value such as "....4..34"). Hence, our next task is to check whether the conversion from a *String* to a *Number* succeeded. If conversion did not succeed, the value of origAmount will be NaN (not-a-number). Hence, we can say that the value is valid when it is *not* NaN:

```
if (!isNaN(origAmount)) {
```

If the value is valid, we check which currency is selected in the drop-down list using currencyPicker.selectedItem.data. The selectedItem property stores a reference to the currently selected item in the ComboBox, which is one of the objects in the dataProvider array we created earlier. To determine which object is selected, we consult that object's data property, which will be one of: null, "US," "UK," or "EU." If the data property is null, no item is selected and we should not attempt to convert the currency:

```
if (currencyPicker.selectedItem.data != null) {
```

If, on the other hand, data is not null, we use a *switch* statement to determine whether data is "US," "UK," or "EU." Within the *case* block for each of those possibilities, we perform the conversion to the selected currency:

```
switch (currencyPicker.selectedItem.data) {
  case "US":
    convertedAmount = origAmount / CurrencyConverter.rateUS;
    break;
  case "UK":
    convertedAmount = origAmount / CurrencyConverter.rateUK;
    break;
  case "EU":
    convertedAmount = origAmount / CurrencyConverter.rateEU;
    break;
}
```

Once the converted amount has been calculated, we display it in the result TextArea component, as follows:

```
result.text = "Result: " + convertedAmount;
```

When no currency has been selected, we display a warning in the result component:

```
result.text = "Please select a currency.";
```

Similarly, when the amount entered in the input component is not valid, we display a warning in the result component:

```
result.text = "Original amount is not valid.";
```

Exporting the Final Application

Our currency converter application is ready for testing and deployment. To specify the name of the movie to create (*CurrencyConverter.swf*), follow these steps:

1. With *CurrencyConverter.fla* open, choose File → Publish Settings → Formats.
2. Under the File heading, for Flash (.*swf*), enter **../deploy/CurrencyConverter.swf**.
3. Click OK.
4. To test our application in the Flash authoring tool's Test Movie mode, select Control → Test Movie.

For our application, we'll export to Flash Player 7 format (the default in Flash MX 2004), but you could also export to Flash Player 6 format if you expect your visitors to be using that version of the Flash Player. The v2 components officially require Flash Player 6.0.79.0 or higher, but in my tests the currency converter application worked happily in Flash Player 6.0.40.0 as well.

Handling Component Events

In this chapter, we handled component events in two different ways:

- With a generic listener object (in the case of the TextInput component):

```
var enterHandler:Object = new Object();
enterHandler.enter = function (e:Object):Void {
  thisConverter.convert();
}
input.addEventListener("enter", enterHandler);
```

- With an event handler function (in the case of the Button component):

```
convertButton.clickHandler = function (e:Object):Void {
  thisConverter.convert();
};
```

Handling component events with generic listener objects in ActionScript 2.0 is somewhat analogous to handling Java Swing component events with anonymous inner classes. In Swing, an anonymous instance of an anonymous inner class is created simply to define a method that responds to a component event. In ActionScript 2.0, an instance of the generic *Object* class is created for the same reason (to define a component-event-handling method). But in ActionScript 2.0, the anonymous class is not required because new methods can legally be added dynamically to instances of the *Object* class at runtime.

In general, the listener object approach is favored over the event handler function approach, primarily because multiple listener objects can receive events from the same component, whereas only one event handler function can be defined for a component at a time. This makes listener objects more flexible and scalable than event handler functions. Hence, Macromedia formally discourages use of event handler functions. However, you'll definitely see both approaches thriving in the wild. The older v1 components that shipped with Flash MX did not support listener objects, so all older v1 code uses event handler functions. The v2 components support event handler functions for backward compatibility. Moving forward, you should use listener objects rather than event handler functions. That said, even if you're not working with components, you'll still encounter event handler functions when working with the Flash Player's built-in library of classes. Many of the built-in classes, including *MovieClip*, *Sound*, *XML*, and *XMLSocket* use event handler functions as their only means of broadcasting events.

As an alternative to defining an event handler function on a component instance, you can also use a so-called *listener function*, which logically lies somewhere between an event handler function and a listener object. A listener function is a standalone function (i.e., a function not defined on any object) registered to handle a component event. For example, our earlier event handler function for the Convert Button component looked like this:

```
convertButton.clickHandler = function (e:Object):Void {
  thisConverter.convert();
}
```

The analogous listener function would be:

```
function convertClickHandler (e:Object):Void {
  thisConverter.convert();
};
convertButton.addEventListener("click", convertClickHandler);
```

Listener functions are preferred over event handler functions because multiple listener functions can be registered to handle events for the same component. However, when using listener functions, you should be careful to delete the function once it is no longer in use. Or, to avoid cleanup work, you might simply pass a function literal to the *addEventListener( )* method of the component in question, as follows:

```
convertButton.addEventListener("click", function (e:Object):Void {
  thisConverter.convert();
});
```

However, using this function literal approach prevents you from ever removing the listener function from the component's listener list. Hence, when registering for an event that you may later want to stop receiving, you should not use the preceding function literal approach.

Whether you're using a listener object, an event handler function, or a listener function, the fundamental goal is the same: to map an event from a component to a method call on an object. For example, in our Convert button example, we want to map the button's click event to our *CurrencyConverter* object's *convert( )* method. Yet another way to make that mapping would be to define a *click( )* method on the *CurrencyConverter* class and register the *CurrencyConverter* instance to handle button click events. Here's the *click( )* method definition:

```
public function click (e:Object):Void {
  convert();
}
```

And here's the code that would register the *CurrencyConverter* instance to receive click events from the Convert button:

```
convertButton.addEventListener("click", this);
```

In the preceding approach, because the *click( )* method is called on the *CurrencyConverter* instance, the *click( )* method can invoke *convert( )* directly, without the need for the thisConverter local variable that was required earlier. However, problems arise when the *CurrencyConverter* instance needs to respond to more than one Button component's click event. To differentiate between our Convert button and, say, a Reset button, we'd have to add cumbersome *if* or *switch* statements to our *click( )* method, as shown in the following code. For this example, assume that the instance properties convertButton and resetButton have been added to the *CurrencyConverter* class.

```
public function click (e:Object):Void {
  if (e.target == convertButton) {
    convert();
  } else if (e.target == resetButton) {
    reset();
  }
}
```

Rather than forcing our *CurrencyConverter* class to handle multiple like-named events from various components, we're better off reverting to our earlier generic listener object system, in which each generic object could happily forward events to the appropriate methods on *CurrencyConverter*. For example:

```
// Convert button handler
var convertClickHandler:Object = new Object();
convertClickHandler.click = function (e:Object):Void {
  thisConverter.convert();
}
convertButton.addEventListener("click", convertClickHandler);
```

```
// Reset button handler
var resetClickHandler:Object = new Object( );
resetClickHandler.click = function (e:Object):Void {
  thisConverter.reset( );
}
resetButton.addEventListener("click", resetClickHandler);
```

To reduce the labor required to create generic listener objects that map component events to object method calls, Mike Chambers from Macromedia created a utility class, *EventProxy*. Using Mike's *EventProxy* class, the preceding code could be reduced to:

```
convertButton.addEventListener("click", new EventProxy(this, "convert"));
resetButton.addEventListener("click", new EventProxy(this, "reset"));
```

The *EventProxy* class, shown in Example 12-2, does a good, clean job of mapping a component event to an object method call. However, the convenience of *EventProxy* comes at a price: reduced type checking. For example, in the following line, even if the current object (this) does not define the method *convert( )*, the compiler does not generate a type error:

```
convertButton.addEventListener("click", new EventProxy(this, "convert"));
```

Hence, wherever you use the *EventProxy* class, remember to carefully check your code for potential datatype errors. For more information on *EventProxy*, see: *http://www.markme.com/mesh/archives/004286.cfm*.

Example 12-2. The EventProxy class

```
class EventProxy {
  private var receiverObj:Object;
  private var funcName:String;

  /**
   * receiverObj  The object on which funcName will be called.
   * funcName     The function name to be called in response to the event.
   */
  function EventProxy(receiverObj:Object, funcName:String) {
    this.receiverObj = receiverObj;
    this.funcName = funcName;
  }

  /**
   * Invoked before the registered event is broadcast by the component.
   * Proxies the event call out to the receiverObj object's method.
   */
  private function handleEvent(eventObj:Object):Void {
    // If no function name has been defined...
    if (funcName == undefined) {
      // ...pass the call to the event name method
      receiverObj[eventObj.type](eventObj);
    } else {
```

Example 12-2. The EventProxy class (continued)

```
      // ...otherwise, pass the call to the specified method name
      receiverObj[funcName](eventObj);
    }
  }
}
```

To avoid the type checking problem presented by the *EventProxy* class, you can use the rewritten version of Mike Chambers' original class, shown in Example 12-3. The rewritten version uses a function reference instead of a string to access the method to which an event is mapped. Hence, to use the rewritten *EventProxy* class, we pass a method instead of a string as the second constructor argument, like this:

```
    // No quotation marks around convert! It's a reference, not a string!
    convertButton.addEventListener("click", new EventProxy(this, convert));
```

Because the *convert( )* method is accessed by reference, the compiler generates a helpful error if the method doesn't exist.

Example 12-3. The Rewritten EventProxy class

```
class EventProxy {
  private var receiverObj:Object;
  private var funcRef:Function;

  /**
   * receiverObj  The object on which funcRef will be called.
   * funcName     A reference to the function to call in response
   *              to the event.
   */
  function EventProxy(receiverObj:Object, funcRef:Function) {
    this.receiverObj = receiverObj;
    this.funcRef = funcRef;
  }

  /**
   * Invoked before the registered event is broadcast by the component.
   * Proxies the event call out to the receiverObj object's method.
   */
  private function handleEvent(eventObj:Object):Void {
    // If no function name has been defined...
    if (funcRef == undefined) {
      // ...pass the call to the event name method
      receiverObj[eventObj.type](eventObj);
    } else {
      // ...otherwise, pass the call to the specified method using
      // Function.call().
      funcRef.call(receiverObj, eventObj);
    }
  }
}
```

As evidenced by the sheer number of event-handling techniques just discussed, the v2 component-event-handling architecture is very flexible. But it also suffers from a general weakness: it allows type errors to go undetected in two specific ways.

First, any component's events can be handled by any object of any class. The compiler does not (indeed cannot) check whether an event-consuming object defines the method(s) required to handle the event(s) for which it has registered. In the following code, if the convertClickHandler object does not define the required *click( )* method, no error occurs at compile time:

```
var convertClickHandler:Object = new Object();
// Oops! Forgot the second "c" in "click," but no compiler error occurs!
convertClickHandler.clik = function (e:Object):Void {
  thisConverter.convert();
}
convertButton.addEventListener("click", convertClickHandler);
```

In other words, in the v2 component architecture there's no well-known manifest of the events a component broadcasts and no contract between the event source and the event consumer to guarantee that the consumer actually defines the events broadcast by the source.

Second, event objects themselves are not represented by individual classes. All event objects are instances of the generic *Object* class. Hence, if you misuse an event object within an event-handling method, the compiler, again, does not generate type errors. For example, in the following code (which, so far, contains no type errors), we disable a clicked button by setting the button's enabled property to false via an event object. We access the button through the event object's target property, which always stores a reference to the event source:

```
convertClickHandler.click = function (e:Object):Void {
  thisConverter.convert();
  e.target.enabled = false;
}
```

But if the programmer specifies the wrong property name for target (perhaps due to a typographical error or a mistaken assumption), the compiler does not generate a type error:

```
convertClickHandler.click = function (e:Object):Void {
  thisConverter.convert();
  e.source.enabled = false;  // Wrong property name! But no compiler error!
  e.trget.enabled = false;   // Oops! A typo, but no compiler error!
}
```

In addition to suppressing potential compiler errors, the lack of typed event objects in the v2 component architecture effectively hides the information those objects contain. If the architecture used formal event classes, such as, say, *Event* or *ButtonEvent*, the programmer could quickly determine what information is available for an event simply by examining the v2 component class library. As things stand, such information can be found only in the documentation (which may be incomplete) or in an event-broadcasting component's raw source code (which is laborious to read).

One way to help make an application's handling of v2 component events more obvious is to define specific classes for event-consumer objects rather than using generic objects. For example, to handle events for the Convert button, an instance of the Button component, in our *CurrencyConverter* application, we might create a custom *ConvertButtonHandler* class as follows:

```
import org.moock.tools.CurrencyConverter;

class org.moock.tools.ConvertButtonHandler {
  private var converter:CurrencyConverter;

  public function ConvertButtonHandler (converter:CurrencyConverter) {
    this.converter = converter;
  }

  public function click (e:Object):Void {
    converter.convert();
  }
}
```

Then, to handle the Button component events for the Convert button, we'd use:

```
convertButton.addEventListener("click", new ConvertButtonHandler(this));
```

By encapsulating the button-event-handling code in a separate class, we make the overall structure of the application more outwardly apparent. We also isolate the button-handling code, making it easier to change and maintain. However, in simple applications, using a separate class can require more work than it's worth. And it doesn't alleviate the other event type checking problems discussed earlier (namely, the compiler's inability to type check event-consumer objects and event objects).

In Java, every aspect of the Swing component event architecture includes type checking. Event consumers in Java must implement the appropriate event listener interface, and event objects belong to custom event classes. In simple Flash applications, Java's additional component event architecture would be cumbersome and hinder rapid, lightweight development. However, for more complex situations, Java's strictness would be welcome. Therefore, we'll see how to implement Java-style events in ActionScript 2.0 classes in Chapter 19. And we'll learn more about generating and handling custom user interface events in Chapter 18.

For reference, Table 12-1 summarizes the various component-event-handling techniques discussed in this chapter.

Table 12-1. Component-event-handling techniques

Technique	Example	Notes

Generic listener object	`var convertClickHandler:Object = new Object();`
	`convertClickHandler.click = function (e:Object):Void {`
	`  thisConverter.convert();`
	`}`
	`convertButton.addEventListener("click",`
	`convertClickHandler);`
		Generally, the preferred means of handling component events

Typed listener object	`convertButton.addEventListener("click", new` `ConvertButtonHandler(this));`	Same as generic listener object, but exposes event-handling code more explicitly

EventProxy class	`convertButton.addEventListener("click", new`
	`EventProxy(this, "convert"));`
	
	or
	
	`convertButton.addEventListener("click", new`
	`EventProxy(this, convert));`
		Functionally the same as generic listener object, but more convenient and easier to read

Listener function	`convertButton.addEventListener("click", function`
	`(e:Object):Void {`
	`  thisConverter.convert();`
	`});`
		The lesser evil of the two function-only event-handling mechanisms

Event handler function	`convertButton.clickHandler = function (e:Object):Void {`
	`  thisConverter.convert();`
	`}`
		The least-desirable means of handling component events; discouraged by Macromedia

Components Complete

We've come to the end of our look at a component-based ActionScript 2.0 application. If you want to see the currency converter in action, you can download all the files discussed in this chapter from *http://moock.org/eas2/examples*. For a lot more information on both using and authoring components, see Flash's online Help (Help → Using Components) and the components section of Macromedia's Flash Developer Center at *http://www.macromedia.com/devnet/mx/flash/components.html*.

In the next chapter, we'll continue our exploration of controlling and creating visual assets by studying *MovieClip* subclasses.

CHAPTER 13

MovieClip Subclasses

From an application development perspective, a *movie clip* is a self-contained multimedia object with a timeline for changing state (you can think of animation in a movie clip as a rapid succession of visual state changes). Movie clips can contain graphics, video, and audio. They are, hence, perfect for creating the audio/visual elements of an application—so much so, that every one of Flash's own components are, in fact, descendents of the *MovieClip* class.

We've already seen lots of examples of how movie clips can be used in OOP. Most of these have involved object composition, in which a movie clip instance is stored in an instance property and used by a class to represent something visual on screen. In the composition model, the class that uses the movie clip does not inherit from the *MovieClip* class. For example, in the *Box* class from Example 4-6, we create a movie clip in which we draw a square shape. We store that movie clip in an instance property of the *Box* class, but the *Box* class does not inherit from the *MovieClip* class (i.e., it does not extend *MovieClip*).

As an alternative to object composition, we can use inheritance to marry one of our own classes to the *MovieClip* class. When taking the inheritance approach, we should feel confident that the custom class in question really "Is-A" kind of *MovieClip*. In other words, only when an application calls for a class whose instances can be used exactly like *MovieClip* instances but also require their own special features should we consider making that class a subclass of *MovieClip*.

Let's put our *Box* class to this test. In our first implementation, the *Box* class used a movie clip to render *Box* instances on screen, but it did not inherit from *MovieClip*. Should it have? To answer that question, we must ask whether a *Box* instance is a specialized variety of *MovieClip*. If *Box* instances need all of the features of *MovieClip* instances, then the *Box* class could sensibly be a *MovieClip* subclass. If not, a *Box* isn't really a specialized variety of *MovieClip*, so it probably shouldn't be a *MovieClip* subclass.

Do *Box* instances need all the features of *MovieClip* instances? Do they need to be dragged with the mouse? No. Do they need to be able to create text fields? No. Should we be able to check the number of bytes loaded by a *Box* instance? Or set the mask over a box? No and no. None of these features are immediate requirements of the *Box* class. Furthermore, a *Box* instance doesn't need a timeline or the timeline control methods of the *MovieClip* class. It doesn't seem as if a *Box* "Is-A" *MovieClip*. In fact, a *Box* more likely "Is-A" *Shape*! If, in a larger application, we made the *Box* class a *MovieClip* subclass, then it wouldn't be able to inherit from a more natural superclass, such as *Shape*. Our original composition-based design was probably the better choice.

The warning here is a refrain from Chapter 6—don't inherit from a class just to borrow some of its functionality; make sure the "Is-A" relationship exists before extending a class. If you're creating a new kind of generic multimedia class that uses most or all of the features of *MovieClip*, by all means subclass *MovieClip*. (The Flash UI Components fall into that category.) But if you're just trying to draw something to the screen, make sure you prudently consider composition before opting for an inheritance implementation.

Now that we've considered when to subclass *MovieClip*, let's see how to subclass *MovieClip*.

The Duality of MovieClip Subclasses

Every *MovieClip* subclass has two parts: a movie clip symbol and a corresponding ActionScript 2.0 class. Like any other subclass, a *MovieClip* subclass uses the extends keyword to inherit from *MovieClip*:

```
class SomeClass extends MovieClip {
}
```

However, a *MovieClip* subclass must also be represented physically in a Flash document Library by a movie clip symbol. The movie clip symbol in the Library specifies the class that represents it, thus coupling the symbol and *MovieClip* subclass together. In the vast majority of cases, this symbol-to-class relationship is a one-to-one relationship. That is, a single movie clip symbol is associated with a single *MovieClip* subclass. In fact, it's not even possible to associate a single symbol with more than one class. However, multiple movie clip symbols can legally each associate itself with the same *MovieClip* subclass. This allows different symbols, each with its own artwork, to adopt the behavior defined by a single class. However, in most cases, associating multiple movie clip symbols with a single *MovieClip* subclass is bound to become confusing. Use this "many symbols to one class" approach with caution.

To create instances of a *MovieClip* subclass, we do not use the *new* operator as we would with a typical class. Instead, instances of the movie clip subclass's *symbol* (not the subclass itself) are created either manually in the authoring tool or programmatically via *attachMovie( )* or *duplicateMovieClip( )*. It is, hence, not possible to create a functioning *MovieClip* subclass without a corresponding movie clip symbol in the Library of a *.fla* file.

Note that the Flash community uses the term "movie clip" to refer to both movie clip instances on stage and movie clip symbols in the Library. The difference is usually clear from context. For example, if I say, "All movie clips must be stored as symbols in the Library." you understand that I mean "all movie clip *symbols* must be stored in the Library." But in this chapter, loose terminology can get us in trouble. So I'll differentiate explicitly between "movie clip instances on stage" and "movie clip symbols in the Library" whenever necessary.

Let's see how this all works in practice by creating a real *MovieClip* subclass. The example files discussed in this chapter are available at *http://moock.org/eas2/examples*.

Avatar: A MovieClip Subclass Example

Our example *MovieClip* subclass, named *Avatar*, is an on-screen representation of a user in a chat room or a game.

For the purposes of this example, we assume that the relationship between our *Avatar* class and the *MovieClip* class is a natural "Is-A" inheritance relationship. In other words, the *Avatar* class doesn't need to inherit from some other class, and users of our *Avatar* class need to treat each *Avatar* instance like a *MovieClip* instance (drag it, manage its depth, mask it, etc.). These assumptions are, in truth, a bit farfetched. The *Avatar* class could quite appropriately be implemented using composition, as we'll show later. For the sake of learning, however, we'll show how to implement the class with inheritance first. (The present difficulty is that any class simple enough to use as an example is, by its very simplicity, probably a better candidate for composition than inheritance.)

The AvatarSymbol Movie Clip

As we learned earlier, every *MovieClip* subclass has a corresponding movie clip symbol. Our *Avatar* class's movie clip symbol is called *AvatarSymbol*. It contains a graphical depiction of the user in three different states: Idle, Sad, and Happy. The three states correspond to three labeled frames in *AvatarSymbol*'s timeline. To change the state of the avatar, we position *AvatarSymbol*'s playhead at the appropriate frame in its timeline. Figure 13-1 shows *AvatarSymbol*'s timeline and the contents of its first frame, the Idle state.

Here are the steps we follow to create the *AvatarSymbol* movie clip, which we'll later associate with the *Avatar* class (see "Linking AvatarSymbol to the Avatar Class"):

1. Create a new Flash document named *AvatarDemo.fla*.
2. Select Insert → New Symbol.

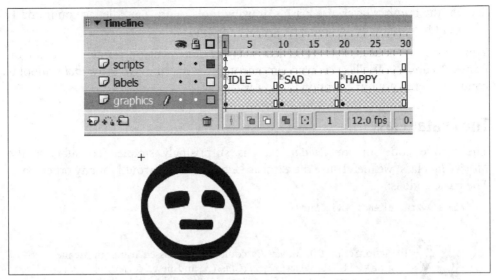

Figure 13-1. The AvatarSymbol timeline

3. For the symbol Name, enter **AvatarSymbol**. The name is arbitrary, but by convention, you should name the symbol *Class*Symbol where *Class* is the name of the class with which you expect to associate the symbol.

4. For the symbol's Behavior type, select Movie Clip.

5. Click OK. Flash automatically enters Edit mode for the *AvatarSymbol* symbol.

Here are the steps we follow to build *AvatarSymbol*'s timeline and contents:

1. Double-click *Layer 1* and rename it to *graphics*.

2. Select frame 30 of the *graphics* layer.

3. Choose Insert → Timeline → Frame (F5).

4. Using Insert → Timeline → Layer, create two new layers, and name them *labels* and *scripts*.

5. With frame 1 of the *scripts* layer selected, enter the following code into the Actions panel (F9):

   ```
   stop( );
   ```

6. Using Insert → Timeline → Blank Keyframe (F7), create blank keyframes on the *labels* and *graphics* layers at keyframes 10 and 20.

7. With frame 1 of the *labels* layer selected, in the Properties panel, under Frame, change <Frame Label> to **IDLE**.

8. With frame 10 of the *labels* layer selected, in the Properties panel, under Frame, change <Frame Label> to **SAD**.

9. With frame 20 of the *labels* layer selected, in the Properties panel, under Frame, change <Frame Label> to **HAPPY**.

10. On the *graphics* layer, use Flash's drawing tools to draw an idle face on frame 1, a sad face on frame 10, and a happy face on frame 20.

You may have noticed that we added a *stop( )* statement on frame 1 but not on frames 10 and 20. We'll see why in a moment. Now that the *AvatarSymbol* symbol is complete, let's turn our attention to the *Avatar* class.

The Avatar Class

The source code for the *Avatar* class is surprisingly simple. To subclass the *MovieClip* class, we merely use the extends keyword, as we would for any other class. The basic code is:

```
class Avatar extends MovieClip {
}
```

 In ActionScript 1.0, *MovieClip* could be subclassed using an arcane nest of #initclip, *Object.registerClass( )*, and new *MovieClip( )* calls. In ActionScript 2.0, the Flash authoring tool handles all that dirty work. Syntactically, *MovieClip* is extended like any other class, with the extends keyword.

The *Avatar* class defines two instance methods:

init( )
> Initializes each *Avatar* instance

setState( )
> Sets the avatar's state using one of three constants (class properties)—IDLE, SAD, and HAPPY.

Example 13-1 shows the *Avatar* class in its entirety.

Example 13-1. Avatar, a MovieClip subclass

```
class Avatar extends MovieClip {
  public static var HAPPY:Number = 0;
  public static var SAD:Number = 1;
  public static var IDLE:Number = 2;

  public function init ():Void {
    setState(Avatar.HAPPY);
  }

  public function setState(newState:Number):Void {
    switch (newState) {
      case Avatar.HAPPY:
        this.gotoAndStop("HAPPY");
        break;
      case Avatar.SAD:
        this.gotoAndStop("SAD");
        break;
```

Example 13-1. Avatar, a MovieClip subclass (continued)

```
      case Avatar.IDLE:
        this.gotoAndStop("IDLE");
        break;
    }
  }
}
```

Notice that the class has no constructor function. Instances of *MovieClip* subclasses are not created using the standard constructor call syntax (using the *new* operator), so there's no need to provide a constructor function. Our *init( )* method fulfills the traditional role of the constructor and should be called on each *Avatar* instance directly after it's created. (You can use constructor functions with *MovieClip* subclasses but, as we'll learn shortly, doing so can be cumbersome and error prone.)

The *Avatar.init( )* method calls *setState( )* to set each *Avatar* instance's initial state to Avatar.HAPPY. In the *setState( )* method, we see the real marriage between the *Avatar* class and the *AvatarSymbol* movie clip; *setState( )* changes the visual state of an *Avatar* instance by positioning the playhead of the associated movie clip instance. For example, in the expression this.gotoAndStop("HAPPY"), the current object (this) is the instance of the *AvatarSymbol* movie clip. Thus, *setState( )* sends the movie clip instance's playhead to the frame labeled *HAPPY*.

> Within *MovieClip* subclass .as files, you must use this explicitly with *MovieClip* methods whose names collide with corresponding global functions. For example, you must use *this.gotoAndStop( )* not *gotoAndStop( )*. The affected *MovieClip* methods are: *duplicateMovieClip( )*, *getURL( )*, *gotoAndPlay( )*, *gotoAndStop( )*, *loadMovie( )*, *loadVariables( )*, *nextFrame( )*, *play( )*, *prevFrame( )*, *removeMovieClip( )*, *startDrag( )*, *stop( )*, *stopDrag( )*, and *unloadMovie( )*.
>
> To be safe, you should always use this when invoking any *MovieClip* method on the current object.

Observant (or perhaps, confused) readers may notice that there is no instance property that stores the *Avatar* instance's state. How then is the state stored? In fact, it isn't. Changes to the *Avatar* instance's state are represented on screen via the associated clip's timeline, but that state is never retrieved, so it is not stored in an instance property. In one sense, the state is "stored" implicitly by the clip's playhead position. At any given time, the frame displayed in the associated clip corresponds with the *Avatar* instance's state. Although we could, in theory, use the MovieClip._currentframe property to check the playhead's position, thus retrieving the state, we should not do so in practice. If the state of an *Avatar* instance needs to be retrieved, we should define a state instance property to store the instance's current state.

You may have noticed that the *AvatarSymbol* movie clip includes a *stop( )* command on frame 1 but not on frames 10 and 20. That initial *stop( )* command ensures that the playhead stops at frame 1 (the Idle state) when the clip first loads. What about stopping at frame 10 or 20 when the state of the clip changes to the Happy or Sad state? Here is another case in which the implementation for the movie clip symbol depends in part on the code you expect to write in the associated class. Because *setState( )* invokes *MovieClip.gotoAndStop( )*, we don't need a separate *stop( )* command at frames 10 and 20. If, however, *setState( )* invoked *gotoAndPlay( )* instead of *gotoAndStop( )*, we'd need separate *stop( )* commands in frames 10 and 20 of our movie clip (or perhaps shortly thereafter if the state change included an animation).

With practice, you'll learn how to design and coordinate a *MovieClip* subclass and its associated movie clip symbol. The degree and type of integration required depends on the responsibilities you assign to each element. As much as possible, you should keep logic and data in the class and use the symbol for display only.

Linking AvatarSymbol to the Avatar Class

To associate the *AvatarSymbol* movie clip with the *Avatar* class, we must set the *AvatarSymbol*'s so-called "AS 2.0 Class" in the Flash authoring tool, as follows:

1. Select the *AvatarSymbol* movie clip in *AvatarDemo.fla*'s Library.
2. Select the pop-up Options menu in the top-right corner of the Library panel, and choose the Linkage option.
3. In the Linkage Properties dialog box, for Linkage, select Export for ActionScript.
4. In the Linkage Properties dialog box, for Identifier, enter **AvatarSymbol**.
5. In the Linkage Properties dialog box, for AS 2.0 Class, enter **Avatar**.
6. Click OK.

If our *Avatar* class were part of a package—say *org.moock.chat*—then in Step 5, we would enter the fully qualified class name, *org.moock.chat.Avatar*, instead of the unqualified class name, *Avatar*. Notice that in the Linkage Properties dialog box, we chose to export the *AvatarSymbol* movie clip in frame 1. If we had wanted to preload the *AvatarSymbol* movie clip and the *Avatar* class, we'd have followed the instructions we used to preload a component in Chapter 12.

Now that we've created a movie clip symbol and linked it to a *MovieClip* subclass, we can create instances of the symbol that combine its own content with the class's behavior. Let's see how.

Creating Avatar Instances

We create an instance of a *MovieClip* subclass by creating an instance of the associated library symbol using *attachMovie( )* (exactly as we create a normal *MovieClip* instance). Here's the code:

```
var av:Avatar = Avatar(someMovieClip.attachMovie("AvatarSymbol",
                                                  "avatar", 0));
```

The instance of the library symbol (*AvatarSymbol*) is physically added to the Stage and also reflected back to ActionScript in the form of the object returned by *attachMovie( )*. The returned object is an instance of the subclass (*Avatar*), while the on-stage movie clip is an instance of the symbol (*AvatarSymbol*).

Flash's use of the term "instance" to describe the relationship that an on-stage movie clip has to its library symbol is unfortunate in an OOP discussion. An on-stage movie clip "instance" is better described as a "physical incarnation" of its library symbol. That physical incarnation is not an "instance" of the library symbol in the OOP sense. That is, the library symbol is not a class; it is a graphical template. However, a physical incarnation of a movie clip symbol is always represented in ActionScript by a corresponding instance of a class, in the traditional OOP sense. Specifically, the ActionScript representation of the physical incarnation of a movie clip is an instance either of the *MovieClip* class or of a *MovieClip* subclass such as *Avatar*. (Say that ten times fast!)

Bearing in mind the subtle but important distinction between a *MovieClip* instance and a movie clip symbol's physical incarnation on stage, let's revisit the preceding instance-creation code:

```
var av:Avatar = Avatar(someMovieClip.attachMovie("AvatarSymbol",
                                                  "avatar", 0));
```

When that code runs, a physical incarnation of the *AvatarSymbol* symbol is attached (added) to the Stage, inside the existing physical movie clip referenced by the variable someMovieClip. The physical incarnation of *AvatarSymbol* is named "avatar" and is placed on depth 1 of someMovieClip. The *attachMovie( )* method then returns an ActionScript object that we will use to control the physical incarnation we just created. That ActionScript object is an instance of our *Avatar* class. We store it in a variable named av. So technically there are two "instances" here: the on-stage instance of the *AvatarSymbol* movie clip symbol and the ActionScript object (instance) whose class is *Avatar*. However, in a more casual discussion (and elsewhere in this book), you'll often find these two instances treated as one and the same.

Dual-instance issues aside, notice that in our instance-creation code we cast the return value of *attachMovie( )* to the *Avatar* type. The cast is necessary because *attachMovie( )*'s return type is *MovieClip*, but the object returned in this case is actually an *Avatar* instance. For example, this code generates a type mismatch error:

```
var av:Avatar = someMovieClip.attachMovie("AvatarSymbol",
                                          "avatar", 0);
```

But this code does not cause an error because we're telling the compiler that the return value of *attachMovie( )* will, in this case, be an *Avatar* instance:

```
var av:Avatar = Avatar(someMovieClip.attachMovie("AvatarSymbol",
                                                 "avatar", 0));
```

Note that the preceding cast is an (unsafe) downcast. If we were being more cautious, we'd use:

```
var av:Avatar;
var temp_mc:MovieClip = someMovieClip.attachMovie("AvatarSymbol",
                                                  "avatar", 0);
// Verify that the cast will succeed at runtime before attempting it.
if (temp_mc instanceof Avatar) {
  av = Avatar(temp_mc);
} else {
  trace("Warning: could not cast temp_mc to type Avatar.")
}
```

For full information on casting, see Chapter 3.

The instance-creation code discussed in this section can be used in the *AvatarDemo.fla*, in any class loaded by *AvatarDemo.fla*, or, more generally, in any class that has access to both the *Avatar* class and the *AvatarSymbol* movie clip symbol. When a *MovieClip* subclass is reused across many projects, consider compiling it as a component, which includes both the class and the symbol in a single file. For details on creating components, see Help → Using Components → Creating Components in Flash's online Help.

Initializing Avatar Instances

To initialize our new *Avatar* instance, we invoke *init( )* on it, as follows:

```
av.init();
```

Creating *Avatar* instances with the *attachMovie( )* syntax can be ungainly because we have to specify the *AvatarSymbol* and the name of that symbol's physical incarnation ("avatar") in the call. Furthermore, requiring developers to call *init( )* on each *Avatar* is sure to lead to errors. To smooth the instance-creation process, we'll create a class method, *createAvatar( )*. The *createAvatar( )* method creates and initializes a new *Avatar* instance, wrapping the *attachMovie( )* and *init( )* calls into a single call for the end developer. Here's the code:

```
public static function createAvatar (name:String, target:MovieClip,
                                     depth:Number):Avatar {
  var av:Avatar = Avatar(target.attachMovie("AvatarSymbol", name, depth));
  av.init();
  return av;
}
```

The *createAvatar( )* method conveniently supplies the name of the symbol associated with the *Avatar* class, so users of the class don't need to know or remember that it's *AvatarSymbol*. The method also invokes *init( )* on the new instance after it's created, so we can be sure *init( )* will always be invoked on new *Avatar* instances. Here's how we'd use the *createAvatar( )* method:

```
var av:Avatar = Avatar.createAvatar("avatar", someMovieClip, 0);
```

The *createAvatar( )* method also gives us the flexibility to define parameters for use during instance initialization, exactly like a constructor function. For example, we could easily add parameters to *createAvatar( )* that set the new instance's initial position:

```
public static function createAvatar (name:String, target:MovieClip,
                                     depth:Number, x:Number,
                                     y:Number):Avatar {
  var av:Avatar = Avatar(target.attachMovie("AvatarSymbol", name, depth));
  av.init(x, y);
  return av;
}

public function init (x:Number, y:Number):Void {
  setState(Avatar.HAPPY);
  this._x = x;
  this._y = y;
}
```

Our avatar-creation code would now look like this:

```
var av:Avatar = Avatar.createAvatar("avatar", someMovieClip, 0, 100, 100);
```

which is much tidier and easier to understand than:

```
var av:Avatar = someMovieClip.attachMovie("AvatarSymbol", "avatar", 0);
av.init(100, 100);
```

For another example of a *MovieClip* subclass that uses an instance-creation method, see the *UIObject.createClassObject( )* method and the *Menu.createMenu( )* method in Flash's online Help, under Help → Using Components → Components Dictionary → UIObject and Help → Using Components → Components Dictionary → Menu (Flash Professional Only).

The *MovieClip.attachMovie( )* method supports a parameter, initObj, that can transfer properties to a new movie clip at creation time. For code clarity, I recommend against requiring initObj as part of a class design. Instead, I prefer to use a method such as *createAvatar( )* with a helper method, *init( )*, to handle instance initialization (as shown in the preceding example).

Here's the code for the completed *Avatar* class, showing the new *createAvatar( )* method and updated *init( )* method in context with the rest of the class:

```
class Avatar extends MovieClip {
  public static var HAPPY:Number = 0;
  public static var SAD:Number = 1;
  public static var IDLE:Number = 2;

  public static function createAvatar (name:String, target:MovieClip,
                                       depth:Number, x:Number,
                                       y:Number):Avatar {
    var av:Avatar = Avatar(target.attachMovie("AvatarSymbol", name, depth));
    av.init(x, y);
    return av;
  }
```

```
public function init (x:Number, y:Number):Void {
  setState(Avatar.HAPPY);
  this._x = x;
  this._y = y;
}

public function setState(newState:Number):Void {
  switch (newState) {
    case Avatar.HAPPY:
      this.gotoAndStop("HAPPY");
      break;
    case Avatar.SAD:
      this.gotoAndStop("SAD");
      break;
    case Avatar.IDLE:
      this.gotoAndStop("IDLE");
      break;
  }
 }
}
```

Avatar: The Composition Version

Now that we've seen how to implement *Avatar* as a *MovieClip* subclass, let's consider an alternative using object composition. This time, the *Avatar* class does not inherit from *MovieClip*. Instead, it creates an instance of *AvatarSymbol* and stores it in an instance property, av_mc. (Well, technically, the ActionScript object representation of that instance is stored in av_mc, but here is an example in which making a distinction between the symbol instance and the ActionScript object would make the discussion awkward, albeit more technically accurate. My editor tells me to "Avoid precision where it merely sacrifices clarity." So I will here and elsewhere in this book.)

Example 13-2 shows a revised version of the *Avatar* class. This version defines a constructor because, now that *Avatar* is no longer a subclass of *MovieClip*, instances are instantiated with *new*. The *AvatarSymbol* clip instance is created in the *Avatar* constructor, which replaces the *createAvatar( )* method. Because initialization is usually performed in a class's constructor function, we put some of the code from *init( )* in the constructor and move the rest to a new method, *setPosition( )*.

Example 13-2. The composition-based Avatar class

```
class Avatar {
  public static var HAPPY:Number = 0;
  public static var SAD:Number = 1;
  public static var IDLE:Number = 2;

  private var av_mc:MovieClip;

  public function Avatar (name:String, target:MovieClip,
                         depth:Number, x:Number, y:Number) {
```

Example 13-2. The composition-based Avatar class (continued)

```
    av_mc = target.attachMovie("AvatarSymbol", name, depth);
    setState(Avatar.HAPPY);
    setPosition(x, y);
  }

  public function setState(newState:Number):Void {
    switch (newState) {
      case Avatar.HAPPY:
        av_mc.gotoAndStop("HAPPY");
        break;
      case Avatar.SAD:
        av_mc.gotoAndStop("SAD");
        break;
      case Avatar.IDLE:
        av_mc.gotoAndStop("IDLE");
        break;
    }
  }

  public function setPosition (x:Number, y:Number):Void {
    av_mc._x = x;
    av_mc._y = y;
  }
}
```

In many ways, the composition version of the *Avatar* class is cleaner and more flexible than its *MovieClip* subclass counterpart—cleaner because it uses fewer methods and a traditional constructor, more flexible because it can easily change the av_mc to some other movie clip symbol if required. However, the *MovieClip* subclass version would still be preferable in the following situations:

- When *Avatar* instances need to belong to the *MovieClip* datatype (e.g., for the sake of polymorphism)
- When the *Avatar* class and the *AvatarSymbol* movie clip symbol need to be packaged together as a component for distribution
- When *Avatar* instances need most of the methods of the *MovieClip* class (in which case the "Is-A" relationship is legitimate)

Issues with Nested Assets

Movie clip symbols can contain other nested movie clips, text fields, or components (i.e., elements attached to the clip symbol during authoring or at runtime). To access and use these nested assets, we must sidestep two issues.

Properties and Methods of Nested Assets Initially Undefined

The Flash Player takes an "outside-in" approach to component and movie clip initialization. When initializing a movie clip hierarchy in a movie, the Flash Player starts with the outermost clip in the hierarchy, defines its custom properties and methods, then moves on to its child clips, defines their custom properties and methods, and so on. As a result, immediately after a clip is constructed, it can see its parent's custom methods and properties, but it cannot see its children's custom methods and properties.

For example, consider a movie clip symbol, *ChatRoomSymbol*, that represents a chat room. It contains the following component instances:

outgoing

> A TextInput component for outgoing messages

incoming

> A TextArea component for incoming messages

userList

> A List component for the list of users in the room

Suppose we use a *ChatRoomSymbol* instance via composition in a class, *ChatRoom*, as follows:

```
class ChatRoom {
  private static var chatroomID:Number = 0;
  private var chat_mc:MovieClip;

  public function ChatRoom (target:MovieClip, depth:Number) {
    // Create clip instance.
    chat_mc = target.attachMovie("ChatRoomSymbol",
                                 "chatroom" + ChatRoom.chatroomID++,
                                 depth);
    chat_mc.userList.dataProvider = [{label:"Colin", data:"User1"},
            {label:"Derek", data:"User2"},
            {label:"James", data:"User3"}];
  }
}
```

The *ChatRoom* constructor creates an instance of the *ChatRoomSymbol* movie clip symbol and stores it in the property chat_mc. (By now, you should know that it actually stores the ActionScript object representation of the *ChatRoomSymbol* instance, so I'll no longer make the distinction.) The constructor then attempts to populate the nested userList List component by assigning a value to its dataProvider property:

```
chat_mc.userList.dataProvider = [{label:"Colin", data:"User1"},
        {label:"Derek", data:"User2"},
        {label:"James", data:"User3"}];
```

But the assignment has no effect because the userList component's properties and methods are not yet functional! To overcome this problem, we must use *setInterval()* to poll the userList component until its custom properties and methods are defined.

Once we detect the existence of a single userList method, we can be sure that all of its properties and methods are available. In fact, we can also be sure that every other nested component is, likewise, ready for use. By the time a single frame passes, the custom properties and methods of all nested assets will be initialized.

The following new code for the *ChatRoom* class shows how to poll for the existence of a userList List component instance's method. The new code uses an *init( )* method to initialize nested components. The *init( )* method is called by the function passed to *setInterval( )* as soon as the *userList.addItem( )* method is defined. Notice that the function passed to *setInterval( )* is, itself, passed a reference to the current object, this. This technique allows the function passed to *setInterval( )* to invoke the *init( )* method on the current object. Without the reference to this, the nested function called by *setInterval( )* would have no access to the current object and could not invoke *init( )*.

```
class ChatRoom {
  private static var chatroomID:Number = 0;
  private var chat_mc:MovieClip;

  public function ChatRoom (target:MovieClip, depth:Number) {
    // Create clip instance.
    chat_mc = target.attachMovie("ChatRoomSymbol",
                                 "chatroom" + ChatRoom.chatroomID++,
                                 depth);
    // Wait until nested clips are initialized before
    // performing any operations on them.
    var initInt = setInterval(function (cr:ChatRoom):Void {
      if (cr.chat_mc.userList.addItem != undefined) {
        cr.init();
        clearInterval(initInt);
      }
    }, 10, this);
  }

  public function init ():Void {
    // Hardcode some dummy data for this example.
    setUserList([{label:"Colin", data:"User1"},
                 {label:"Derek", data:"User2"},
                 {label:"James", data:"User3"}]);
  }

  public function setUserList (list:Array):Void {
    chat_mc.userList.dataProvider = list;
  }
}
```

When you want to access the custom properties and methods of an asset nested in a movie clip immediately after creating that clip, you should use the preceding *setInterval( )* technique. If, however, you want to use a *native* property or method of the *MovieClip* class (e.g., *gotoAndPlay( )*), then you do not have to use *setInterval( )*. Native properties and methods are immediately available on all nested assets.

Nested Assets Not Automatically Recognized by Compiler

Assets nested in a movie clip symbol are not automatically available to a corresponding *MovieClip* subclass as instance properties. That is, a *MovieClip* subclass cannot refer to assets nested inside its associated movie clip symbol unless the subclass explicitly declares those assets as instance properties.

For example, consider a *LoginSymbol* movie clip symbol that contains two text fields, userName and password. The *LoginSymbol*'s corresponding *MovieClip* subclass is *Login*. The *Login* class wants to set the default contents of the userName and password text fields. If we use the following *Login* class code:

```
class Login extends MovieClip {
  public function Login () {
    userName.text = "Enter your name.";
    password.text = "Enter your password.";
  }
}
```

the compiler generates the following errors:

```
There is no property with the name 'userName'.
        userName.text = "Enter your name.";
There is no property with the name 'password'.
        password.text = "Enter your password.";
```

We know that the *LoginSymbol* movie clip symbol contains the required text fields, but the compiler doesn't have any way of knowing. The compiler bases its type checking on the *Login* class definition, not the contents of the *LoginSymbol* movie clip symbol. To work around this problem, we simply declare the userName and password text fields as instance properties, like this:

```
class Login extends MovieClip {
  public var userName:TextField;  // Declare userName
  public var password:TextField;  // Declare password

  public function Login () {
    userName.text = "Enter your name.";
    password.text = "Enter your password.";
  }
}
```

A Note on MovieClip Sub-subclasses

Nothing officially prevents a *MovieClip* subclass from being subclassed. For example, hearkening back to the *Avatar* class, if we wanted to create an *Avatar* whose mood changed randomly, we could create a *RandomAvatar* class that inherits from *Avatar*. However, the *RandomAvatar* class would need to be associated with its own library movie clip symbol because, as we learned earlier, a movie clip symbol can specify only a single AS 2.0 Class association. Hence, while the *RandomAvatar* class would inherit the behavior of the *Avatar* class, it would not inherit *Avatar*'s physical movie clip symbol. Hence, to create the *RandomAvatar* class, we'd have to create a completely separate symbol, *RandomAvatarSymbol*, that is a duplicate of *AvatarSymbol*.

Duplicating a symbol merely for the sake of subclassing is neither practical nor wise in most cases. The better approach is (yet again) to use composition. When a class uses a movie clip symbol via composition, the class can easily be subclassed, allowing reuse both of its code and of the movie clip symbol associated via composition. Example 13-3 shows how we could create the *RandomAvatar* class as a subclass of the *Avatar* class shown earlier in Example 13-2. Neither *Avatar* nor *RandomAvatar* are *MovieClip* subclasses. We use composition to associate them with a movie clip symbol.

Example 13-3. RandomAvatar, an Avatar subclass

```
class RandomAvatar extends Avatar {
  private var randomInt:Number;

  public function RandomAvatar (name:String, target:MovieClip,
                                depth:Number, x:Number, y:Number) {
    super(name, target, depth, x, y);
    startRandom();
  }

  public function startRandom ():Void {
    randomInt = setInterval (function (av:RandomAvatar):Void {
      var r:Number = Math.floor(Math.random() * 3);
      av.setState(r);
    }, 500, this);
  }

  public function stopRandom ():Void {
    clearInterval(randomInt);
  }
}
```

For comparison, the example files for the inheritance and composition versions of the *RandomAvatar* class are posted at *http://moock.org/eas2/examples*.

Curiouser and Curiouser

MovieClip subclasses are an enigmatic aspect of object-oriented Flash development. As we've seen, given the option, it's often better to use composition to associate a class with a movie clip symbol rather than to extend *MovieClip*. In the next chapter, however, we'll be forced to use *MovieClip* subclasses in an equally (if not more) enigmatic situation: distributing class libraries.

Distributing Class Libraries

This chapter discusses various techniques for sharing a group of classes (i.e., a *class library*) among multiple projects and possibly multiple developers. Before we start, a warning: Flash MX 2004's class distribution features are not particularly refined; by far the easiest way to share classes is to simply distribute the source code. We'll cover this easiest case first, before we learn how to share classes without distributing source code, as you may want to do when selling a professional class library.

The term *class library* is a generic programming term that simply means a group of classes. Don't confuse it with a *.fla* file's Library, the Flash Library panel, shared libraries (used to share Library assets at authoring time), or runtime shared libraries (used to share Library assets at runtime). Each of those terms is unique to the Flash environment and not part of the current discussion.

Nor do class libraries have anything to do with the packages discussed in Chapter 9, despite the fact that both terms happen to relate to the grouping of classes. The term "class library" is just programmer jargon for an arbitrary group of classes distributed to a team or to the world at large. A package, on the other hand, is a formal, syntactic namespace in which to define a class (in order to prevent naming conflicts with other classes).

In ActionScript a class library can be distributed to other developers simply as a bunch of source *.as* files, in a *.swf* file, or in a *.swc* file. We'll cover all three approaches in this chapter.

Sharing Class Source Files

Probably the most common reason for sharing classes is to reuse them across multiple projects. For example, suppose you work in a small web shop called Spider Services, whose web site is *http://www.spiderservices.com* (while I was writing this book, a company named Spider Solutions LTD registered that domain, but let's pretend Spider Services is a fictitious shop). You've made a *TextAnimation* class to handle various text effects. You want to use the *TextAnimation* class on two sites you're working on, Barky's Pet Supplies and Mega Bridal Depot. Rather than place a copy of the class file (that is, the *.as* file) in each project folder, you should store the class file centrally and merely refer to it from each project. For example, on Windows, you could store the *TextAnimation.as* class file in the following location:

   c:\data\actionscript\com\spiderservices\effects\TextAnimation.as

To make the *TextAnimation* class accessible to both projects, you'd add the directory *c:\data\actionscript* to Flash MX 2004's global classpath (under Edit → Preferences → ActionScript → Language → ActionScript 2.0 Settings).

If there were several members on your team, you might think it would be handy to store your class on a central server so everyone would be able to use it. For example, your team might want to store all shared classes on a server called *codecentral*, in a directory matching the company's domain name (*\com\spiderservices*):

   \\codecentral\actionscript\com\spiderservices\effects\TextAnimation.as

That practice is highly perilous and is not recommended.

 If you store your classes on a central server and allow developers to modify them directly, the developers are liable to overwrite one another's changes. Furthermore, if the clock of the server and the clock of a programmer's personal computer are not in perfect sync, then the latest version of the class might not be included in the movie at compile time. To avoid these problems, you should always use version control software to manage your class files when working on a team. One popular (and free!) option is CVS (see *http://www.cvshome.org*).

On large projects, you might also want to automate the *.swf* export process using a build tool such as Apache Ant (*http://ant.apache.org*). To do so, you'd have to execute a command-line JSFL script to tell Flash to create the *.swf* for each *.fla* file in your project(s). Complete coverage of command-line compilation is outside the scope of this book (and is still in its infancy), but here's a quick sample that gives the general flavor of it on Windows:

```
// Code in exportPetSupplies.jsfl:
// ================================
// Open the .fla file.
var doc = fl.openDocument("file:///c|/data/projects/pet/petsupplies.fla");
// Export the .swf file.
doc.exportSWF("file:///c|/data/projects/pet/petsupplies.swf", true);
// Quit the Flash MX 2004 authoring tool (optional).
fl.quit(false);

// Command issued on command line from /pet/ directory:
// =====================================================
"c:\program files\macromedia\flash mx 2004\flash.exe" exportPetSupplies.jsfl
```

For this command to work, Flash MX 2004 must not be running. After the command is issued, the compiled *petsupplies.swf* movie appears in the directory *c:\data\ projects\pet*.

Loading Classes at Runtime

When working with multiple *.swf* files that make use of the same class, compiling the class into every *.swf* is a waste of space. When file size is a concern, you can prevent such redundancies by externalizing the class library into a separate *.swf* file and loading it at runtime. Once the library has loaded the first time, it is cached on the end user's machine and can be reused by other *.swf* files without being downloaded again.

 A class library loaded at runtime is known as a *dynamic class library*.

To create a dynamic class library, we compile the desired classes into a *.swf* file. We then use *loadMovie( )* to load that *.swf* into any movie that needs the classes. However, in order for this technique to work, we must be sure that the classes in the class library are excluded from the movies that load them. To prevent runtime-loaded classes from being compiled into the movies that load them, we use an *exclusion XML file*. The exclusion XML file lets a *.fla* file access classes locally for the sake of compile-time type checking but prevents those classes from being included in the exported *.swf* file, thus allowing them to be loaded at runtime.

To see how to create a runtime-loaded class library, we'll return to our earlier Spider Services *TextAnimation* class example.

Here are the general tasks we have to complete:

1. Create the classes in the class library (in our case, just the *TextAnimation* class).
2. Create the *.swf* file that will contain the classes in the class library.
3. Create the movie that loads the class library *.swf* file.
4. Create the exclusion XML file.

Now let's look at each task individually. The source files discussed in the next few sections can be downloaded from *http://moock.org/eas2/examples*.

Create the classes in the class library

The first step in creating a class library is to create the classes that it will contain. Our sole class is called *TextAnimation*, stored in the file *c:\data\actionscript\com\spiderservices\effects\TextAnimation.as*. Here's the source for the *TextAnimation* class. For this example, our focus is class library building, so we won't show the actual text animation code in the class; we'll just provide a *trace( )* statement in the class constructor to verify that the class is working:

```
class com.spiderservices.effects.TextAnimation {
  public function TextAnimation () {
    trace("Imagine a text effect with great majesty.");
  }
}
```

Now that our class library is complete, we can create the *.swf* file that will contain it.

Create the class library .swf file

To make the class library *.swf* file, follow these steps:

1. Create the following working directory for the class library source files: *c:\data\ spiderservices\spidercore*. In this case, we use the name of the company, *spider-services*, as a general folder name for all projects and *spidercore* as the name of the folder that will contain our class library *.swf* file (the class library contains the "core" classes for most Spider Services projects, so we call it *spidercore*).

2. Add the directory *c:\data\actionscript* to Flash MX 2004's global classpath using Edit → Preferences → ActionScript → Language → ActionScript 2.0 Settings. With the *c:\data\actionscript* directory in the global classpath, we'll be able to access our *TextAnimation* class when we export our class library *.swf* file.

3. Create a new *.fla* file named *spidercore_runtime.fla* in the following location: *c:\data\ spiderservices\spidercore\spidercore_runtime.fla*. We'll export the class library *.swf* file from *spidercore_runtime.fla*. We use the word "runtime" in the document's name to indicate that our class library will be loaded and used at runtime.

4. On frame 1 of *spidercore_runtime.fla*, add the following code:

   ```
   com.spiderservices.effects.TextAnimation;
   ```

   By referring to the *TextAnimation* class in our *.fla* file, we force the class to be included in our class library *.swf* file. Each class in the class library should be listed on frame 1. The compiler finds and includes all dependent classes automatically (for example, if the *TextAnimation* class uses a *Tween* class, then the *Tween* class will be included in the *spidercore_runtime.swf* file automatically). This conveniently relieves us from finding and individually including all classes upon which *TextAnimation* is dependent.

5. Use Insert → Timeline → Keyframe to add a new keyframe at frame 2 of the main timeline of *spidercore_runtime.fla*.

6. On frame 2 of *spidercore_runtime.fla*, add the following code:

   ```
   // Notify the parent movie clip that the class library
   // has finished loading.
   _parent.spidercoreLoaded();
   stop();
   ```

7. Select File → Export → Export Movie to create *spidercore_runtime.swf* in the same directory as *spidercore_runtime.fla*. Be sure to specify ActionScript 2.0 in the publish settings when you export the *.swf* file.

8. Save the *spidercore_runtime.fla* file.

Now that our class library .*swf* file is ready, we can use it in any movie. Let's do that next.

Create the movie that loads the class library .swf file

For this example, the movie that loads *spidercore_runtime.swf* is the homepage of Barky's Pet Supplies. To create the homepage movie, follow these steps:

1. Create the following working directory for the Barky's Pet Supplies project: *c:\ data\spiderservices\barkys*. As usual, we place company-related files in the folder *spiderservices* and project files in a subfolder named after the current project (in this case, *barkys*).

2. Create a new .*fla* file named *barkyshome.fla* in the following location: *c:\data\spiderservices\barkys\barkyshome.fla*.

3. On frame 1 of *barkyshome.fla*, add the following code:

```
import com.spiderservices.effects.TextAnimation;

// This function is called when the class library finishes loading.
function spidercoreLoaded ():Void {
  // Classes are loaded. It's now safe to proceed with the application.
  // Just to prove everything's working, make a TextAnimation instance.
  var ta:TextAnimation = new TextAnimation();
}

// Load class library.
this.createEmptyMovieClip("spidercore", 0);
this.spidercore.loadMovie("../spidercore/spidercore_runtime.swf");
```

Our Barky's homepage movie is ready to use the class library, but there's a problem. If we use it in its current state, it will automatically include the *TextAnimation* class file in the *barkyshome.swf* movie! We don't want that to happen because we'll be loading that class at runtime via *spidercore_runtime.swf*, and we don't want to load the class twice for no reason. Hence, we now need to create a special XML file that tells the compiler not to include the class *TextAnimation* in *barkyshome.swf*.

You might assume we could prevent the *TextAnimation* class from being included in *barkyshome.swf* simply by removing the path *c:\data\actionscript* from the global classpath. In fact, that would work but would also prevent the compiler from finding the *TextAnimation* class for the sake of type checking! Hence, type errors would occur and our *barkyshome.swf* file wouldn't be compiled. So, even though we're loading classes at runtime, we still need access to the source files for those classes at authoring time. Later in this chapter, we'll see how to ship a dynamic class library without also shipping source code.

Create the exclusion XML file

The exclusion file specifies which classes should not be compiled into the associated *.swf* file. We want to prevent those classes that will be loaded dynamically at runtime from being compiled into the applicable *.swf*.

To make the exclusion XML file, follow these steps:

1. Create a new text file named *barkyshome_exclude.xml* in the following location: *c:\data\spiderservices\barkys\barkyshome_exclude.xml*.

   The precise name of the exclusion file in this step is very important. It must exactly match the name of the *.fla* file to which it applies, followed by *_exclude.xml*.

2. The exclusion file prevents the specified class(es) from being compiled into the associated *.swf* file. To prevent the *TextAnimation* class from being compiled into the *.swf* file, add the following code to *barkyshome_exclude.xml*:

   ```
   <excludeAssets>
     <asset name="com.spiderservices.effects.TextAnimation"></asset>
   </excludeAssets>
   ```

   Here's a hypothetical exclusion file that shows how to exclude more than one class. It excludes the *TextAnimation* class as well as the hypothetical classes *Tween* and *Randomizer*:

   ```
   <excludeAssets>
     <asset name="com.spiderservices.effects.TextAnimation"></asset>
     <asset name="com.spiderservices.effects.Tween"></asset>
     <asset name="com.spiderservices.util.Randomizer"></asset>
   </excludeAssets>
   ```

3. Save the *barkyshome_exclude.xml* file.

By listing the *TextAnimation* class in an <asset> tag, we force it to be excluded from our *barkyshome.swf* file. Each class in the *spidercore_runtime.swf* class library should be listed in its own <asset> tag.

 The compiler does not automatically exclude dependent classes. For example, if our *spidercore* class library contains a *Tween* class that is used by *TextAnimation*, but the *barkyshome_exclude.xml* file does not list *Tween* as an exclusion in an <asset> tag, the *Tween* class is included in the *barkyshome.swf* file (which is undesirable and unnecessary because the code resides in the class library too).

You must name each and every class you want excluded in its own <asset> tag, and there are no wildcards to help you exclude a whole package.

Our *spidercore* class library is now ready for use!

Try it out

We can test our dynamic class library by exporting a *.swf* file from *barkyshome.fla* using Control → Test Movie (Ctrl-Enter on Windows or Cmd-Enter on Mac). The *barkyshome.swf* file will not include the *TextAnimation* class but will have access to it via the loaded dynamic class library, *spidercore_runtime.swf*. Remember that the class library loads because we told it to on frame 1 of *barkyshome.fla*:

```
// Load class library.
this.createEmptyMovieClip("spidercore", 0);
this.spidercore.loadMovie("../spidercore/spidercore_runtime.swf");
```

If you're following along at home, you should see this text appear in the Output panel:

```
Imagine a text effect with great majesty.
```

Note that if we were to load another class library with its own version of the class *com.spiderservices.effects.TextAnimation*, the second version of the class would not overwrite the first version; it would be ignored. To prevent that kind of name collision, you should always keep your classes in a uniquely named package, particularly when working with dynamic class libraries.

Sharing Classes Without Sharing Source Files

Earlier we learned that it's easiest to share a class library simply by distributing class files (that is, *.as* files). However, you may not want to share a class library in that way for two reasons:

- You don't want to distribute your source files because they're proprietary.

- You want your code to compile faster. (That is, your core classes don't change much, so you don't want them recompiled every time you export a *.swf* file— you're happy using precompiled versions of the classes.)

Both of these concerns are valid. However, given the work involved in distributing a class library without distributing its source files, you should consider the following factors before you take the no-source plunge:

- No code in a *.swf* file is safe. Several Flash decompilers that can strip source code from a *.swf* file are available, but not obfuscators that can absolutely, 100% prevent source code theft. At best, efforts to protect source code in a *.swf* are a deterrent only, merely costing the would-be thief extra work.

- The time saved by using precompiled libraries may be consumed by the extra time required to maintain a no-source code library. Your mileage may vary. (Maybe you should upgrade your computer instead and make all compiling faster?)

The remainder of this chapter explains how to distribute a class library without distributing its source files. Hold on to your hat. The ride's about to get a little bumpy.

Runtime Versus Compile Time

Once you've determined that you must distribute a no-source class library, you need to decide whether the library should be incorporated at compile time or loaded at runtime. A class library loaded at compile time is known as a *static class library* (contrast this with a *dynamic class library*, which, as we learned earlier, is a class library loaded at runtime). In Flash MX 2004, a static class library takes the form of a component *.swc* file, which is added to a *.fla* file at authoring time. As we saw earlier, a dynamic class library takes the form of a *.swf* file, such as *spidercore_runtime.swf*. Dynamic class libraries are loaded into the Flash Player via *loadMovie( )*. The pros and cons in Table 14-1 should help you decide which kind of library you should use in your application.

Table 14-1. Comparing static class libraries with dynamic class libraries

Library type	Pros	Cons
Dynamic library	• No need to recompile *.swfs* that incorporate the class library when the class library *.swf* changes (you need to recompile the dynamic library only once, not recompile the *.swfs* that include it) • Reduces overall file size when used across multiple *.swf* files • Loaded only if necessary, incurring download cost when actually used or not at all if not used	• Harder to create, maintain, use, and distribute • Easier to steal
Static library	• Easier to create, maintain, use, and distribute • Harder to steal	• Need to recompile all *.swf* files that use the library if library changes • Adds to file size of every *.swf* • Completely included in every *.swf* file that incorporates the library, whether or not all the classes in the library are referenced at runtime

Whether you prefer to use a static class library or a dynamic class library, if you want to ship a class library without also shipping the source code, you'll need to build a static class library to start with. In the case of shipping a dynamic class library without also shipping source code, you must provide the static class library for the sake of compile-time type checking. Hence, we'll learn how to create a static class library first.

Creating a No-Source Compile-time Class Library

A compile-time class library (a.k.a. a static class library) takes the form of a Flash MX 2004 component, which includes the following:

- The compiled bytecode for the classes in the library
- An *intrinsic* class definition file for each class in the library (this provides type checking information to the compiler)
- An optional icon *.png* file for use in the Flash MX 2004 Components panel

In Flash MX 2004, components are fundamentally visual entities. They are subclasses of the *MovieClip* class and intended primarily as reusable GUI widgets. The type of class library we want to build, by contrast, is not visual at all. It is simply a collection of code that can be added to an application. Hence, shipping a nonvisual class library as a component is, in part, an exercise of fitting a square peg into a round hole. That is, some aspects of the component-creation process are obviously not related to the basic task of shipping class libraries. However, these aspects are required due to the architecture of components in Flash MX 2004. What matters in the end is that it all works.

To learn how to create a compile-time class library as a component, we'll return to our fictitious web shop, Spider Services. This time, suppose we want to ship our *TextAnimation* class in a compile-time class library, which we'll again call *spidercore*. Here are the general tasks we have to complete:

1. Create the classes in the class library (in our case, just the *TextAnimation* class).
2. Create the component icon (in our case, a little spider) as a *.png* file.
3. Create the component class, called *ClassLoader*.
4. Create the component.
5. Distribute the component to other developers, providing instructions on how to use it.

Now let's look at each task individually. The source files discussed in the next several sections can be downloaded at *http://moock.org/eas2/examples*.

Note that some steps in the following sections are repeated from the earlier section "Loading Classes at Runtime." If you have completed the procedures in that section already, you can skip some of the steps in the following sections.

Create the classes in the class library

The first step in creating a class library is to create the classes themselves. Refer to the earlier section "Create the classes in the class library," which I shan't repeat here.

Create the component icon

We're going to give our component an icon, not only for cosmetic appearances in the Flash MX 2004 Components panel but also so that we have an image to put in our

---

component symbol. As we'll soon see, the component symbol should not be empty, otherwise instances of it will not show up on stage at authoring time. Note that for components created simply to contain a class library, such as ours, it's appropriate to use the same icon for the Components panel and for the content of the component itself. The similarity helps draw a connection between the component in the Library of a *.fla* file and an instance of the component placed on the Stage.

To create the component icon, follow these steps:

1. Create the following working directory for the component source files: *c:\data\spiderservices\spidercore*. (You will have done this step already if you completed the procedures earlier under "Loading Classes at Runtime.")

2. Create an 18 x 18–pixel image and save it in *.png* format using, say, Adobe Photoshop, Macromedia Fireworks, or your favorite image editor. Our image is a little illustration of a spider, as seen in Figure 14-1.

3. Save the image as *c:\data\spiderservices\spidercore\spidercore.png*.

Figure 14-1. Our component icon

Create the component class

We must now create the class that will be associated with our component. Because our component's only purpose is to load other classes, our component class simply lists the classes we want to include in our class library. The component class is called *ClassLoader* because loading classes is its only purpose. Here's the source code for the *ClassLoader* class, which is stored in a file named *ClassLoader.as* in the directory *c:\data\actionscript\com\spiderservices*:

```
[IconFile("spidercore.png")]

class com.spiderservices.ClassLoader extends MovieClip {

  public function setSize () {
    _width = 18;
    _height = 18;
  }

  public function doNothing ():Void {
    // Trick the compiler into including
    // the TextAnimation class in the component.
    com.spiderservices.effects.TextAnimation;
  }
}
```

The *ClassLoader* class has four key features:

- It uses a *component metadata tag* to specify the name of the image icon, *spider-core.png*, to use in the Flash MX 2004 Components panel. (A component metadata tag tells the compiler something about a component, and you need not concern yourself with the technical details for the purposes of this discussion. For more information, see Using Components → Creating Components → Component Metadata in the online Help.)

  ```
  [IconFile("spidercore.png")]
  ```

- It extends *MovieClip*. This is a necessary evil required by the Flash MX 2004 component architecture.

  ```
  class com.spiderservices.ClassLoader extends MovieClip {
  ```

- It implements a *setSize( )* method, indicating how an instance of the component should be sized on the Stage. This is another necessary evil required by the Flash MX 2004 component architecture.

  ```
  public function setSize () {
    _width = 18;
    _height = 18;
  }
  ```

- In a dummy method, *doNothing( )*, *ClassLoader* lists all the classes that should be included in our class library. Listing the classes forces the compiler to include them when generating the component. The compiler finds and includes all dependent classes automatically (for example, if the *TextAnimation* class uses a *Tween* class, then the *Tween* class will be included in the spidercore component automatically).

  ```
  public function doNothing ():Void {
    com.spiderservices.effects.TextAnimation;
  }
  ```

The preceding four features are, in truth, quite bizarre—you likely wouldn't expect the *ClassLoader* class to be required at all! At least, once the general structure is in place, it rarely needs to be altered (so you can forget how strange creating the class loader was after it's done).

Create the component

Now that the *ClassLoader* class is ready, we can create our spidercore component, which is what will contain the class library we'll distribute to the world.

The spidercore component is a movie clip symbol with a so-called *component definition* that transforms it from a plain old movie clip into a component. The movie clip symbol resides in a *.fla* file (*spidercore.fla*), which we'll create specifically for the purpose of producing the spidercore component.

To create *spidercore.fla*, follow these steps:

1. Create a new *.fla* file in the following location: *c:\data\spiderservices\spidercore\ spidercore.fla*. (Note that the *spidercore.png* must be in the same folder as the *spidercore.fla* file in order for the spidercore component icon to be included with the component.)

2. Add *c:\data\actionscript* to the global classpath using Edit → Preferences → ActionScript → Language → ActionScript 2.0 Settings. (Again, you might have done this step already.)

To create the spidercore component, follow these steps:

1. In the *spidercore.fla* file, choose Insert → New Symbol (Ctrl-F8) to create a new movie clip symbol.

2. Name the new symbol **spidercore**.

3. In the *spidercore.fla* Library, right-click (Windows) or Cmd-click (Mac) the spidercore symbol and select the Linkage option.

4. Under Linkage, be sure the Export for ActionScript and Export in First Frame options are checked.

5. For the Linkage Identifier, enter **spidercore**.

6. For AS 2.0 Class, enter **com.spiderservices.ClassLoader**.

7. Click OK to accept the Linkage settings specified in Steps 4–6.

8. In the *spidercore.fla*'s Library, right-click (Windows) or Cmd-click (Mac) the spidercore symbol and select Component Definition from the contextual menu.

9. In the Component Definition dialog box, for AS 2.0 Class, enter **com. spiderservices.ClassLoader**.

10. Under Options, check Display in Components Panel.

11. For Tool Tip Text, enter **SpiderCore Class Library**.

12. Click OK to accept the Component Definition settings specified in Steps 9–11.

Now we must place some arbitrary content in the spidercore symbol so that instances of it can appear on the Stage at authoring time. If we skip this important step, instances on the Stage will completely disappear when deselected! To add content to the spidercore symbol, follow these steps:

1. To edit the spidercore symbol, double-click it in the *spidercore.fla* document's Library.

2. Select File → Import → Import to Stage (Ctrl-R in Windows or Cmd-R on Mac).

3. Choose the spidercore image file: *c:\data\spiderservices\spidercore\spidercore.png*.

4. Ensure that the image appears in the spidercore symbol, with its top-left corner aligned to the symbol's registration point, which is indicated by a small crosshair in the center of the symbol.

5. Save the *spidercore.fla* file.

Our component is now complete. All that's left to do is export its *.swc* file, which is the compiled component that we'll distribute to the world. Follow these steps:

1. In the *spidercore.fla*'s Library, right-click (Windows) or Cmd-click (Macintosh) on the spidercore symbol and select Export SWC File from the contextual menu.

2. Save the *.swc* file as *c:\data\spiderservices\spidercore\spidercore.swc*.

The exported *spidercore.swc* file is our finished class library component. We can now give the component to other developers to add to their Flash MX 2004 Components panel, for inclusion in any *.fla* file.

Distribute the component to developers

Anyone who wishes to use the class library must obtain a copy of *spidercore.swc* and install it in Flash MX 2004. Here's the set of instructions we include in our class library documentation to help users install the spidercore component:

1. Open the following folder, substituting your operating-system user account name for *USER* and your Flash language code for *LANGUAGE_CODE,* such as "en" for English:

   On Windows

   c:\Documents and Settings\USER/Local Settings\Application Data/Macromedia\Flash MX 2004\LANGUAGE_CODE\Configuration\Components

   Note that the *Local Settings* folder is a hidden folder that must be revealed explicitly in Windows File Explorer using Tools → Folder Options → View → Advanced Settings → Files and Folders → Hidden Files and Folders → Show Hidden Files and Folders.

   On Mac

   HD:/Users/USER/Library/Application Support/Macromedia/Flash MX 2004/ LANGUAGE_CODE/Configuration/Components/

2. In the *Components* folder, create a new folder named *Spider Services*.

3. Copy *spiderservices.swc* to *Components/Spider Services*.

4. If you are currently running the Flash authoring tool, click the Components panel's pop-up Options menu (top right of the panel) and select Reload.

   The spidercore component should now appear in the Components panel.

Try it out

Let's try using our spidercore component by adding it to a movie. We'll pretend we're creating a web site for the Mega Bridal Depot, and we want to use the text animation effect in our *spidercore* class library. Follow these steps:

1. Install the spidercore component in the Components panel as described in the preceding section.

2. Create the following working directory for the Mega Bridal Depot project: *c:\data\spiderservices\megabridaldepot*.

3. Create a new *.fla* file named *mbd_home.fla* in the following location: *c:\data\spiderservices\megabridaldepot\mbd_home.fla*.

4. Drag an instance of the spidercore component from the Components panel to the Stage of *mbd_home.fla*.

5. Delete the instance you just dragged to the Stage. (The component is required in the *.fla* file's Library only, not on stage.)

6. Be sure never to change the Linkage settings for the component. The settings should always be set to Export for ActionScript and Export in First Frame. To change the frame on which the classes in the component are exported, use File → Publish Settings → ActionScript Version → Settings → Export Frame for Classes.

7. On frame 1 of *Layer 1* in *mbd_home.fla*, add the following code:

```
import com.spiderservices.effects.TextAnimation;
var textani:TextAnimation = new TextAnimation( );
```

8. Export a test *.swf* file from *mbd_home.fla* using Control → Test Movie (Ctrl-Enter on Windows or Cmd-Enter on Mac).

If you followed the preceding steps correctly, the Output panel should display:

```
Imagine a text effect with great majesty.
```

Creating a No-Source Runtime Class Library

Earlier in this chapter, under "Loading Classes at Runtime," we learned that a runtime-loaded class library can save overall file size when the same classes are used across multiple *.swf* files. However, the implementation we studied earlier for runtime class libraries required users of the library to have access to the library's source code.

By combining a no-source compile-time class library with a runtime class library, we can distribute a runtime class library without distributing any class source code. Here's the technique:

1. Create a class library *.swf* file, *someLib_runtime.swf*, as described earlier under "Loading Classes at Runtime."

2. Create a class library component, *someLib*, as described under "Creating a No-Source Compile-time Class Library."

3. Create a *.fla* file, *someApp.fla*, that loads *someLib_runtime.swf*, as described under "Loading Classes at Runtime."

4. Add the *someLib* component to *someApp.fla*, as described under "Distribute the component to developers."

5. Create an exclusion XML file, *someApp_exclude.xml*, for *someApp.fla*, as described earlier under "Loading Classes at Runtime."

6. Select File → Export → Export movie to export *someApp.swf* from *someApp.fla*.

Because of the *someApp_exclude.xml* file, the movie *someApp.swf* will not contain the classes included in the *someLib* component. Instead, *someApp.swf* will load the classes from *someLib_runtime.swf*.

Look, Mom! No source!

Solving Real OOP Problems

The past two chapters explained some of the nitty-gritty mechanical details of producing code in the Flash MX 2004 authoring environment. For the remainder of this book (Part III), we'll return to a more generalized study of OOP. Up next, *design patterns*—widely accepted solutions to specific architectural problems in object-oriented programming.

Design Pattern Examples in ActionScript 2.0

Part III explores a variety of approaches to various programming situations. You'll learn how to apply proven and widely accepted object-oriented programming strategies—known as *design patterns*—to Flash. Once you've tried working with the patterns presented in Part III, you'll have confidence consulting the larger body of patterns available online and in other literature. You'll have the skills to draw on other widely recognized object-oriented practices.

Introduction to Design Patterns

We've covered a lot of territory, both theoretical and practical throughout the first two parts of this book. By now you should have a firm grasp on ActionScript 2.0 syntax and fundamentals, as well as higher-order concepts such as classes, inheritance, composition, and exception handling, plus housekeeping details such as packages, class libraries, and components. So you're well on your way to being a skilled object-oriented programmer. But you may be wondering how to design an application. You're in luck. This chapter is our first stop on our journey through object-oriented design. By the end of Part III, you should be comfortable architecting relationships between classes to address a variety of common scenarios. With time, you'll learn to expand and apply this knowledge to other problems.

At the beginning of every program is a problem, probably one that other programmers have faced before. A *design pattern* is a widely accepted description, with a recommended solution, of a design or architectural problem in object-oriented programming. Given a specific requirement, a design pattern describes, in general terms, how to structure interacting classes to meet that requirement. In other words, the pattern provides a general blueprint to follow when implementing some aspect of a program.

Design patterns are, by their very nature, generic solutions. For example, one pattern, named *Observer*, describes how to update many objects when a single object changes state. Another pattern, named *Singleton*, describes how to ensure that a program creates only a single instance of a class, not multiple instances. The Observer and Singleton patterns each describes a generalized structure that has a myriad of specific uses. For example, the Observer pattern might be used to keep a pie chart and a bar chart in sync, or it might be used to let multiple objects respond to the completion of a game.

A design pattern does not describe the entire structure of an application. For example, a complete architecture for a tile-based adventure game is not a design pattern. Neither does a design pattern describe a specific algorithm or procedure in an application. For example, a path-finding algorithm used by monsters in an adventure game to find their prey is not a design pattern. Design patterns live somewhere between the complete application and the low-level algorithm. They describe how classes and objects should communicate in a generalized situation that might occur in any kind of program. Furthermore, a specific program will often combine several design patterns to build a complex whole from a group of simpler parts.

By programming with design patterns, we profit from the collective experience of the OOP community, exploiting known tricks and avoiding common pitfalls. We also make our code more familiar to other programmers. Design patterns are part of the common OOP vernacular, so we can use them to more quickly and effectively discuss the general implementation of a program. For example, when we tell another knowledgeable programmer, "The log in this application is a Singleton," he immediately understands the structure to which we're referring without even looking at the code. What might have taken half an hour to explain without reference to an existing design pattern took only a few seconds.

Many of the design patterns that exist in OOP today were first documented by Erich Gamma, Richard Helm, Ralph Johnson, and John Vlissides. In 1994, those four authors published the canonical *Design Patterns: Elements Of Reusable Object-Oriented Software* (Addison-Wesley). The book, known affectionately as *GoF* (Gang of Four), defined a formal system for describing a design pattern and presented 23 patterns, many of which are still well-known and commonly used today.

The formal design pattern format laid out by GoF includes four general parts: the pattern name, the problem, the solution, and the consequences. Those general parts are broken down into the following sections:

Pattern Name and Classification
Intent
Also Known As
Motivation
Applicability
Structure
Participants
Collaborations
Consequences
Implementation
Sample Code
Known Uses
Related Patterns

Our consideration of design patterns in ActionScript is informal, so it doesn't use the preceding categories. Similarly, many design patterns include formal UML (Unified Modeling Language) diagrams, but this book doesn't use UML. The emphasis here is on the concepts, not the formal notation. If you've never heard of UML or design patterns before but you've understood Parts I and II of this book, you'll be able to keep up quite easily.

If after finishing Part III, you're keen to learn more about design patterns, you should definitely purchase a copy of GoF. The theory in that book is language agnostic, but the examples focus on C++ and Smalltalk.

Here's an excerpt from GoF that introduces the concept of design patterns. It should give you a feel for the tone of the book (while also giving the present text an opportunity to pay homage to its groundbreaking work):

> [Design patterns are] descriptions of communicating objects and classes that are customized to solve a general design problem in a particular context.
>
> A design pattern names, abstracts, and identifies the key aspects of a common design structure that make it useful for creating reusable object-oriented design. The design pattern identifies the participating classes and instances, their roles and collaborations, and the distribution of responsibilities. Each design pattern focuses on a particular object-oriented design problem or issue. It describes when it applies, whether it can be applied in view of other object-oriented design constraints, and the consequences and trade-offs of its use.

If you know Java (or are willing to learn a little), you might also try *Applying UML and Patterns: An Introduction to Object-Oriented Analysis and Design and the Unified Process,* by Craig Larman (Prentice Hall). For a good resource showing source code in Java for many design patterns, see: *http://www.fluffycat.com/java/patterns.html*. Java's syntax is quite similar to ActionScript 2.0, so the site should be intelligible even to Flash programmers who don't know Java.

Bring on the Patterns

The remainder of this book studies four design patterns that are particularly applicable to the problems that arise in Flash, showing how to use them to structure sections of an ActionScript 2.0 application. First we'll study two canonical design patterns, Observer and Singleton (both of which come from GoF). Then we'll move on to two quasi-patterns, Model-View-Controller (MVC) and the *delegation event model*. MVC is a combination of patterns that grew out of the Smalltalk language and is used to structure user interfaces. The delegation event model is a core Java pattern that describes how to implement events and event handling.

Among the large number of formal and informal design patterns available today, the four patterns presented in this section were chosen because:

- They're extremely well-known and relatively easy to understand.
- They address event architectures, an important part of OOP that affects nearly every application.
- They demonstrate tangible, practical ways to develop user interfaces in OOP, which is perhaps the most important aspect of Flash application development.

The Observer pattern is up first, so put on your thinking caps and let's get started.

CHAPTER 16
The Observer Design Pattern

[The Observer pattern defines] a one-to-many dependency between objects so that when one object changes state, all its dependents are notified and updated automatically.

——from *Design Patterns: Elements of Reusable Object-Oriented Software* (the so-called *GoF* book discussed in Chapter 15)

Effectively, the Observer pattern is an all-purpose event-broadcasting mechanism. It lets a class broadcast generic updates to registered listeners, much as you could ask your local movie retailer to call you when a DVD you're interested in arrives. It could be used in anything from a mail application (when a new email is received) to a video game (when an enemy dies).

In the Observer pattern, changes in the state of one object (the *subject*) are broadcast to other interested objects (the *observers*). Each observer object indicates that it is interested in receiving broadcasts by registering with the subject. When the subject changes, it tells its current list of observers that it changed.

The Observer pattern is perfect for rendering multiple representations of a single body of data. For example, consider a weather-reporting application with a class, *WeatherReporter*, that stores the latest weather report. On screen are two representations of the weather report, each handled by its own class. The *TextReport* class describes the weather in text, such as:

Temperature: 29C, Probability of Precipitation: 20%

A separate *GraphicReport* class represents the weather with icons (a thermometer icon for temperature and a pie chart for the probability of precipitation).

When the weather application starts, instances of *TextReport* and *GraphicReport* register to receive updates from the *WeatherReporter* object. When the weather data changes, the *WeatherReporter* (the subject) broadcasts the latest weather to its list of observers, in this case the *TextReport* and *GraphicReport* instances. Each object is responsible for independently handling the update in its own way. The *TextReport* instance generates a text message whereas the *GraphicReport* instance displays weather icons. New classes can be added to the application at any time to handle the weather data in other ways. For example, a *SoundReport* class could play the sound of rain when it's raining, and an *EmailReport* class could use a server-side script to send out email when the weather report is updated.

Importantly, nothing about the *WeatherReporter* class needs to change to allow new types of observers to receive updates from it. Observer classes can be added, changed, and removed without affecting any other part of the application. Furthermore, the *WeatherReporter* class doesn't need to know the identity of the listeners (observers), such as the *TextReport* and *GraphicReport* classes. The datatype of the observers doesn't matter as long as they can handle updates provided by *WeatherReporter*. In other words, in the Observer pattern, the subject and its observers are *loosely coupled*, making the application easy to modify and extend. If we weren't using the Observer pattern, we might tightly couple the *WeatherReporter* class with the *TextReport* and *GraphicReport* classes. We might have the *WeatherReporter* class invoke methods found only in those classes, such as *TextReport.updateTextOutput( )* and *GraphicReport.changeWeatherIcons( )*. In this hypothetical, tightly coupled implementation, our architecture is much more difficult to change. If we want to add a new output class, we have to change *WeatherReporter* to call the new class's specific update method. And if we want to change the name of, say, *GraphicReport.changeWeatherIcons( )*, we have to update the code that calls that method in *WeatherReporter*. The Observer pattern protects us from that work.

Figure 16-1 depicts the general relationships between the *WeatherReporter*, *TextReport*, and *GraphicReport* objects in our hypothetical weather application.

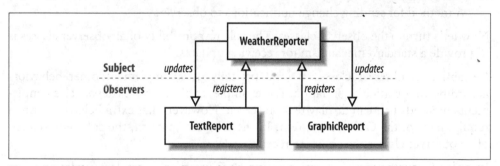

Figure 16-1. Observer pattern weather application example

Now let's take a look at how to implement the Observer pattern, first by studying its general structure, then by creating a real example—an application log. As we progress through the chapter, try to remember the simplicity of the pattern. If you feel bogged down by code details, come back to Figure 16-1 and remind yourself that in the Observer pattern we're just trying to make one class broadcast changes to other classes. Once we establish a code base for the pattern, it takes relatively little effort to create new implementations of Observer.

The source code discussed in this chapter is available at *http://moock.org/eas2/ examples*.

Implementing Observer in ActionScript 2.0

The responsibilities of the subject class in the Observer pattern are as follows:

- Maintain a list of dependent observers
- Provide methods for adding (registering) and removing (unregistering) observer objects
- Send notifications to observers

To create the subject class, we'll follow Java's implementation and define a base class, *Observable*, that any would-be subject class can extend. The *Observable* class provides the basic services required of all subject classes. Specifically, *Observable* defines the following properties and methods:

observers

> An instance property that holds an array of observers

addObserver( )

> A method for adding a new observer to the observers array

removeObserver( )

> A method for removing an observer from the observers array

notifyObservers( )

> A method for sending change notifications to observers

Now let's turn to the observer classes. The sole responsibility of all observer classes is to provide a standard mechanism for receiving updates.

Certainly, an observer class can (and typically does) implement other behaviors according to a particular situation. For example, our earlier *TextReport* class implements methods that can display text on screen. However, that extra behavior is not a requirement of the Observer pattern. In the Observer pattern, the sole requirement of an observer class is the ability to receive updates.

In order to guarantee that every observer class provides a standard update mechanism, we'll create an *Observer* interface that defines an *update( )* method. Classes that wish to register with a subject (using *addObserver( )*) must implement the *Observer* interface and define an *update( )* method. When the subject changes state (i.e., has a message to broadcast), it calls *notifyObservers( )*, which invokes *update( )* on all observers. Each observer's *update( )* method responds to the change as it sees fit.

If you're thinking ahead, you may already be wondering how the observers know what changed in the subject. For example, in our hypothetical weather application, the subject, *WeatherReporter*, sends an update whenever the weather report changes.

How do the observers (*TextReport* and *GraphicReport*) obtain that updated weather information? There are two options, known as the *push* and *pull* models.

In the push model, the updated information is pushed to the observers via an *info object*. The info object is sent to observers by the subject's *notifyObservers( )* method. Each observer receives the info object as an argument to its *update( )* method. For example, if the *WeatherReporter* class were to use the push model, it would report weather changes by invoking *update( )* on *TextReport* and *GraphicReport*, as usual, but would also pass *update( )* an object with, say, temperature and precipitation properties. The *TextReport* and *GraphicReport* classes would process the object in their respective *update( )* methods.

In the pull model, the observers are expected to retrieve the information they want via getter methods defined by the subject. For example, if the *WeatherReporter* class were to use the pull model, it might define methods such as *getTemperature( )* and *getPrecipitation( )*. The *TextReport* and *GraphicReport* classes would then be responsible for implementing an *update( )* method that used *getTemperature( )* and *getPrecipitation( )* to retrieve the latest weather information.

Both the push and pull models have their pros and cons. The pull model requires observers to manually determine what has changed every time an update is received, which can be inefficient. In the push model, observers are told explicitly what changed, but that requires the subject to know the needs of its observers. The more the subject must know about its observers, the harder it is to modify observers without affecting the subject.

Our implementation of the Observer pattern supports both push and pull models. That is, the basic facilities required to send an info object at notification time are available but optional.

Figure 16-2 shows the architecture of our Observer implementation. The *Observable* class is the base class for all subjects. Subject classes (such as *WeatherReporter*) extend *Observable*. Observer classes (such as *TextReport*) implement the *Observer* interface and use *addObserver( )* to register with the subject. When a change in the subject occurs, the subject class invokes *update( )* on all *Observer* instances in its observers array.

Example 16-1 shows the source code for the *Observable* class, which we've chosen to place in the *util* package (following Java's lead). In addition to the features we've discussed, the *Observable* class in Example 16-1 provides several other conveniences:

- The *countObservers( )* method, which returns the number of observers in the observers array.
- The *clearObservers( )* method, used to remove all observers with a single, crushing blow.

- A Boolean property, changed, and the following supporting methods *setChanged( )*, *clearChanged( )*, and *hasChanged( )*. The changed property is used to specify and check whether the subject has changed since the last notification. We use changed when, for the sake of efficiency, we want to broadcast a single notification for multiple state changes in the subject (for an example, see the *ClockModel* class in Chapter 18).

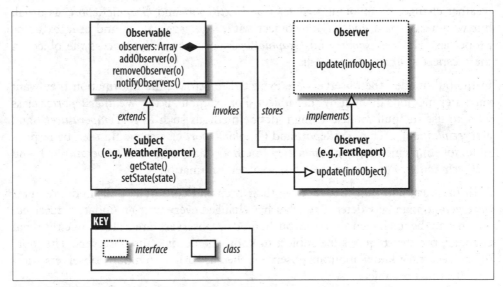

Figure 16-2. Observer pattern implementation

For an explanation of the *Observable* class's source code, consult the comments in Example 16-1. Note, however, that you don't need to know *Observable*'s internals very deeply. The *Observable* class is a reusable utility that never changes. We treat it as a black box that we simply extend when implementing the Observer pattern.

Example 16-1. The Observable class

```
import util.Observer;

/**
 * A Java-style Observable class used to represent the "subject"
 * of the Observer design pattern. Observers must implement the Observer
 * interface and register to observe the subject via addObserver().
 */
class util.Observable {
  // A flag indicating whether this object has changed.
  private var changed:Boolean = false;
  // A list of observers.
  private var observers:Array;

  /**
   * Constructor function.
   */
```

Example 16-1. The Observable class (continued)

```
  */
  public function Observable () {
    observers = new Array();
  }

  /**
   * Adds an observer to the list of observers.
   * @param   o   The observer to be added.
   */
  public function addObserver(o:Observer):Boolean {
    // Can't add a null observer.
    if (o == null) {
      return false;
    }

    // Don't add an observer more than once.
    for (var i:Number = 0; i < observers.length; i++) {
      if (observers[i] == o) {
        // The observer is already observing, so quit.
        return false;
      }
    }

    // Put the observer into the list.
    observers.push(o);
    return true;
  }

  /**
   * Removes an observer from the list of observers.
   *
   * @param   o   The observer to remove.
   */
  public function removeObserver(o:Observer):Boolean {
    // Find and remove the observer.
    var len:Number = observers.length;
    for (var i:Number = 0; i < len; i++) {
      if (observers[i] == o) {
        observers.splice(i, 1);
        return true;
      }
    }
    return false;
  }

  /**
   * Tell all observers that the subject has changed.
   *
   * @param   infoObj   An object containing arbitrary data
   *                    to pass to observers.
   */
  public function notifyObservers(infoObj:Object):Void {
```

Example 16-1. The Observable class (continued)

```
  // Use a null info object if none is supplied.
  if (infoObj == undefined) {
    infoObj = null;
  }

  // If the subject hasn't changed, don't bother notifying observers.
  if (!changed) {
    return;
  }

  // Make a copy of the observers array. We do this to ensure
  // the list doesn't change while we're processing it.
  var observersSnapshot:Array = observers.slice(0);

  // This change has been processed, so unset the changed flag.
  clearChanged( );

  // Invoke update( ) on all observers. Count backward because
  // it's faster, and order doesn't matter in this case.
  for (var i:Number = observersSnapshot.length-1; i >= 0; i--) {
    observersSnapshot[i].update(this, infoObj);
  }
}

/**
 * Removes all observers from the observer list.
 */
public function clearObservers( ):Void {
  observers = new Array( );
}

/**
 * Indicates that the subject has changed.
 */
private function setChanged( ):Void {
  changed = true;
}

/**
 * Indicates that the subject has either not changed or
 * has notified its observers of the most recent change.
 */
private function clearChanged( ):Void {
  changed = false;
}

/**
 * Checks if the subject has changed.
 *
 * @return   true if the subject has changed,
 *           as determined by setChanged( ).
 */
```

Example 16-1. The Observable class (continued)

```
  public function hasChanged():Boolean {
    return changed;
  }

  /**
   * Returns the number of observers in the observer list.
   *
   * @return   An integer: the number of observers for this subject.
   */
  public function countObservers():Number {
    return observers.length;
  }
}
```

Example 16-2 shows the source code for the *Observer* interface, which resides in the *util* package along with *Observable*. The *Observer* interface is simple, containing only one method: *update( )*. We use *Observer* to guarantee that any class that registers for updates from a subject implements the standard *update( )* method. Notice that the *update( )* method defines two parameters, o and infoObj. The parameter o contains a reference to the subject that changed. It is used to distinguish changes in one subject from changes in another, as well as to access changed data in the subject (if the subject is using the pull model to update its observers). The parameter infoObj receives the optional info object provided by the subject if the subject is using the push model to broadcast changes to its observers. Note that although a single observer can, in theory, register with multiple subjects (and our code accommodates such a circumstance), in practice, a single observer typically registers with only one subject. An observer registered with multiple subjects must use awkward conditionals (*if/else* or *switch* statements) to distinguish between those subjects at update time. When a program reaches that level of complexity, it's often better to implement full-scale event handling, as described in Chapter 19.

Example 16-2. The Observer interface

```
import util.Observable;

/**
 * The interface that must be implemented by all observers of an
 * Observable object.
 */
interface util.Observer {
  /**
   * Invoked automatically by an observed object when it changes.
   *
   * @param   o        The observed object (an instance of Observable).
   * @param   infoObj  An arbitrary data object sent by
   *                    the observed object.
   */
  public function update(o:Observable, infoObj:Object):Void;
}
```

Logger: A Complete Observer Example

Now that we've implemented the core of the Observer pattern, let's put it to use in a real-world example—an application log. To create the log, we'll define four classes: *Logger*, *LogMessage*, *OutputPanelView*, and *TextFieldView*, all of which reside in the *logger* package. The *Logger* class is our subject. The *OutputPanelView* and *TextFieldView* classes are our observers. The *LogMessage* class is our info object.

Any class in the application can send a message to the *Logger* class. The receipt of a new message constitutes a change in the *Logger* class's state, causing it to broadcast the change (i.e., the message) to all *Logger* observers. In our case, the *Logger* observers are *OutputPanelView* and *TextFieldView*. The *OutputPanelView* renders log messages to the Output panel in Flash's Test Movie mode. The *TextFieldView* renders log messages to a text field on the movie's Stage, allowing them to be seen at runtime in the Flash Player.

Our *Logger* class uses the push model to broadcast messages. When a message arrives, *Logger* creates a *LogMessage* instance and passes that instance on to its list of observers. Each *LogMessage* provides methods for retrieving the text and severity of the message logged. *LogMessage* instances can have one of five severities, represented by the integers 0 through 4, as follows: FATAL (0), ERROR (1), WARN (2), INFO (3), and DEBUG (4). The severity-level integers are stored in static properties of the *Logger* class. They can be converted to human-readable strings via the *Logger.getLevelDesc( )* method.

The *Logger* class provides a filter for suppressing log messages. Using *Logger.setLevel( )*, a *Logger* instance can set a severity level, which determines whether messages should be broadcast or discarded. Messages with a severity level greater than the *Logger*'s severity level are not broadcast to observers. For example, if a message has a severity of 4 (DEBUG), but the *Logger*'s severity level is 3 (INFO), the message is not broadcast. The *Logger* class's filter lets us easily change the quantity and granularity of messages of a log from a central location. During development, we might use a log severity level of 4 (broadcast all messages), but in the final application, we might use a log severity level of 1 (broadcast ERROR and FATAL messages only).

The LogMessage Class

Let's start our examination of our log's source code with the *LogMessage* class, a simple class for setting and retrieving the text and severity of a logged message. The *LogMessage* class defines the following members:

msg
> An instance property that stores the text of the message

level
> An instance property that stores the message severity level

---

setLevel( )

A method for setting the message severity level

getLevel( )

A method for retrieving the message severity level

setMessage( )

A method for setting the message text

getMessage( )

A method for retrieving the message text

As we'll see later, the *Logger* class creates *LogMessage* instances when broadcasting a change notification to its observers. Example 16-3 shows the source code for the *LogMessage* class.

Example 16-3. The LogMessage class

```
/**
 * A log message. Sent by the Logger instance to all registered
 * log observers when a new log message is generated.
 */
class logger.LogMessage {
  // The text of the message sent to the log.
  private var msg:String;
  // The severity level of this message.
  private var level:Number;

  /**
   * LogMessage Constructor
   */
  public function LogMessage (m:String, lev:Number) {
    setMessage(m);
    setLevel(lev);
  }

  /**
   * Sets the log message.
   */
  public function setMessage (m:String):Void {
    msg = m;
  }

  /**
   * Returns the log message.
   */
  public function getMessage ():String {
    return msg;
  }

  /**
   * Sets the severity level for this message.
   */
  public function setLevel (lev:Number):Void {
    level = lev;
```

Example 16-3. The LogMessage class (continued)

```
  }

  /**
   * Returns the severity level for this message.
   */
  public function getLevel ():Number {
    return level;
  }
}
```

Now let's move on to *OutputPanelView*, a class that receives *LogMessage* instances from *Logger* and generates corresponding on-screen messages.

The OutputPanelView Class

The *OutputPanelView* class displays log messages in the Output panel in Flash's Test Movie mode. It implements the *Observer* interface from Example 16-2 and defines only one property and one method:

log

An instance property that stores a reference to the *Logger* instance being observed

update( )

The all-important method used by *Logger* to broadcast messages to the *OutputPanelView* instance

By convention, all observer classes should store an instance of the subject they are observing. They use that reference to pull changes from the subject or to set the subject's state. In our case, the *Logger* class broadcasts its updates using the push model, so the log property in *OutputPanelView* is not actually used. However, we maintain it as a matter of good form and for the sake of possible future updates to the *OutputPanelView* class.

Example 16-4 shows the source code for the *OutputPanelView* class. Pay special attention to the *update( )* method, which receives a *LogMessage* instance as an argument and uses it to display log messages in the Output panel. Notice that the generic infoObj instance received by *update( )* is cast to the *LogMessage* datatype before it is used so that the compiler can perform type checking on it. (Technically, the cast is not necessary in this case because the *Object* class is dynamic, so invoking non-*Object* methods on infoObj would not cause an error.)

Example 16-4. The OutputPanelView class

```
import util.Observer;
import util.Observable;
import logger.Logger;
import logger.LogMessage;
```

Example 16-4. The OutputPanelView class (continued)

```
/**
 * An observer of the Logger class. When a movie is played in
 * the Flash authoring tool's Test Movie mode, this class displays
 * log messages in the Output panel.
 */
class logger.OutputPanelView implements Observer {
  // The log (subject) that this object is observing.
  private var log:Logger;

  /**
   * Constructor
   */
  public function OutputPanelView (l:Logger) {
    log = l;
  }

  /**
   * Invoked when the log changes. For details, see the
   * Observer interface.
   */
  public function update (o:Observable, infoObj:Object):Void {
    // Cast infoObj to a LogMessage instance for type checking.
    var logMsg:LogMessage = LogMessage(infoObj);
    trace(Logger.getLevelDesc(logMsg.getLevel()) + ": " +
                          logMsg.getMessage());
  }

  public function destroy ():Void {
    log.removeObserver(this);
  }
}
```

Now let's look at our log's other observer class, *TextFieldView*.

The TextFieldView Class

The *TextFieldView* class displays log messages in a text field in the Flash movie rather than in the Output panel.

The basic structure of *TextFieldView* is identical to *OutputPanelView*. Like *OutputPanelView*, *TextFieldView* defines a log property and an *update( )* method. It also adds a new method, *makeTextField( )*, which creates an on-screen *TextField* instance in which to display messages. And it adds a new property, out, which stores a reference to the text field created by *makeTextField( )*. The *TextFieldView* constructor defines seven parameters:

l

A reference to the *Logger* instance that will be observed

target

The movie clip in which to create the text field

depth
> The depth in target on which to create the text field

x
> The horizontal position of the text field

y
> The vertical position of the text field

w
> The width of the text field

h
> The height of the text field

Example 16-5 shows the code for the *TextFieldView* class. Once again, pay special attention to the *update( )* method, which receives log messages and handles the important task of displaying them on screen.

Example 16-5. The TextFieldView class

```
import util.Observer;
import util.Observable;
import logger.Logger;
import logger.LogMessage;

/**
 * An observer of the Logger class. This class displays
 * messages sent to the log in an on-screen text field.
 */
class logger.TextFieldView implements Observer {
  // The log that this object is observing.
  private var log:Logger;
  // A reference to the text field.
  private var out:TextField;

  /**
   * TextFieldView Constructor
   */
  public function TextFieldView (l:Logger,
                                 target:MovieClip,
                                 depth:Number,
                                 x:Number,
                                 y:Number,
                                 w:Number,
                                 h:Number) {
    log = l;
    makeTextField(target, depth, x, y, w, h);
  }

  /**
   * Invoked when the log changes. For details, see the
   * Observer interface in Example 16-2.
   */
```

Example 16-5. The TextFieldView class (continued)

```
public function update (o:Observable, infoObj:Object):Void {
  // Cast infoObj to a LogMessage instance for type checking.
  var logMsg:LogMessage = LogMessage(infoObj);
  // Display the log message in the log text field.
  out.text += Logger.getLevelDesc(logMsg.getLevel())
            + ": " + logMsg.getMessage() + "\n";
  // Scroll to the bottom of the log text field.
  out.scroll = out.maxscroll;
}

/**
 * Creates a text field in the specified movie clip at
 * the specified depth. Log messages are displayed in the text field.
 */
public function makeTextField (target:MovieClip,
                               depth:Number,
                               x:Number,
                               y:Number,
                               w:Number,
                               h:Number):Void {
  // Create the text field.
  target.createTextField("log_txt", depth, x, y, w, h);
  // Store a reference to the text field.
  out = target.log_txt;
  // Put a border on the text field.
  out.border = true;
  // Make the text in the text field wrap.
  out.wordWrap = true;
}

public function destroy ():Void {
  log.removeObserver(this);
  out.removeTextField();
}
}
```

The completion of the *TextFieldView* class is a eureka! moment in which we can clearly see the fruits of our labor. With both the *TextFieldView* and *OutputPanelView* classes implemented, we now have two separate displays based on the same information source. When the *Logger* class receives a message, it doesn't have to worry about how the message is rendered. Instead, it merely broadcasts the message to its observers. The rendering and processing of the messages are handled by two completely separate observer classes. In our current example, we render the log in two ways, but once the general logging system is in place, it is trivial to add more log-rendering classes. For example, we could add a class that sends the log to a server-side database. Or we could add a class that archives the log locally and provides searching and arbitrary access to log messages. Each class neatly encompasses its own responsibilities. And the *Logger* class doesn't care whether there are three log-processor (observer) classes, a hundred such classes, or none.

Now let's put the final piece in the Observer puzzle, the *Logger* class.

The Logger Class

As the subject of our Observer implementation, the *Logger* class extends the *Observable* class, using it to handle the grunt work of managing observers and broadcasting state changes (in this case, log messages).

Here's the skeleton for the *Logger* class:

```
class logger.Logger extends Observable {
}
```

To ensure that each application creates only one *Logger* instance, we use the Singleton design pattern, which we'll study in the next chapter. The following aspects of the *Logger* class are all part of the Singleton design pattern; we'll skip consideration of these items for now and return to them next chapter:

- The *Logger* class stores an instance of itself in a static property called log

  ```
  private static var log:Logger = null;
  ```

- The *Logger* constructor function is private so that *Logger* instances cannot be created by outside code

- *Logger* instances can be created only via *Logger.getLog()*

  ```
  public static function getLog():Logger {
    if (log == null) {
      log = new Logger();
    }
    return log;
  }
  ```

As we learned earlier, the *Logger* class maintains a log severity level that is used to filter log messages. The severity levels are stored in static properties, as follows:

```
public static var FATAL:Number = 0;
public static var ERROR:Number = 1;
public static var WARN:Number  = 2;
public static var INFO:Number  = 3;
public static var DEBUG:Number = 4;
```

Human-readable strings describing the severity levels are stored in the property levelDescriptions:

```
public static var levelDescriptions = ["FATAL", "ERROR", "WARN", "INFO", "DEBUG"];
```

The current severity level is stored in an instance property, logLevel:

```
private var logLevel:Number;
```

To allow the log severity level to be set, the *Logger* class defines a *setLevel()* method:

```
public function setLevel(lev:Number):Void {
  lev = Math.floor(lev);
  if (lev >= Logger.FATAL && lev <= Logger.DEBUG) {
    logLevel = lev;
    info("Log level set to: " + lev);
    return;
```

```
    }
    warn("Invalid log level specified.");
}
```

To allow the log severity level to be retrieved, the *Logger* class defines a *getLevel( )* method:

```
public function getLevel():Number {
  return logLevel;
}
```

A human-readable string representing a given log level can be retrieved via the class method *getLevelDesc( )*:

```
public static function getLevelDesc(level:Number):String {
  return levelDescriptions[level];
}
```

By default, the *Logger* constructor sets each *Logger* instance's severity level to 3 (INFO):

```
private function Logger () {
  setLevel(Logger.INFO);
}
```

And now the code we've been waiting for. To allow messages to be sent to the log, the *Logger* class provides five methods, corresponding to the five log levels: *fatal( )*, *error( )*, *warn( )*, *info( )*, and *debug( )*. To send a message to the log, we first create a *Logger* instance:

```
var log:Logger = Logger.getLog();
```

Then we pass the message to be sent to the desired message-sending method. For example, the following code sends the message, "Something went wrong," with a severity of ERROR:

```
log.error("Something went wrong");
```

The following code sends a message, "Application started!" with a severity of INFO:

```
log.info("Application started!");
```

The most recent message sent to the log is stored in the instance property `lastMsg`:

```
private var lastMsg:LogMessage;
```

The methods *fatal( )*, *error( )*, *warn( )*, *info( )*, and *debug( )* are all structured identically. Let's look at the code for the *info( )* method to see how a log message is handled. Remember that the five message-sending methods are the state-change methods of the subject in our Observer pattern. As such, they follow a basic structure that all state-change methods in an Observer implementation follow. Here's the code for *info( )*, with comments explaining each line:

```
public function info(msg:String):Void {
  // If the filter level is at least "INFO"...
  if (logLevel >= Logger.INFO) {
```

```
    // ...then  broadcast the message to observers.

    // Using the supplied message string (msg),
    // create a LogMessage instance to send to observers.
    // The LogMessage instance is the info object of this
    // notification. Store the LogMessage instance in
    // lastMsg for later retrieval.
    lastMsg = new LogMessage(msg, Logger.INFO);

    // Indicate that the subject has changed state.
    setChanged( );

    // Use notifyObservers( ) to invoke update( ) on all Logger
    // observers, passing the LogMessage instance as an argument.
    // For the source code of notifyObservers( ), see Example 16-1.
    notifyObservers(lastMsg);
  }
}
```

The basic structure of the *Logger.info( )* method is:

- Perform state change (i.e., set lastMsg)
- Create info object
- Register state change in subject (via *setChanged( )*)
- Broadcast change notification (via *notifyObservers( )*)

All state-change methods in *Observable* subclasses use the preceding structure.

Example 16-6 shows the code for *Logger* in its entirety.

Example 16-6. The Logger class

```
import util.Observable;
import logger.LogMessage;

/**
 * A general log class. Use getLog( ) to create an app-wide instance.
 * Send messages with fatal( ), error( ), warn( ), info( ), and debug( ).
 * Add views for the log with addObserver( ) (views must implement Observer).
 *
 * @version 1.0.0
 */
class logger.Logger extends Observable {
  // Static variable. A reference to the log instance (Singleton).
  private static var log:Logger = null;

  // The possible log levels for a message.
  public static var FATAL:Number = 0;
  public static var ERROR:Number = 1;
  public static var WARN:Number  = 2;
  public static var INFO:Number  = 3;
  public static var DEBUG:Number = 4;
```

Example 16-6. The Logger class (continued)

```
  private var lastMsg:LogMessage;

  // The human-readable descriptions of the preceding log levels.
  public static var levelDescriptions = ["FATAL", "ERROR",
                                          "WARN", "INFO", "DEBUG"];

  // The zero-relative filter level for the log. Messages with a level
  // above logLevel are not passed on to observers.
  // Default is 3, "INFO" (only DEBUG messages are filtered out).
  private var logLevel:Number;

  /**
   * Logger Constructor
   */
  private function Logger () {
    // Show "INFO" level messages by default.
    setLevel(Logger.INFO);
  }

  /**
   * Returns a reference to the log instance.
   * If no log instance exists yet, creates one.
   *
   * @return    A Logger instance.
   */
  public static function getLog():Logger {
    if (log == null) {
      log = new Logger();
    }
    return log;
  }

  /**
   * Returns a human-readable string representing the specified log level.
   */
  public static function getLevelDesc(level:Number):String {
    return levelDescriptions[level];
  }

  /**
   * Sets the message filter level for the log.
   *
   * @param    lev    The level above which messages are filtered out.
   */
  public function setLevel(lev:Number):Void {
    // Make sure the supplied level is an integer.
    lev = Math.floor(lev);
    // Set the log level if it's one of the acceptable levels.
    if (lev >= Logger.FATAL && lev <= Logger.DEBUG) {
      logLevel - lev;
      info("Log level set to: " + lev);
      return;
```

Example 16-6. The Logger class (continued)

```
  }
  // If we get this far, the log level isn't valid.
  warn("Invalid log level specified.");
}

/**
 * Returns the message filter level for the log.
 */
public function getLevel():Number {
  return logLevel;
}

/**
 * Returns the most recent message sent to the log.
 */
public function getLastMsg():LogMessage {
  return lastMsg;
}

/**
 * Sends a message to the log, with severity "FATAL".
 */
public function fatal(msg:String):Void {
  // If the filter level is at least "FATAL", broadcast
  // the message to observers.
  if (logLevel >= Logger.FATAL) {
    // Construct the log message object.
    lastMsg = new LogMessage(msg, Logger.FATAL);

    // Pass the message on to observers.
    setChanged();
    notifyObservers(lastMsg);
  }
}

/**
 * Sends a message to the log, with severity "ERROR".
 */
public function error(msg:String):Void {
  // If the filter level is at least "ERROR", broadcast
  // the message to observers.
  if (logLevel >= Logger.ERROR) {
    lastMsg = new LogMessage(msg, Logger.ERROR);

    setChanged();
    notifyObservers(lastMsg);
  }
}

/**
 * Sends a message to the log, with severity "WARN".
 */
```

Example 16-6. The Logger class (continued)

```
public function warn(msg:String):Void {
  // If the filter level is at least "WARN", broadcast
  // the message to observers.
  if (logLevel >= Logger.WARN) {
    lastMsg = new LogMessage(msg, Logger.WARN);

    setChanged( );
    notifyObservers(lastMsg);
  }
}

/**
 * Sends a message to the log, with severity "INFO".
 */
public function info(msg:String):Void {
  // If the filter level is at least "INFO", broadcast
  // the message to observers.
  if (logLevel >= Logger.INFO) {
    lastMsg = new LogMessage(msg, Logger.INFO);

    setChanged( );
    notifyObservers(lastMsg);
  }
}

/**
 * Sends a message to the log, with severity "DEBUG".
 */
public function debug(msg:String):Void {
  // If the filter level is at least "DEBUG", broadcast
  // the message to observers.
  if (logLevel >= Logger.DEBUG) {
    lastMsg = new LogMessage(msg, Logger.DEBUG);

    setChanged( );
    notifyObservers(lastMsg);
  }
}
}
```

Notice that the five message-sending methods in the *Logger* class—*fatal( )*, *error( )*, *warn( )*, *info( )*, and *debug( )*—all contain nearly identical code. In this example, we'll accept that redundancy in order to repeatedly demonstrate the general structure of a state-change method. However, in a real-world version of the *Logger* class, we'd move the repeated code to a centralized method that checks the log level and notifies observers when appropriate. We'd call our centralized method *handleMessage( )* and have each of the message-sending methods use it to validate and broadcast messages, as shown next:

```
// The new handleMessage( ) method.
public function handleMessage(msg:String, msgSeverity:Number):Void {
```

```
    if (logLevel >= msgSeverity) {
      lastMsg = new LogMessage(msg, msgSeverity);

      setChanged( );
      notifyObservers(lastMsg);
    }
  }

  // Here's a revised message-sending method, debug( ),
  // showing how handleMessage( ) would be used. (Other
  // message-sending methods are not shown.)
  public function debug(msg:String):Void {
    handleMessage(msg, Logger.DEBUG);
  }
```

Inheritance Misuse?

As we've just seen, in our implementation of the *Logger* class, we extend *Observable*. In our situation, the *Logger* class doesn't need to inherit from any other class, so it can extend *Observable* without issue. But what if the *Logger* class were already a subclass of some other class (say, *MessageManager*)? It wouldn't be able to inherit from the *Observable* class! Here, we encounter a classic misuse of inheritance—extending a class simply to borrow its functionality. We first saw this kind of misuse in Chapter 6 and later showed how to avoid it in Chapter 8, under "Multiple Type Inheritance with Interfaces." Specifically, the *Logger* class doesn't have a legitimate "Is-A" relationship with the *Observable* class. That is, the *Logger* class is not a specialized kind of update broadcaster. Other classes won't use it in place of *Observable* for its additional broadcast features. On the contrary, the *Logger* class manages an application log and just happens to need the update broadcasting functionality found in *Observable*. In short, we've used inheritance to arrange a marriage of convenience between the *Logger* and *Observable* classes.

In a much more flexible implementation of the Observer pattern, we would define the *Observable* datatype as an interface, not as a concrete class. We would then create an implementation of that interface in a class named *ObservableSubject*. The *ObservableSubject* class would have all the features of the *Observable* class from Example 16-1. Our *Logger* class would not extend *ObservableSubject*. Instead, it would implement the *Observable* interface and make use of *ObservableSubject* via composition (exactly as the *Rectangle* class from Chapter 8 implemented *Serializable* and used the *Serializer* class via composition). The *Logger* class would then be able to inherit from a more natural superclass (again, perhaps a generic *MessageManager* class).

So, knowing that we're misusing inheritance in our *Logger* example, should we now alter our Observer implementation to allow subjects such as *Logger* to use a base class such as *ObservableSubject* via composition instead of inheritance? That depends on the situation. The composition approach is undeniably more flexible (adding justification to Sun's recommendation that every class that can be extended should also be usable via composition!). However, the composition approach is also more complex. In a simple application, that complexity can translate to unnecessary development time and source code that's harder to digest. Hence, a good rule to follow is one we've seen several times already: Never Add Functionality Early (for details on this and other Extreme Programming rules, see *http://www.extremeprogramming.org/rules.html*). So far our *Logger* class doesn't need to inherit from any other class, so we don't need to worry that we're "misusing" inheritance. We can wait until the program we're creating requires another subject that cannot inherit from *Observable* because it already inherits from another class. That's a good time to implement the composition version of Observer.

In this chapter, we'll stick with our inheritance-based Observer implementation. For comparison, however, Example 16-7 presents the composition-based version. Differences from the inheritance version are shown in bold. Refer to Chapter 8 for an explanation of the basic structure of composition. Note that the composition-based implementation of Observer uses, verbatim, the previous versions of the *Observer* interface and the *LogMessage*, *OutputPanelView*, and *TextFieldView* classes. The source code for those items is, hence, not repeated in Example 16-7. You can download the code shown in Example 16-7 from *http://moock.org/eas2/examples*.

Example 16-7. Implementing the Observer pattern using composition

```
// Code in Observable.as. This is the new Observable interface.
import util.Observer;
interface util.Observable {
  public function addObserver(o:Observer):Boolean;
  public function removeObserver(o:Observer):Boolean;
  public function notifyObservers(infoObj:Object):Void;
  public function clearObservers():Void;
  public function hasChanged():Boolean;
  public function setChanged():Void;
  public function clearChanged():Void;
  public function countObservers():Number;
}


// Code in ObservableSubject.as. The ObservableSubject class is nearly
// identical to the previous Observable class, save for the commented
// sections in bold. Note that ObservableSubject implements the new
// Observable interface. Hence, the Observable interface must be imported.
import util.Observer;
import util.Observable;
class util.ObservableSubject implements Observable {
  private var changed:Boolean = false;
  private var observers:Array;

  // Constructor function, this time named ObservableSubject.
  public function ObservableSubject () {
    observers = new Array();
  }
```

Example 16-7. Implementing the Observer pattern using composition (continued)

```
public function addObserver(o:Observer):Boolean {
  if (o == null) {
    return false;
  }
  for (var i:Number = 0; i < observers.length; i++) {
    if (observers[i] == o) {
      return false;
    }
  }
  observers.push(o);
  return true;
}

public function removeObserver(o:Observer):Boolean {
  var len:Number = observers.length;
  for (var i:Number = 0; i < len; i++) {
    if (observers[i] == o) {
      observers.splice(i, 1);
      return true;
    }
  }
  return false;
}

public function notifyObservers(infoObj:Object):Void {
  if (infoObj == undefined) {
    infoObj = null;
  }
  if (!changed) {
    return;
  }
  var observersSnapshot:Array = observers.slice(0);
  clearChanged();
  for (var i:Number = observersSnapshot.length-1; i >= 0; i--) {
    observersSnapshot[i].update(this, infoObj);
  }
}

public function clearObservers():Void {
  observers = new Array();
}

public function setChanged():Void {
  changed = true;
}

public function clearChanged():Void {
  changed = false;
}

public function hasChanged():Boolean {
  return changed;
```

Example 16-7. Implementing the Observer pattern using composition (continued)

```
  }

  public function countObservers( ):Number {
    return observers.length;
  }
}


// Code in Logger.as.
import util.Observable;        // Import the new Observable interface.
import util.ObservableSubject;   // Import the new ObservableSubject class.
import util.Observer;
import logger.LogMessage;

// Implement Observable, but don't extend ObservableSubject!
class logger.Logger implements Observable {
  // An ObservableSubject instance, used to broadcast updates to observers.
  private var subj:ObservableSubject;

  private static var log:Logger = null;
  public static var FATAL:Number = 0;
  public static var ERROR:Number = 1;
  public static var WARN:Number = 2;
  public static var INFO:Number  = 3;
  public static var DEBUG:Number = 4;
  private var lastMsg:LogMessage;
  public static var levelDescriptions = ["FATAL", "ERROR",
                                         "WARN", "INFO", "DEBUG"];
  private var logLevel:Number;

  // Create the ObservableSubject instance in the constructor.
  private function Logger ( ) {
    subj = new ObservableSubject( );
    setLevel(Logger.INFO);
  }

  public static function getLog( ):Logger {
    if (log == null) {
      log = new Logger( );
    }
    return log;
  }

  public static function getLevelDesc(level:Number):String {
    return levelDescriptions[level];
  }

  public function setLevel(lev:Number):Void {
    // Make sure the supplied level is an integer.
    lev = Math.floor(lev);
    // Set the log level if it's one of the acceptable levels.
    if (lev >= Logger.FATAL && lev <= Logger.DEBUG) {
      logLevel = lev;
```

```
      info("Log level set to: " + lev);
      return;
    }
    // If we get this far, the log level isn't valid.
    warn("Invalid log level specified.");
  }

  public function getLevel():Number {
    return logLevel;
  }

  public function getLastMsg():LogMessage {
    return lastMsg;
  }

  public function fatal(msg:String):Void {
    if (logLevel >= Logger.FATAL) {
      // Construct the log message object.
      lastMsg = new LogMessage(msg, Logger.FATAL);

      // Pass the message on to observers.
      setChanged();
      notifyObservers(lastMsg);
    }
  }

  public function error(msg:String):Void {
    if (logLevel >= Logger.ERROR) {
      lastMsg = new LogMessage(msg, Logger.ERROR);

      setChanged();
      notifyObservers(lastMsg);
    }
  }

  public function warn(msg:String):Void {
    if (logLevel >= Logger.WARN) {
      lastMsg = new LogMessage(msg, Logger.WARN);

      setChanged();
      notifyObservers(lastMsg);
    }
  }

  public function info(msg:String):Void {
    if (logLevel >= Logger.INFO) {
      lastMsg = new LogMessage(msg, Logger.INFO);

      setChanged();
      notifyObservers(lastMsg);
    }
  }
```

```
  public function debug(msg:String):Void {
    if (logLevel >= Logger.DEBUG) {
      lastMsg = new LogMessage(msg, Logger.DEBUG);

      setChanged();
      notifyObservers(lastMsg);
    }
  }

  // Wrapper methods for ObservableSubject methods follow. These methods
  // subcontract their work out to the ObservableSubject instance, subj.
  public function addObserver(o:Observer):Boolean {
    return subj.addObserver(o);
  }

  public function removeObserver(o:Observer):Boolean {
    return subj.removeObserver(o);
  }

  public function notifyObservers(infoObj:Object):Void {
    subj.notifyObservers(infoObj);
  }

  public function clearObservers():Void {
    subj.clearObservers();
  }

  public function setChanged():Void {
    subj.setChanged();
  }

  public function clearChanged():Void {
    subj.clearChanged();
  }

  public function hasChanged():Boolean {
    return subj.hasChanged();
  }

  public function countObservers():Number {
    return subj.countObservers();
  }
}
```

Using the Logger Class

Now that we've seen how our subject (*Logger*) and its observers (*OutputPanelView* and *TextFieldView*) work individually, let's put them all together to form a functional logging system. The code in this section could go on a frame in the timeline of a *.fla* file or in a class (an *.as* file). Furthermore, the code works equally well with both the inheritance-based and composition-based implementations of the Observer pattern shown in this chapter.

First, we import the *logger* package (so we can refer to the *Logger*, *LogMessage*, *OutputPanelView*, and *TextFieldView* classes in that package directly):

```
import logger.*;
```

Then, we create a variable, log, to store our application's *Logger* instance:

```
var log:Logger;
```

Then we create the *Logger* instance:

```
log = Logger.getLog();
```

Next, we create two variables to store our *Logger* observers:

```
var outputLogView:OutputPanelView;
var textLogView:TextFieldView;
```

Then we create our observer instances, passing each the *Logger* instance for this application:

```
outputLogView = new OutputPanelView(log);
textLogView = new TextFieldView(log, someMovieClip, 0, 50, 50, 300, 200);
```

Finally, we use *addObserver( )* to register our observers to receive updates from the *Logger* instance:

```
log.addObserver(outputLogView);
log.addObserver(textLogView);
```

Our log's ready to go! Let's now try logging some messages:

```
log.fatal("This is a non-recoverable problem.");
log.error("This is a serious problem that may be recoverable.");
log.warn("This is something to look into, but probably isn't serious.");
log.info("This is a general bit of application information.");
log.debug("This is a note that helps track down a bug.");
```

If we executed the preceding code, the *debug( )* message wouldn't appear because the *Logger* instance filters out *debug( )* messages by default. To enable all messages for the log, we'd use:

```
log.setLevel(Logger.DEBUG);
```

If you want to see the log work on your own computer, you can download the example files from *http://moock.org/eas2/examples*.

Memory Management Issues with Observer

In Chapter 5, we learned that event-listener objects registered with an event source must always unregister from that source before being deleted. The same holds true in the Observer pattern—observers must unregister with their subject before being deleted. For example, suppose we create an *OutputPanelView* object and register it to observe a *Logger* instance (as shown in the previous section):

```
var outputLog:OutputPanelView = new OutputPanelView(log);
log.addObserver(outputLog);
```

Later in the program, we decide we no longer want to print log messages to the Output panel, so we delete the variable outputLog. But even with outputLog deleted, messages continue to appear in the Output panel! Why? Because the *Logger* class stores a reference to *OutputPanelView* instance, and deleting the variable outputLog does not remove that reference. We must unregister the reference with *Logger* before deleting outputLog, as follows:

```
log.removeObserver(outputLog);
delete outputLog;
```

To formalize the process of unregistering an observer from its subject, we implement a *destroy( )* method on the observer class. For example, the following code shows how we implement *destroy( )* for *OutputPanelView*:

```
public function destroy ():Void {
  log.removeObserver(this);
}
```

The *destroy( )* method's main responsibility is to unregister the observer from its subject; however, *destroy( )* can also be used to generally clean up assets used by the observer class. For example, the following code shows the implementation of *destroy( )* we use for the *TextFieldView* class. Here, the *destroy( )* method performs unregistration and also removes the log text field from the screen:

```
public function destroy ():Void {
  log.removeObserver(this);
  out.removeTextField( );
}
```

A similar warning applies to the subject class in the Observer pattern. A subject must be deleted only after ensuring that its observers no longer refer to it. As we've seen in this chapter, each observer class stores a reference to its subject. For example, both the *OutputPanelView* and the *TextFieldView* classes store a reference to the *Logger* class in the property log. If we want to delete a *Logger* instance, we first have to remove the reference to it in both *OutputPanelView* and *TextFieldView* (assuming instances of those classes are observing the *Logger* instance). This requires *OutputPanelView* and *TextFieldView* to implement a new method, *releaseSubject( )*, which sets the property log to null:

```
public function releaseSubject():Void {
  log = null;
}
```

The *Observable* class then implements a corresponding method, *destroy( )*, which calls *releaseSubject( )* on its observers prior to deletion:

```
public function destroy ( ):Void {
  var observersSnapshot:Array = observers.slice(0);

  // Invoke releaseSubject( ) on all observers.
  for (var i:Number = observersSnapshot.length-1; i >= 0; i--) {
    observersSnapshot[i].releaseSubject( );
  }
}
```

We can then safely delete a subject by first invoking *destroy( )* on it:

```
theLog.destroy( );
delete theLog;
```

Note that we don't have to manually remove the subject's list of observers; deleting the subject also deletes its observers array automatically.

In situations in which the observers do not need arbitrary access to the subject they are observing, the observers need not store a reference to the subject at all. Instead, a reference to the subject can be passed to the observers via the *update( )* method (either as a separate argument or as a property of the info object). The observers can then access the subject at update time via the parameters passed to the *update( )* method and then immediately discard the reference to the subject. This prevents dangling references to deleted subjects in observers.

Beyond Observer

In the real world, many classes broadcast events. For example, many of Flash's built-in classes (*Mouse*, *Selection*, *XML*, *Stage*, *TextField*, and so on) broadcast events. The Observer pattern provides one generic blueprint for event broadcasting, but in practice most classes that broadcast events use a more complex event architecture structure. You can use Observer to good effect in simple, self-contained cases such as our application log or, say, to update objects when a stock ticker changes. You might also use Observer when implementing internal state management for a user interface component such as a slider bar or, as we'll see in Chapter 18, a clock. But for more complex event handling, you'll very likely want a more flexible, feature-rich event architecture such as the delegation event model discussed in Chapter 19. See that chapter for a detailed comparison between the Observer pattern and the delegation event model.

That completes our study of the Observer pattern. In the next chapter, we'll return to our *Logger* class to study its instance-creation process.

The Singleton Design Pattern

[The Singleton pattern's purpose is to] ensure a class has only one instance, and provide a global point of access to it.

—from *Design Patterns: Elements of Reusable Object-Oriented Software* (the so-called *GoF* book discussed in Chapter 15)

Sometimes an application needs only a single instance of a particular class and should not create more than that one instance. For example, an order form might need one *FormProcessor*. A game might need one *LevelManager*. A text editor might need one *GUIBuilder*. Or a chat might need one *SocketManager*. In each of those applications, creating more than one instance of the *FormProcessor*, *LevelManager*, *GUIBuilder*, or *SocketManager* classes could cause problems. For example, having multiple *SocketManager*s might lead to multiple open socket connections, which would waste resources and potentially disrupt communications. To prevent an application from creating more than one instance of a class and to give various parts of the application access to that one instance we use the Singleton pattern.

Implementing Singleton in ActionScript 2.0

The Singleton pattern has a relatively simple implementation, particularly considering its general usefulness. Most of the pattern implementation resides in a class we'll refer to as the *Singleton* class (i.e., the class being limited to a single instance). The remainder of the implementation involves the external access to the lone *Singleton* instance.

The *Singleton* class has four main facets (shown in a generic implementation in Example 17-1):

- A class property, _instance, that stores the lone instance of the class
- A private constructor, *Singleton ( )*, that creates the lone instance

- An instance-retrieval method, *getInstance( )*, that returns a reference to the lone instance
- Typical instance methods, such as *doSomething( )*, and properties (none shown in Example 17-1) that implement the behavior of the class

Example 17-1 shows the source code for a generic *Singleton* class. Read it over, then we'll consider each of its features in turn.

Example 17-1. The Singleton class

```
class Singleton {
  private static var _instance:Singleton = null;

  private function Singleton () {
  }

  public static function getInstance():Singleton {
    if (Singleton._instance == null) {
      Singleton._instance = new Singleton();
    }
    return Singleton._instance;
  }

  public function doSomething ():Void {
    trace("doSomething() was called");
  }
}
```

To store the lone instance of the *Singleton* class, we create a *private*, *static* property, _instance, which we initialize to null. The _instance property must be *private* so that it cannot be accessed outside of the *Singleton* class or its subclasses. And it must be *static* so that it can be accessed by the class method *getInstance( )*.

To retrieve the lone instance of the *Singleton* class, other classes use the class method *Singleton.getInstance( )*. When called, the *getInstance( )* method checks _instance to see whether an instance of the *Singleton* class exists already. If the _instance property is null, then no instance has yet been created, so the *getInstance( )* method creates one and returns it. If, on the other hand, an instance already exists, the *getInstance( )* method simply returns the existing instance without creating a new one.

In our *Singleton* class example, the constructor is empty. Despite that fact, the constructor definition is extremely important because it specifies that the constructor is *private* (i.e., cannot be accessed outside the *Singleton* class or its subclasses). Omitting the constructor altogether causes Flash to implicitly create a public constructor, which would allow multiple *Singleton* instances to be created. When a class's constructor is private, you can use the *new* operator to create an instance of the class from within the class or its subclasses; however, external attempts to create an instance of the class using the *new* operator cause an error. For example, when the following code appears outside the Singleton class (and outside any of its subclasses):

```
var s:Singleton = new Singleton();
```

it causes this error:

```
The member is private and cannot be accessed.
```

Thus, any class that wishes to create a *Singleton* instance is forced to use the *Singleton.getInstance( )* method, which guarantees that only one *Singleton* instance is ever created.

Notice that because the *Singleton* instance is stored in a property of the same class, it is automatically accessible to any other class that can access *Singleton*. (In theory, we could have made our instance accessible to the application by defining it as a global variable, but that global variable's name might conflict with another global variable.)

Here's how we'd use our *Singleton* class, somewhere in our application:

```
var s:Singleton = Singleton.getInstance( );
s.doSomething( );
```

In some cases, it's not necessary to store the *Singleton* instance in a variable or property. When we have only temporary need of the *Singleton* instance, we could reduce the previous code to:

```
Singleton.getInstance().doSomething( );
```

Now that we've seen how the Singleton pattern is implemented in general, let's look at a specific *Singleton* implementation example—the *Logger* class from Chapter 16.

The Singleton Pattern in the Logger Class

In Chapter 16, we created an application log using the Observer pattern. That application required a single, central logging facility, which we implemented in the *Logger* class. Now let's return to the *Logger* class and look at the specific code in it that implements the Singleton pattern. By using Singleton, the *Logger* class guarantees that the application using it creates only a single log, even if there are multiple observers displaying the log output in various ways.

Example 17-2 shows the relevant section of the *Logger* class, omitting code that is not directly part of the Singleton pattern. (For the full *Logger* class listing, see Example 16-6 in Chapter 16.)

Example 17-2. The Singleton pattern in the Logger class

```
class logger.Logger extends Observable {
  private static var log:Logger = null;

  private function Logger () {
    setLevel(Logger.INFO);
  }

  public static function getLog():Logger {
    if (log == null) {
      log = new Logger();
```

Example 17-2. The Singleton pattern in the Logger class (continued)

```
    }
    return log;
  }
}
```

Let's compare the *Logger* class with the generic Singleton implementation from Example 17-1. The *Logger*'s log property stores the single *Logger* instance and is equivalent to Example 17-1's _instance property. As in Example 17-1, the *Logger* class constructor is *private*, but this time the constructor actually performs a useful action (setting the log level). Finally, the *Logger.getLog( )* method provides access to the *Logger* instance in log, exactly as *getInstance( )* does in Example 17-1.

To send a testing debug message to the log, we use:

```
import logger.Logger;
var log:Logger = Logger.getLog( );
log.debug("Testing...testing...");
```

Or, more succinctly:

```
import logger.Logger;
Logger.getLog( ).debug("Testing...testing...");
```

No matter where the preceding code appears in our application, the log message is guaranteed to be routed through the same, lone *Logger* instance. Hence, we can be sure that all log messages in the application are processed in the same way (i.e., are handled by the same *Logger* observers).

Singleton Versus Class Methods and Class Properties

You might wonder why we wouldn't implement the *Logger* class's functionality entirely in class methods and class properties. That is, why not design *Logger* to be used directly through class methods instead of through a solitary instance? The Singleton pattern is used in favor of a class that simply groups class methods and class properties together for two key reasons.

First, flexibility. Once established, the Singleton pattern is very easy to change from a "sole-instance" implementation to a multiple-instance implementation. For example, if down the road we decide to use separate *Logger* instances to log different aspects of our application, we can easily update the *Logger* class to allow the creation of multiple instances. In contrast, moving functionality from class methods and class properties to individual instances would be much more work.

Second, inheritance. As we've just seen with the *Logger* class, the Singleton pattern works freely with inheritance. For example, our *Logger* class (a Singleton) extends *Observable* without issue. In contrast, a class used solely through its class members cannot meaningfully extend a class used through its instances. If *Logger* were used entirely through class methods, it could not inherit the functionality of the *Observable* class because *Observable* must be instantiated to work. The inverse is also true: a class comprised solely of class members is difficult to extend (sometimes prohibitively so) because of the scope issues described in Chapter 6.

The Singleton pattern gives us the benefits of centralized access to some aspect of a program without the limitations of class methods and class properties.

A Warning Against Singletons as Globals

Beware that the Singleton pattern can turn an object-oriented program into a series of haphazard global functions and variables, negating most of the benefits of OOP. You should use the Singleton pattern when you need to limit the number of instances created by a class, not just when you want to access something globally. If you are tempted to use a Singleton simply as a repository for global variables, you should stop, rethink the problem, and try to fit the services you're implementing into some logically encapsulated structure with the rest of your program. When code is spread loosely around in global variables and functions, it's much harder to maintain, extend, and understand than when it's neatly packed into self-contained units. For further reading on this topic, see:

Global Variables Are Bad, from the Portland Pattern Repository's Wiki
    http://c2.com/cgi/wiki?GlobalVariablesAreBad

Use Your Singletons Wisely, by J. B. Rainsberger
    http://www-106.ibm.com/developerworks/webservices/library/co-single.html

On to User Interfaces

Now that we've studied two relatively simple design patterns (Observer and Singleton), we're ready to move on to a more complex pattern, Model-View-Controller (which, itself, is actually a group of patterns). Model-View-Controller is of particular interest to Flash developers because it suggests how to structure the classes that create and manage a user interface.

The Model-View-Controller Design Pattern

In the MVC paradigm the user input, the modeling of the external world, and the visual feedback to the user are explicitly separated and handled by three types of object, each specialized for its task.

———from *Applications Programming in Smalltalk-80(TM): How to use Model-View-Controller (MVC)*, by Steve Burbeck, available at: *http://st-www.cs.uiuc.edu/users/ smarch/st-docs/mvc.html*

The Model-View-Controller (MVC) design pattern separates user interface code into three distinct classes:

Model
> Stores the data and application logic for the interface

View
> Renders the interface (usually to the screen)

Controller
> Responds to user input by modifying the model

For example, in a toggle button, the model would store the state of the button (on or off), the view would draw the button on screen, and the controller would set the state of the button in the model (to on or off) when the button is clicked. But an interface need not be visual. In some cases, the view might play a sound or, as a non-ActionScript example, the view might make a video game controller vibrate.

MVC originated in the Smalltalk language and has been used widely for years in many different incarnations. Though the basic principles of the pattern are easy to understand, its details are complex enough to foster an enormous amount of debate and contradictory implementations. In this chapter, we'll study a relatively traditional implementation of the pattern, bearing in mind that there is no single "right" way to implement MVC.

The basic principle of MVC is the separation of responsibilities. In an MVC application, the model class concerns itself only with the application's state and logic. It has no interest in how that state is represented to the user or how user input is received. By contrast, the view class concerns itself only with creating the user interface in response to generic updates it receives from the model. It doesn't care about application logic nor about the processing of input; it just makes sure that the interface reflects the current state of the model. Finally, the controller class is occupied solely with translating user input (provided by the view) into updates that it passes to the model. It doesn't care how the input is received or what the model does with those updates.

Separating the code that governs a user interface into the model, view, and controller classes yields the following benefits:

- Allows multiple representations (views) of the same information (model)
- Allows user interfaces (views) to be easily added, removed, or changed, at both compile time and runtime
- Allows response to user input (controller) to be easily changed, at both compile time and runtime
- Promotes reuse (e.g., one view might be used with different models)
- Allows multiple developers to simultaneously update the interface, logic, or input of an application without affecting other source code
- Helps developers focus on a single aspect of the application at a time

Despite those benefits, not all user interfaces are best implemented with MVC. For example, in Chapter 12 we built a simple currency converter application using a single class, *CurrencyConverter*. The conceptual responsibilities of the model, view, and controller were still manifest in that application, but they were encompassed by a single class. The currency converter application was so simple that the cost of implementing formal MVC outweighed the benefits.

 Design patterns offer more benefits to larger projects than to smaller ones, but the concepts in a pattern like MVC can still inform the design of simple applications like the currency converter.

The MVC pattern can be applied to a single user interface element (like a button), to a group of user interface elements (like a control panel), or to an entire application. This chapter uses MVC to create a clock that combines three user interface elements: a digital display, an analog display, and a toolbar for starting, stopping, and resetting the clock.

The General Architecture of MVC

Before we study our specific clock example, let's explore the general structure of the MVC design pattern.

Communication in MVC

Although the model, view, and controller classes in MVC are intentionally segregated, they must communicate regularly. The model must send notifications of state changes to the view. The view must register the controller to receive user interface events and, possibly, request data from the model. The controller must update the model and, possibly, update the view in response to user input.

To facilitate this communication, each object in MVC must store a reference to the other object(s) with which it interacts. Specifically, the model instance needs a reference to the view instances that render it, while the view and controller each needs a reference to the model and reciprocal references to each other. Figure 18-1 shows how the objects in MVC reference one another. The diamond shape in the figure represents a composition relationship, in which one object stores an instance of another.

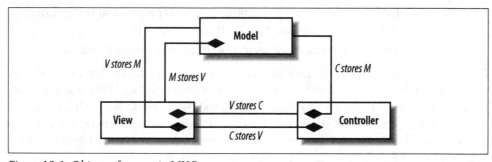

Figure 18-1. Object references in MVC

Communication proceeds in a single direction (as shown in Figure 18-2) through the object references shown in Figure 18-1, as follows:

1. The view receives user input and passes it to the controller.
2. The controller receives user input from the view.
3. The controller modifies the model in response to user input (or, in some cases, the controller modifies the view directly and does not update the model at all).
4. The model changes based on an update from the controller.
5. The model notifies the view of the change.
6. The view updates the user interface, (i.e., presents the data in some way, perhaps by redrawing a visual component or by playing a sound).

Figure 18-2 depicts the MVC communication cycle. The starting point for the cycle is typically the receipt of user input. However, another part of the program could also start the cycle by modifying the model directly (perhaps in response to new data arriving from a server).

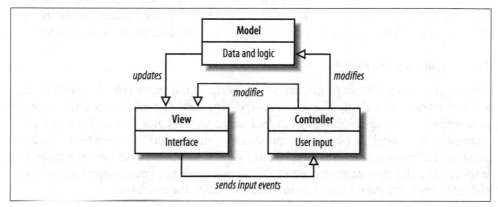

Figure 18-2. The MVC communication cycle

Note that Figure 18-2 shows the simplest case of MVC, with a single model, a single view, and a single controller. However, it's not uncommon for an application to provide two or more views for a single model. For example, in our MVC clock implementation, we'll use one model to manage the time, but we'll have three views—one to represent the clock in digital format, one to represent the clock in analog format, and one to display buttons that start, stop, and reset the clock. You may wonder how these buttons qualify as a view of the clock given that they do not represent the time. Views do not necessarily have to represent the entire model and need not even represent the same information (the way the analog and digital views do). As we'll see later, the buttons in our clock do not indicate the current time; instead, the button states reflect whether the clock is currently running, which is simply another aspect of the model.

While an MVC implementation may contain multiple views per model, every view has exactly one controller instance and vice versa. Each view's controller is dedicated to that view's sole service.

> The view and the controller form an indivisible pair. MVC requires that each view has a controller (even if it is just the placeholder value, null) and each controller has a view.

Some views do not allow user input. For example, a view might be a simple graph that cannot be edited. When a view accepts no user input, it does not need a controller to translate user input into model updates. Hence, views that do not allow user input have either null in place of a controller or a controller that does nothing in response to user input.

Class Responsibilities in MVC

As we've already learned, responsibilities in an MVC implementation are divided among the model, view, and controller. By the end of this chapter, you should be mumbling the MVC mantra to yourself at the grocery store—"the model manages data and logic, the view creates the interface, and the controller processes user input." Those general responsibilities break down into many specific tasks, covered next.

Responsibilities of the model

The model stores data in properties and provides application-specific methods that set and retrieve that data. The data-management methods are not generic; they are customized per application and must be known to the controller and the view. For example, the model in our clock application defines methods specific to a clock, such as *setTime( )* and *stop( )*. Controllers in MVC are custom written to manipulate a specific model; for example, a controller in our clock application must know about the *setTime( )* and *stop( )* methods in order to modify the model.

The model's data can be changed externally by an outside class or internally by its own logic. For example, the time of our clock's model might be reset by the controller in response to user input, or it might be updated because, internally, it detects the passing of a second. (It might be monitoring the operating system's built-in clock or, as in our upcoming example, tracking the passing milliseconds itself.)

The model must also provide a way for views to register and unregister themselves, and it must manage a list of registered views. Whenever the model determines that its state has changed meaningfully, it must notify all registered views.

Finally, the model implements the logic of the MVC triad. For example, the model in our clock application implements a *tick( )* method that runs once per second, updating the time. The model might also provide data validation services and other application-specific utilities, such as loading the current time from a server-side application.

Responsibilities of the view

The view must create the user interface and keep it up-to-date. The view listens for state changes in the model; when the model changes, the view updates the interface to reflect the change. For example, in our clock application, when the time changes, the model notifies the three registered views. In response, the analog clock view positions the hands of a traditional clock, while the digital clock view sets the numbers in its digital display. The third, "buttons" view (*ClockTools*) changes the appearance of the buttons to indicate whether the clock is running or has been stopped.

Each view must forward all input events to its controller. It should not process any inputs itself. For example, our analog clock view might allow the user to set the time by dragging the hands of the clock. When the hands are dragged, the view merely forwards the input information to the controller, and the controller decides what to do.

Depending on the specific implementation, the view might query the model for its state in order to determine what changed when an update is received. The view never changes the model but can retrieve information from it. For example, our clock's model might tell its views that the time changed, and the views, in response, might invoke *getTime( )* on the model to determine the new time. Alternatively (and more commonly), the model might send the new time to the views directly in an info object at update time. You should recognize these two options as the push and pull models discussed in Chapter 16 for the Observer pattern. See that chapter for details.

You may be wondering whether the MVC design pattern as presented makes sense architecturally. It may seem odd that, if the user changes something in the view, instead of responding immediately, the view passes the input to the controller, which passes it to the model, which notifies the view of the change, and finally the view requests the details of the change from the model and renders them for the user. Wouldn't it be easier to skip all the detailed communication and just have the view update itself whenever the user makes a change? In some sense that may be easier, and in a simple application it might be appropriate. As an application becomes more complex, however, the MVC pattern offers significant benefits. For example, in the case of our clock implementation, in which there are multiple views, the architecture allows changes in one view to be detected by and reflected in all views. Therefore, you don't have to write code to make the analog clock view notify or update the digital clock view (or vice versa). Furthermore, the logic is centralized in the model, which prevents code duplication and allows us to add or remove views at runtime with minimal effort. For example, you could add a view that displays time in 24-hour (a.k.a. military) format instead of 12-hour (a.m./p.m.) format. Complex applications demand this type of flexibility, and MVC provides the structure to implement it.

Responsibilities of the controller

The controller listens for notifications from the view based on user input and translates that input into changes in the model. In some cases, the controller makes logical decisions about the input before making a corresponding change to the model. For example, our clock application has a Reset button that resets the time to midnight. When the button is clicked, the clock controller translates the input conceptually from "Reset button clicked" to the command "Set model's time to 00:00:00."

In some special cases, the controller might also instruct the view to make changes to the user interface by calling methods on the view. The changes are sent directly to the view only when they are purely cosmetic and have no effect on the model. For example, if a user interface has buttons to alphabetize a list of names in ascending and descending order, the controller may legitimately call the appropriate sort methods on the view when those buttons are clicked. Calling the sort methods is legitimate because it does not change the underlying data stored in the model (i.e., the list of names); only the presentation of that data changes.

What Creates the MVC Classes?

Through all this talk of the model, view, and controller, we still haven't seen how to make instances of those classes. That's partly because there's no single, definitive way to instantiate the classes in MVC. In our clock example, we'll create a single class, *Clock*, which instantiates the model, its views, and their controllers. Our *Clock* class sets up the MVC classes as follows:

- Create the model
- Create views
- Register views with the model

Notice that the controllers are missing from the preceding list because they are created by their respective views.

Hence, our *Clock* class forms a wrapper around the MVC triad, packaging it into a tidy, self-contained unit. However, that's definitely not the only approach possible. At least one Java implementation suggests that the controller class should create the model, and possibly the view, in its constructor!

In our example code, we'll follow the traditional (Smalltalk) implementation of MVC, in which the model and view(s) are created by some containing class, and then the model and controller are registered for each view. When the controller for a view is not specified, the view class creates a default controller for itself automatically.

A Generalized MVC Implementation

Now that we've learned the theoretical structure of MVC, let's explore a real-world MVC implementation. To get started, we'll create a basic MVC framework that can be reused across many projects. We'll store our core structure in a package called *mvc*. The classes and interfaces in the *mvc* package are:

View
    An interface all views must implement

Controller
    An interface all controllers must implement

AbstractView
    A generic implementation of the *View* interface

AbstractController
    A generic implementation of the *Controller* interface

You'll notice that the model class is conspicuously absent from our *mvc* package. That's because the model-view relationship in MVC is essentially the same as the Observer pattern we studied in Chapter 16. Hence, we'll use the core code from our existing Observer implementation rather than rewriting similar code for our MVC implementation. The model class in our MVC architecture will be a subclass of *Observable*, which resides in the package *util*. The Observer pattern provides the basic services for the model-view relationship—views register with the model using *addObserver( )* and *removeObserver( )*, and the model sends updates via the standardized method *update( )*, implemented by each view. Hence, in order to register with a model, every view class must implement the *util.Observer* interface in addition to implementing the *mvc.View* interface.

By definition, to use the *Observable* class as the basis of our model class, the model class must extend *Observable*. If we want our model class to inherit from a different class, we'd have to use the composition-based implementation of the Observer pattern, from Example 16-7.

The View Implementation

Example 18-1 shows the *View* interface in our *mvc* package. The *View* interface defines the basic services every *View* class must offer, namely:

- Methods to set and retrieve the controller reference
- Methods to set and retrieve the model reference
- A method that returns the default controller for the view

Notice that references to the controller in Example 18-1 must be instances of a class that implements the *Controller* interface. References to the model must be instances of a class that extends *Observable* (or, in the composition-based version of the Observer pattern, that implements the *Observable* interface).

Example 18-1. The View interface

```
import util.*;
import mvc.*;

/**
 * Specifies the minimum services that the view
 * of a Model-View-Controller triad must provide.
 */
interface mvc.View {
  /**
   * Sets the model this view is observing.
   */
  public function setModel (m:Observable):Void;

  /**
   * Returns the model this view is observing.
   */
  public function getModel ( ):Observable;

  /**
   * Sets the controller for this view.
   */
```

Example 18-1. The View interface (continued)

```
  public function setController (c:Controller):Void;

  /**
   * Returns this view's controller.
   */
  public function getController ():Controller;

  /**
   * Returns the default controller for this view.
   */
  public function defaultController (model:Observable):Controller;
}
```

To make the *View* interface easy to implement, we provide *AbstractView*, a class that implements the basic services defined by the *View* interface (namely, managing interactions with the controller and model). The *AbstractView* class also implements the *Observer* interface. To create a real view class in an MVC application, we need simply extend *AbstractView* and add code to build and update a user interface. The core MVC grunt work in any real view class is taken care of by *AbstractView*.

Example 18-2 shows the code for the *AbstractView* class. Typically, subclasses of *AbstractView* will create a user interface at construction time and modify that user interface from the *update()* method.

Notice that an instance of the model class must be passed to *AbstractView*'s constructor. Without that reference, the view cannot query the model for its state. An instance of the controller class can also be passed to the view constructor. However, if you don't supply a controller instance, the *AbstractView* class uses *defaultController()* to create the controller automatically the first time it is requested (i.e., the first time *getController()* is invoked). Each *AbstractView* subclass is expected to override *defaultController()*, providing a reference to its own default controller.

Example 18-2. The AbstractView class

```
import util.*;
import mvc.*;

/**
 * Provides basic services for the view of a Model-View-Controller triad.
 */
class mvc.AbstractView implements Observer, View {
  private var model:Observable;      // A reference to the model.
  private var controller:Controller;  // A reference to the controller.

  public function AbstractView (m:Observable, c:Controller) {
    // Set the model.
    setModel(m);

    // If a controller was supplied, use it. Otherwise let the first
    // call to getController() create the default controller.
```

Example 18-2. The AbstractView class (continued)

```
    if (c !== undefined) {
      setController(c);
    }
  }

  /**
   * Returns the default controller for this view.
   */
  public function defaultController (model:Observable):Controller {
    return null;
  }

  /**
   * Sets the model this view is observing.
   */
  public function setModel (m:Observable):Void {
    model = m;
  }

  /**
   * Returns the model this view is observing.
   */
  public function getModel ():Observable {
    return model;
  }

  /**
   * Sets the controller for this view.
   */
  public function setController (c:Controller):Void {
    controller = c;
    // Tell the controller this object is its view.
    getController().setView(this);
  }

  /**
   * Returns this view's controller.
   */
  public function getController ():Controller {
    // If a controller hasn't been defined yet...
    if (controller === undefined) {
      // ...make one. Note that defaultController() is normally overridden
      // by AbstractView's subclass so that it returns the appropriate
      // controller for the view.
      setController(defaultController(getModel()));
    }
    return controller;
  }

  /**
   * A do-nothing implementation of the Observer interface's
   * update() method. Subclasses of AbstractView provide a concrete
```

Example 18-2. The AbstractView class (continued)

```
 * implementation for this method.
 */
 public function update(o:Observable, infoObj:Object):Void {
 }
}
```

Now that we have our view defined, let's define the controller.

The Controller Implementation

Example 18-3 shows the *Controller* interface in our *mvc* package. The *Controller* interface defines the basic services every *Controller* class must offer, namely:

- Methods to set and retrieve the view reference
- Methods to set and retrieve the model reference

In the *Controller* interface, references to the view must be instances of any class that implements the *View* interface. References to the model must be instances of any class that extends *Observable*.

Example 18-3. The Controller interface

```
import util.*;
import mvc.*;

/**
 * Specifies the minimum services that the controller of
 * a Model-View-Controller triad must provide.
 */
interface mvc.Controller {
  /**
   * Sets the model for this controller.
   */
  public function setModel (m:Observable):Void;

  /**
   * Returns the model for this controller.
   */
  public function getModel ():Observable;

  /**
   * Sets the view this controller is servicing.
   */
  public function setView (v:View):Void;

  /**
   * Returns this controller's view.
   */
  public function getView ():View;
}
```

To make controller classes easy to create, we provide *AbstractController*, a class that implements the basic services defined by the *Controller* interface to manage interactions with the view and model. To create a real controller class in an MVC application, we need to extend *AbstractController* and add input-handling code. The core MVC grunt work in any real controller is taken care of by *AbstractController*.

Example 18-4 shows the code for the *AbstractController* class. Typically, subclasses of *AbstractController* implement input event-handling methods that translate user input received from the view into model modification notices sent to the model.

Example 18-4. The AbstractController class

```
import util.*;
import mvc.*;

/**
 * Provides basic services for the controller of
 * a Model-View-Controller triad.
 */
class mvc.AbstractController implements Controller {
  private var model:Observable;    // A reference to the model.
  private var view:View;           // A reference to the view.

  /**
   * Constructor
   *
   * @param   m   The model this controller's view is observing.
   */
  public function AbstractController (m:Observable) {
    // Set the model.
    setModel(m);
  }

  /**
   * Sets the model for this controller.
   */
  public function setModel (m:Observable):Void {
    model = m;
  }

  /**
   * Returns the model for this controller.
   */
  public function getModel ():Observable {
    return model;
  }

  /**
   * Sets the view that this controller is servicing.
   */
  public function setView (v:View):Void {
    view = v;
  }
```

Example 18-4. The AbstractController class (continued)

```
  /**
   * Returns this controller's view.
   */
  public function getView ( ):View {
    return view;
  }
}
```

An MVC Clock

With our core MVC structure in place, we can create a real-world MVC application—a clock with analog and digital displays. The default MVC framework and source files for the clock are available at *http://moock.org/eas2/examples*.

Figure 18-3 shows the graphical user interface for the clock. Notice that in addition to the analog and digital displays, the clock includes buttons to start, stop, and reset the clock's time.

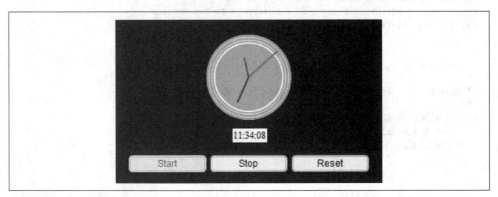

Figure 18-3. The Clock graphical user interface

Our clock application includes seven classes, as follows:

Clock
> The main application class, which creates the MVC clock

ClockModel
> The model class, which tracks the clock's time

ClockUpdate
> An info object class that stores update data sent by *ClockModel* to all views

ClockAnalogView
> A view class that presents the analog clock display

ClockDigitalView
> A view class that presents the digital clock display

ClockTools
A view class that presents the Start, Stop, and Reset buttons
ClockController
A controller class that handles button input

Figure 18-4 shows how our application's classes integrate into the core MVC structure we built earlier in this chapter.

In Figure 18-4, note that *ClockUpdate* instances are info objects sent by the *ClockModel* to its views (*ClockAnalogView*, *ClockDigitalView*, and *ClockTools*) at update time. The *View* interface specifies operations for registering the model (*ClockModel*) and controller (*ClockController*), while the *Observer* interface specifies the operation used by the model (*ClockModel*) to send updates to its views (again, *ClockAnalogView*, *ClockDigitalView*, and *ClockTools*). The *ClockAnalogView* and *ClockDigitalView* classes use null for their controller while the *ClockTools* class uses a *ClockController* instance for its controller. Finally, Figure 18-4 does not show the *Clock* class, which creates the clock using the *ClockModel* class and its views.

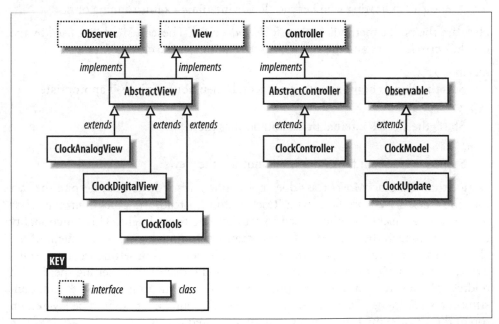

Figure 18-4. Clock application architecture

We've already looked at the supporting classes and interfaces in the *mvc* and *util* packages. The classes specific to the clock application are all stored in the package *mvcclock*. Let's look at them one at a time.

The ClockModel Class

The *ClockModel* class extends *Observable*. It provides methods for setting the time and runs an internal ticker that updates the time once per second. Whenever the time changes, the *ClockModel* class uses *notifyObservers( )* to broadcast the change to all registered views.

Here are the properties defined by the *ClockModel* class. Remember that the model class's properties represent its current state.

hour
> The current hour, from 0 (midnight) to 23 (11 p.m.)

minute
> The current minute, from 0 to 59

second
> The current second, from 0 to 59

isRunning
> A Boolean indicating whether the clock's internal ticker is running or not

Here are the public methods of the *ClockModel* class. These methods are used by the *ClockController* class and the *Clock* class to manipulate the clock's data:

setTime( )
> Sets the clock's hour, minute, and second, then notifies views if appropriate

start( )
> Starts the clock's internal ticker and notifies the views

stop( )
> Stops the clock's internal ticker and notifies the views

Notice that the *ClockModel* class does not define a *reset( )* method, despite the fact that the clock's user interface has a Reset button. Instead, the *ClockController* class defines a *resetClock( )* method, used to set the time to midnight. This functionality does not belong in the *ClockModel* class because it is not a logical requirement of the clock's basic operation. That is, the clock provides a means of setting the time, starting it, and stopping it—other classes can and should decide that "setting the time to midnight" constitutes a so-called "reset," while setting the time to, say, 6 p.m. constitutes a *setToDinnerTime( )* operation. These value judgments should be layered on top of the clock's core functionality, not incorporated into it.

Here are the private methods of the *ClockModel* class. These methods are used internally by the *ClockModel* class to update the time and to validate data:

isValidHour( )
> Checks whether a number is a valid hour (i.e., an integer from 0 to 23)

isValidMinute( )
> Checks whether a number is a valid minute (i.e., is an integer from 0 to 59)

---

isValidSecond( )

    Checks whether a number is a valid second (i.e., is an integer from 0 to 59)

tick( )

    Increments the second property by 1

The range-checking functions are properly implemented as private methods of the model class so that all updates from all controllers use the same data validation. Thus, we minimize duplicate code, standardize the notion of valid clock data, and simplify maintenance.

Note that although the clock class itself determines that, say, 25 is not a legal hour, it is up to the controller classes to format the time into 24-hour format before sending change requests to the model. Each controller must take responsibility for formatting the data according to the requirements of the model. For example, if a view accepts text input, the controller is responsible for converting the text string into a number before sending the time update to the model.

To register views and notify them when the time changes, the *ClockModel* class relies on its superclass's methods: *addObserver( )*, *removeObserver( )*, and *notifyObservers( )*.

Example 18-5 shows the code for the *ClockModel* class. In particular, note the *setTime( )* method's use of *setChanged( )* to indicate whether an update should be broadcast when the time is set. If *setTime( )* is called but the new time specified is the same as the existing time, then no update is sent. An update is sent only if the time has actually changed. (In this case, the time must change by at least one second. Implementing a version that issues updates more frequently, such as every tenth of a second, is left as an exercise for the reader. Naturally, you wouldn't bother unless you were implementing a digital display that displayed the fractional seconds or some other view that relied on the greater resolution.) Updates take the form of a *ClockUpdate* object passed to each view's *update( )* method. The *setChanged( )* method is inherited from the *Observable* class, discussed in Chapter 16.

Example 18-5. The ClockModel class

```
import util.Observable;
import mvcclock.*;

/**
 * Represents the data of a clock (i.e., the model of the
 * Model-View-Controller triad).
 */
class mvcclock.ClockModel extends Observable {
  // The current hour.
  private var hour:Number;
  // The current minute.
  private var minute:Number;
  // The current second.
  private var second:Number;
  // The interval identifier for the interval that
```

Example 18-5. The ClockModel class (continued)

```
// calls tick( ) once per second.
private var tickInterval:Number;
// Indicates whether the clock is running or not.
private var isRunning:Boolean;

/**
 * Constructor
 */
public function ClockModel ( ) {
  // By default, set the clock time to the current system time.
  var now:Date = new Date( );
  setTime(now.getHours(), now.getMinutes(), now.getSeconds( ));
}

/**
 * Starts the clock ticking.
 */
public function start ( ):Void {
  if (!isRunning) {
    isRunning = true;
    tickInterval = setInterval(this, "tick", 1000);

    var infoObj:ClockUpdate = new ClockUpdate(hour, minute,
                                         second, isRunning);
    setChanged( );
    notifyObservers(infoObj);
  }
}

/**
 * Stops the clock ticking.
 */
public function stop ( ):Void {
  if (isRunning) {
    isRunning = false;
    clearInterval(tickInterval);

    var infoObj:ClockUpdate = new ClockUpdate(hour, minute,
                                         second, isRunning);
    setChanged( );
    notifyObservers(infoObj);
  }
}

/**
 * Sets the current time (i.e., the hour, minute, and second properties).
 * Notifies observers (views) of any change in time.
 *
 * @param   h   The new hour.
 * @param   m   The new minute.
 * @param   s   The new second.
 */
```

Example 18-5. The ClockModel class (continued)

```
public function setTime (h:Number, m:Number, s:Number):Void {
  if (h != null && h != hour && isValidHour(h)) {
    hour = h;
    setChanged( );
  }

  if (m != null && m != minute && isValidMinute(m)) {
    minute = m;
    setChanged( );
  }

  if (s != null && s != second && isValidSecond(s)) {
    second = s;
    setChanged( );
  }

  // If the model has changed, notify views.
  if (hasChanged( )) {
    var infoObj:ClockUpdate = new ClockUpdate(hour, minute,
                                              second, isRunning);
    // Push the changed data to the views.
    notifyObservers(infoObj);
  }
}

/**
 * Checks to see if a number is a valid hour
 * (i.e., an integer in the range 0 to 23).
 *
 * @param    h    The hour to check.
 */
private function isValidHour (h:Number):Boolean {
  return (Math.floor(h) == h && h >= 0 && h <= 23);
}

/**
 * Checks to see if a number is a valid minute
 * (i.e., an integer in the range 0 to 59).
 *
 * @param    m    The minute to check.
 */
private function isValidMinute (m:Number):Boolean {
  return (Math.floor(m) == m && m >= 0 && m <= 59);
}

/**
 * Checks to see if a number is a valid second
 * (i.e., an integer in the range 0 to 59).
 *
 * @param    s    The second to check.
 */
private function isValidSecond (s:Number):Boolean {
  return (Math.floor(s) == s && s >= 0 && s <= 59);
```

Example 18-5. The ClockModel class (continued)

```
}

/**
 * Makes time pass by adding a second to the current time.
 */
private function tick ():Void {
  // Get the current time.
  var h:Number = hour;
  var m:Number = minute;
  var s:Number = second;

  // Increment the current second, adjusting
  // the minute and hour if necessary.
  s += 1;
  if (s > 59) {
    s = 0;
    m += 1;
    if (m > 59) {
      m = 0;
      h += 1;
      if (h > 23) {
        h = 0;
      }
    }
  }

  // Set the new time.
  setTime(h, m, s);
}
}
```

Notice that our *ClockModel* class defines methods for setting the current time but does not define any methods for retrieving it. That's because the clock's time is pushed to all views via a *ClockUpdate* object; views do not need to query the state of the model in our example. However, we could just as sensibly have required views to retrieve the new time from the model. Typically, the push system (in this case, sending the time) is used if pulling information from the model (in this case, retrieving the time) is too processor intensive. That limitation doesn't apply here, so both the push and pull systems are appropriate.

The ClockUpdate Class

The *ClockUpdate* class is a simple data holder used to transfer the state of the *ClockModel* to views when the time changes or the clock is started or stopped. It defines four properties—hour, minute, second, and isRunning—which are accessed directly. To avoid distracting from the issues at hand, we won't implement accessor methods such as *getMinute( )* for these properties. The *ClockUpdate* class is simply a data vessel, used like an associative array or a hash, so the direct property access is arguably appropriate.

Example 18-6 shows the code for the *ClockUpdate* class.

Example 18-6. The ClockUpdate class

```
/**
 * An info object sent by the ClockModel class to
 * its views when an update occurs. Indicates the
 * time and whether or not the clock is running.
 */
class mvcclock.ClockUpdate {
  public var hour:Number;
  public var minute:Number;
  public var second:Number;
  public var isRunning:Boolean;

  public function ClockUpdate (h:Number, m:Number, s:Number, r:Boolean) {
    hour = h;
    minute = m;
    second = s;
    isRunning = r;
  }
}
```

The ClockAnalogView and ClockDigitalView Classes

The *ClockAnalogView* and *ClockDigitalView* classes extend *AbstractView*, which implements the *Observer* and *View* interfaces. They are display-only views; that is, the user interface they create has no inputs and therefore needs no controller. Accordingly, neither *ClockAnalogView* nor *ClockDigitalView* overrides the *AbstractView.defaultController( )* method. Both classes simply use null as their controller, as returned by the *AbstractView.defaultController( )* method. If you were to make the clock hands on the analog display draggable, you would implement an appropriate controller class to notify the model of the specified input obtained via the view's GUI. Likewise, if the hours, minutes, and seconds of the digital clock were editable, you would implement an appropriate controller for that view as well.

The *ClockAnalogView* class is responsible for rendering the clock as a traditional circle with moving hands. The *ClockDigitalView* class is responsible for rendering the clock as a numeric display. Both classes have the same basic structure, which includes the following two public methods:

makeClock( )
    Creates the visual display of the clock at construction time
update( )
    Handles updates from the *ClockModel* by setting the appropriate time on screen

In addition to those two methods, the *ClockDigitalView* class defines two private utility methods—*formatTime12( )* and *formatTime24( )*—for adjusting the format of the time to 12-hour or 24-hour display (the analog view always displays 12-hour time). Each view is responsible for translating raw information provided by the model into some particular interface representation. Hence, the time-formatting methods belong in the *ClockDigitalView* class, not in a hypothetical controller for that class (whose job would be to process input) nor in the model class (whose job is to manage raw data, not to transform that data for the needs of some particular rendering). That said, formatting time is a particularly common operation that might be required throughout an application. We might, therefore, have alternatively chosen to implement the time-formatting methods in a general utility class, say *DateFormat*. Indeed, date- and time-formatting functionality is built directly into many languages, but is not built into ActionScript.

The *ClockDigitalView* class creates its user interface entirely via code in the *makeClock( )* method (there are no author-time movie clips). The *ClockAnalogView* class, by contrast, creates its user interface by attaching an instance of a movie clip symbol (*ClockAnalogViewSymbol*) from the Flash document's Library. We won't cover the creation of that symbol in detail here except to say that it contains a circle shape and three movie clips that represent the hands of the clock: hourHand_mc, minuteHand_mc, and secondHand_mc. To see the *ClockAnalogViewSymbol*, download the sample files from *http://moock.org/eas2/examples*. The analog clock is an excellent demonstration of Flash's unique ability to combine hand-drawn graphics with OOP code. Readers of *ActionScript for Flash MX: The Definitive Guide* may recognize some of the code in Example 18-7 from the analog clock developed in Example 13-7 of that book, which is posted at *http://moock.org/asdg/codedepot*. Recipe 10.8 in the *ActionScript Cookbook*, by Joey Lott (O'Reilly), also implements an analog clock created entirely on-the-fly.

Example 18-7 shows the code for the *ClockAnalogView* class, which implements the analog display of the time.

Example 18-7. The ClockAnalogView class

```
import util.*;
import mvcclock.*;
import mvc.*;

/**
 * An analog clock view for the ClockModel class. This view has no user
 * inputs, so no controller is required.
 */
class mvcclock.ClockAnalogView extends AbstractView {
  // Contains an instance of ClockAnalogViewSymbol, which
  // depicts the clock on screen.
  private var clock_mc:MovieClip;

  /**
   * Constructor
   */
  public function ClockAnalogView (m:Observable, c:Controller,
```

Example 18-7. The ClockAnalogView class (continued)

```
                            target:MovieClip, depth:Number,
                            x:Number, y:Number) {
  // Invoke superconstructor, which sets up MVC relationships.
  // This view has no user inputs, so no controller is required.
  super(m, c);

  // Create UI.
  makeClock(target, depth, x, y);
}

/**
 * Creates the movie clip instance that will display the
 * time in analog format.
 *
 * @param   target   The clip in which to create the movie clip.
 * @param   depth    The depth at which to create the movie clip.
 * @param   x     The movie clip's horizontal position in target.
 * @param   y     The movie clip's vertical position in target.
 */
public function makeClock (target:MovieClip, depth:Number,
                           x:Number, y:Number):Void {
  clock_mc = target.attachMovie("ClockAnalogViewSymbol",
             "analogClock_mc", depth);
  clock_mc._x = x;
  clock_mc._y = y;
}


/**
 * Updates the state of the on-screen analog clock.
 * Invoked automatically by ClockModel.notifyObservers().
 *
 * @param   o    The ClockModel object that is broadcasting an update.
 * @param   infoObj  A ClockUpdate instance describing the changes that
 *                   have occurred in ClockModel.
 */
public function update (o:Observable, infoObj:Object):Void {
  // Cast the generic infoObj to the ClockUpdate datatype.
  var info:ClockUpdate = ClockUpdate(infoObj);

  // Display the new time.
  var dayPercent:Number = (info.hour>12 ? info.hour-12 : info.hour) / 12;
  var hourPercent:Number = info.minute/60;
  var minutePercent:Number = info.second/60;
  clock_mc.hourHand_mc._rotation = 360 * dayPercent
                                   + hourPercent * (360 / 12);
  clock_mc.minuteHand_mc._rotation = 360 * hourPercent;
  clock_mc.secondHand_mc._rotation = 360 * minutePercent;

  // Dim the display if the clock isn't running.
  if (info.isRunning) {
    clock_mc._alpha = 100;
  } else {
```

Example 18-7. The ClockAnalogView class (continued)

```
    clock_mc._alpha = 50;
  }
 }
}
```

Example 18-8 shows the code for the *ClockDigitalView* class, which implements the digital display of the time. In *ClockDigitalView*, for the sake of contrast, we create the clock interface entirely in code. Specifically, *ClockDigitalView.makeClock( )* creates a text field in which we display the time. If desired, we could also have made the earlier *ClockAnalogView* entirely in code instead of using the authoring tool approach, in which we create the clock as a movie clip (*ClockAnalogViewSymbol*). Both approaches are valid Flash development practices. You might choose to draw your interface manually in the Flash authoring tool to save time (if the code equivalent would be complex) or to allow the interface to be redesigned by a nonprogrammer.

Example 18-8. The ClockDigitalView class

```
import util.*;
import mvcclock.*;
import mvc.*;

/**
 * A digital clock view for ClockModel. This view has no user
 * inputs, so no controller is required.
 */
class mvcclock.ClockDigitalView extends AbstractView {
  // The hour format.
  private var hourFormat:Number = 24;
  // The separator character in the clock display.
  private var separator:String = ":";
  // The text field in which to display the clock, created by makeClock( ).
  private var clock_txt:TextField;

  /**
   * Constructor
   */
  public function ClockDigitalView (m:Observable,  c:Controller,
                                    hf:Number, sep:String, target:MovieClip,
                                    depth:Number, x:Number, y:Number) {
    // Invoke superconstructor, which sets up MVC relationships.
    super(m, c);

    // Make sure the hour format specified is legal. If it is, use it.
    if (hf == 12) {
      hourFormat = 12;
    }

    // If a separator was provided, use it.
    if (sep != undefined) {
      separator = sep;
    }
```

Example 18-8. The ClockDigitalView class (continued)

```
      // Create UI.
      makeClock(target, depth, x, y);
  }

  /**
   * Creates the onscreen text field that will display the
   * time in digital format.
   *
   * @param    target   The clip in which to create the text field.
   * @param    depth    The depth at which to create the text field.
   * @param    x    The text field's horizontal position in target.
   * @param    y    The text field's vertical position in target.
   */
  public function makeClock (target:MovieClip, depth:Number,
                             x:Number, y:Number):Void {
    // Make the text field.
    target.createTextField("clock_txt", depth, x, y, 0, 0);
    // Store a reference to the text field.
    clock_txt = target.clock_txt;
    // Assign text field characteristics.
    clock_txt.autoSize = "left";
    clock_txt.border = true;
    clock_txt.background = true;
  }

  /**
   * Updates the state of the on-screen digital clock.
   * Invoked automatically by ClockModel.
   *
   * @param    o    The ClockModel object that is broadcasting an update.
   * @param    infoObj   A ClockUpdate instance describing the changes that
   *                     have occurred in ClockModel.
   */
  public function update (o:Observable, infoObj:Object):Void {
    // Cast the generic infoObj to the ClockUpdate datatype.
    var info:ClockUpdate = ClockUpdate(infoObj);

    // Create a string representing the time in the appropriate format.
    var timeString:String = (hourFormat == 12)
            ?
            formatTime12(info.hour, info.minute, info.second)
            :
            formatTime24(info.hour, info.minute, info.second);

    // Display the new time in the clock text field.
    clock_txt.text = timeString;

    // Dim the color of the display if the clock isn't running.
    if (info.isRunning) {
      clock_txt.textColor = 0x000000;
```

Example 18-8. The ClockDigitalView class (continued)

```
  } else {
    clock_txt.textColor = 0x666666;
  }
}

/**
 * Returns a formatted 24-hour time string.
 *
 * @param    h    The hour, from 0 to 23.
 * @param    m    The minute, from 0 to 59.
 * @param    s    The second, from 0 to 59.
 */
private function formatTime24 (h:Number, m:Number, s:Number):String {
  var timeString:String = "";

  // Format hours...
  if (h < 10) {
    timeString += "0";
  }
  timeString += h + separator;

  // Format minutes...
  if (m < 10) {
    timeString += "0";
  }
  timeString += m + separator;

  // Format seconds...
  if (s < 10) {
    timeString += "0";
  }
  timeString += String(s);

  return timeString;
}

/**
 * Returns a formatted 12-hour time string (not including AM or PM).
 *
 * @param    h    The hour, from 0 to 23.
 * @param    m    The minute, from 0 to 59.
 * @param    s    The second, from 0 to 59.
 */
private function formatTime12 (h:Number, m:Number, s:Number):String {
  var timeString:String = "";

  // Format hours...
  if (h == 0) {
    timeString += "12" + separator;
  } else if (h > 12) {
    timeString += (h - 12) + separator;
  } else {
```

Example 18-8. The ClockDigitalView class (continued)

```
      timeString += h + separator;
  }

  // Format minutes...
  if (m < 10) {
    timeString += "0";
  }
  timeString += m + separator;

  // Format seconds...
  if (s < 10) {
    timeString += "0";
  }
  timeString += String(s);

  return timeString;
  }
}
```

We've now seen two view classes that do not accept user input and therefore have no controller. Next, we'll consider a view class, *ClockTools*, which accepts user input and shows how to process that input with a controller.

The ClockTools Class

Like the *ClockAnalogView* and *ClockDigitalView* classes, the *ClockTools* class is a view for *ClockModel*, so it extends *AbstractView*. The *ClockTools* class creates the Start, Stop, and Reset buttons below the analog and digital clock display, as shown in Figure 18-3. A *.fla* file that uses *ClockTools* must contain the Flash MX 2004 Button component in its Library and have it exported for ActionScript (see Chapter 12 for information on components).

Unlike *ClockAnalogView* and *ClockDigitalView*, the *ClockTools* view includes a functional controller to process user input. The general structure of *ClockTools* follows the structure of *ClockAnalogView* and *ClockDigitalView—ClockTools* has a *makeTools( )* method that creates the user interface and an *update( )* method that makes changes to that interface based on *ClockModel* updates. However, the *makeTools( )* method does more than just render the user interface; it also creates the all-important connection from that interface to the controller (and, indeed, creates the controller itself).

Because *ClockTools* has a functional controller, it also overrides the *AbstractView. defaultController( )* method. The *ClockTools.defaultController( )* method returns an instance of *ClockController*, the default controller for the *ClockTools* view.

Example 18-9 shows the code for the *ClockTools* class. Read it through, then we'll study the important *makeTools( )* and *update( )* methods in detail.

Example 18-9. The ClockTools class

```
import util.*;
import mvcclock.*;
import mvc.*;
import mx.controls.Button;

/**
 * Creates a user interface that can control a ClockModel.
 */
class mvcclock.ClockTools extends AbstractView {
  private var startBtn:Button;
  private var stopBtn:Button;
  private var resetBtn:Button;

  /**
   * Constructor
   */
  public function ClockTools (m:Observable, c:Controller,
                            target:MovieClip, depth:Number,
                            x:Number, y:Number) {
    // Invoke superconstructor, which sets up MVC relationships.
    super(m, c);

    // Create UI.
    makeTools(target, depth, x, y);
  }

  /**
   * Returns the default controller for this view.
   */
  public function defaultController (model:Observable):Controller {
    return new ClockController(model);
  }

  /**
   * Creates a movie clip instance to hold the Start, Stop,
   * and Reset buttons and also creates those buttons.
   *
   * @param    target   The clip in which to create the tools_mc clip.
   * @param    depth    The depth at which to create the tools_mc clip.
   * @param    x    The tools clip's horizontal position in target.
   * @param    y    The tools clip's vertical position in target.
   */
  public function makeTools (target:MovieClip, depth:Number,
                            x:Number, y:Number):Void {
    // Create a container movie clip.
    var tools_mc:MovieClip = target.createEmptyMovieClip("tools", depth);
    tools_mc._x = x;
    tools_mc._y = y;

    // Create UI buttons in the container clip.
    startBtn = tools_mc.createClassObject(Button, "start", 0);
    startBtn.label = "Start";
```

Example 18-9. The ClockTools class (continued)

```
    startBtn.enabled = false;
    startBtn.addEventListener("click", getController( ));

    stopBtn = tools_mc.createClassObject(Button, "stop", 1);
    stopBtn.label = "Stop";
    stopBtn.enabled = false;
    stopBtn.move(startBtn.width + 5, startBtn.y);
    stopBtn.addEventListener("click", getController( ));

    resetBtn = tools_mc.createClassObject(Button, "reset", 2);
    resetBtn.label = "Reset";
    resetBtn.move(stopBtn.x + stopBtn.width + 5, startBtn.y);
    resetBtn.addEventListener("click", getController( ));
  }

  /**
   * Updates the state of the user interface.
   * Invoked automatically by ClockModel.
   *
   * @param   o    The ClockModel object that is broadcasting an update.
   * @param   infoObj   A ClockUpdate instance describing the changes that
   *                    have occurred in ClockModel.
   */
  public function update (o:Observable, infoObj:Object):Void {
    // Cast the generic infoObj to the ClockUpdate datatype.
    var info:ClockUpdate = ClockUpdate(infoObj);

    // Enable the Start button if the clock is stopped, or
    // enable the Stop button if the clock is running.
    if (info.isRunning) {
      stopBtn.enabled = true;
      startBtn.enabled = false;
    } else {
      stopBtn.enabled = false;
      startBtn.enabled = true;
    }
  }
}
```

The *ClockTools.makeTools( )* method creates three Button component instances: one that starts the clock, one that stops it, and one that resets it. The *click* event of each Button instance is handled by the *ClockTools* controller, *ClockController*. Let's examine one button, Start, to see how it is wired to the *ClockController*.

First, we create an empty container movie clip, tools_mc, in which to store all three buttons. The tools_mc clip is attached to target, a movie clip instance specified when the *ClockTools* view is instantiated.

```
    var tools_mc:MovieClip = target.createEmptyMovieClip("tools", depth);
```

Next, we create the Start button instance inside tools_mc, using *createClassObject( )* (which we studied in Chapter 12). We store the Start button instance in the property startBtn so that we can access it later when it's time to update the interface. The instance name of the button, "start", will be used later in the *ClockController* class to uniquely identify the button:

```
startBtn = tools_mc.createClassObject(Button, "start", 0);
```

Now we add the text on the button (i.e., its *label*) and disable the button. By default, the clock will be running, so the Start button should be disabled at the outset:

```
startBtn.label = "Start";
startBtn.enabled = false;
```

Finally, we make the crucial connection between the view and the controller by specifying the controller as the listener object for the Start button's *click* event. This implies (indeed, demands) that the controller defines a method named *click( )* which will be invoked when the Start button is clicked.

```
startBtn.addEventListener("click", getController());
```

Notice that the *makeTools( )* method does not refer to the *ClockController* class directly. It retrieves the controller instance via *getController( )*. If a controller already exists, it is returned; if not, an instance of the default controller is created and returned. By specifying and accessing the controller indirectly via *getController( )*, we maintain the loose coupling between the view and the controller, giving us the flexibility to change the controller at runtime (or to rewrite a new implementation in the future with little disturbance of existing code). For example, at any point in the program, we could use setController(*SomeOtherController*) to completely replace the current controller, which in turn would change the interface's response to user input. If, on the other hand, we had hardcoded the controller reference, as follows:

```
startBtn.addEventListener("click", new ClockController());
```

we would not be able to change the controller at runtime.

The *ClockTools.update( )* method, unlike *ClockAnalogView.update( )* and *ClockDigitalView.update( )*, does not simply display the current time. Instead, it disables the Start or Stop button depending on whether the clock is running. If the clock is running, only the Stop and Reset buttons are enabled. If the clock is stopped, only the Start and Reset buttons are enabled:

```
if (info.isRunning) {
  stopBtn.enabled = true;
  startBtn.enabled = false;
} else {
  stopBtn.enabled = false;
  startBtn.enabled = true;
}
```

It's a common misconception that a view is always a literal representation of the model's data. While *ClockAnalogView* and *ClockDigitalView* create literal representations of the *ClockModel*, the *ClockTools* view does not. In general, then, a view depicts a user interface whose display depends on the state of the model but isn't necessarily a direct visualization of the model. Here, the button states depend on whether the clock is running, not on the current time. That is, this view depicts the model's isRunning property, which is equally as valid as the other views depicting the hour, minute, and second properties.

Now let's move on to the *ClockController* class, which handles input for *ClockTools*. Again, the *ClockAnalogView* and *ClockDigitalView* views use the default controller created by *AbstractView*, but our *ClockTools* class creates its own controller.

The ClockController Class

The *ClockController* class extends *AbstractController*. It provides event handling for the user interface created by the *ClockTools* view.

To change the state of the *ClockModel*, the *ClockController* class defines the following methods:

> *startClock( )*
> *stopClock( )*
> *resetClock( )*
> *setTime( )*
> *setHour( )*
> *setMinute( )*
> *setSecond( )*

Notice that many of the preceding methods are wrappers over methods in the *ClockModel* class. Some of them act as direct pass-through methods (e.g., *startClock( )* and *stopClock( )*), whereas others add some convenience functionality (e.g., the ability to independently set a single aspect of the time, such as the hour, minute, or second).

But the real duty of the *ClockController* class is fulfilled by its *click( )* method, which handles events from the buttons created by the *ClockTools* class. Before we look at the full class listing for *ClockController*, let's take a detailed look at the *click( )* method:

```
public function click (e:Object):Void {
  switch (e.target._name) {
    case "start":
      startClock( );
      break;
    case "stop":
      stopClock( );
      break;
    case "reset":
      resetClock( );
      break;
  }
}
```

The *click( )* method is set up like any component-event-handling method. It accepts a single argument, e, which contains details about the event as well as a very important reference back to the component that generated the event. In the case of the *click( )* method, the property e.target gives us a reference back to the Button component that generated the *click( )* event. The property e.target._name tells us the instance name of that button—either "start", "stop", or "reset". (Recall that we set each button's instance name when we created it in the *ClockTools.makeTools( )* method.) Depending on that instance name, we invoke the appropriate method, either *startClock( )*, *stopClock( )* or *resetClock( )*.

Note that the *click( )* handler is implemented in the controller rather than the view. Some alternative MVC variations implement event handlers in the view and then pass input to the controller, but in our implementation, we emphasize the separation between the view's "interface rendering" role and the controller's "input processing" role. Notice also that a single view and a single controller implement the event handling for all three buttons. That is, the *click( )* handler distinguishes between buttons using the event object, e, passed to it. In this case, it would be overkill to implement separate views and controllers for each of the three buttons, but it wouldn't be insane to do so. MVC can be as nested and granular as the program needs it to be. For example, in a ComboBox component (i.e., a pull-down menu), each individual item in the ComboBox might implement MVC while the entire ComboBox also implements MVC.

Finally, notice that the view is a listener in the model's list of registered listeners (subscribing to the *update* event) and the controller is a listener in the view's list of registered listeners (subscribing to the *click* event). In our example, the model doesn't subscribe to any events. Its methods are invoked manually by *ClockController* and internally by *setInterval( )*.

As an example, here's the event sequence for the Reset button:

1. User clicks on the Reset button, generating a *click* event.
2. *ClockController.click( )* receives and interprets the event, eventually calling *ClockModel.setTime( )* with zeros for the hour, minute, and second.
3. *ClockModel* receives the command from the controller and changes the time accordingly.
4. The *ClockModel.notifyObservers( )* method broadcasts an *update* event (containing a *ClockUpdate* info object) to all registered views.
5. All three views—*ClockAnalogView*, *ClockDigitalView*, and *ClockTools*—receive the *update* event and refresh their user interface elements accordingly.
   a. *ClockAnalogView* resets both hands to 12 o'clock.
   b. *ClockDigitalView* resets the digital display to "00:00:00".
   c. *ClockTools* makes sure all its buttons are correct (in this case, the Stop and Start button states would depend on whether the clock was running when it was reset).

The sequence would be similar for the Start and Stop buttons, except that the views would update differently according to the *ClockUpdate* object representing the model's state. Notice that none of the views updates its display until notified by the model. But it all happens so quickly that the analog and digital displays appear to reset instantly when the Reset button is clicked.

Now let's look at the *click( )* method in the context of the complete *ClockController* class, shown in Example 18-10.

Example 18-10. The ClockController class

```
import mvcclock.ClockModel;
import mvc.*;
import util.*;

/**
 * Makes changes to ClockModel's data based on user input.
 * Provides general services that any view might find handy.
 */
class mvcclock.ClockController extends AbstractController {

  /**
   * Constructor
   *
   * @param   cm   The model to modify.
   */
  public function ClockController (cm:Observable) {
    super(cm);
  }

  /**
   * Starts the clock ticking.
   */
  public function startClock ():Void {
    ClockModel(getModel()).start();
  }

  /**
   * Stops the clock ticking.
   */
  public function stopClock ():Void {
    ClockModel(getModel()).stop();
  }

  /**
   * Resets the clock's time to 12 midnight (0 hours).
   */
  public function resetClock ():Void {
    setTime(0, 0, 0);
  }

  /**
   * Changes the clock's time.
```

Example 18-10. The ClockController class (continued)

```
 *
 * @param    h    The new hour, from 0 to 23.
 * @param    m    The new minute, from o to 59.
 * @param    s    The new second, from 0 to 59.
 */
public function setTime (h:Number, m:Number, s:Number):Void {
  ClockModel(getModel( )).setTime(h, m, s);
}

// As these next three methods show, the controller can provide
// convenience methods to change data in the model.

/**
 * Sets just the clock's hour.
 *
 * @param    h    The new hour.
 */
public function setHour (h:Number):Void {
  ClockModel(getModel( )).setTime(h, null, null);
}

/**
 * Sets just the clock's minute.
 *
 * @param    m    The new minute.
 */
public function setMinute (m:Number):Void {
  ClockModel(getModel( )).setTime(null, m, null);
}

/**
 * Sets just the clock's second.
 *
 * @param    s    The new second.
 */
public function setSecond (s:Number):Void {
  ClockModel(getModel( )).setTime(null, null, s);
}

/**
 * Handles events from the Start, Stop, and Reset buttons
 * of the ClockTools view.
 */
public function click (e:Object):Void {
  switch (e.target._name) {
    case "start":
      startClock( );
      break;
    case "stop":
      stopClock( );
      break;
    case "reset":
```

Example 18-10. The ClockController class (continued)

```
        resetClock( );
        break;
    }
  }
}
```

The *ClockController* class is fairly generic. It could, in theory, be extended to provide event handling for other clock-related classes as well. For example, if the *ClockAnalogView* class allowed its hands to be dragged, methods could be added to *ClockController* to handle the clock-hand drag events. In that case, each view would have its own instance of *ClockController*. Alternatively, separate controller classes could be created to handle the drag events. Or, the *ClockTools* class and the *ClockAnalogView* class could use different controllers that inherit from a single *ClockController* super-class, which would define a set of methods common to both classes.

Putting It All Together: The Clock Class

The pieces of our MVC clock are now complete. All that's left to do is assemble them into a functional application. The final assembly of our application occurs in the *Clock* class, our primary class that performs the following tasks:

- Creates the *ClockModel* instance
- Creates the clock views (*ClockAnalogView*, *ClockDigitalView*, *ClockTools*)
- Registers the clock views to receive updates from the *ClockModel*
- Optionally sets the clock's time
- Starts the clock ticking

All the preceding tasks occur in the *Clock* class's constructor function. However, because the clock needs to run as a standalone application, the *Clock* class also defines a *main( )* method that starts the clock application. For information on creating and using a *main( )* method as an application entry point, see Chapter 11.

Example 18-11 shows the code for the *Clock* class.

Example 18-11. The Clock class

```
import mvcclock.*

/**
 * An example Model-View-Controller (MVC) clock application.
 */
class mvcclock.Clock {
  // The clock data (i.e., the model).
  private var clock_model:ClockModel;

  // Two different displays of the clock's data (i.e., views).
  private var clock_analogview:ClockAnalogView;
```

Example 18-11. The Clock class (continued)

```
  private var clock_digitalview:ClockDigitalView;

  // A toolbar for controlling the clock (also a view).
  private var clock_tools:ClockTools;

  /**
   * Clock constructor
   *
   * @param   target   The movie clip to which the digital and
   *                    analog views will be attached.
   * @param   h   The initial hour, 0 to 23, at which to set the clock.
   * @param   m   The initial minute, 0 to 59, at which to set the clock.
   * @param   s   The initial second, 0 to 59, at which to set the clock.
   */
  public function Clock (target:MovieClip, h:Number, m:Number, s:Number) {
    // Create the data model.
    clock_model = new ClockModel();

    // Create the digital clock view, which uses a default controller.
    clock_digitalview = new ClockDigitalView(clock_model, undefined,
                                   24, ":", target, 0, 253, 265);
    clock_model.addObserver(clock_digitalview);

    // Create the analog clock view, which uses a default controller.
    clock_analogview = new ClockAnalogView(clock_model, undefined,
                                   target, 1, 275, 200);
    clock_model.addObserver(clock_analogview);

    // Create the clock tools view, which creates its own controller.
    clock_tools = new ClockTools(clock_model, undefined, target,
                          2, 120, 300);
    clock_model.addObserver(clock_tools);

    // Set the time.
    clock_model.setTime(h, m, s);

    // Start the clock ticking.
    clock_model.start();
  }

  /**
   * System entry point. Starts the clock application running.
   */
  public static function main (target:MovieClip, h:Number,
                            m:Number, s:Number) {
    var clock:Clock = new Clock(target, h, m, s);
  }
}
```

To start our clock application in motion, we invoke *Clock.main( )* on a frame of a *.fla* file (presumably the frame following any preloader). For example:

```
// Import the package containing the Clock class.
import mvcclock.Clock;
// Attach the clock to someClip. The time defaults to the system time.
Clock.main(someClip);
```

As mentioned earlier, the *.fla* file's Library must contain a movie clip symbol named *ClockAnalogViewSymbol*, and it must contain the Button UI component. (To add the Button component to the Library, drag an instance of it from the Components panel to the Stage, and then delete the instance from the Stage.)

In the preceding example, if we had chosen to set the time of the clock to 3:40:25 a.m., we'd have used:

```
Clock.main(someClip, 3, 40, 25);
```

In either case, a clip referenced by the variable or instance name "someClip" must exist on the timeline.

To create a clock set to 3:40:25 p.m. and attach it to the current timeline, we can use:

```
Clock.main(this, 15, 40, 25);
```

Alternatively, we could create an instance of the *Clock* class directly (skipping the *main( )* method) like this:

```
var c:Clock = new Clock(this, 15, 40, 25);
```

We'd need to use that approach when creating a clock as part of a larger application. The *main( )* method approach simply lets us use the clock as a standalone application.

Further Exploration

Because our clock is an MVC application, it is incredibly flexible. New interfaces, input responses, and functionality can easily be added to the clock. If you're keen to experiment with MVC in ActionScript, try the following exercises:

- Create a view that can display a different time zone.
- Create a new view that displays a creative representation of the hours, minutes, and seconds of the clock—perhaps use shapes on screen to represent the time: circles for the hours, triangles for the minutes, and squares for the seconds.
- Create a new view that makes a ticking sound every second and, at the top of every hour, gongs to indicate the current time.
- Add components to the *ClockTools* view that let the user set the current time.

- Change the *ClockModel* so that it updates by polling the computer's system time instead of by counting milliseconds with *setInterval( )*. Hint: you'll need the *Date( )* class.
- Change the clock so it can display hundredths of a second, like a stopwatch.
- Let the user set the time by dragging the analog hands or editing the digital display.

If you'd like to continue reading about the MVC design pattern, see the following online articles:

Steve Burbeck's canonical Applications Programming in Smalltalk-80(TM): How to use Model-View-Controller (MVC)
    http://st-www.cs.uiuc.edu/users/smarch/st-docs/mvc.html

John Hunt's You've got the model-view-controller (excellent article with complete example source in Java)
    http://www.jaydeetechnology.co.uk/planetjava/tutorials/swing/Model-View-Controller.PDF

Richard Baldwin's Implementing The Model-View-Controller Paradigm using Observer and Observable
    http://www.dickbaldwin.com/java/Java200.htm

Sun's Java BluePrints: Model-View-Controller
    http://java.sun.com/blueprints/patterns/MVC-detailed.html

In the next (and final) chapter, we'll continue our coverage of interclass update mechanisms by studying the delegation event model.

The Delegation Event Model

> [In the delegation event model,] an event is propagated from a "Source" object to a "Listener" object by invoking a method on the listener and passing in the instance of the event subclass which defines the event type generated.
>
> ——from Sun's *Java AWT: Delegation Event Model* (*http://java.sun.com/j2se/1.4.1/docs/guide/awt/1.3/designspec/events.html*)

In Chapter 16, we used the Observer pattern to structure a group of objects so that when one changes state, the others are automatically notified. As we learned in Chapter 16, the Observer pattern is intentionally generic, emphasizing loose coupling between the object that changes (the *subject*) and the objects being notified of the change (the *observers*). In this chapter, we'll apply the concepts of the Observer pattern to a more specific situation: implementing events for a class. Our event implementation will follow Java's *delegation event model*, a general design for event broadcasting.

The delegation event model framework we'll develop in this chapter can be used to implement event broadcasting for any class. For example, a *Chat* class might use it to implement *onChatMessage( )* or *onUserNameChanged( )* events. An interactive *WorldMap* class might likewise implement *onCountryClick( )*, *onCountryRollover( )*, and *onCountryRollout( )* events. Or a *ChessGame* class might implement *onCheckMate( )*, *onPieceTaken( )*, and *onMove( )* events. In each case, the delegation event model provides a basic structure for the event source (*Chat*, *WorldMap*, and *ChessGame*) and the event listeners (objects that register to receive events from an event source).

As usual, the code discussed in this chapter is available at *http://moock.org/eas2/examples*.

Structure and Participants

The delegation event model has three main participants:

Event source
  An object that notifies other objects of some specific occurrence (i.e., some event)
Event listeners
  The objects that are notified by the event source when an event occurs
Event object
  An object that describes the nature of the event

An *event* is any predetermined occurrence that the *event source* considers significant enough to tell other objects about—anything from the clicking of the mouse to the ending of a game to the submission of an order form. To notify an *event listener* of an event, the event source invokes an agreed-upon method on it. The *event object* is passed to the agreed-upon method by the event source, giving the event listener access to information about the event.

In a minimal delegation event model implementation, the event source, event listeners, and event object participants break down into the classes and interfaces described in the following sections.

The Event Source

The event source includes the following classes:

Event source class
  The class whose instances broadcast events to event listeners (the class can have any name)
EventListenerList
  A utility class used by the event source to manage event listeners

The *EventListenerList* class resides in the *event* package, but the event source class can reside in any package. The event source class has the following responsibilities:

• Register and unregister event listener objects

• Broadcast events to event listeners (by invoking agreed-upon methods on them)

• Pass an event description (in the form of an event object) to event listeners at event time

For example, earlier we mentioned a hypothetical *Chat* class with two events, *onChatMessage( )* and *onUserNameChanged( )*. As an event source, instances of the *Chat* class would manage objects interested in receiving those events. At event time, a *Chat* class instance would invoke either *onChatMessage( )* or *onUserNameChanged( )* (as appropriate) on all registered listeners. In the former case, the *Chat* instance might send the chat message text using the messageText property of the event object. In the latter, it would send, perhaps, the old username and the new username using the oldUserName and newUserName properties of the event object.

The Event Object

The event object includes the following classes:

EventObject
A foundation class that provides basic services for all event objects

A subclass of EventObject
Describes a specific event

The *EventObject* class resides in the *event* package (along with the *EventListenerList* class), but the *EventObject* subclass can reside in any package. The event object describes an event. That is, the object stores information about the event in its properties, which it makes accessible either directly or via accessor methods. The event object also provides event listeners with a reference to the event source.

In our *Chat* class example, the *EventObject* subclass might be called *ChatEvent*. It would define the following properties: messageText, messageSender, oldUserName, and newUserName.

The Event Listener

The event listener includes (at least) two interfaces and one class:

EventListener
A marker interface that all event listener interfaces must extend (a marker interface is simply an empty interface that does not define any methods and is used for the sake of semantics only; see Chapter 8)

EventListener subinterface
A subinterface that catalogs the event source's events

The event listener class
A class that implements the *EventListener* subinterface

The *EventListener* interface resides in the *event* package (along with the *EventObject* and *EventListenerList* classes), but the *EventListener* subinterface and class can reside in any package.

The event listener class defines the methods that are invoked by the event source when events occur. The *EventListener* subinterface specifies the set of event methods that must be implemented by every event listener class. At event time, the event source invokes one of those methods on each listener object; each listener then has the opportunity to respond in some application-specific way.

In our ongoing hypothetical *Chat* example, the *EventListener* interface might look like this:

```
import event.EventListener;

interface ChatListener extends EventListener {
```

```
    public function onChatMessage (e:ChatEvent):Void;
    public function onUserNameChanged (e:ChatEvent):Void;
}
```

Notice that the event object passed to each event method is a *ChatEvent* instance.

One of the event listener classes in our *Chat* example might be *ChatGUI*, a class responsible for displaying the chat interface on screen. The *ChatGUI* class would implement both *onChatMessage( )* and *onUserNameChanged( )*. Here's a skeletal example of what the *ChatGUI* class might look like:

```
class ChatGUI implements ChatListener {
    // Properties and methods used to render the interface not shown.
    // Constructor also not shown.
    public function onChatMessage (e:ChatEvent):Void {
        displayMessage(e.messageSender, e.messageText);
    }

    public function onUserNameChanged (e:ChatEvent):Void {
        updateUserList(e.oldUserName, e.newUserName);
    }
}
```

Are Observer and Delegation Event Model Equivalent?

Structurally, the delegation event model has much in common with the Observer pattern. The Observer pattern's two basic participants—the subject class and the observer classes—correspond to the delegation event model's event source class, which broadcasts events, and event listener classes, which receive event notifications. But are the two designs the same?

Not exactly. The delegation event model is designed to broadcast specific, known events rather than generic updates. In Observer, the subject broadcasts updates to observers by invoking a generic *update( )* method. But in the delegation event model, the event source broadcasts a specific type of event by invoking a custom method on its listeners. Listeners receiving the event must implement an interface that defines the method invoked by the event source. Furthermore, in the delegation event model, any class can broadcast events; the event source need not be a subclass of some base event-broadcasting class, such as *Observable*. The info object (which is optional in the Observer pattern) is formally required by the delegation event model, and its identity is known to both the event source and the event listeners. Finally, in Observer, the subject should broadcast an update only in response to a state change. Events, by contrast, can be broadcast for any reason deemed appropriate by the event source.

Generally speaking, the Observer pattern works well as an internal update mechanism within a discrete system, such as maintaining the state of a single toggle button or a tile on a chessboard. In the preceding chapter, we saw Observer used effectively within the MVC pattern. Observer worked perfectly as a means of maintaining the internal state of our clock.

By contrast, the delegation event model is typically appropriate when the granularity of events matters (i.e., when events should correspond to individual methods rather than a single *update( )* method). Event granularity is desirable for event sources that have a wide variety of unknown event listeners, as is often the case for publicly distributed components. For example, a SliderBar component might use the delegation event model to broadcast *onChanged( )*, *onDragged( )*, and *onReleased( )* events to the world, but internally, it might maintain its own visual appearance using Observer as part of MVC.

The Flow of Logic

Figure 19-1 shows the structure and logic flow of the delegation event model in diagrammatic form. The steps shown in the figure are as follows:

1. An instance of the event source (*EventSourceClass*) is created.
2. The event source creates and stores an instance of *EventListenerList*.
3. An instance of the event listener (*EventListenerClass*) is created and registers to receive events from the event source.
4. The event listener is stored by the event source's *EventListenerList*.
5. An event occurs and is broadcast by the event source as follows:
   a. The event source creates an event object (*EventObject*) instance describing the event.
   b. The event source invokes the appropriate method (*onEventName( )*) on all registered event listeners, passing along the event object that describes the event.
6. Each event listener processes the event in its own way, using the event object to determine how to respond to the event.

In Figure 19-1, italic type indicates the part of a name that is customized per implementation. The names used reflect the formal convention for the delegation event model. The parameter, 1, passed to *addEventTypeListener( )* and *removeEventTypeListener( )* in Figure 19-1 is the listener to be added or removed.

Later, in Figure 19-2, we'll compare the abstract roles shown in Figure 19-1 with real examples.

Core Implementation

To provide a foundation for delegation event model implementations, we'll create the *event* package, which contains two classes and an interface, as we saw earlier:

EventListenerList
    A utility class used by the event source to manage event listeners

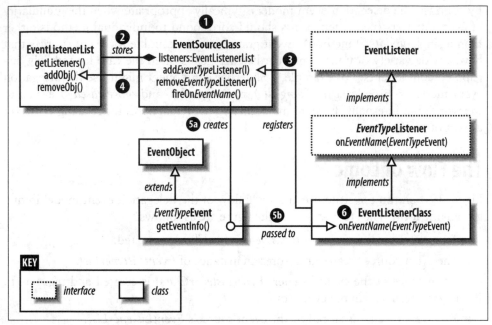

Figure 19-1. Logic flow in the delegation event model

EventObject
    A foundation class that provides basic services for all event objects

EventListener
    A marker interface that all event listener interfaces must extend

Let's see how those items look in real code.

The EventListenerList Class

The *EventListenerList* class stores *EventListener* objects in an array and defines three methods to manage those objects:

addObj( )
    Places a new object in the array (if it isn't already in the array)

removeObj( )
    Removes an object from the array

getListeners( )
    Returns a copy of the array (used by the event source during event broadcast)

Recall our earlier *Chat* example, in which the event source was the *Chat* class. In that example, an instance of the *Chat* class would create an *EventListenerList* instance to contain listener objects that implement the *ChatListener* interface. At event time, the *Chat* instance would invoke the appropriate event method on all objects in the *EventListenerList*.

Example 19-1 shows the code for the *EventListenerList* class.

Example 19-1. The EventListenerList class

```
import event.*;

/**
 * Manages a list of objects registered to receive events (i.e., instances
 * of a class that implements EventListener). This class is used by an event
 * source to store its listeners.
 */
class event.EventListenerList {
  // The listener objects.
  private var listeners:Array;

  /**
   * Constructor
   */
  public function EventListenerList () {
    // Create a new array in which to store listeners.
    listeners = new Array();
  }

  /**
   * Adds a listener to the list.
   *
   * @param    l    The listener to add. Must implement EventListener.
   */
  public function addObj (l:EventListener):Boolean {
    // Search for the specified listener.
    var len:Number = listeners.length;
    for (var i:Number = len; --i >= 0; ) {
      if (listeners[i] == l) {
        return false;
      }
    }

    // The new listener is not already in the list, so add it.
    listeners.push(l);
    return true;
  }

  /**
   * Removes a listener from the list.
   *
   * @param    l    The listener to remove. Must implement EventListener.
   */
  public function removeObj (l:EventListener):Boolean {
    // Search for the specified listener.
    var len:Number = listeners.length;
    for (var i = len;  i >= 0, ) {
      if (listeners[i] == l) {
        // We found the listener, so remove it.
        listeners.splice(i, 1);
```

Example 19-1. The EventListenerList class (continued)

```
      // Quit looking.
      return true;
    }
  }
  return false;
}

/**
 * Returns the complete list of listeners, used during event notification.
 */
public function getListeners ():Array {
  // Return a copy of the list, not the list itself.
  return listeners.slice(0);
}
}
```

In addition to managing event listeners in an *EventListenerList* instance, the event source must broadcast an event description to its listeners at event time. The description takes the form of an *EventObject* subclass. Let's create the *EventObject* class next.

The EventObject Class

The *EventObject* class is the parent of all classes that describe an event. It provides a reference to its event source, which lets event listeners retrieve data from the event source or perform actions on it. Subclasses of *EventObject* define properties that describe an event and often provide methods to access those properties.

The *EventObject* class defines a single method, *getSource( )*, which returns a reference to the event source that created the current *EventObject* instance.

The event source reference is supplied to the *EventObject* via its constructor. As we described earlier, our chat application's *EventObject* subclass would be *ChatEvent*, which would define the properties: messageText, messageSender, oldUserName, and newUserName.

Example 19-2 shows the code for the *EventObject* class.

Example 19-2. The EventObject class

```
/**
 * The base class for an object describing an event.
 * EventObject instances are passed to event methods defined
 * by classes that implement EventListener.
 * Each kind of event should be represented by an EventObject subclass.
 *
 * Each EventObject instance stores a reference to its event source,
 * which is the object that generated the event.
 */
class event.EventObject {
  // The source of the event.
```

Example 19-2. The EventObject class (continued)

```
  private var source:Object;

  /**
   * Constructor
   *
   * @param   src   The source of the event.
   */
  public function EventObject (src:Object) {
    source = src;
  }

  /**
   * Returns the source of the event.
   */
  public function getSource ():Object {
    return source;
  }
}
```

In order to receive an event notice (and with it, an *EventObject* instance), an event listener object must be an instance of a class that implements the appropriate event listener interface. The event source class determines which interface its event listeners must implement. All specific event listener interfaces are subclasses of the generic *EventListener* interface, described next.

The EventListener Interface

The *EventListener* interface is a so-called marker interface (as explained in Chapter 8). It simply tags a class as being part of the delegation event model structure. Each implementation of the delegation event model must supply an *EventListener* subinterface listing all methods that can be triggered by the event source. Listener classes wishing to register to receive events from a particular event source must implement that source's corresponding *EventListener* subinterface. For example, suppose the class *OrderForm* is an event source and the class *FormValidator* is an event listener. In order to receive events from *OrderForm*, the *FormValidator* class would have to implement, say, *FormListener*. The *FormListener* interface would extend *EventListener* and define the *OrderForm*'s events—perhaps *onFormSubmit( )* and *onFormReset( )*.

Example 19-3 shows the code for the *EventListener* interface.

Example 19-3. The EventListener interface

```
/**
 * This is a marker interface that marks a class as an event
 * listener. All event listener interfaces should extend this interface.
 */
interface event.EventListener { }
```

NightSky: A Delegation Event Model Example

Now that we have established a foundation for delegation event model implementations, let's use it in a real example: a starry night sky with animated shooting stars. The code discussed in this section is available at *http://moock.org/eas2/examples*. This example breaks from earlier examples in this book, which focused primarily on application development. Here, we see how OOP and design patterns can be applied to motion graphics as well as application development. Of course, a random event generator is also perfect for video games, which make heavy use of OOP.

The Event Source

The event source for our example is *Randomizer*, a class that triggers an event named *onRandomAction( )* at random intervals. Every *n* seconds, the *onRandomAction( )* event has a user-defined chance of occurring. For example, a specific *Randomizer* instance might, every 5 seconds, have a 1-in-20 chance of triggering *onRandomAction( )*.

The *onRandomAction( )* event typically activates some random behavior in *Randomizer*'s listeners, such as the blinking of a cartoon character's eyes, the spawning of a random monster in a game, or, as in our case, the appearance of a shooting star animation in a night sky. The *Randomizer* class is a generally handy utility, so we store it in the package *util*.

The EventListener Subinterface

The *EventListener* subinterface in our example is *RandomizerListener*. The *Randomizer* class broadcasts only a single event, so the *RandomizerListener* interface defines only a single method—*onRandomAction( )*. Classes wishing to receive *Randomizer* events must implement *RandomizerListener* and define an *onRandomAction( )* method. The *RandomizerListener* interface resides in the package *util*, along with the *Randomizer* class.

The EventObject Subclass

Each event broadcast by *Randomizer* is described by a *RandomizerEvent* instance (*RandomizerEvent* is an *EventObject* subclass). The *RandomizerEvent* class provides a single method, *getTimeSinceLast( )*, which reports the elapsed time since the previous *onRandomAction( )* event was generated. The *RandomizerEvent* class resides in the package *util*, along with the *Randomizer* class and *RandomizerListener* interface.

The Event Listener Class

Our night sky application's event listener class is *NightSky*. It implements the *RandomizerListener* interface and defines an *onRandomAction( )* method. When *NightSky* is constructed, it creates a sky background. Each time *Randomizer* invokes *onRandomAction( )* on *NightSky*, the *NightSky* class creates a shooting star animation over the sky background.

The Overall Structure

Figure 19-2 shows the structure of the night sky application. Compare Figure 19-2 with the generic delegation event model structure shown earlier in Figure 19-1. Specifically, *Randomizer* is our *EventSourceClass*, *RandomizerListener* is our *EventTypeListener*, *RandomizerEvent* is our *EventTypeEvent*, and *NightSky* is our *EventListenerClass*. The parameter, 1, passed to *addRandomizerListener( )* and *removeRandomizerListener( )* in Figure 19-2 is the listener to be added or removed.

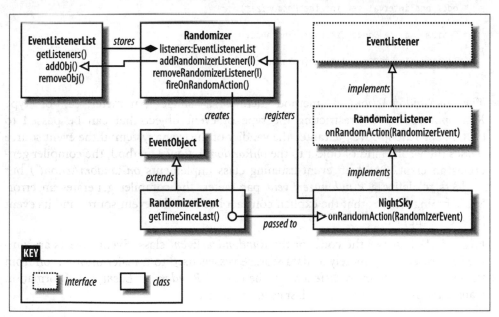

Figure 19-2. Night sky application structure

Now let's take a closer look at the code in the night sky application.

Randomizer, RandomizerListener, and RandomizerEvent

The *Randomizer* and *RandomizerEvent* classes and the *RandomizerListener* interface work together to provide event-broadcast services for the *Randomizer* class. Conceptually, every delegation event model implementation will have the same three participants—a class that generates events (*Randomizer*), a class that describes those events

(*RandomizerEvent*), and an interface that states the events (*RandomizerListener*). Let's work through the code for these participants in reverse order, starting with *RandomizerListener*.

The *RandomizerListener* interface and its single method, *onRandomAction( )*, are shown in Example 19-4.

Example 19-4. The RandomizerListener interface

```
import event.*;
import util.*;

/**
 * Lists the methods that must be implemented by
 * an object that wants to be notified of Randomizer events.
 */
interface util.RandomizerListener extends EventListener {
  /**
   * Triggered when a random event has occurred (according to the
   * odds and interval set for the Randomizer).
   *
   * @param   e   A RandomizerEvent instance.
   */
  public function onRandomAction (e:RandomizerEvent):Void;
}
```

The *onRandomAction( )* method defines a single parameter, e, of type *RandomizerEvent*. By restricting the type of event object that can be passed to *onRandomAction( )*, we guarantee the validity of the event system: if the event source passes the wrong kind of object to the *onRandomAction( )* method, the compiler generates an error. Or, if an event-listening class implements *onRandomAction( )* but neglects to define a *RandomizerEvent* parameter, the compiler generates an error. Static typing ensures that the explicit contract between the event source and its event listeners is upheld.

Example 19-5 shows the code for the *RandomizerEvent* class. Event objects are simple in nature, acting merely as data-storage vessels used to transfer information from the event source to event listeners. In the case of *RandomizerEvent*, the information transferred is the time since the last event occurred.

Example 19-5. The RandomizerEvent class

```
import event.*;
import util.*;

/**
 * An event object describing a Randomizer event.
 */
class util.RandomizerEvent extends EventObject {
  // The number of milliseconds since the last event was broadcast.
  private var timeSinceLast:Number;
```

Example 19-5. The RandomizerEvent class (continued)

```
/**
 * Constructor
 *
 * @param  src   The event source (a Randomizer instance).
 * @param  timeSinceLast  The number of milliseconds since the last event.
 */
public function RandomizerEvent (src:Randomizer, timeSinceLast:Number) {
  // Always pass event source to superclass constructor!
  super(src);

  // Record the time since the last event.
  this.timeSinceLast = timeSinceLast;
}

/**
 * Returns the time since the last event.
 */
public function getTimeSinceLast ():Number {
  return timeSinceLast;
}
}
```

Notice that the *RandomizerEvent* constructor receives two arguments: `src`, a reference to the *Randomizer* instance that created the *RandomizerEvent*, and `timeSinceLast`, the time elapsed since the last event.

```
function RandomizerEvent (src:Randomizer, timeSinceLast:Number) {
  super(src);
  this.timeSinceLast = timeSinceLast;
}
```

In the constructor body, we pass the `src` reference to the *RandomizerEvent*'s superclass constructor. There, the reference is stored for access by the event listener receiving the *RandomizerEvent* object.

> Passing the event source reference to the *EventObject* constructor is a required step that must not be skipped. If you do not pass the event source to the *EventObject* constructor, recipients of the event will not have access to the object that generated the event.

Example 19-6 shows the code for the *Randomizer* class. Read it over, then we'll study the important sections in detail.

Example 19-6. The Randomizer class

```
import event.*;
import util.*;

/**
```

Example 19-6. The Randomizer class (continued)

```
 * Generates random events.
 */
class util.Randomizer {
  // The event listeners that will receive events.
  private var listenerList:EventListenerList;
  // The time in milliseconds between checks for a random event.
  private var randInterval:Number;
  // The time of the last random event.
  private var lastEventTime:Date;

  /**
   * Constructor
   *
   * @param  interval  The time in milliseconds to wait between
   *                   checks for a random event.
   * @param  odds      The likelihood an event will be triggered at
   *                   each check. An event has a 1-in-odds chance of
   *                   being triggered.
   */
  public function Randomizer (interval:Number, odds:Number) {
    // Create an EventListenerList to manage listeners.
    listenerList = new EventListenerList();

    // Initialize the time of the most recent event.
    lastEventTime = new Date();

    // Start checking for events.
    start(interval, odds);
  }

  /**
   * Register an object to receive random events.
   */
  public function addRandomizerListener (l:RandomizerListener):Boolean {
    return listenerList.addObj(l);
  }

  /**
   * Unregister an event listener object.
   */
  public function removeRandomizerListener (l:RandomizerListener):Boolean {
    return listenerList.removeObj(l);
  }

  /**
   * Start an interval to check for random events.
   *
   * @param  interval  The time in milliseconds to wait between
   *                   checks for a random event.
   * @param  odds      The likelihood an event will be triggered at
   *                   each check.
   */
```

Example 19-6. The Randomizer class (continued)

```
public function start (interval:Number, odds:Number):Boolean {
  if (interval > 0 && odds > 1) {
    // Call this.check( ) every interval milliseconds.
    randInterval = setInterval(this, "check", interval, odds);
    return true;
  }
  return false;
}

/**
 * Stop checking for random events.
 */
public function stop ( ):Void {
  clearInterval(randInterval);
}

/**
 * Restart the event-checking interval, possibly with new odds.
 *
 * @param  interval  The time in milliseconds to wait between
 *                   checks for a random event.
 * @param  odds      The likelihood an event will be triggered at
 *                   each check.
 */
public function restart (interval:Number, odds:Number):Void {
  stop( );
  start(interval, odds);
}

/**
 * Checks to see if a random event occurs, based on the
 * current odds.
 *
 * @param  odds      The likelihood an event will be triggered at
 *                   each check.
 */
private function check (odds:Number):Void {
  // Local variables.
  var rand:Number = Math.floor(Math.random( ) * odds);
  var now:Date = new Date( );
  var elapsed:Number;

  // If the random event occurs...
  if (rand == 0) {
    // Determine the elapsed time since the last event.
    elapsed = now.getTime() - lastEventTime.getTime( );
    lastEventTime = now;

    // Fire the event.
    fireOnRandomAction(elapsed);
  }
}
```

Example 19-6. The Randomizer class (continued)

```
/**
 * Invokes onRandomAction( ) on all listeners.
 *
 * @param  elapsed   The amount of time since the last event notification.
 */
private function fireOnRandomAction (elapsed:Number):Void {
  // Create an object to describe the event.
  var e:RandomizerEvent = new RandomizerEvent(this, elapsed);
  // Get a list of the current event listeners.
  var listeners:Array = listenerList.getListeners( );

  // Broadcast the event to all listeners.
  for (var i:Number = 0; i < listeners.length; i++) {
    // Notice that we don't cast to RandomizerListener here.
    // For an explanation of why the cast isn't required, see
    // "Array Elements and Type Checking," in Chapter 3.
    listeners[i].onRandomAction(e);
  }
}
}
```

Much of the *Randomizer* class code relates to the internal task of checking odds at specific time intervals, which is not our current focus. From the perspective of the delegation event model, we're concerned only with the listenerList property and the *addRandomizerListener( )*, *removeRandomizerListener( )*, and *fireOnRandomAction( )* methods, used to manage event listener objects and broadcast the *onRandomAction* event.

When a *Randomizer* instance is constructed, it creates an *EventListenerList* instance, which it stores in the property listenerList:

```
listenerList = new EventListenerList( );
```

The *EventListenerList* instance manages the *Randomizer* class's event listeners. To register an object to receive *Randomizer* events, we pass it to *addRandomizerListener( )*, which, in turn passes it to *listenerList.addObj( )*. The *listenerList.addObj( )* method is what actually adds the object to the list of event listeners for the current *Randomizer* instance:

```
public function addRandomizerListener (l:RandomizerListener):Boolean {
  return listenerList.addObj(l);
}
```

To stop an object from receiving *Randomizer* events, we pass it to *removeRandomizerListener( )*, which, like *addRandomizerListener( )*, delegates its work to the listenerList object:

```
public function removeRandomizerListener (l:RandomizerListener):Boolean {
  return listenerList.removeObj(l);
}
```

Both *addRandomizerListener( )* and *removeRandomizerListener( )* return a Boolean indicating whether the registration or unregistration attempt succeeded. Registration succeeds (and *addRandomizerListener( )* returns true) if the object registering is not already registered. If the object is already registered, *addRandomizerListener( )* returns false. Unregistration will fail if the object being unregistered is not in the list of currently registered event listeners.

Notice, again, that static typing ensures that only instances of classes that implement *RandomizerListener* can register to receive events from *Randomizer*. If a non-*RandomizerListener* is passed to *addRandomizerListener( )* or *removeRandomizerListener( )*, the compiler generates a type mismatch error. Hence, all registered listeners are guaranteed to define the *onRandomAction( )* method, which *Randomizer* uses when broadcasting its event.

When it's time for the *Randomizer* class to broadcast an event, it invokes *fireOnRandomAction( )*, passing the amount of time since the last event to that method:

```
private function fireOnRandomAction (elapsed:Number):Void {
  var e:RandomizerEvent = new RandomizerEvent(this, elapsed);
  var listeners:Array = listenerList.getListeners();
  for (var i:Number = 0; i < listeners.length; i++) {
    listeners[i].onRandomAction(e);
  }
}
```

In the *fireOnRandomAction( )* method, we first create a *RandomizerEvent* instance and pass it two arguments—a reference to the current *Randomizer* instance and information describing the event, in this case, the time elapsed since the previous event:

```
var e:RandomizerEvent = new RandomizerEvent(this, elapsed);
```

Next, we retrieve the list of currently registered listeners from the listenerList:

```
var listeners:Array = listenerList.getListeners();
```

Finally, we invoke *onRandomAction( )* on all registered listeners, passing each the event object we created earlier:

```
for (var i:Number = 0; i < listeners.length; i++) {
  listeners[i].onRandomAction(e);
}
```

Thus, the event is broadcast, and each listener happily determines its own appropriate response. For example, if we were using a *Randomizer* to control monsters in an adventure game, each monster (each listener object) could pick some random behavior—perhaps *attackPlayer( )*, *flee( )*, or *defend( )*. Or in our shooting star example, when the *Randomizer* instance invokes *onRandomAction( )* on our *NightSky* instance, the *NightSky* instance responds by displaying a shooting star.

Multiple event types from a single event source

Before we move on to the use of our *Randomizer* class, it's worth noting that a single event source can legitimately define more than one kind of event. For example, in Java (from whence the delegation event model originates), the all-purpose user interface class, *Component*, defines two categories of mouse events: one for mouse motion and one for mouse input (i.e., mouseclicks). To register an object for mouse motion events in Java, we first ensure that it implements the *MouseMotionListener* interface, then we pass it to *Component.addMouseMotionListener( )*. To register an object for mouse input events, we first ensure that it implements the *MouseListener* interface, then we pass it to *Component.addMouseListener( )*. The same event source, *Component*, manages both types of events, keeping separate track of its event listeners by using two separate registration routines and two separate listener lists.

When an event source defines multiple types of events, its listeners can flexibly sign up to receive only a particular category of events, ignoring other events that are not of interest. To receive both events, however, a listener object must register twice (once for each event).

The NightSky Class

In our delegation event model example, the *NightSky* class is the event listener class; it receives events from *Randomizer*. In order to become eligible to receive *Randomizer* events, *NightSky* implements *RandomizerListener*.

Example 19-7 shows the code for the *NightSky* class.

Example 19-7. The NightSky class

```
import util.*;

/**
 * Creates a sky full of stars and listens for Randomizer
 * events to create random shooting stars.
 */
class nightsky.NightSky implements RandomizerListener {
  // The movie clip in which to create the sky.
  private var target:MovieClip;
  // The sky movie clip.
  private var sky_mc:MovieClip;
  // The depth, in target, at which to create the sky. Defaults to 0.
  private var skyDepth:Number = 0;
  // The depth, in sky_mc, at which to create shooting stars. Defaults to 0.
  private var starDepth:Number = 0;

  /**
   * Constructor
   */
  public function NightSky (target:MovieClip,
                            skyDepth:Number, starDepth:Number) {
```

Example 19-7. The NightSky class (continued)

```
    this.target = target;
    this.skyDepth = skyDepth;
    this.starDepth = starDepth;
    makeSkyBG( );
  }

  /**
   * Responds to random events from a Randomizer object.
   * Creates a shooting star in the sky.
   *
   * @param   e    An object that describes the event.
   */
  public function onRandomAction (e:RandomizerEvent):Void {
    trace("New shooting star! Time since last star: "
          + e.getTimeSinceLast( ));
    makeShootingStar( );
  }

  /**
   * Creates a sky graphic by attaching a movie clip with the
   * linkage identifier of "skybg".
   */
  private function makeSkyBG ( ):Void {
    sky_mc = target.attachMovie("skybg", "skybg", skyDepth);
  }

  /**
   * Creates a shooting star by attaching a movie clip with the
   * linkage identifier of "shootingstar".
   */
  private function makeShootingStar ( ):Void {
    // Create the shooting star in the sky movie clip.
    sky_mc.attachMovie("shootingstar",
                       "shootingstar" + starDepth, starDepth);
    // Randomly position the shooting star.
    sky_mc["shootingstar" + starDepth]._x = Math.floor(Math.random( )
                             * target.skybg._width);
    sky_mc["shootingstar" + starDepth]._y = Math.floor(Math.random( )
                             * target.skybg._height);
    // Put the next shooting star on a higher depth.
    starDepth++;
  }
}
```

The *NightSky* class uses what should now be familiar techniques to create an instance of a movie clip symbol depicting a sky background, namely *MovieClip. attachMovie( )*.

Our focus in Example 19-7 is the *onRandomAction( )* method, which handles *onRandomAction* events from *Randomizer*. The method is simple—when the random event occurs, it creates a shooting star by invoking *makeShootingStar( )*. For debugging purposes, *onRandomAction( )* also displays the time elapsed since the last shooting star was created.

```
public function onRandomAction (e:RandomizerEvent):Void {
  trace("New shooting star! Time since last star: " + e.getTimeSinceLast());
  makeShootingStar();
}
```

Reader exercise: try modifying the code so that the chance of a shooting star appearing dynamically decreases or increases depending on the amount of time elapsed since the last star. Hint—use e.getSource( ) to access the *Randomizer.restart( )* method.

Using NightSky in an Application

To use the *NightSky* class in an application, we create an instance of *Randomizer* and an instance of *NightSky*, then we use *addRandomizerListener( )* to register the *NightSky* instance as a listener with the *Randomizer* instance. The following code shows the technique:

```
import nightsky.*;
import util.*;

var sky:NightSky = new NightSky(bg_mc, 1, 0);
var starRandomizer:Randomizer = new Randomizer(1000, 3);
starRandomizer.addRandomizerListener(sky);
```

The *NightSky* instance (sky) creates a sky graphic in the movie clip bg_mc at depth 1. Shooting stars in the sky will start appearing on depth 0. The *Randomizer* instance (starRandomizer) has a one-in-three chance of triggering *onRandomAction( )* every second (i.e., every 1000 milliseconds).

The preceding code could appear in a class as part of a larger OOP application, or it could be placed directly on a frame in the timeline of a *.fla* file. Either way, the *.fla* that uses the *NightSky* instance must export two movie clip symbols, one for the sky ("skybg") and one for the shooting stars ("shootingstar").

For a working version of the night sky example, see *http://moock.org/eas2/examples*.

Other Event Architectures in ActionScript

Neither ActionScript's built-in classes, nor the Flash v2 components use the delegation event model in its entirety. Both do use an event listener model but without an *EventListener* interface or a formal *EventObject* class. For information on handling events from ActionScript's built-in classes, see *ActionScript for Flash MX: The Definitive Guide* (O'Reilly). For information on handling events from the Flash v2 components, see Chapter 12 and Help → Using Components → Working with Components → About Component Events. The core v2 component architecture comes with its own event-dispatching facilities. To learn how to implement events for a component that is based on the v2 component architecture, see Help › Using Components → Creating Components → Handling Events.

From Some Place to Some OtherPlace

This book has reached its end, but your journey as a programmer continues. Over the preceding 19 chapters, you've learned many different programming tools and techniques; it's now up to you to experiment with them. Take what you've learned and explore your own ideas and projects. If you've previously spent most of your time in Flash, don't feel limited to it. Most of the concepts in this book are applicable to many other languages. Your basic OOP ActionScript training will serve you well in Java, C++, Perl, and Visual Basic, just to name a few. Don't be afraid to venture into that territory.

Programming is an art form. As such, it comes with all the frustrations and elation of sculpture, writing, painting, or music. And it's subject to the primary law of creativity: there is no final destination. With every day you program, you'll express something new and learn more along the way. The process never stops.

In the Preface, I wrote that "This book wants you to use object-oriented programming in your daily Flash work. It wants you to reap the benefits of OOP—one of the most important revolutions in programming history. It wants you to understand ActionScript 2.0 completely." I hope this book achieved that goal. And I hope you had some fun in the process.

With that, I'm off to race cars over the network with my friend Hoss from Scotland. He has hometown advantage because the track is Edinburgh, his real-life hometown. The game is *Project Gotham Racing 2* and the network infrastructure is *Microsoft XBox Live*. Quite a programming marvel, in case you're looking for inspiration. Or I suppose, alternatively, you could go look at pictures from the robot programmed to drive around on Mars. What a world...

Appendixes

The appendixes include:

ActionScript 2.0 Language Quick Reference

The following reference lists the datatypes recognized by the ActionScript 2.0 compiler for the built-in classes, objects, global properties, and global functions in Flash Player 7. This list will help you preemptively avoid type mismatch errors when declaring datatypes. Or, if you've encountered a compiler error because you've used a built-in class, object, property, or function with the wrong datatype, this list will help you find the correct datatype and fix the error. Remember that if the datatype is specified as *Object*, the compiler will accept data of any datatype. See Chapter 3 for complete information on datatypes in ActionScript 2.0.

The ActionScript compiler retrieves datatype information at compile time from so-called intrinsic files, which catalog the methods and properties supported by each class. You can find the intrinsic files in your Flash program installation folder, under *Flash MX 2004\en\First Run\Classes*.

Numerous errors plague the intrinsic files that shipped with Flash MX 2004 and Flash MX Professional 2004 (both the original version and the 7.0.1 updated version). Hence, in those versions of the authoring tool, the compiler will incorrectly skip type checking for some items and report mistaken datatype errors for others. Macromedia is aware of the problem and intends to update the intrinsic files in a future version of the authoring tool.

In response to the general problem of errors in the intrinsic files, I've chosen to list the correct datatypes for all items in this appendix, not the erroneous datatypes found in the intrinsic files. For example, according to the *Boolean.as* intrinsic file that shipped with Flash MX 2004 and Flash MX Professional 2004 (versions 7.0.0 and 7.0.1), the return type of *Boolean.valueOf( )* is *Number*. But in this appendix, we've listed the return type as *Boolean*, which is the correct return type for *Boolean.valueOf( )*.

When this appendix contradicts an intrinsic file, I'll make a special note so you won't be surprised by the compiler's behavior. For example, in the case of *Boolean. valueOf( )*, I'll point out that the intrinsic files for versions 7.0.0 and 7.0.1 of the authoring tool use *Number* not *Boolean* as the return type. It's then up to you to conclude that, say, assigning *true.valueOf( )* to a variable of type *Boolean* will (mistakenly) generate an error, as shown here:

```
// Generates a (mistaken) error in versions 7.0.0 and 7.0.1 of
// Flash MX 2004 and Flash MX Professional 2004.
var val:Boolean = true.valueOf( );

**Error** Scene=Scene 1, layer=Layer 1, frame=1:Line 1: Type mismatch in
assignment statement: found Number where Boolean is required.
```

To work around the mistaken error, leave the variable val in the preceding code example untyped or, alternatively, fix your installation's *Boolean.as* intrinsic file manually by following these steps:

1. Open the following file, substituting your operating system user account name for *USER* and your Flash language code for *LANGUAGE_CODE* such as "en" for English:

   On Windows:

   > *c:\Documents and Settings\USER\Local Settings\Application Data\Macromedia\Flash MX 2004\LANGUAGE_CODE\Configuration\Classes\Boolean.as*

   Note that the *Local Settings* folder is a hidden folder that must be revealed explicitly in Windows File Explorer using Tools → Folder Options → View → Advanced Settings → Files and Folders → Hidden Files and Folders → Show Hidden Files and Folders.

   On Mac:

   > *HD:/Users/USER/Library/Application Support/Macromedia/Flash MX 2004/ LANGUAGE_CODE/Configuration/Classes/Boolean.as*

2. In the file *Boolean.as*, change the following line:

   ```
   function valueOf( ):Number;
   ```

   to:

   ```
   function valueOf( ):Boolean;
   ```

3. Save the file *Boolean.as*.

You should also be sure to check for updated intrinsic files from Macromedia at *http:// www.macromedia.com/support/flash*. I'll post news of any updates on my blog (*http:// www.moock.org/blog*) and my mailing list (*http://www.moock.org/moockupdates*).

In general, I've done my best to represent the correct datatype in anticipation of future corrected intrinsic files. That said, to confirm the datatypes used by the compiler in your specific installation of the Flash authoring tool, you should always consult the appropriate intrinsic file. If you want to know which version of Flash you currently have installed, use Help → About Flash.

Throughout this appendix, items marked with * are those that Macromedia erroneously omitted from the intrinsic files for Flash MX 2004 and Flash MX Professional 2004, versions 7.0.0 and 7.0.1. In those versions of the authoring tool, no type checking is performed on items marked with *. Future versions of the authoring tool will likely have updated intrinsic files and perform type checking on items marked with *.

Only core classes and objects defined by the Flash Player itself are presented in this appendix. Other classes, such as classes for Flash Remoting or Flash UI Components, are not listed. You can find datatype information for components in the component source files, stored in Flash's program installation folder, in the following locations: *Flash MX 2004\en\First Run\Classes\mx\controls*, *Flash MX 2004\en\First Run\Classes\mx\containers*, and *Flash MX 2004\en\First Run\Classes\mx\managers*.

For a description of the items in this reference, consult the Flash MX 2004 online Help and O'Reilly's *ActionScript for Flash MX: The Definitive Guide* (note, however, that depending on the edition, some items presented here may not be listed in that book).

The following classes are new in Flash MX 2004 and Flash MX Professional 2004. They cannot be used when exporting to Flash Player 6 format:

> *ContextMenu*
> *ContextMenuItem*
> *MovieClipLoader*
> *PrintJob*
> *TextField.StyleSheet*
> *TextSnapshot*

Global Properties

Global properties store information that relates generally to the Flash Player environment and are accessible to any scope in a movie.

> _focusRect:Boolean*
> _global:Object
> _highquality:Number*
> Infinity:Number
> NaN:Number
> _quality:String*
> _root:MovieClip[a]
> _soundbuftime:Number*
> $version:String*

[a] Datatype listed as *Object* in 7.0.0 and 7.0.1

The following global property is never type checked:

> _level*n*

Global Functions

Global functions provide commands that relate generally to the Flash Player environment and are accessible to any scope in a movie.

Boolean(*value*:Object):Boolean*

call( ):Void*

clearInterval(*id*:Number):Void

Date( ):String*

duplicateMovieClip(*target*:String, *newName*:String, *depth*:Number):Void*

escape(*value*:String):String

eval(*expr*:String):Object*

fscommand(*command*:String, *parameters*:String):Void*

getProperty(*movieClip*:Object, *property*:Object):Object*

getTimer( ):Number*

getURL(*url*:String, *window*:String, *method*:String):Void*

getVersion( ):String*

gotoAndPlay(*frameNumOrLabel*:Object):Void*

gotoAndPlay(*scene*:Object, *frameNumOrLabel*:Object):Void*

gotoAndStop(*frameNumOrLabel*:Object):Void*

gotoAndStop(*scene*:Object, *frameNumOrLabel*:Object):Void*

int(*num*:Number):Number*

isFinite(*value*:Object):Boolean

isNaN(*value*:Object):Boolean

loadMovie(*url*:String, *target*:Object, *method*:String):Void*

loadMovieNum(*url*:String, *level*:Number, *method*:String):Void*

loadVariables(*url*:String, *target*:Object, *method*:String):Void*

loadVariablesNum(*url*:String, *level*:Number, *method*:String):Void*

nextFrame( ):Void*

nextScene( ):Void*

Number(*value*:Object):Number

parseFloat(*value*:String):Number

parseInt(*value*:String, *radix*:Number):Number

play( ):Void*

prevFrame( ):Void*

prevScene( ):Void*

print(*target*:Object, *boundingBox*:String):Void*

printAsBitmap(*target*:Object, *boundingBox*:String):Void*

printAsBitmapNum(*level*:Number, *boundingBox*:String):Void*

printNum(*level*:Number, *boundingBox*:String):Void*

random(*number*:Number):Number*

removeMovieClip(*target*:Object):Void*

setInterval(*function*:Object, *interval*:Object, *arg1*:Object, *...argn*:Object):
Number[a]

setInterval(*object*:Object, *method*:Object, *interval*:Object, *arg1*:Object, ...
argn:Object):Number[a]

setProperty(*movieClip*:Object, *property*:Object, *value*:Object):Void*
startDrag(*target*:Object, *lockCenter*:Boolean, *left*:Number, *top*:Number,
    right:Number, *bottom*:Number):Void*
stop():Void*
stopAllSounds():Void*
stopDrag():Void*
String(*value*:Object):String*
targetPath(*mc*:MovieClip):String*
toggleHighQuality():Void*
trace(*value*:String):Void
unescape(*value*:String):String
unloadMovie(*target*:Object):Void*
unloadMovieNum(*level*:Number):Void*
updateAfterEvent():Void*

a *setInterval()* has two forms with differing numbers of parameters, so all parameter types are specified
as *Object* to accept any datatype.

Accessibility Class

The *Accessibility* class provides tools for developing advanced accessible UI components.

> At runtime, the *Accessibility* class is actually a standalone, predefined
> object, not a class. However, it is treated as a class by the compiler for the
> sake of type checking. Hence, the *Accessibility* class has no constructor.

Constructor

None

Class methods

isActive():Boolean
sendEvent(*mc*:MovieClip, *childID*:Object, *event*:Object, *isNonHtml*:Boolean):Void[a]
updateProperties():Void

a No type specified for the *childID* parameter in 7.0.0 and 7.0.1

Arguments Class   Extends Array

The *Arguments* class provides access to function arguments, the current function, and the
calling function.

Note that datatype information for the *Arguments* class is stored in the intrinsic file *Func-
tionArguments.as*. Instances of the *Arguments* class are created automatically by
ActionScript and made available within each executing function. Hence, the *Arguments*
class has no constructor.

Instance properties

callee:Function[a]
caller:Function[a]

[a] Incorrectly listed as an instance method in 7.0.0 and 7.0.1

Elements are accessed as follows but not type checked:

arguments[*index*]

Array Class

The *Array* class provides support for ordered lists of data.

Constructor

Array()*
Array(*len*:Object)*
Array(*elem0*:Object, *elem1*:Object, *elem2*:Object,...*elemn*:Object)*

Class properties

The following class properties are supported for arrays in Flash Player 7 and later:

CASEINSENSITIVE:Number
DESCENDING:Number
NUMERIC:Number
RETURNINDEXEDARRAY:Number
UNIQUESORT:Number

Instance properties

length:Number

Instance methods

concat(*value*:Object):Array
join(*delimiter*:String):String
pop():Object
push(*value*:Object):Number[a]
reverse():Void
shift():Object
slice(*startIndex*:Number, *endIndex*:Number):Array
sort(*compare*:Object, *options*:Number):Array[b]
sortOn(*key*:Object, *options*:Number):Array[c]
splice(*startIndex*:Number, *deleteCount*:Number, *value*:Object):Array
toString():String[d]
unshift(*value*:Object):Number

[a] Datatype for *value* not listed in 7.0.0 and 7.0.1
[b] Datatype for *compare* not listed in 7.0.0 and 7.0.1
[c] Datatype for *key* not listed in 7.0.0 and 7.0.1
[d] This method overrides the default *Object.toString()*.

Boolean Class

The *Boolean* class acts as a wrapper class for primitive Boolean data.

Constructor

Boolean(*value*:Object)*

Instance methods

toString():String
valueOf():Boolean[a]

[a] Return type incorrectly listed as *Number* in 7.0.0 and 7.0.1

Button Class

The *Button* class provides control over instances of button symbols in a movie. Note that the following properties are not defined by the *Button* class but are erroneously listed in the *Button. as* intrinsic file for Flash MX 2004 and Flash MX Professional 2004 in versions 7.0.0 and 7.0.1.

_currentframe
_droptarget
_framesloaded
_totalframes

The legitimate properties and methods of the *Button* class are listed next.

Constructor

None (use the authoring tool to create buttons)

Instance properties

_alpha:Number	trackAsMenu:Boolean
enabled:Boolean	_url:String
_focusrect:Boolean	useHandCursor:Boolean
_height:Number	_visible:Boolean
_name:String	_width:Number
_parent:MovieClip	_x:Number
_quality:String[a]	_xmouse:Number
_rotation:Number	_xscale:Number
_soundbuftime:Number[b]	_y:Number
tabEnabled:Boolean	_ymouse:Number
tabIndex:Number	_yscale:Number
_target:String	

[a] Synonym for global property _quality
[b] Synonym for global property _soundbuftime

Instance methods

getDepth():Number

Event handlers

onDragOut():Void
onDragOver():Void
onKeyDown():Void
onKeyUp():Void
onKillFocus(*newFocus*:Object):Void
onPress():Void

onRelease():Void
onReleaseOutside():Void
onRollOut():Void
onRollOver():Void
onSetFocus(*oldFocus*:Object):Void

Camera Class

The *Camera* class provides support to capture video from a video camera. It is used primarily with Macromedia Flash Communication Server.

Constructor

None (instances are created with *Camera.get( )*)

Class properties

names:Array

Instance properties

activityLevel:Number
bandwidth:Number
currentFps:Number
fps:Number
height:Number
index:Number
keyFrameInterval:Number
loopback:Boolean

motionLevel:Number
motionTimeOut:Number
muted:Boolean
name:String
nativeModes:Array
quality:Number
width:Number

Class methods

get(*index*:Number):Camera

Instance methods

setKeyFrameInterval(*keyFrameInterval*:Number):Void
setLoopback(*compress*:Boolean):Void
setMode(*width*:Number, *height*:Number, *fps*:Number, *favorArea*:Boolean):Void
setMotionLevel(*motionLevel*:Number, *timeOut*:Number):Void
setQuality(*bandwidth*:Number, *quality*:Number):Void

Event handlers

onActivity(*active*:Boolean):Void
onStatus(*infoObject*:Object):Void

Color Class

The *Color* class provides control over movie clip color values.

Constructor

new Color (*target*:Object)[a]

[a] The *target* parameter is not listed in 7.0.0 and 7.0.1.

Instance methods

getRGB():Number
getTransform():Object
setRGB(*offset*:Number):Void
setTransform(*transformObject*:Object):Void

ContextMenu Class

The *ContextMenu* class provides control over the Flash Player context menu, which is accessed via right-click (Windows) or Ctrl-click (Mac). This class is available in Flash Player 7 and later only.

Constructor

ContextMenu(*callbackFunction*:Function)[a]

[a] Datatype for *callbackFunction* not listed in 7.0.0 and 7.0.1

Instance properties

builtInItems:Object

Instance methods

copy():ContextMenu
hideBuiltInItems():Void

Event handlers

onSelect(*item*:Object, *item_menu*:ContextMenu):Void[a]

[a] Incorrectly listed as a property in 7.0.0 and 7.0.1

ContextMenuItem Class

An instance of the *ContextMenuItem* class represents an item in the Flash Player's context menu. This class is available in Flash Player 7 and later only.

Constructor

ContextMenuItem(*caption*:String, *callbackFunction*:Function, *separatorBefore*: Boolean, *enabled*:Boolean, *visible*:Boolean)[a]

[a] Datatypes for constructor parameters not listed in 7.0.0 and 7.0.1

Instance properties

caption:String
enabled:Boolean
separatorBefore:Boolean
visible:Boolean

Instance methods

copy():ContextMenuItem

Event handlers

onSelect(*obj*:Object, *menuItem*:ContextMenuItem):Void[a]

[a] Incorrectly listed as a property in 7.0.0 and 7.0.1

Date Class

The *Date* class provides the current time and structured support for date information.

Constructor

Date()
Date(*milliseconds*:Number)
Date(*year*:Number, *month*:Number, *date*:Number, *hour*:Number, *min*:Number, *sec*:Number, *ms*:Number)

Class methods

UTC(*year*:Number, *month*:Number, *date*:Number, *hour*:Number, *min*:Number, *sec*:Number, *ms*:Number):Number

Instance methods

getDate():Number
getDay():Number
getFullYear():Number
getHours():Number
getMilliseconds():Number
getMinutes():Number
getMonth():Number
getSeconds():Number
getTime():Number
getTimezoneOffset():Number

getYear():Number
setDate(*value*:Number):Void
setFullYear(*value*:Number):Void
setHours(*value*:Number):Void
setMilliseconds(*value*:Number):Void
setMinutes(*value*:Number):Void
setMonth(*value*:Number):Void
setSeconds(*value*:Number):Void
setTime(*value*:Number):Void
setUTCDate(*value*:Number):Void

getUTCDate( ):Number	setUTCFullYear(*value*:Number):Void
getUTCDay( ):Number	setUTCHours(*value*:Number):Void
getUTCFullYear( ):Number	setUTCMilliseconds(*value*:Number):Void
getUTCHours( ):Number	setUTCMinutes(*value*:Number):Void
getUTCMilliseconds( ):Number	setUTCMonth(*value*:Number):Void
getUTCMinutes( ):Number	setUTCSeconds(*value*:Number):Void
getUTCMonth( ):Number	setYear(*value*:Number):Void
getUTCSeconds( ):Number	toString( ):String
getUTCYear( ):Number[a]	valueOf( ):Number

[a] Undocumented

Function Class

The *Function* class provides an object-oriented representation of ActionScript functions.

Constructor

None (use the function keyword to create functions)

Instance properties

prototype:Object*

Instance methods

apply(*thisArg*:Object, *args*:Array)
call(*thisArg*:Object)

Key Class

The *Key* class is used to determine the state of keys on the keyboard.

 At runtime, the *Key* class is actually a standalone, predefined object, not a class. However, it is treated as a class by the compiler for the sake of type checking. Hence, the *Key* class has no constructor.

Constructor

None

Class properties

The following properties are all datatype *Number*:

ALT	DOWN	INSERT	SHIFT
BACKSPACE	END	LEFT	SPACE
CAPSLOCK	ENTER	PGDN	TAB
CONTROL	ESCAPE	PGUP	UP
DELETEKEY	HOME	RIGHT	

Class methods

addListener(*listener*:Object):Void
getAscii():Number
getCode():Number
isDown(*code*:Number):Boolean
isToggled(*code*:Number):Boolean
removeListener(*listener*:Object):Boolean

Events broadcast to listeners

onKeyDown():Void*
onKeyUp():Void*

LoadVars Class

The *LoadVars* class is used to export variables to, or import variables from, an external source.

Constructor

LoadVars()

Instance properties

contentType:String
loaded:Boolean

Instance methods

addRequestHeader(*header*:Object, *headerValue*:String):Void[a]
decode(*queryString*:String):Void
getBytesLoaded():Number
getBytesTotal():Number
load(*url*:String):Boolean
send(*url*:String, *target*:String, *method*:String):Boolean
sendAndLoad(url:String, target, *method*:String):Boolean
toString():String[b]

[a] Supported in Flash Player 6.0.65.0 and later
[b] Overrides *Object.toString()*

Event handlers

onData(*src*:String):Void
onLoad(*success*:Boolean):Void

LocalConnection Class

The *LocalConnection* class is used to transmit data directly between movies running on the same system.

Constructor

LocalConnection( )

Instance methods

close( ):Void
connect(*connectionName*:String):Boolean
domain( ):String
send(*connectionName*:String, *methodName*:String, *args*:Object):Boolean

Event handlers

allowDomain(*domain*:String):Boolean
allowInsecureDomain(*domain*:String):Boolean[a]
onStatus(*infoObject*:Object):Void

[a] Supported in Flash Player 7 and later

Math Class

The *Math* class provides access to mathematical functions and constants.

 At runtime, the *Math* class is actually a standalone, predefined object, not a class. However, it is treated as a class by the compiler for the sake of type checking. Hence, the *Math* class has no constructor.

Constructor

None

Class properties

The following properties are all datatype *Number*:

E	LN2	LOG2E	SQRT1_2
LN10	LOG10E	PI	SQRT2

Class methods

abs(*value*:Number):Number
acos(*value*:Number):Number
asin(*value*:Number):Number
atan(*value*:Number):Number
atan2(*value1*:Number, *value2*:Number):Number
ceil(*value*:Number):Number
cos(*value*:Number):Number
exp(*value*:Number):Number
floor(*value*:Number):Number
log(*value*:Number):Number
max(*value1*:Number, *value2*:Number):Number

min(*value1*:Number, *value2*:Number):Number
pow(*value1*:Number, *value2*:Number):Number
random( ):Number
round(*value*:Number):Number
sin(*value*:Number):Number
sqrt(*value*:Number):Number
tan(*value*:Number):Number

Microphone Class

The *Microphone* class is used to capture audio from a microphone. It is used primarily with Macromedia Flash Communication Server.

Constructor

None (instances are created using *Microphone.get( )*)

Class properties

names:Array

Instance properties

activityLevel:Number
gain:Number
index:Number
muted:Boolean
name:String

rate:Number
silenceLevel:Number
silenceTimeOut:Number
useEchoSuppression:Boolean

Class methods

get(*index*:Number):Microphone

Instance methods

setGain(*gain*:Number):Void
setRate(*rate*:Number):Void
setSilenceLevel(*silenceLevel*:Number, *timeOut*:Number):Void
setUseEchoSuppression(*useEchoSuppression*:Boolean):Void

Event handlers

onActivity(*active*:Boolean):Void
onStatus(*infoObject*:Object):Void

Mouse Class

The *Mouse* class is used to access mouse events and control mouse pointer visibility.

At runtime, the *Mouse* class is actually a standalone, predefined object, not a class. However, it is treated as a class by the compiler for the sake of type checking. Hence, the *Mouse* class has no constructor.

Constructor

None

Class methods

addListener(*listener*:Object):Void
hide():Number
removeListener(*listener*:Object):Boolean
show():Number

Events broadcast to listeners

onMouseDown():Void
onMouseMove():Void
onMouseUp():Void

MovieClip Class

The *MovieClip* class is a classlike datatype for main movies and movie clips.

Constructor

None (use *createEmptyMovieClip( )*, *attachMovie( )*, *duplicateMovieClip( )*, or the authoring tool to create instances)

Instance properties

_alpha:Number	tabEnabled:Boolean
_currentframe:Number	tabIndex:Number
_droptarget:String	_target:String
enabled:Boolean	_totalframes:Number
focusEnabled:Boolean	trackAsMenu:Boolean
_focusrect:Boolean	_url:String
_framesloaded:Number	useHandCursor:Boolean
_height:Number	_visible:Boolean
hitArea:Object	_width:Number
_lockroot:Boolean[a]	_x:Number
_name:String	_xmouse:Number
_parent:MovieClip	_xscale:Number
_quality:String[b]	_y:Number
_rotation:Number	_ymouse:Number
_soundbuftime:Number[c]	_yscale:Number
tabChildren:Boolean	

a Supported in Flash Player 7 and later
b Synonym for global property _quality
c Synonym for global property _soundbuftime

Instance methods

attachAudio(*id*:Object):Void
attachMovie(*id*:String, *name*:String, *depth*:Number, *initObject*:Object):MovieClip
beginFill(*rgb*:Number, *alpha*:Number):Void
beginGradientFill(*fillType*:String, *colors*:Array, *alphas*:Array, *ratios*:Array,
    matrix:Object):Void
clear():Void
createEmptyMovieClip(*name*:String, *depth*:Number):MovieClip
createTextField(*instanceName*:String, *depth*:Number, *x*:Number, *y*:Number,
    width:Number, *height*:Number):Void
curveTo(*controlX*:Number, *controlY*:Number, *anchorX*:Number,
    anchorY:Number):Void
duplicateMovieClip(*name*:String, *depth*:Number, *initObject*:Object):MovieClip
endFill():Void
getBounds(*targetCoordinateSpace*:Object):Object[a]
getBytesLoaded():Number
getBytesTotal():Number
getDepth():Number
getInstanceAtDepth(*depth*:Number):MovieClip[b]
getNextHighestDepth():Number[b]
getSWFVersion():Number*[b]
getTextSnapshot():TextSnapshot[b]
getURL(*url*:String, *window*:String, *method*:String):Void
globalToLocal(*pt*:Object):Void
gotoAndPlay(*frame*:Object):Void
gotoAndStop(*frame*:Object):Void
hitTest():Boolean
lineStyle(*thickness*:Number, *rgb*:Number, *alpha*:Number):Void
lineTo(*x*:Number, *y*:Number):Void
loadMovie(*url*:String, *method*:String):Void
loadVariables(*url*:String, *method*:String):Void
localToGlobal(*pt*:Object):Void
moveTo(*x*:Number, *y*:Number):Void
nextFrame():Void
play():Void
prevFrame():Void
removeMovieClip():Void
setMask(*mc*:Object):Void
startDrag(*lockCenter*:Boolean, *left*:Number, *top*:Number, *right*:Number,
    bottom:Number):Void
stop():Void
stopDrag():Void

swapDepths(*mc*:Object):Void
unloadMovie():Void
valueOf():Object*

a Datatype for *targetCoordinateSpace* not listed in 7.0.0 and 7.0.1
b Supported in Flash Player 7 and later

Event handlers

onData():Void
onDragOut():Void
onDragOver():Void
onEnterFrame():Void
onKeyDown():Void
onKeyUp():Void
onKillFocus(*newFocus*:Object):Void
onLoad():Void
onMouseDown():Void

onMouseMove():Void
onMouseUp():Void
onPress():Void
onRelease():Void
onReleaseOutside():Void
onRollOut():Void
onRollOver():Void
onSetFocus(*oldFocus*:Object):Void
onUnload():Void

MovieClipLoader Class

The *MovieClipLoader* class is used to load a *.swf* file or JPEG image into a movie clip and report on its download progress. Available in Flash Player 7 and later only.

Constructor

MovieClipLoader()

Instance methods

addListener(*listener*:Object):Boolean
getProgress(*target*:Object):Object
loadClip(*url*:String, *target*:Object):Boolean
removeListener(*listener*:Object):Boolean
unloadClip(*target*:Object):Boolean

Events broadcast to listeners

onLoadComplete(*target*:Object):Void
onLoadError(*target*:Object, *errorCode*:String):Void
onLoadProgress(*target*:Object, *bytesLoaded*:Number, *bytesTotal*:Number):Void
onLoadStart(*target*:Object):Void

NetConnection Class

The *NetConnection* class is used to play streaming *.flv* (video) files. Note that when used with Macromedia Flash Communication Server or Macromedia Flash Remoting, the *NetConnection* class supports more methods. For details, see the documentation for those products. See also *Flash Remoting: The Definitive Guide* by Tom Muck (O'Reilly).

Constructor

NetConnection( )

Instance properties

isConnected:Boolean
uri:String

Instance methods

addHeader( )
call(*remoteMethod*:String, *resultObject*:Object):Void
close( ):Void
connect(*targetURI*:String):Boolean

Event handlers

onResult(*infoObject*:Object):Void
onStatus(*infoObject*:Object):Void

NetStream Class

The *NetStream* class offers control over a streaming *.flv* (video) file.

Constructor

NetStream(*connection*:NetConnection)

Instance properties

bufferLength:Number
bufferTime:Number
bytesLoaded:Number
bytesTotal:Number
currentFps:Number
liveDelay:Number
time:Number

Instance methods

attachAudio(*theMicrophone*:Microphone):Void
attachVideo(*theCamera*:Camera, *snapshotMilliseconds*:Number):Void
close( ):Void
pause(*flag*:Boolean):Void
play(*name*:Object, *start*:Number, *len*:Number, *reset*:Object)
publish(*name*:Object, *type*:String):Void
receiveAudio(*flag*:Boolean):Void
receiveVideo(*flag*:Object):Void
seek(*offset*:Number):Void
send(*handlerName*:String):Void

setBufferTime(*bufferTime*:Number)

Event handlers

onResult(*streamId*:Number)
onStatus(*info*:Object):Void

Number Class

The *Number* class is a wrapper class for primitive numeric data.

Constructor

Number(*value*:Object)

Class properties

MAX_VALUE:Number   NEGATIVE_INFINITY:Number
MIN_VALUE:Number   POSITIVE_INFINITY:Number
NaN:Number

Object Class

Th *Object* class is the base class for all other classes and the class for generic objects.

Constructor

Object( )

Class properties

prototype:Object

Instance properties

constructor:Object
__proto__:Object

Class methods

registerClass(*name*:String, theClass:Function):Boolean

Instance methods

addProperty(*name*:String, *getter*:Function, *setter*:Function):Boolean
hasOwnProperty(*name*:String):Boolean[a]
isPropertyEnumerable(*name*:String):Boolean[a]
isPrototypeOf(*theClass*:Object):Boolean[a]
toLocaleString( ):String[a]
toString( ):String
unwatch(*name*:String):Boolean
valueOf( ):Object
watch(*name*:String, *callback*:Function, *userData*:Object):Boolean

[a] Undocumented

PrintJob Class

The *PrintJob* class is used to print content from a movie, including dynamic and off-screen content. It offers more functionality and detailed control than the global *print( )* function. Available in Flash Player 7 and later only.

Constructor

PrintJob( )

Instance properties

orientation:String
pageHeight:Number
pageWidth:Number
paperHeight:Number
paperWidth:Number

Instance methods

addPage(*target*:Object, *printArea*:Object, *options*:Object, *frameNum*:Number):Boolean
send( ):Void
start( ):Boolean

Selection Class

The *Selection* class provides control over text field selections and movie input focus.

At runtime, the *Selection* class is actually a standalone, predefined object, not a class. However, it is treated as a class by the compiler for the sake of type checking. Hence, the *Selection* class has no constructor.

Constructor

None

Class methods

addListener(*listener*:Object):Void
getBeginIndex():Number
getCaretIndex():Number
getEndIndex():Number
getFocus():String
removeListener(*listener*:Object):Boolean
setFocus(*newFocus*:Object):Boolean
setSelection(*beginIndex*:Number, *endIndex*:Number):Void

Events broadcast to listeners

onSetFocus(*oldFocus*:Object, *newFocus*:Object):Void

SharedObject Class

The *SharedObject* class supports local data storage and remote data transmission.

Constructor

None (instances are created with *SharedObject.getLocal( )* or *SharedObject.getRemote( )*)

Instance properties

data:Object

Class methods

getLocal(*name*:String, *localPath*:String):SharedObject
getRemote(*name*:String, *remotePath*:String, *persistence*:Object):SharedObject

Instance methods

close():Void
connect(*myConnection*:NetConnection):Boolean
flush(*minDiskSpace*:Number):Object
getSize():Number
send(*handlerName*:String):Void
setFPS(*updatesPerSecond*:Number):Boolean

Event handlers

onStatus(*infoObject*:Object):Void
onSync(*objArray*:Array):Void

Sound Class

The *Sound* class offers external sound-loading tools and control over sounds in a movie.

Constructor

Sound(*target*)

Instance properties

duration:Number
id3:Object
ID3:Object[a]
position:Number

[a] Refers to id3 property

Instance methods

attachSound(*id*:String):Void
getBytesLoaded():Number
getBytesTotal():Number
getPan():Number
getTransform():Object
getVolume():Number
loadSound(*url*:String, *isStreaming*:Boolean):Void
onSoundComplete():Void
setPan(*value*:Number):Void
setTransform(*transformObject*:Object):Void
setVolume(*value*:Number):Void
start(*secondOffset*:Number, *loops*:Number):Void
stop(*linkageID*:String):Void

Event handlers

onID3():Void[a]
onLoad(*success*:Boolean):Void

[a] Supported in Flash Player 7 and later

Stage Class

The *Stage* class provides access to a movie's size, scale settings, and alignment.

 At runtime, the *Stage* class is actually a standalone, predefined object, not a class. However, it is treated as a class by the compiler for the sake of type checking. Hence, the *Stage* class has no constructor.

Constructor

None

Class properties

align:String

height:Number
scaleMode:String
showMenu:Boolean
width:Number

Class methods

addListener(*listener*:Object):Void
removeListener(*listener*:Object):Void

Events broadcast to listeners

onResize( ):Void

String Class

The *String* class is a wrapper class for the string primitive datatype.

Constructor

String(*string*:String)

Instance properties

length:Number

Class methods

fromCharCode(*code_point1*, ... *code_pointn*):String[a]

[a] Code points are not type checked, but should be type *Number*.

Instance methods

charAt(*index*:Number):String
charCodeAt(*index*:Number):Number
concat( ):String
indexOf(*value*:String, *startIndex*:Number):Number
lastIndexOf(*value*:String, *startIndex*:Number):Number
slice(*index1*:Number, *index2*:Number):String
split(*delimiter*:String):Array
substr(*index1*:Number, *index2*:Number):String
substring(*index1*:Number, *index2*:Number):String
toLowerCase( ):String
toUpperCase( ):String

System Class

The *System* class offers access to Flash Player and system settings and specifications.

At runtime, the *System* class is actually a standalone, predefined object, not a class. However, it is treated as a class by the compiler for the sake of type checking. Hence, the *System* class has no constructor.

Constructor

None

Properties

exactSettings:Boolean[a]
useCodepage:Boolean

[a] Supported in Flash Player 7 and later

Methods

setClipboard(*text*:String):Void[a]
showSettings(*tabID*:Number):Void

[a] Supported in Flash Player 7 and later

System.capabilities Class

The *System.capabilities* class offers information about the Flash Player and its host system.

At runtime, the *System.capabilities* class is actually a standalone, predefined object, not a class. However, it is treated as a class by the compiler for the sake of type checking. Hence, the *System.capabilities* class has no constructor.

At runtime, the *System.capabilities* class is a property of the *System* object, but at compile-time, the compiler treats *capabilities* as a class in the *System* package. These peculiarities are the unfortunate consequence of updating Flash's built-in class and object library from ActionScript 1.0 to ActionScript 2.0.

Constructor

None

Class properties

avHardwareDisable:Boolean[a]
hasAccessibility:Boolean
hasAudio:Boolean
hasAudioEncoder:Boolean
hasEmbeddedVideo:Boolean[b]
hasMP3:Boolean
hasPrinting:Boolean[b]
hasScreenBroadcast:Boolean[c]
hasScreenPlayback:Boolean[c]
hasStreamingAudio:Boolean[b]
hasStreamingVideo:Boolean[b]
hasVideoEncoder:Boolean
input:String
isDebugger:Boolean

language:String
localFileReadDisable:Boolean[a]
manufacturer:String
os:String
pixelAspectRatio:Number
playerType:String[a]
screenColor:String
screenDPI:Number
screenResolutionX:Number
screenResolutionY:Number
serverString:String
version:String
windowlessDisable:Boolean[d]

[a] Supported in Flash Player 7 and later
[b] Supported in Flash Player 6.0.65.0 and later
[c] Supported in Flash Player 6.0.79.0 and later
[d] Undocumented

System.security Class

The *System.security* class is used to set cross-domain movie permissions.

 At runtime, the *System.security* class is actually a standalone, pre-defined object, not a class. However, it is treated as a class by the compiler for the sake of type checking. Hence, the *System.security* class has no constructor.

At runtime, the *System.security* class is a property of the *System* object, but at compile time, the compiler treats *security* as a class in the *System* package. These peculiarities are the unfortunate consequence of updating Flash's built-in class and object library from ActionScript 1.0 to ActionScript 2.0.

Constructor
None

Class methods

```
allowDomain(domain1, ...domainn ):Voida
allowInsecureDomain(domain1, ...domainn ):Voidb
loadPolicyFile(URL:String):Voidc
```

[a] Parameters not type checked

[b] Supported in Flash Player 7 and later; parameters not type checked

[c] No type specified for URL in 7.0.0 and 7.0.1

TextField Class

The *TextField* class is used to display and manipulate text on screen.

Note that the following properties are not defined by the *TextField* class but are erroneously listed in the *TextField.as* intrinsic file for Flash MX 2004 and Flash MX Professional 2004 in versions 7.0.0 and 7.0.1.

```
_currentframe
_droptarget
_focusrect
_framesloaded
_totalframes
```

The legitimate properties and methods of the *TextField* class are listed next.

Constructor

None (use *MovieClip.createTextField( )* or the authoring tool to create instances)

Instance properties

_alpha:Number
autoSize:String
background:Boolean
backgroundColor:Number
border:Boolean
borderColor:Number
bottomScroll:Number
condenseWhite:Boolean
embedFonts:Boolean
_height:Number
hscroll:Number
html:Boolean
htmlText:String
length:Number
maxChars:Number
maxhscroll:Number
maxscroll:Number
mouseWheelEnabled:Boolean*c
multiline:Boolean
_name:String
_parent:MovieClip
password:Boolean
_quality:Stringd
restrict:String

_rotation:Number
scroll:Number
selectable:Boolean
_soundbuftime:Numbera
StyleSheet:TextField.StyleSheetb
tabEnabled:Boolean
tabIndex:Number
_target:String
text:String
textColor:Number
textHeight:Number
textWidth:Number
type:String
_url:String
variable:String
_visible:Boolean
_width:Number
wordWrap:Boolean
_x:Number
_xmouse:Number
_xscale:Number
_y:Number
_ymouse:Number
_yscale:Number

a Synonym for global property _soundbuftime

b Supported in Flash Player 7 and later. The syntax *TextField.StyleSheet* is a special case allowed only in the built-in classes. In ActionScript 2.0, you cannot create nested classes such as *TextField.StyleSheet*.

c Supported in Flash Player 7 and later

d Synonym for global property _quality

Class methods

getFontList():Array

Instance methods

addListener(*listener*:Object):Boolean
getDepth():Number
getNewTextFormat():TextFormat
getTextFormat(*beginIndex*:Number, *endIndex*:Number):TextFormat
removeListener(*listener*:Object):Boolean
removeTextField():Void
replaceSel(*newText*:String):Void
replaceText(*beginIndex*:Number, *endIndex*:Number, *newText*:String):Void
setNewTextFormat(*tf*:TextFormat):Void
setTextFormat():Void

Event handlers

    onChanged(*changedField*:TextField):Void
    onKillFocus(*newFocus*:Object):Void
    onScroller(*scrolledField*:TextField):Void
    onSetFocus(*oldFocus*:Object):Void

Events broadcast to listeners

    onChanged(*changedField*:TextField):Void
    onScroller(*scrolledField*:TextField):Void

TextField.StyleSheet Class

The *TextField.StyleSheet* class provides CSS stylesheet support for a text field. Available in Flash Player 7 and later only.

 At runtime, the *StyleSheet* class is actually defined as a static property of the *TextField* class. Classes can be made properties of other classes only in ActionScript 1.0. In ActionScript 2.0, it is illegal to assign a class as a property of another class. Therefore, for the sake of type checking, the compiler must treat *StyleSheet* as a class in the *TextField* package.

Constructor

    StyleSheet( )

Instance methods

    clear( ):Void
    getStyle(*name*:String):Object
    getStyleNames( ):Array
    load(*url*:String):Boolean
    parse(*cssText*:String):Boolean
    parseCSS(*cssText*:String):Boolean
    setStyle(*name*:String, *style*:Object):Void
    transform(*style*:Object):TextFormat

Event handlers

    onLoad(*success*:Boolean):Void

TextFormat Class

The *TextFormat* class retrieves or sets a text field's visual formatting.

Constructor

    TextFormat(*font*:String, *size*:Number, *textColor*:Number, *bold*:Boolean,
        italic:Boolean, *underline*:Boolean, *url*:String, *window*:String, *align*:String,
        leftMargin:Number, *rightMargin*:Number, *indent*:Number, *leading*:Number)

Instance properties

align:String
blockIndent:Number
bold:Boolean
bullet:Boolean
color:Number
font:String
indent:Number
italic:Boolean

leading:Number
leftMargin:Number
rightMargin:Number
size:Number
tabStops:Array
target:String
underline:Boolean
url:String

Instance methods

getTextExtent(*text*:String):Object

TextSnapshot Class

The *TextShapshot* class represents static text fields in a movie. Available in Flash Player 7 and later only.

Constructor

None (create instances using *MovieClip.getTextSnapshot( )*)

Instance methods

findText(*startIndex*:Number, *textToFind*:String, *caseSensitive*:Boolean):Number
getCount( ):Number
getSelected(*start*:Number, *end*:Number):Boolean
getSelectedText(*includeLineEndings*:Boolean):String
getText(*start*:Number, *end*:Number, *includeLineEndings*:Boolean):String
hitTestTextNearPos(*x*:Number, *y*:Number, *closeDist*:Number):Number
setSelectColor(*color*:Number):Void
setSelected(*start*:Number, *end*:Number, *select*:Boolean):Void

---

Video Class

The *Video* class provides control over captured or streaming video.

Constructor

None (create Video instances with the authoring tool)

Instance properties

deblocking:Number
height:Number
smoothing:Boolean
width:Number

Instance methods

```
attachVideo(source:Object):Void
clear():Void
```

XML Class

The *XML* class provides DOM-based support for XML-structured data.

Constructor

```
XML(text:String)
```

Instance properties

```
contentType:String
docTypeDecl:String
ignoreWhite:Boolean
loaded:Boolean
status:Number
xmlDecl:String
```

Instance methods

```
addRequestHeader(header:Object, headerValue:String):Void[a]
createElement(name:String):XMLNode
createTextNode(value:String):XMLNode
getBytesLoaded():Number
getBytesTotal():Number
load(url:String):Boolean
parseXML(value:String):Void
send(url:String, target:String, method:String):Boolean
sendAndLoad(url:String, result:XML):Void
```

[a] Supported in Flash Player 6.0.65.0 and later

Event handlers

```
onData(src:String):Void
onLoad(success:Boolean):Void
```

XMLNode Class

The *XMLNode* class is the superclass of the *XML* class. It contains operations required by a node in an XML DOM tree.

Constructor

```
XMLNode(type:Number, value:String)
```

Instance properties

attributes:Object
childNodes:Array
firstChild:XMLNode
lastChild:XMLNode
nextSibling:XMLNode
nodeName:String
nodeType:Number
nodeValue:String
parentNode:XMLNode
previousSibling:XMLNode

Instance methods

appendChild(*newChild*:XMLNode):Void
cloneNode(*deep*:Boolean):XMLNode
hasChildNodes():Boolean
insertBefore(*newChild*:XMLNode, *insertPoint*:XMLNode):Void
removeNode():Void
toString():String

XMLSocket Class

The *XMLSocket* class provides support for a persistent client/server TCP/IP connection, typically used to implement multiuser applications. For numerous examples, see *http:// www.moock.org/unity*.

Constructor

XMLSocket()

Instance methods

close():Boolean
connect(*url*:String, *port*:Number):Boolean
send(*data*:Object):Boolean

Event handlers

onClose():Void
onConnect(*success*:Boolean):Void
onData(*src*:String):Void
onXML(*src*:XML):Void

Differences from ECMAScript Edition 4

Table B-1 reflects important *intentional* differences between Flash ActionScript 2.0 and the ECMAScript Edition 4 standard (available at: *http://www.mozilla.org/js/ language/es4*). At the time of writing, the ECMAScript Edition 4 specification is still very much under development; hence, additional important differences may not be listed here, and certainly many minor differences are not listed. Most of ActionScript 2.0's divergences from the ECMAScript Edition 4 standard are the result of either the standard's ongoing volatility or an architectural limitation imposed by the Flash Player platform. Finally, Table B-1 does not reflect any bugs that may exist in Action-Script's implementation of the standard.

Table B-1. Differences between ECMAScript Edition 4 and ActionScript 2.0

Topic	Description
Code in class definition block	In ActionScript 2.0, class definition blocks can contain only variable and function definitions. In ECMAScript 4, "A Class Definition's Block is evaluated just like any other Block, so it can contain expressions, statements, loops, etc. Such statements that do not contain declarations do not contribute members to the class being declared, but they are evaluated when the class is declared."
Nested classes	ActionScript 2.0 does not allow any form of nested classes. ECMAScript 4 allows a class to be defined as a static member of another class.
Class attributes	ActionScript 2.0 does not support ECMAScript 4's *final* class attribute, but adds its own custom attribute, *intrinsic*. See Chapter 4.
Method overriding	ActionScript 2.0 has no overriding restrictions. ECMAScript 4 requires an overriding method to use the *override* attribute and to have the same name, number of parameters, and parameter types as the overridden method. See Chapter 6.
Property enumeration	According to the ECMAScript 4 specification, instance properties should be nonenumerable unless they are defined with the *enumerable* attribute. In ActionScript 2.0, instance properties become enumerable once assigned a value. ActionScript 2.0 does not support the *enumerable* attribute. See Chapter 4. Refer to the *Object.isPropertyEnumerable( )* method.
Interfaces	ECMAScript 4 does not include ActionScript 2.0's *interface* construct. See Chapter 8.

Table B-1. Differences between ECMAScript Edition 4 and ActionScript 2.0 (continued)

Topic	Description
Member access	ActionScript 2.0 provides only two levels of member access: *private* and *public*. In Action-Script 2.0, *private* members are accessible to subclasses. In ECMAScript 4, members can be *private*, *internal*, or *public*, where *internal* means package access only and *private* means class access only (not subclass).
Packages	Packages are part of ActionScript 2.0 but were removed from the ECMAScript 4 specification due to time constraints. ActionScript 2.0's implementation of packages depends on the file-system (like Java), not on ECMAScript 4's *package* statement. The semantics of the *import* statement in ActionScript 2.0 vary slightly from those in ECMAScript 4. See Chapter 9.

Index

Symbols

{ } (curly braces)
  delineating statement block, 83, 84
  interface method declarations and, 227
( ) (function call) operator, 16
  invoking accessor methods without, 106
. (dot) operator, 16
  referring to specific class in a
      package, 239
  replacing [] operator with, 57
. (dot), representing current directory, 245
[] operator, type checking and, 57

A

abstract classes, not supported, 213
AbstractController class (example), 397
AbstractView class (example), 394–396
access control modifiers
  ActionScript, Java, and C++, 70
  differences between ECMAScript 4 and
      ActionScript 2.0, 479
  public and private constructor
      functions, 114
  public and private method
      attributes, 89–91
  public and private property attributes,
      69, 70
  visibility modifiers vs., 70
Accessibility class, 451
accessor methods, 94–98, 105–109
  creating in ActionScript 1.0, 107
  getter, 91, 97

inability to define as private, 106
  setter, 94
    return values, 96
actions layer (see scripts layer)
ActionScript 1.0
  changes to, in Flash Player 7, 11
  in Flash Player 6 and 7, 8
  MovieClip, subclassing, 320
  packages, simulating, 248
ActionScript 2.0, xx
  ActionScript 1.0 vs., xx
  differences from ECMAScript Edition
      4, 478
  in Flash Player 6 and 7, 8
  links to resources, xxiii
  object-oriented programming syntax, xvii
  unit testing tool, 31
addObj( ) (EventListenerList), 428
addProperty( ) (Object), 107
algorithms, design patterns vs., 349
animations, using timeline for, 287
API (application programming interface)
  ActionScript 2.0 interface vs., 224
  changes to, 138
  class code revision and, 126
  designing, 126
application framework, OOP, 283–290
  classes, 285
  directory structure, 284
  document timeline, 287
  exported .swf file, 289
  .fla file (Flash document), 284
  projects in Flash MX Professional
      2004, 290

We'd like to hear your suggestions for improving our indexes. Send email to *index@oreilly.com*.

D

data and logic, management by MVC model
   class, 390
datatypes, 17
   ActionScript 2.0, quick
      reference, 447–477
   ActionScript, online primer, 24
   built-in classes, information for, 54
   casting
      compile-time, leniency of AS2, 52
      conversion vs., 52
      member selection and, 51
      problems with, 52
      runtime support, 49
      terminology, 48
   converting numbers to strings, 27
   declaration of
      method parameters and return
         values, 34–36
      for properties, 67
      variables and properties, 32
   defined by interfaces, 224
   dynamic typing, 28
   indicating for method parameters, 81
   multidatatype classes, interfaces and, 226
   multiple type inheritance with
      interfaces, 232–236
   overridden instance methods and, 169
   post-colon syntax, 36
   property, 66
   redeclaring, 33
   return type, defining for method return
      value, 81
   static typing, 4
      reasons for, 30, 31
      weak, 29
   strict, static, and strong typing, 29
   strongly typed languages, 29
   subclasses as subtypes, 162
   type and subtype, 160
   type checking, 24–58
      ActionScript 2.0 features for, 10
      built-in dynamic classes, 40
      casting, 45–54
      circumventing type checking, 41–45
      compatible types, 36–40
      declaring datatypes, 25
      fixing datatype mismatch error, 27
      incompatible types, 26
      mistaken datatype assumption, 25
      quirks and limitations of, 55–58
      static typing, 28
      Void, 82
Date class, 17, 456, 457
   getDay( ), 27
   problems casting to Date type, 52
debugging messages, using to distinguish
      among exceptions, 259
declarations
   class, 60
   interface methods, 227
declaring datatypes, 25
   method or parameters and return
      values, 34–36
   post-colon syntax, 36
   variables and properties, 32
delegation event model, 227, 351, 423–443
   core implementation, 427–431
      EventListener interface, 431
      EventListenerList class, 428–430
      EventObject class, 430
   flow of logic, 427
   NightSky (example), 432–442
      event source, Randomizer class, 432
      NightSky class, 433, 440–442
      overall structure, 433
      Randomizer class, 435–440
      RandomizerEvent class, 432, 434
      RandomizerListener interface, 432,
         434
   structure and participants, 423–427
      event object, 425
      event source, 424
      Observer pattern vs., 426
deleting
   class resources, 149–151
   event-listener objects, 378
   objects, 86
depths, movie clips, 128
   unique, supplying for ImageViewer class
      instances, 132
derived class, 160
design patterns, xviii, 125, 349–351
   benefits of, 387
   definition of, 351
   delegation event model, 351, 423–443
      core implementation, 427–431
      flow of logic, 427
      structure and participants, 423–427

extending classes
   inheritance relationship, setting up, 159
   MovieClip, subclasses, 317
   nonextendable built-in classes, 199
extends keyword, 4, 75, 230
Extreme Programming (web site), 126

F

file extension for class files (.as), 4
final classes, not supported, 214
final property attribute, 74
finally block (see try/catch/finally statements)
fixed properties, 65
Flash
   components and movie clips, 21
   components, using (online help), 283
   design patterns, xviii
   example code and online resources, xxii
   .fla files
      accessing packaged class through
         classpath, 245–247
      application state frames, adding to
         timeline, 288
      class files, accessing through
         classpath, 247
      creating, 134
      timeline, OOP application, 287
   object-oriented applications, starting, 19
   procedural and OOP, support of, 20
   versions, xxi
      naming conventions in this book, xxii
Flash Exchange, v1 component update for
      ActionScript 2.0, 6
Flash MX 2004
   bug in catch block parameters, 264
   code hints, 30
   components, v2, 6–8
      listing of v1 and v2 components, 7
   datatype information for built-in
      classes, 55
   intrinsic files, errors in, 447–449
   static class library, 339
Flash MX Professional 2004, xxi
   .as (class) file, creating, 216
   .as file, creating, 129
   components, 6
      complete listing of, 7
   creating a class, 286
   intrinsic files, errors in, 447–449
   projects in, 290

Screens feature, 23
Visual Basic–style forms-based
      development (Screens), 287
visual development, online help for, 283
Flash Player
   retrieving MP3 files for playback in, 81
   setting version for a movie, 9
   .swf file versions, changing ActionScript
      for, 11
   version 4
      slash syntax, 10, 12
   version 6
      ActionScript 1.0 and 2.0 in, 8
      extraneous superclass constructor
         invocation, 197
      movies upgraded to Flash Player 7, 11
      runtime casting in .swf files, not
         supported, 50
      .swf files exported to, 10, 135
   version 7, 5
      ActionScript 1.0 and 2.0 in, 8
      array-sorting capabilities, 5
      case sensitivity, strict, 11
      changes to ActionScript 1.0, 11
      features introduced by, 5
      MovieClipLoader class, 146
      nested exception bug, 274
      required for ActionScript 2.0 exception
         handling, 250
      string conversion, 11
      undefined values, 11
flowing text around images, 5
for-in loops, enumerating properties with, 79
Forms, 23
frames, 20
   as application states, 287
   application state, adding to .fla file
      timeline, 288
   export frame for movie classes, 287
   labeled, AvatarSymbol (example), 318
   later than 1, classes exported on, 293
fully qualified references, 240
function call operator ( ), 16
   invoking accessor methods without, 106
function keyword, 83
function keyword, method attributes and, 88
function libraries, stored by built-in
      classes, 200
Function objects, 9
function statement, 81

functions, 14
  constructor (see constructor functions)
  declaring parameters and return value
      datatypes, 34–36
  event handler, 308
  Function class, 457
  global, 450, 451
  listener, 309
  nesting in methods, 101–105
    access to local variables and
        parameters, 102
    current object, accessing, 103–105
  wrapping, 133
  (see also methods)

G

getDay( ) (Date), 27
getListeners( ) (EventListenerList), 428
getSource( ) (EventObject), 430
getter and setter method syntax, 4
getter methods, 94, 97, 105–109
  automatic invocation by setter
      method, 108
  creating in ActionScript 1.0, 107
  defining, 105
  invoking without function call operator
      ( ), 106
global classpath, 245
  adding new directory to, 247
  class files in, 286
global functions, 450–451
global properties, 449
global variables
  class definitions as, 135
  class properties vs., 75
  inability to type, 55
globals, Singletons as, 385
gModeler, 161
gotoAndPlay( ) (MovieClip), 24
granularity, 256
  determining for exception types, 257–264
graphics application displaying shapes
      (example), 204–206
GUIs (graphical user interfaces)
  ActionScript 2.0 interfaces vs., 224
  currency converter application, 300–306
  Java Component class, 440
  MVC design pattern
    benefits of, 387
    management by view class, 390
  (see also currency converter application)

H

Has-A relationship, 209, 212
hierarchy, class, 161, 203
  (see also inheritance)
HTML page that includes movie, 289

I

icons, creating for components, 340
ID3 v2 tag, 5
identifiers
  ActionScript 2.0 reserved words as, 10
  case sensitivity, changes in Flash Player
      7, 11
image loading events, methods that
      handle, 148
images in text fields, support for, 5
ImageViewer class (example), 124–157
  creating the class, steps in, 124
  designing, 125–129
    functional requirements,
        establishing, 125
    functional requirements to
        code, 126–129
  download site for code, 152
  implementation, version 1, 129–133
  implementation, version 2, 138–141
    completed code, 142–145
    redesign, summary of, 141
    using in Flash movie, 145
  implementation, version 3, 146–157
    completed code, 151–157
  using in a Flash movie, 124, 134–138
    exporting and testing .swf file, 135
    .fla file, 134
    instantiating timeline to frame 15, 137
    preloading the class, 136
  (see also ImageViewerDeluxe subclass)
ImageViewerDeluxe subclass
      (example), 215–223
  autosizing the image viewer, 218–222
  setPosition( ) and setSize( ) methods, 217
  skeleton of, 216
  using, 223
implementation
  ActionScript 2.0 class (see classes, writing;
      ImageViewer class)
  interfaces, 224, 226, 228
implements keyword, 4, 226, 228
implicit casting, 49
import keyword, 240

MovieClip class, 24, 461–463
    composition vs. inheritance, 211–213
    extended by ClassLoader, 342
    improved depth management methods, 5
    subclasses, 316–331
        ActionScript 1.0, 320
        Avatar class (example), 318–327
        movie clip symbol and ActionScript
            class, 317
        nested assets, issues with, 327–330
        subclassing of, 330
        this (keyword), using, 321
MovieClipLoader class, 5, 146, 463
    listener list, 150
    methods to handle image loading
        events, 148
movies
    Flash Player 6–format movie upgraded to
        Flash Player 7–format, 11
    Flash Player 7–format, 5
    format for OOP application, 289
    setting ActionScript and Flash Player
        versions, 9
    size, scale settings, and alignment (Stage
        class), 468
    (see also .swf files)
MP3 files
    external, retrieving for playback in Flash
        Player, 81
    ID3 v2 tag, support for, 5
multithreaded languages, finally block
    in, 270
MVC (see Model-View-Controller)
MX family of products, xxi

N

name property (Error class), 251
namespace collision, 238
    importing classes with same name from
        different packages, 241
namespaces, 238
    nested packages in, 239
naming conflicts, 238
    interface method names, 229
    managing for parameters/properties, 86
    package or class, avoiding, 243
    properties and local variables with same
        name, 100
naming conventions
    interfaces, 229
    interfaces and their .as files, 228
    packages, 239, 243

NaN (not-a-number) values, 307
nested assets, issues with, 327–330
    not automatically recognized by
        compiler, 330
    properties and methods, initially
        undefined, 328–329
nested classes, 478
nested exceptions, 271–275
    bug in Flash Player 7, 274
nested functions, 101–105
    access to local variables and parameters
        defined in a method, 102
    accessing current object from, 103–105
nesting packages, 239
NetConnection class, 463
NetStream class, 464
new MovieClip( ) calls, ActionScript 1.0, 320
new operator, 15
    MovieClip subclass instances and, 317
    parameter values passed to constructor
        function, 116
not-a-number (NaN) values, 307
null datatype, 39
    casting to, 50
    placeholder for missing method
        arguments, 111
nullifying a method, 171
Number class, 465
numbers
    converting to strings, 27
    problems casting to Number type, 52

O

Object class, 38, 465
    addProperty( ), 107
    event objects as instances of, 313
    registerClass( ), 5, 320
    root class of built-in hierarchy, 161
object composition (see composition)
object references, using local variables instead
    of, 100
object-oriented design (OOD), 19–23
object-oriented programming (OOP), xvii,
    13–23
    ActionScript 1.0 vs. 2.0, xx
    ActionScript 2.0 features, 3
    application framework, 283–290
        classes, 285
        directory structure, 284
        document timeline, 287
        exported .swf file, 289
        .fla file (Flash document), 284

TextField class, 472–474
TextField.StyleSheet class, 474
TextFieldView class (example), 363–365
TextShapshot class, 475
this (keyword), 84–88
  class methods and, 92
  constructor functions, using in, 119
  managing parameter/property name
    conflicts, 86
  MovieClip subclass methods, using
    with, 321
  passing current object to a method, 84
  redundant use of, 87
  resolving property/local variable naming
    conflicts, 100
throw statement, 4, 250, 251
  datatypes of generated exceptions, 261
  try/catch block, searching call stack
    for, 264
throwing an exception, 250
  (see also exceptions)
timeline, 20
  application state
    adding to .fla file timeline, 288
    changing, 316
    creating, 287
  labeled frames corresponding to
    application states, 318
  placing components in, 294
timeline-based code
  instantiating ImageViewer to frame
    15, 137
  overuse of, 22
  procedural programming for, 20
  type checking and, 55
toString( )
  Error class, 251, 253
  Object class, 162
try/catch/finally statements, 4, 252
  catch blocks, 252
  control flow changes in, 275–277
  finally block, 268–270
    circumstances for execution, 268
    cleanup after code execution, 269
    in multithreaded languages, 270
    in single-threaded ActionScript, 270
  Flash bug in catch block parameters, 264
  handling different kinds of errors, 255
  nested, 271–275
    bug in Flash Player 7, 274
  searching call stack to match thrown
    exception, 264–267

throwing an error directly from try
  block, 254
try block with multiple catch blocks, 256
type casting (see casting)
type checking, 24–58
  built-in dynamic classes, 40
  casting, 45–54
    compile-time, leniency of AS2, 52
    conversion vs., 52
    member selection and, 51
    problems with, 52
    runtime support, 49
    terminology, 48
  circumventing, 41–45
  compatible types, 36–40
    handling any datatype, 38
    null and undefined, 39
  datatype information for built-in
    classes, 54
  dynamic binding vs, 204
  incompatible types, 26
  manual, at runtime, 206
  method parameters and return values, 82
  quirks and limitations of, 55–58
    [] operator, 57
    array elements, 58
    global variables, 55
    timeline code, 55
    XML instances, 56
  static typing, reasons for using, 30–31
  strict, static, and strong typing, 29
  type syntax, 31–36
    declaring method parameter and
      return value datatypes, 34–36
    declaring variable and property
      datatypes, 32
    items applied to, 31
    post-colon syntax, 36
  weak static typing and, 29
  (see also datatypes)
type mismatch errors (see datatypes; type
  checking)

U

UIObject class, createClassObject( ), 325
UML (Unified Modeling Language), 161
  design patterns, use in, 350
uncaught exceptions, 267
undefined datatype, 39
  ActionScript 1.0, changes to in Flash
    Player 7, 11

About the Author

Colin Moock is an independent web guru with a passion for networked creativity and expression. He is the author of the well-known guide to Flash programming, *ActionScript for Flash MX: The Definitive Guide* (O'Reilly). A web professional since 1995, Moock runs one of the Web's most venerable Flash developer sites, *http://www.moock.org*. He spends most of his time pursuing his cardinal interest, multiuser application development, and working on Unity (*http://www.moock.org/unity*), moock.org's complete commercial framework for creating and deploying multiuser applications for Macromedia Flash.

Colophon

Our look is the result of reader comments, our own experimentation, and feedback from distribution channels. Distinctive covers complement our distinctive approach to technical topics, breathing personality and life into potentially dry subjects.

The animal on the cover of *Essential ActionScript 2.0* is the coral snake (*Micrurus fulvius tenere*). This highly dangerous snake is found in the southeastern states of North America and can also be found in Mexico. It likes wet, humid, and thick foliage-littered forests, but can be found in any environment.

The coral snake is recognized by its vibrant red, yellow and black bands. These colors ward off would-be attackers. On the head and tail are bands of black and yellow; on the midsection are black, yellow, and red bands. The red bands are always adjacent to the yellow bands. The average length of a snake is 24 inches, with a maximum length of 47 inches. The coral snake is the only venomous snake in North America to hatch its young from eggs.

Coral snakes have short, grooved, and hollow fangs located at the front of the mouth. They feed on lizards and other snakes. Coral snakes bite their prey to inject neurotoxic venom, which paralyzes the victim; however, unlike snakes of the viper family, which use a stabbing method, when a coral snake bites its victim, it hangs on for a long time to inject as much venom as possible. Coral snakes are seldom seen, due to their habit of living underground, or in cracks and crevices, and their nocturnal tendencies. Coral snakes usually do not bite humans unless handled. If a human or pet is bitten, treatment should take place as soon as possible, since coral snake bites are often fatal.

Sarah Sherman was the production editor and proofreader, and Norma Emory was the copyeditor for *Essential ActionScript 2.0*. Colleen Gorman and Claire Cloutier provided quality control. Ellen Troutman-Zaig wrote the index.

Ellie Volckhausen designed the cover of this book, based on a series design by Edie Freedman. The cover image is a 19th-century engraving from the Dover Pictorial Archive. Emma Colby produced the cover layout with QuarkXPress 4.1 using Adobe's ITC Garamond font.

David Futato designed the interior layout. This book was converted by Julie Hawks to FrameMaker 5.5.6 with a format conversion tool created by Erik Ray, Jason McIntosh, Neil Walls, and Mike Sierra that uses Perl and XML technologies. The text font is Linotype Birka; the heading font is Adobe Myriad Condensed; and the code font is LucasFont's TheSans Mono Condensed. The illustrations that appear in the book were produced by Robert Romano and Jessamyn Read using Macromedia FreeHand 9 and Adobe Photoshop 6. The tip and warning icons were drawn by Christopher Bing. This colophon was written by Janet Santackas.

O'REILLY®

Essential ActionScript 2.0

 Macromedia Flash, already the de facto standard for delivering multimedia over the Web, is used increasingly to develop web-based applications (so-called Rich Internet Applications). Introduced in Flash MX 2004 and Flash MX Professional 2004, ActionScript 2.0 is a major upgrade to Flash's scripting language, which radically improves object-oriented development in Flash by formalizing objected-oriented programming (OOP) syntax and methodology.

Essential ActionScript 2.0, from the author of the widely acclaimed *ActionScript for Flash MX: The Definitive Guide*, covers not only ActionScript 2.0 syntax, but also object-oriented design and object-oriented programming. This book is targeted at ActionScript developers who want to know how ActionScript 2.0 development differs from ActionScript 1.0, how to upgrade legacy code to ActionScript 2.0, and how to take maximum advantage of ActionScript 2.0 and its OOP features. If you are an experienced OOP developer coming from another language such as Java or C++, *Essential ActionScript 2.0* shows you how to leverage your OOP knowledge in Flash.

Part I teaches object-oriented concepts, syntax, and usage in ActionScript 2.0. It covers strict datatyping, type casting, classes, objects, methods, properties, inheritance, composition, interfaces, classpaths, packages, and exception handling. Beyond teaching mere basics, it helps you to properly design and structure your code.

Part II teaches best practices for setting up and architecting an object-oriented project, plus how user interface components and movie clip subclasses fit into a well-structured Flash application. You'll learn how to structure entire applications and exchange code with other developers to help you build more stable, scalable, and extensible applications.

Part III teaches you to apply proven and widely accepted object-oriented programming strategies—known as design patterns—to Flash. After a brief introduction to design patterns, this section covers the Observer, Singleton, and Model-View-Controller design patterns, plus the delegation event model, with particular attention to their implementation in ActionScript 2.0.

"This book delivers a complete education in harnessing the power of ActionScript 2.0, coupled with the best practices for doing so. Colin illustrates not just how to write ActionScript but how to write great ActionScript."

—Gary Grossman, Flash Architect and Creator of ActionScript, Macromedia

Visit O'Reilly on the Web at *www.oreilly.com*

ISBN 0-596-00652-7
US $39.95
CAN $57.95

90000

9 780596 006525

6 36920 00652 7